T0214297

Communications in Computer and Information Science 1222

Commenced Publication in 2007
Founding and Former Series Editors:
Simone Diniz Junqueira Barbosa, Phoebe Chen, Alfredo Cuzzocrea,
Xiaoyong Du, Orhun Kara, Ting Liu, Krishna M. Sivalingam,
Dominik Ślęzak, Takashi Washio, Xiaokang Yang, and Junsong Yuan

Editorial Board Members

Joaquim Filipe ⓘ
  Polytechnic Institute of Setúbal, Setúbal, Portugal
Ashish Ghosh
  Indian Statistical Institute, Kolkata, India
Igor Kotenko ⓘ
  *St. Petersburg Institute for Informatics and Automation of the Russian
  Academy of Sciences, St. Petersburg, Russia*
Raquel Oliveira Prates ⓘ
  Federal University of Minas Gerais (UFMG), Belo Horizonte, Brazil
Lizhu Zhou
  Tsinghua University, Beijing, China

More information about this series at http://www.springer.com/series/7899

Ana Fred · Ana Salgado ·
David Aveiro · Jan Dietz ·
Jorge Bernardino · Joaquim Filipe (Eds.)

Knowledge Discovery, Knowledge Engineering and Knowledge Management

10th International Joint Conference, IC3K 2018
Seville, Spain, September 18–20, 2018
Revised Selected Papers

 Springer

Editors
Ana Fred
Instituto de Telecomunicações
University of Lisbon
Lisbon, Portugal

David Aveiro (iD)
University of Madeira
Funchal, Portugal

Jorge Bernardino
University of Coimbra
Coimbra, Portugal

Ana Salgado
Federal University of Pernambuco
Recife, Brazil

Jan Dietz
Delft University of Technology
Delft, The Netherlands

Joaquim Filipe
Polytechnic Institute of Setúbal/INSTIC
Setúbal, Portugal

ISSN 1865-0929   ISSN 1865-0937 (electronic)
Communications in Computer and Information Science
ISBN 978-3-030-49558-9   ISBN 978-3-030-49559-6 (eBook)
https://doi.org/10.1007/978-3-030-49559-6

© Springer Nature Switzerland AG 2020
This work is subject to copyright. All rights are reserved by the Publisher, whether the whole or part of the material is concerned, specifically the rights of translation, reprinting, reuse of illustrations, recitation, broadcasting, reproduction on microfilms or in any other physical way, and transmission or information storage and retrieval, electronic adaptation, computer software, or by similar or dissimilar methodology now known or hereafter developed.
The use of general descriptive names, registered names, trademarks, service marks, etc. in this publication does not imply, even in the absence of a specific statement, that such names are exempt from the relevant protective laws and regulations and therefore free for general use.
The publisher, the authors and the editors are safe to assume that the advice and information in this book are believed to be true and accurate at the date of publication. Neither the publisher nor the authors or the editors give a warranty, expressed or implied, with respect to the material contained herein or for any errors or omissions that may have been made. The publisher remains neutral with regard to jurisdictional claims in published maps and institutional affiliations.

This Springer imprint is published by the registered company Springer Nature Switzerland AG
The registered company address is: Gewerbestrasse 11, 6330 Cham, Switzerland

Preface

The present book includes extended and revised versions of a set of selected papers from the 10th International Joint Conference on Knowledge Discovery, Knowledge Engineering and Knowledge Management (IC3K 2018), held in Seville, Spain, September 18–20, 2018.

IC3K 2018 received 167 paper submissions from 44 countries, of which 18% were included in this book. The papers were selected by the event chairs and their selection was based on a number of criteria that include the classifications and comments provided by the Program Committee members, the session chairs' assessment, and also the program chairs' global view of all papers included in the technical program. The authors of selected papers were then invited to submit a revised and extended version of their papers having at least 30% innovative material.

The purpose of the IC3K is to bring together researchers, engineers, and practitioners working in the areas of Knowledge Discovery, Knowledge Engineering, and Knowledge Management. IC3K is composed of three colocated conferences, each specialized in at least one of the aforementioned main knowledge areas.

The papers selected to be included in this book contribute to the understanding of relevant trends of current research on Knowledge Discovery, Knowledge Engineering, and Knowledge Management. They include the ongoing extension of application areas of ontologies, the quality assessment of ontological models, and a focus on formalization.

We would like to thank all the authors for their contributions and also to the reviewers who have helped to ensure the quality of this publication.

September 2018

Ana Fred
Ana Salgado
David Aveiro
Jan Dietz
Jorge Bernardino
Joaquim Filipe

Organization

Conference Chair

Joaquim Filipe   Polytechnic Institute of Setúbal, INSTICC, Portugal

Program Co-chairs

KDIR

Ana Fred   Instituto de Telecomunicações, University of Lisbon, Portugal

KEOD

Jan Dietz   Delft University of Technology, The Netherlands
David Aveiro   University of Madeira, Madeira-ITI, Portugal

KMIS

Jorge Bernardino   Polytechnic of Coimbra, ISEC, Portugal
Ana Salgado   Federal University of Pernambuco, Brazil

KDIR Program Committee

Sherief Abdallah   British University in Dubai, UAE
Amir Ahmad   United Arab Emirates University, UAE
Mayer Aladjem   Ben-Gurion University of the Negev, Israel
Maria Aramburu Cabo   Jaume I University, Spain
Eva Armengol   IIIA CSIC, Spain
Zeyar Aung   Masdar Institute of Science and Technology, UAE
Vladan Babovic   National University of Singapore, Singapore
Vladimir Bartik   Brno University of Technology, Czech Republic
Gloria Bordogna   CNR, Italy
Amel Borgi   Université de Tunis El Manar, Institut Supérieur d'Informatique, LIPAH, Tunisia

Jesús Carrasco-Ochoa   INAOE, Mexico
Arnaud Castelltort   LIRMM, France
Keith Chan   The Hong Kong Polytechnic University, Hong Kong
Chien Chen   National Taiwan University College of Management, Taiwan, China
Zhiyuan Chen   University of Maryland Baltimore County, USA
Patrick Ciarelli   Universidade Federal do Espírito Santo, Brazil
Paulo Cortez   University of Minho, Portugal
Ingemar Cox   University of Copenhagen, Denmark

Luis M. de Campos	University of Granada, Spain
Emanuele Di Buccio	University of Padua, Italy
Thanh-Nghi Do	Can Tho University, Vietnam
Antoine Doucet	University of La Rochelle, France
Markus Endres	University of Augsburg, Germany
Iaakov Exman	The Jerusalem College of Engineering (JCE), Israel
Ana Fred	Instituto de Telecomunicações, University of Lisbon, Portugal
Susan Gauch	University of Arkansas, USA
Angelo Genovese	Università degli Studi di Milano, Italy
Rosario Girardi	Federal University of the State of Rio de Janeiro, Brazil
Rosalba Giugno	University of Catania, Italy
Nuno Gonçalves	Polithecnical Institute of Setúbal, Portugal
Francesco Gullo	UniCredit R&D, Italy
Jennifer Harding	Loughborough University, UK
Beatriz de la Iglesia	University of East Anglia, UK
Roberto Interdonato	DIMES, Università della Calabria, Italy
Szymon Jaroszewicz	Polish Academy of Sciences, Poland
Mouna Kamel	IRIT, France
Ron Kenett	Samuel Neaman Institute, Israel
Margita Kon-Popovska	Ss Cyril and Methodius University, Macedonia
Donald Kraft	Colorado Technical University, USA
Nuno Lau	Universidade de Aveiro, Portugal
Anne Laurent	LIRMM, Montpellier University, France
Carson Leung	University of Manitoba, Canada
Chun Li	Hong Kong Baptist University, Hong Kong
Jerry Chun-Wei Lin	Western Norway University of Applied Sciences, Norway
Giovanni Livraga	Università degli Studi di Milano, Italy
J. Martínez-Trinidad	Instituto Nacional de Astrofísica, Óptica y Electrónica, Mexico
Sérgio Matos	University of Aveiro, Portugal
Edson Matsubara	UFMS, Brazil
Misael Mongiovi	Università di Catania, Italy
Stefania Montani	Piemonte Orientale University, Italy
Davide Moroni	ISTI-CNR, Italy
Yashar Moshfeghi	University of Strathclyde, UK
Mitsunori Ogihara	University of Miami, USA
Elias Oliveira	Universidade Federal do Espirito Santo, Brazil
José Oliveira	University of Aveiro, DETI/IEETA, Portugal
Márcia Oliveira	Universidade Federal do Espírito Santo, Brazil
Fabrício Olivetti de França	Universidade Federal do ABC, Brazil
Rui Pedro Paiva	University of Coimbra, Portugal
Krzysztof Pancerz	University of Rzeszow, Poland
Alberto Pinto	LIAAD, INESC-TEC, University of Porto, Portugal
Giovanni Ponti	ENEA, DTE-ICT-HPC, Portici Research Center, Italy

Luigi Pontieri	CNR, Italy
Alfredo Pulvirenti	Universita di Catania, Italy
Marcos Quiles	Federal University of São Paulo (UNIFESP), Brazil
Isabel Ramos	University of Minho, Portugal
Maria Rifqi	Université Panthéon-Assas, France
Antonio Rinaldi	University of Naples Federico II, Italy
Carolina Ruiz	WPI, USA
Ovidio Salvetti	CNR, Italy
Milos Savic	University of Novi Sad, Serbia
Filippo Sciarrone	Roma TRE University, Italy
Zhongzhi Shi	Chinese Academy of Sciences, China
Umberto Straccia	ISTI-CNR, Italy
Ulrich Thiel	Fraunhofer Gesellschaft, Germany
I-Hsien Ting	National University of Kaohsiung, Taiwan, China
Kar Toh	Yonsei University, South Korea
Juan-Manuel Torres-Moreno	École Polytechnique de Montréal, Canada
Predrag Tosic	Washington State University, USA
Alicia Troncoso Lora	Pablo de Olavide University, Spain
Domenico Ursino	Università Politecnica delle Marche, Italy
Xing Wei	Pinterest Inc., USA
JingTao Yao	University of Regina, Canada
Michiko Yasukawa	Gunma University, Japan
Yi Zhang	University of Technology Sydney, Australia

KDIR Additional Reviewers

Kevin Labille	University of Arkansas, USA
Cristiano Russo	Université Paris-Est, France

KEOD Program Committee

Rocío Abascal-Mena	Universidad Autónoma Metropolitana Unidad Cuajimalpa, Mexico
Andreas Abecker	disy Informationssysteme GmbH, Germany
Mamoun Abu Helou	Al-Istiqlal University, Palestine
Alessandro Adamou	Knowledge Media Institute, The Open University, UK
Raian Ali	Hamad Bin Khalifa University, Qatar
Frederic Andres	Research Organization of Information and Systems, Japan
Francisco Antunes	Institute of Computer and Systems Engineering of Coimbra and Beira Interior University, Portugal
David Aveiro	University of Madeira, Madeira-ITI, Portugal
Petra Bago	University of Zagreb, Croatia
Claudio Baptista	Universidade Federal de Campina Grande, Brazil
Jean-Paul Barthes	Université de Technologie de Compiègne, France

Punam Bedi	University of Delhi, India
Ines Ben Messaoud	Laboratory Mir@cl, Tunisia
Alain Bretto	Université de Caen Basse Normandie, France
Vladimír Bureš	University of Hradec Kralove, Czech Republic
Radek Burget	Brno University of Technology, Czech Republic
Davide Ciucci	Università degli Studi di Milano Bicocca, Italy
João Costa	Institute of Computer and Systems Engineering of Coimbra, Portugal
Christophe Cruz	Laboratoire LIB, EA 7534, France
Ananya Dass	New Jersey Institute of Technology, USA
Valeria De Antonellis	Università degli Studi di Brescia, Italy
Jan Dietz	Delft University of Technology, The Netherlands
Erdogan Dogdu	Angelo State University, USA
Pierpaolo D'Urso	Università di Roma La Sapienza, Italy
John Edwards	Aston University, UK
Dieter Fensel	University of Innsbruck, Austria
Manolis Gergatsoulis	Ionian University, Greece
Giancarlo Guizzardi	Federal University of Espirito Santo, Brazil, and Institute for Cognitive Science and Technology, CNR, Italy
Yoan Gutiérrez	University of Alicante, Spain
Christopher Hogger	Imperial College London, UK
Mahmood Hosseini	Bournemouth University, UK
Martina Husáková	University of Hradec Králové, Czech Republic
Dimitris Kanellopoulos	University of Patras, Greece
Sarantos Kapidakis	Ionian University, Greece
Nikos Karacapilidis	University of Patras, Greece
Pinar Karagoz	METU, Turkey
Jakub Klímek	Charles University and Czech Technical University in Prague, Czech Republic
Kouji Kozaki	Osaka Electro-Communication University, Japan
Antoni Ligeza	AGH University of Science and Technology, Poland
Elena Lloret	University of Alicante, Spain
Paulo Maio	Polytechnic of Porto, Portugal
Luca Mazzola	Lucerne University of Applied Sciences (HSLU), Switzerland
Nives Mikelic Preradovic	University of Zagreb, Croatia
Riichiro Mizoguchi	Japan Advanced Institute of Science and Technology, Japan
Andres Montoyo	University of Alicante, Spain
Azah Muda	Universiti Teknikal Malaysia Melaka, Malaysia
Phivos Mylonas	Ionian University, Greece
Jørgen Nilsson	Technical University of Denmark, Denmark
Femke Ongenae	Ghent University, imec, Belgium
Rafael Peñaloza	Free University of Bozen-Bolzano, Italy
Jiajie Peng	Northwestern Polytechnical University (NPU), China

Carlos Periñán-Pascual	Universidad Politécnica de Valencia, Spain
Dimitris Plexousakis	FORTH, Greece
Mihail Popescu	University of Missouri-Columbia, USA
Amar Ramdane-Cherif	Versailles Saint-Quentin-en-Yvelines University, France
Domenico Redavid	University of Bari, Italy
Thomas Risse	University Library Johann Christian Senckenberg, Germany
Oscar Rodríguez Rocha	Inria, France
Colette Rolland	Université Paris 1 Panthéon-Sorbonne, France
Inès Saad	ESC Amiens, France
José Salas	Universidad Católica de la Santísima Concepción, Chile
Fabio Sartori	University of Milano-Bicocca, Italy
Marvin Schiller	Ulm University, Germany
Nuno Silva	Polytechnic of Porto, Portugal
Cesar Tacla	Federal University of Technology in Parana, Brazil
Orazio Tomarchio	University of Catania, Italy
Petr Tucnik	University of Hradec Kralove, Czech Republic
Manolis Tzagarakis	University of Patras, Greece
Rafael Valencia-Garcia	Universidad de Murcia, Spain
Yue Xu	Queensland University of Technology, Australia
Gian Zarri	Sorbonne University, France
Ying Zhao	Naval Postgraduate School, USA
Qiang Zhu	University of Michigan, USA

KEOD Additional Reviewers

Eduardo Fermé	University of Madeira, Portugal
Josiane Hauagge	Mid-West State University (UNICENTRO), Brazil
Elias Kärle	Semantic Technologie Institute (STI) Innsbruck, Austria
Umutcan Simsek	University of Innsbruck, Austria

KMIS Program Committee

Marie-Helene Abel	HEUDIASYC, CNRS, UMR, University of Compiègne, France
Miriam Alves	Institute of Aeronautics and Space, Brazil
Ana Azevedo	CEOS.PP, ISCAP, P.PORTO, Portugal
Joachim Baumeister	denkbares GmbH, Germany
Jorge Bernardino	Polytechnic of Coimbra - ISEC, Portugal
Kelly Braghetto	University of São Paulo, Brazil
Ritesh Chugh	Central Queensland University, Australia
Silvia Dallavalle de Pádua	University of São Paulo, Brazil
Michael Fellmann	Universität Rostock, Germany

Joao Ferreira	ISEL, Portugal
Joan-Francesc Fondevila-Gascón	CECABLE, UPF, URL, UdG, UOC, Spain
Annamaria Goy	University of Torino, Italy
Renata Guizzardi	Universidade Federal do Espírito Santo (UFES), Brazil
Jennifer Harding	Loughborough University, UK
Mounira Harzallah	LS2N, Polytech Nantes, University of Nantes, France
Anca Ionita	University Politehnica of Bucharest, Romania
Nikos Karacapilidis	University of Patras, Greece
Mieczyslaw Klopotek	Polish Academy of Sciences, Poland
Veit Koeppen	Otto-von-Guericke-University Magdeburg, Germany
Tri Kurniawan	Universitas Brawijaya, Indonesia
Katarzyna Kuzmicz	Bialystok University of Technology, Poland
Dominique Laurent	ETIS Laboratory, CNRS, UMR 8051, Cergy-Pontoise University, ENSEA, France
Michael Leyer	University of Rostock, Germany
Antonio Lieto	University of Turin, ICAR-CNR, Italy
Lin Liu	Tsinghua University, China
Xiaobing Liu	Dalian University of Technology, China
Heide Lukosch	Delft University of Technology, The Netherlands
Xiaoyue Ma	Xi'an Jiaotong University, China
Carlos Malcher Bastos	Universidade Federal Fluminense, Brazil
Nada Matta	University of Technology of Troyes, France
Rodney McAdam	University of Ulster, UK
Brahami Menaouer	National Polytechnic School of Oran (ENPOran), Algeria
Christine Michel	INSA, Laboratoire LIRIS, France
Michele Missikoff	ISTC-CNR, Italy
Owen Molloy	National University of Ireland, Ireland
Jean-Henry Morin	University of Geneva, Switzerland
Wilma Penzo	University of Bologna, Italy
José Pérez-Alcázar	University of São Paulo (USP), Brazil
Erwin Pesch	University of Siegen, Germany
Filipe Portela	Centro ALGORITMI, University of Minho, Portugal
Arkalgud Ramaprasad	University of Illinois at Chicago, USA
Marina Ribaudo	Università di Genova, Italy
Colette Rolland	Université Paris 1 Panthéon-Sorbonne, France
Ana Roxin	University of Burgundy, France
Ana Salgado	Federal University of Pernambuco, Brazil
Masaki Samejima	Osaka University, Japan
Christian Seel	University of Applied Sciences Landshut, Germany
Mukhammad Setiawan	Universitas Islam Indonesia, Indonesia
Tijs Slaats	University of Copenhagen, Denmark
Jo Smedley	University of South Wales, UK
Malgorzata Sterna	Poznan University of Technology, Poland
Jeff Tang	The Open University of Hong Kong, Hong Kong

Tan Tse Guan	Universiti Malaysia Kelantan, Malaysia
Shu-Mei Tseng	I-SHOU University, Taiwan, China
Martin Wessner	Darmstadt University of Applied Sciences, Germany
Uffe Wiil	University of Southern Denmark, Denmark
Qiang Zhu	University of Michigan, USA

KMIS Additional Reviewer

| Julian Dörndorfer | University of Applied Sciences Landshut, Germany |

Invited Speakers

Nicola Leone	Università di Calabria, Italy
Xindong Wu	Mininglamp Software Systems, China, and University of Louisiana at Lafayette, USA
Rudi Studer	Karlsruhe Institute of Technology, Germany
Rita Cucchiara	University of Modena and Reggio Emilia, Italy
Oscar Pastor	Universidad Politécnica de Valencia, Spain

Contents

Knowledge Management and Information Sharing

Knowledge Discovery and Information Retrieval

Secure Outsourced kNN Data Classification over Encrypted Data Using Secure Chain Distance Matrices

Nawal Almutairi[1,2], Frans Coenen[1(✉)], and Keith Dures[1]

[1] Department of Computer Science, University of Liverpool, Liverpool, UK
{n.m.almutairi,coenen,dures}@liverpool.ac.uk
[2] Information Technology Department, College of Computer and Information Sciences,
King Saud University, Riyadh, Saudi Arabia
nawalmutairi@ksu.edu.sa

Abstract. The paper introduces the Secure kNN (SkNN) approach to data classification and querying. The approach is founded on the concept of Secure Chain Distance Matrices (SCDMs) whereby the classification and querying is entirely delegated to a third party data miner without sharing either the original dataset or individual queries. Privacy is maintained using two property preserving encryption schemes, a homomorphic encryption scheme and bespoke order preserving encryption scheme. The proposed solution provides advantages of: (i) preserving the data privacy of the parties involved, (ii) preserving the confidentiality of the data owner encryption key, (iii) hiding the query resolution process and (iv) providing for scalability with respect to alternative data mining algorithms and alternative collaborative data mining scenarios. The results indicate that the proposed solution is both efficient and effective whilst at the same time being secure against potential attack.

Keywords: Secure kNN query · Homomorphic encryption · Secure Chain Distance Matrices · Order preserving encryption

1 Introduction

Recent years have witnessed an increase in the adoption of cloud services to store and manage data. There has been an increasing tendency for Data Owners (DOs), enterprises of all kinds, to outsource their data storage to Cloud Service Providers (CSPs) according to some contractual agreement. However, there are increasing concerns that sensitive data, belonging to the DOs, may be inadvertently exposed or misused [30]. These concerns are compounded by legislative requirements for data privacy preservation [6, 11]. This has motivated DOs to encrypt their data prior to outsourcing to CSPs so that the privacy of sensitive information is guaranteed [24].

Although encryption addresses the above data confidentiality issue it imposes limitations on the functionality of the operations that can be applied to the data in that the

© Springer Nature Switzerland AG 2020
A. Fred et al. (Eds.): IC3K 2018, CCIS 1222, pp. 3–24, 2020.
https://doi.org/10.1007/978-3-030-49559-6_1

data can only be processed (queried) by the DOs who are in possession of the encryption keys. There is also an increasing desire, on behalf of DOs, for the benefits of data mining and machine learning to be leveraged from their data. Many CSPs provide a Data Mining as a Service (DMaaS) [5] facility. However, the standard encryption techniques used to preserve data confidentiality means that the application of any data mining task will necessitate some form of data decryption. The research domain of Privacy Preserving Data Mining (PPDM) seeks to address this issue [1, 15].

A variety of PPDM methods have been proposed, including: data anonymisation [26], perturbation [19, 33] and the utilisation of Secure Multi-Party Computation (SMPC) protocols [10]. Using data anonymisation, DOs will remove "personal" attributes that are deemed confidential from the data and then irreversibly generalised the remaining dataset according to some "syntactic" condition. However, examples of breaches data confidentiality, reported in [22, 28, 29], have shown that anonymised data can be "de-anonymised" using quasi-identifier attributes and "linkage attacks" [22]. Data perturbation (or transformation) operates by distorting or randomising the entire dataset by adding noise while maintaining the statistical makeup of the data. However, perturbing the data cannot entirely assure data privacy since most of the methods used allow "reverse engineering" of the original data distribution [13]. Perturbation methods and data anonymisation have also been shown to be unsuitable for many instances of DMaaS; it has been demonstrated that they adversely affect the accuracy of the data analysis [19, 27]. The SMPC-based approach is directed at analysis tasks where the data is distributed, not encrypted, across a number of participating parties; such as a number of DOs, or a single DO and several Query Users (QUs). The SMPC-based approach requires many intermediate computations, using a dedicated SMPC protocol, performed over non-encrypted data and using DO and/or QU local resources, the statistical results of which are then shared. The significant computational and communication overhead that is a feature of the SMPC-based approach has rendered the approach to be infeasible for large datasets and complex data mining activities. Moreover, when using a SMPC-based approach, the involvement of many DOs and/or QUs poses a security risk given the presence of a non-honest party who may launch attacks such as "overlapping attacks" [18] and Chosen-Plaintext Attacks (CPAs) [34]. These PPDM methods do not therefore provide a solution to the desire of DOs to take advantage of the benefits offered by CSPs in a manner whereby data confidentiality can be guaranteed while at the same time allowing the techniques of data analytics to be applied to their data.

The emergence of Property Preserving Encryption (PPE) schemes, such as Homomorphic Encryption (HE) [17], Asymmetric Scalar Product Preserving Encryption (ASPE) [31] and Order Preserving Encryption (OPE) [16, 20], has provided a potential solution to the disadvantages associated with PPDM by permitting cyphertext manipulation without decryption. HE schemes allow simple mathematical operations, such as addition and multiplication, to be applied over encrypted data. ASPE schemes preserve scalar distances across cyphertexts. OPE schemes permit cyphertext comparison. However, although PPE schemes go someway to providing a solution to secure DMaaS they do not provide a complete solution in that, given a particular data mining application, the mathematical operations that are required are currently not all provided by single PPE scheme. This limitation has been addressed in the literature by either:

(i) recourse to data owners whenever unsupported operations are required or (ii) confiding the secret key to non-colluding parties using either a secret sharing techniques, as the case of [23], or using two-distinct CSPs as in the case of [25]. The former solution clearly introduces a computation and communication overhead which renders the approach unsuitable for many instances of DMaaS. In the case of the latter, the existence of two non-colluding parties is not always applicable while at the same time raising security concerns for many DOs as the secret key cannot be revoked even when a party is found to be untrustworthy. The solution presented in this paper is to use two complementary PPE schemes which collectively provide the necessary operations without compromising data confidentiality. More specifically, the proposed solution uses two PPEs: Liu's HE scheme [17] and bespoken Frequency and Distribution Hiding Order Preserving Encryption (FDH-OPE) scheme.

In the context of previous work directed at the use of PPE schemes, a popular DMaaS application, because of its simplicity and because it is used with respect to many application domains [25], is k Nearest Neighbour (kNN) classification/querying [7]. Given a query record q and a prelabeled dataset D held by a CSP, the standard kNN approach, where $k = 1$, operates by finding the class label for the most similar record in D to q, and assigning this label to q. Where $k > 1$, kNN operates by finding the "major" class label amongst k nearest records and assigning this to q. The challenges here is not just efficient data privacy preservation in the context the dataset D belonging to the DO, but also the efficient data privacy preservation associated with the query set Q (or sets $\{q_1, q_2, \dots\}$). The general view is that the query process should be controllable by the DO to whom the prelabeled dataset D belongs. This means that any QU cannot encrypt the records in their query set without first being "approved" by the DO. In many proposed solutions [12,31,32,35,38] the DO is required to either: disclose the encryption key (or at least part of it) to the QUs so as to allow them to encrypt Q, or disclose the key to a Third Party Data Miner (TPDM) which in turn means QUs have to disclose Q to the TPDM (the CSP). Both approaches entail a potential security risk, either because of the wide distribution of the encryption key across QUs or because of the requirement to treat the TPDM as a trusted party. Another challenge is in how to determine securely the data similarity between the records in Q and the records in D. To address the data similarity challenge various techniques have been proposed which rely either on HE schemes that provide only a partial solution and consequently entail recourse to data owners, or make use of SMPC primitives that required DO and QU participation and thus entail an undesired computation and communication overhead.

The work presented in this paper proposes the Secure kNN classification/querying (SkNN) system. The idea is to encrypt the dataset D using Liu's HE scheme [17] while at the same time recasting the dataset into a proxy format. More specifically as a Chain Distance Matrix (CDM), of the form first introduced in [3], which is then encrypted using a proposed FDH-OPE scheme to give a Secure CDM (SCDM). By allowing the two encryption schemes to work in tandem the disadvantages associated with earlier approaches reliant on a single encryption scheme are avoided, and hence SkNN can process queries without requiring data owner participation or recourse to SMPC protocols as in the case of earlier solutions. To ensure data confidentiality the encryption keys are held by the DO and never confided with the QUs or the TPDM. The QUs encrypt their query set Q using a proposed Secure Query Cyphering (SQC) protocol that preserves the privacy of the query record and the confidentiality of the DO's private key. The query process is controllable by the DO, although undertaken by the TPDM without involving the QUs or DO. The proposed SkNN system is fully described and evaluated in the remainder of this paper.

2   Previous Work

This section presents a review of previous work directed at secure kNN data classification and kNN querying. The existing work is directed at different kNN querying scenarios and different level of party involvement, however it can be categorised according to the data confidentiality preserving technique adopted: (i) cryptography [12,31,34,36,38,39], (ii) data perturbation [32,35] and (iii) SMPC protocols [9]. In most cases three categories of party are considered: (i) a Third Party Data Miner (TPDM); (ii) a Data Owner (DO) and (iii) one or more authorised Query Users (QUs) who are permitted to query the outsourced data so as to label their own query records (the set Q). In the remainder of this previous work section a number of previously proposed exemplar secure kNN data classification/querying techniques are discussed, each representing a particular approach in the context of the above categorisation.

In [12] the HE scheme presented in [8] was used to encrypt the DO's data. The encrypted dataset was then outsourced to authorised QUs along with the encryption key whilst the decryption key was sent to the TPDM. The secure kNN data classification was collaboratively conducted by the QUs and the TPDM, thus the query process was not controlled by the DO, therefore raising security concerns. Also the approach featured a considerable communication overhead as a result of interactions between the QUs and the TPDM while queries were being process; most of the computation was conducted using the QUs' local resources. A general principle of DMaaS is that the QU and/or DO should not need to be involved in the processing of a query once the query is launched, the mechanism presented in [12] does not support this principle. Wong et al. [31] proposed an Asymmetric Scalar Product Preserving Encryption (ASPE) scheme which used a random invertible matrix to encrypt the outsourced data. The APSE scheme supported scalar product operations over cyphertext which were used to calculate Euclidean distances between encrypted data records and encrypted query records. However, in this approach the QUs have access to the DO's encryption and decryption keys, hence the DO's data privacy may not be preserved. A similar approach was presented in [38], but providing some limitation on the information concerning encryption keys provided to QUs.

The work presented in [39] addresses the risk of encryption key leakage from QUs; however, the QUs can still learn the partial sum of the numbers in the encryption key belonging to the DO using a legal query, the QUs can also launch uncontrolled queries (queries that are processed without DO approval). Yuan et al. [36] present a secure kNN ($k = 1$) query scheme to address the threat of untrusted QUs and/or TPDMs; however, the QUs directly submit private plain query records to the DO which means that query privacy is not preserved. More recently, Zhu et al. [37] demonstrated that the scheme presented in [36] cannot achieve their declared security, and that the encrypted dataset in [36] can be quickly compromised by untrusted QUs and/or TPDMs.

In [35] a transformation method is used to encode the DO data outsourced to the TPDM. However, as in the case in [31,38], the QUs have access to the encryption and decryption keys, therefore they are assumed to be fully trusted. The trusted QUs encrypt their data records and send queries to the TPDM who conducts an approximate similarity search on the transformed data. The search results are then sent back to the QUs who decrypt the results and determine the label of their query records. The work in [32,34] presents various schemes to securely support approximate kNN for a given query record. In [34], the secure kNN is executed by retrieving the approximated nearest records instead of finding the encrypted exact k-nearest neighbours that requires the QUs to be involved in a substantial amount of computation during the query processing step. The method presented in [34] considers the TPDM as a provider of storage space, no significant work is done by the TPDM. In [32], Random Space (RASP) data perturbation combined with order preserving features are used to preserve data privacy and allow secure kNN querying. Confiding the encryption and decryption key to QUs, or to the TPDM as in the case of [31,32,34,35], significantly increase the risk of key leakage (it is also difficult to revoke a key distributed to QUs should they be deemed untrustworthy). Thus raising a significant security concern, as detailed in [34], whereby QUs can launch Chosen-Plaintext Attacks (CPAs). The QUs are assumed to be completely trusted QUs; this not only in limits the application scope of this approach, but also raises several practical problems. In general, the existing secure kNN query schemes where QUs can access the DO's encryption key are still far from being practical in many situations.

3   System Model

This section introduces the system model and design goals for the proposed Secure kNN classification/querying (SkNN) system. As in the case of earlier work on secure kNN the proposed system features three types of participant: a DO, a TPDM and several QUs as shown in Fig. 1. The TPDM is assumed to have a large but bounded storage and computation capability, and provides outsourcing storage and computation services, for example the TPDM might be a CSP. The DO has a large privet dataset D which consists of r records, $D = \{d_1, \ldots, d_r\}$. Each record d_i has $a + 1$ attribute values; $d_i = \{d_{i,1}, \ldots, d_{i,a}, d_{i,a+1}\}$ where $d_{i,a+1}$ is the class label for data record d_i. The QUs are a set of authorised parties who want to classify their data records $Q = \{q_1, q_2, \ldots\}$. The DO encrypts D using Liu's HE scheme (presented later in Sect. 4) to arrive at D' and sends it to the TPDM so as to take advantage of storage resources and computational ability provided by TPDM as a service. Note that the class label (attribute value $a + 1$) for each record in D is not encrypted. The DO also generates a Secure Chain Distance Matrix (SCDM) encrypted using the proposed FDH-OPE scheme that facilitates secure data similarity determination, this is presented in further detail in Sects. 4 and 5.

The DO delegates the generation of a kNN classification model, using its encrypted outsourced data, to the TPDM, and allows QUs to take advantage of the developed model. To maintain privacy any query $q_i \in Q$ needs to be encrypted by the QU who owns the query, before it is submitted to the TPDM for processing. Clearly to allow q_i to be processed using the kNN model generated using the DO's encrypted data, q_i needs to be encrypted using the same encryption key (held by the DO). Query encryption is thus achieved using a proposed Secure Query Cyphering (SQC) protocol that preserves the privacy of the query record and the confidentiality of DO's private key. To determine the similarity between an encrypted query record q_i' and the encrypted kNN model requires q_i' to be processed in such a way that it is integrated with the SCDM, a process referred to as "binding". The secure binding process is presented in Sect. 6. To make ensure that the querying is controlled by the DO, the binding process requires two records, one generated by the QU ($BindRec_1$) and the other generated by the DO that handles query approval ($BindRec_2$). Once approved query processing is delegated entirely to the TPDM. At the end of which the QU will receive predicted class label for q_i (see Fig. 1).

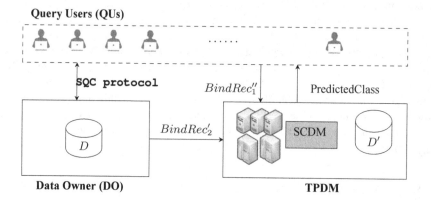

Fig. 1. The SkNN system architecture.

4   Cryptographic Preliminaries

As noted above the proposed SkNN data classification and query process operates using two encryption schemes: (i) the FDH-OPE scheme used to encrypt SCDMs and (ii) Liu's HE scheme used to encrypt the DO's outsourced data and securely exchange the FDH-OPE keys using a dedicated SQC protocol. Both are discussed in further detail in the following two sub-sections, Subsects. 4.1 and 4.2 respectively.

4.1   Frequency and Distribution Hiding Order Preserving Encryption (FDH-OPE)

This sub-section presents the FDH-OPE scheme used to encrypt CDMs, an order preserving scheme. The proposed scheme is an amalgamation of two existing Order Preserving Encryption (OPE) schemes, that of [20] and [16]. The former used to hide the data distribution in generated cyphertexts, the latter used to hide the data frequency. Encrypting data so that the data distribution is hidden requires knowledge of the distribution within the plaintext data, the plaintext intervals where the data density is high, and then generating the cyphertexts in such a way that high density plaintext intervals are dispersed along large cyphertext intervals. The frequency of data is simply hidden by generating different cyphers for the same plaintext value (even when using the same encryption key). The first step in FDH-OPE, is to determine the "interval" of the message space $M = [l, h)$ and the expanded "interval" of the cypher space $C = [l', h')$ in such a way that $M \ll C$ and the l, l', and h, h', are the minimum and maximum interval boundaries for the message and cypher spaces respectively (see Fig. 2). Data distribution hiding comprises two steps, *message space splitting* and *non-linear cypher space expansion* which operate as follows:

Message Space Splitting: The DO randomly splits the message space interval M into t consecutive intervals; $M = \{m_1, \ldots, m_t\}$, where t is a random number. The length of intervals are determined randomly by deciding the minimum and maximum interval boundaries (Fig. 2). The data density for each interval is then calculated as $Dens = \{dens_1, \ldots, dens_t\}$ where $dens_i$ is density of data in message space m_i.

Non-linear Cypher Space Expansion: The DO then splits the cypher space C into t intervals; $C = \{c_1, \ldots, c_t\}$. So that the data distribution is hidden, the length of each cypher space interval c_i is determined according to the density of the data in the corresponding message space interval, $dens_i$, so that message space intervals with high data density will have large corresponding cypher space intervals. For example, if $dens_i > dens_j$ then $|c_i| > |c_j|$. The message space and cypher space interval boundaries are the FDH-OPE encryption keys.

The data frequency is hidden using a "one-to-many" encryption function that maps $x \in m_i$ to an OPE equivalent value $x' \in c_i$. Algorithm 1 gives the pseudo code for the encrypting function. The algorithm commences by determining the message space interval ID, i, within which x is contained (line 2). The interval boundaries (keys) of the ith message and cypher space are then retrieved in lines 3 and 4. These values are used to calculate interval $scale_i$ and sample random value δ_i as per lines 5 and 6, where $Sens$ is a data sensitivity value representing the minimum distance between plaintext values in the dataset to be encrypted (calculated as specified in [16]). The value of δ_i is sampled for each interval so that longer intervals with a larger $scale_i$ value will consequently have a larger δ_i value than in the case of shorter intervals which contribute toward the hiding of the data distribution. The algorithm will exit (line 8) with cyphertext x' calculated as in line 7. The random value δ_i is added so that identical attribute values will not have the same encryption.

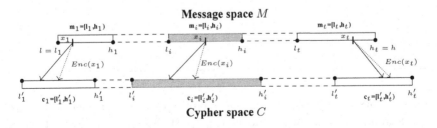

Fig. 2. Message and cypher space splitting.

Algorithm 1. FDH-OPE encryption algorithm.

1: **procedure** $\text{ENC}_i(x, Sens)$
2:     $i \leftarrow \text{IntervalID}(x)$
3:     $[l_i, h_i] \leftarrow \text{Range}(i)$
4:     $[l'_i, h'_i] \leftarrow \text{Range}'(i)$
5:     $scale_i = \frac{(l'_i - h'_i)}{(l_i - h_i)}$
6:     $\delta_i = \text{Random}(0, Sens \times scale_i)$
7:     $x' = l'_i + scale_i \times (x - l_i) + \delta_i$
8:     **Exit** with **x'**
9: **end procedure**

4.2 Liu's Homomorphic Encryption

The Liu's scheme is a symmetric HE scheme that supports cypher addition $\oplus$, cypher multiplication $\otimes$ and the multiplication of cyphertexts by plaintext values $*$. Given a data attribute value v, this is encrypted to m sub-cyphers; $E = \{e_1, \ldots, e_m\}$ where $m \geqslant 3$. The same key (Key) is used for the encryption and decryption processes; $Key(m) = [(k_1, s_1, t_1), \ldots, (k_m, s_m, t_m)]$. The key generation process is as presented in [17]. Algorithm 2 shows the pseudo code for the encryption process, $Encrypt(v, Key(m))$. The pseudo code for the data decryption process, $Decrypt(C, Key(m))$, is given in Algorithm 3.

Algorithm 2. Liu's HE encryption algorithm.

1: **procedure** $\text{ENCRYPT}(v, Key(m))$
2:     $R = [r_{[1]}, \ldots, r_{[m-1]}]$, list of real random numbers
3:     $E =$ Real value array of m elements
4:     $e_1 = k_1 \times t_1 \times v + s_1 \times r_m + k_1 \times (r_1 - r_{m-1})$
5:     **for** $i = 2$ to $m - 1$ **do**
6:         $e_i = k_i \times t_i \times v + s_i \times r_m + k_i \times (r_i - r_{i-1})$
7:     **end for**
8:     $e_m = (k_m + s_m + t_m) \times r_m$
9:     **Exit** with **E**
10: **end procedure**

Algorithm 3. Liu's HE decryption algorithm.

1: **procedure** $\text{DECRYPT}(E, Key(m))$
2:     $t = \sum_{i=1}^{m-1} t_i$
3:     $s = \frac{e_m}{(k_m + s_m + t_m)}$
4:     $v = \frac{(\sum_{i=1}^{m-1}(e_i - s*s_i)/k_i)}{t}$
5:     **Exit** with **v**
6: **end procedure**

Liu's scheme has both security and homomorphic properties. The scheme is semantically secure in that it produces different cyphertexts for the same plaintext on each occasion, even when the same secret key is used. Further detail regarding the security of Liu's scheme is given in Sect. 7. In terms of its homomorphic properties, as noted above, the scheme support $\oplus$, $\otimes$ and $*$ as shown in Eq. 1 (where c is a plaintext value), and thus, by extension, supports cypher subtraction $\ominus$ and division $\oslash$ as shown in Eq. 2.

$$
\begin{aligned}
E \oplus E' &= \{e_1 \oplus e_1', \ldots, e_m \oplus e_m'\} &&= v + v' \\
E \otimes E' &= \{e_1 \otimes e_1', \ldots, e_1 \otimes e_m', \ldots e_m \otimes e_1', \ldots, e_m \otimes e_m'\} &&= v \times v' \quad (1) \\
c * E &= \{c * e_1, \ldots, c * e_m\} &&= c \times v
\end{aligned}
$$

$$
\begin{aligned}
E \ominus E' &= E \oplus (-1 * E') \\
c \oslash E &= \frac{1}{c} * E
\end{aligned}
\quad (2)
$$

5   Secure Chain Distance Matrices (SCDMs)

Liu's scheme described above, does not preserve the data ordering in the generated cyphers. Therefore record comparison, an operation frequently required by many data mining algorithms, cannot be directly applied. To facilitate cyphertext comparison the idea of SCDM, presented recently in [3], was adopted. For the purposed of completeness the SCDM concept is presented in this section.

A SCDM is a 2D matrix that holds the encrypted distances between the attribute values in every *consecutive* data records in a dataset D in whatever ordering the records appear in the dataset. Therefore, the first dimension is $r - 1$, where r is the number of records in D, and the second is the size of the attribute set a. A SCDM has a *linear chain feature* that allows secure derivation of the distances between any pair of data records held in the SCDM without decryption, while at the same time requiring less storage space than that required by alternative distance matrix formalisms, such as the Updatable Distance Matrices (UDMs) proposed in [2]. Given a SCDM a TPDM can determine the similarity between two records, r_x and r_y, where $x \neq y$ as per Eq. 3. In the case of $x = y$ the distance will clearly be 0. The SCDM is generated in two steps: (i) CDM calculation and (ii) CDM encryption:

CDM Calculation: Algorithm 4 gives the CDM Calculation process. The algorithm starts by dimensioning the desired CDM (line 2) according to the dimensions of D received as an input. As noted above, the first dimension is the number of records in dataset minus one ($r - 1$) and the second is the size of attributes set (a). The CDM elements are then populated (lines 3 to 7); element $CDM_{i,j}$ will hold the distance between the jth attribute value in record i and the same attribute value in record $i + 1$ (this can be a negative value).

CDM Encryption: The CDM, as the case of the UDM presented in [2], is essentially a set of linear equation that may support reverse engineering. To preclude the potential of reverse engineering, the CDM needs to be encrypted in such a way that the data distribution and frequency are hidden, while at the same time preserving the ordering in the generated cyphertexts. To this end, the FDH-OPE scheme described in Subsect. 4.1 above was used. The key feature of the encrypted CDM, the SCDM, is that a TPDM now has access to the "distances value ordering" facilitated by the FDH-OPE scheme, but not the original distance values, between the data records. This means that the TPDM can calculate the order of difference between records.

$$Sim(SCDM, r_x, r_y) = \sum_{j=1}^{j=a} \left| \sum_{i=x}^{i=(y-1)} SCDM_{i,j} \right| \tag{3}$$

Algorithm 4. CDM calculation.

1: **procedure** CDMCALCULATION(D)
2:     CDM $= \emptyset$ array of $r-1$ rows and a column
3:     **for** $i = 1$ to $i = r - 1$ **do**
4:         **for** $j = 1$ to $j = a$ **do**
5:             CDM$_{i,j} = d_{i,j} - d_{i+1,j}$
6:         **end for**
7:     **end for**
8:     **Exit** with **CDM**
9: **end procedure**

---

6   Secure Query Processing over Encrypted Data with Query Controllability and Key Confidentiality

This section presents the proposed SkNN data classification and SkNN data querying process designed to achieve the key security requirements of: (i) *key confidentiality* from QUs, (ii) *query controllability*, (iii) *data privacy* and (iv) *query privacy*; without involving the DO and/or QUs while a query is processed and at the same time maintaining the efficiency and accuracy of the data classification. The solution is founded on the concept of SCDMs as described in Sect. 5. The proposed SkNN algorithm consists of three main steps as follows:

1. **Query Encryption:** The secure encryption of the QU's query record to preserve privacy, while maintaining DO encryption key confidentiality. To this end the Secure Query Cyphering (SQC) protocol is used, described in further detail in Subsect. 6.1.
2. **Binding Process:** The "binding" of the encrypted query q' with the SCDM to allow the data similarity between the contents of D' and q' to be determined. The binding process is detailed in Subsect. 6.2 below.
3. **SkNN Data Classification:** Query resolution (classification) conducted in two further steps: (i) nearest neighbour records retrieval and (ii) major class label determination. Both are discussed further in Subsect. 6.3.

6.1   Secure Query Cyphering (SQC) Protocol

The SQC protocol operates between the DO and QUs and is designed to allow the QUs to encrypt a query record, $q_i = \{q_{i,1}, q_{i,2}, \ldots, q_{i,a}\}$, using FDH-OPE, so that a "binding" record can be generated which in turn is utilised by the TPDM to update its SCDM. The binding process and the updating of the SCDM is discussed in the following sub-section, this sub-section presents the SQC protocol. To encrypt the query record q_i, using the FDH-OPE scheme, QU requires the FDH-OPE key. As FDH-OPE is a symmetric scheme, that uses the same key for encryption and decryption, sharing the key with the QU presents a security risk. The idea, instead of providing the FDH-OPE key, is therefore to provide the QU with the parameters to allow FDH-OPE encryption. However, provision of these parameters still presents a security threat. Therefore the parameters are encrypted using Liu's Scheme; recall that this is an HE scheme whose functionality will allow FDH-OPE encryption of q_i without decryption of the parameters. In effect q_i will be double encrypted, firstly using FDH-OPE to give q_i', and secondly using Liu's scheme to give q_i''. Note that the Liu HE scheme keys used with respect to the SQC protocol is different to the Liu HE scheme keys used to encrypt D (see Sect. 3). To distinguish between the two, the former will be referred to as the *Shared Liu* scheme (shared because later in the SkNN process it is shared with the TPDM).

Recall that Using FDH-OPE a value x is encrypted as follows (line 7 of Algorithm 1):

$$x' = l_j' + scale_j \times (x - l_j) + \delta_j \tag{4}$$

where l_j' is the minimum bound for the cypher space interval in question, $scale_j$ is the required scaling between the message space interval and the corresponding cypher space interval, and δ_j is a noise value included to prevent identical values being encrypted in the same way on repeated encryptions. The above can be rewritten as follows (with noise δ_j removed):

$$x' = scale_j \times (x) + (l_j' - (scale_j \times (l_j))) \tag{5}$$

which can be further simplified to

$$x' = scale_j \times (x) + e_j \tag{6}$$

where $e_j = l_j' - (scale_j \times (l_j))$. The parameters $scale_j$ and e_j are calculated by the DO, encrypted using the Shared Liu scheme to give $scale_j'$ and e_j', and sent to the relevant QU. Of course the values of $scale_j$ and e_j are dependent on the interval in which x falls; thus this also needs to be established within the context of the SQC protocol. The SQC protocol to achieve the above can be summarised as follows:

$$q_{i,j}'' = (q_{i,j} * scale') \oplus e' \tag{7}$$

SQC Protocol. Secure Query Cyphering.

1: **DO** generates the Shared Liu key.
2: Using binary questioning with the **QU**, **DO** identifies the FDH-OPE interval ID within which each query attribute value in $q_{i,j} \in q_i$ is contained.
3: **DO** calculates the FDH-OPE values for $scale_j$ and e_j for each attribute value $q_{i,j}$.
4: **DO** encrypts the $scale_j$ and e_j values using the Shared Liu scheme to arrive at $scale'_j$ and e'_j.
5: **DO** sends $scale'_j$ and e'_j to **QU**.
6: Using $scale'_j$ and e'_j, **QU** double encrypts the query attribute values in $q_{i,j} \in q_i$ using the HE properties of Liu's scheme as per Equation 7, the result is q''_i.

6.2 QU Authorisation and Binding

The binding process is the process whereby a query record is incorporated into the SCDM held by the TPDM. Recall that the SCDM contains distances (differences) between corresponding attribute values in a pairs of records. What we wish to do is add the difference between the first record in D held by the DO and the query record q held by the QU without sending either to the TPDM. The binding process is a collaborative process between the DO and a QU, and is required not only to allow a response to QU's query, but also so that the query can be authorised by the DO.

The process starts with the DO generating a random record p of length a, $p = \{p_1, \ldots, p_a\}$. This is then encrypted twice, firstly using the FDH-OPE scheme to give p', and secondly using the Shared Liu scheme to give p'', which is then sent to the relevant QU. The double encryption is required because, to retain the confidentiality of the FDH-OPE key held by the DO, q_i is also double encrypted. QU will then generate a binding record $BindRec_1$ representing the difference between their double encrypted query record q'' and the p''. This is achieved using the Shared Liu scheme properties, thus $BindRec''_1 = q'' \ominus p''$ (as described in Subsect. 4.2). The binding record $BindRec_1$ is then sent to the TPDM (see Fig. 1). At the same time the DO will calculate the binding record $BindRec_2$, representing the distances between p' (single encryption using FDH-OPE) and the first record in their dataset D, also encrypted using FDH-OPE. The binding record, $BindRec_2$, encrypted using FDH-OPE to give $BindRec'_2$, is then sent to the TPDM. The receipt of $BindRec'_2$ by the TPDM from the DO signals "approval" for the query, without this the TPDM will not process the query. The role of DO and QU is now finished.

Once the TPDM has received $BindRec''_1$ and $BindRec'_2$, the TPDM decrypts the double encrypted $BindRec''_1$, using the Shared Liu scheme, to give $BindRec'_1$. Both binding records remain encrypted using FDH-OPE. The TPDM then creates a $Pivot$ record by adding $BindRec'_1$ to $BindRec'_2$. The $Pivot$ record will now hold the distance between the query record q and the first record in $d_1 \in D$ without either being confided to the TPDM, or each other. The pivot record is then added to the SCDMs. The similarity between the query record q_i (at index 1 in the updated SCDM) and the xth record in dataset is calculated using Eq. 8.

$$Sim(SCDM, Q, r_x) = \sum_{j=1}^{j=a} \left| \sum_{i=1}^{i=(x)} SCDM_{i,j} \right| \tag{8}$$

6.3 Third Party Data Classification

The processing (classification) of queries from an authorised QUs (note that the DO may also be a QU) is entirely delegated to the TPDM (CSP). The main purpose of using a TPDM is because: (i) the limited computing resource and technical expertise that DOs are anticipated to have, the assumption is that the DO's core business is not data analytics, but some other form of commerce where data is generated which the DO is prepared to share for commercial gain; and (ii) that DOs and QUs are likely to want avail themselves of the analytical capabilities offered using a mobile device of some kind. Using a TPDM for query resolution also provides the additional benefit that query outcomes are not shared with the DO. Algorithm 6 shows the pseudo code for SkNN data classification. The inputs are: (i) the SCDM on completion of the binding process whereby the distance between the query record and the first record in D has been inserted at index 1 ($SCDM_1$), (ii) the encrypted dataset D' and (iii) the desired value for k. The SkNN process comprises two stages: (i) secure NN retrieval (lines 2 to 6) and (ii) determination of the major class label (line 7 which call procedure given in lines 10 to 17). The first stage starts with the calculation of the similarity between query record q' and each other record $d'_j \in D'$ as per Eq. 8. The calculated distance, together with the associated class label held at $d'_{j,a+1}$, is added to the neighbour list N (line 5). The second stage, determining the major class label, is commenced by ordering the neighbour list according to the $dist$ values (line 11). Recall that the FDH-OPE scheme used to encrypt the SCDM is an order preserving encryption scheme, thus facilitating secure data ordering. The first k elements in the neighbour list are then used to create list C that holds counts of the number of records in the first k elements in N that correspond to each label featured in the first k elements in N. The maximum class label is returned as the query label (line 13).

Algorithm 6. Secure kNN classification algorithm.

1: **procedure** SKNN($SCDM, D', k$)
2:     $N = \emptyset$
3:     **for** $j = 1$ to $j = |D'|$ **do**
4:         $dist = \text{Sim}(SCDM, 1, j)$
5:         $N = N \cup < dist, d'_{[j,a+1]} >$
6:     **end for**
7:     $predictedClass = \text{majorClassLabel}(N, k)$
8:     **Exit** with $predictedClass$
9: **end procedure**
10: **procedure** MAJORCLASSLABEL(N, k)
11:     Order N using $N < dist >$
12:     $C = \{c_1, \dots, c_l\}$
13:     **for** $i = 1$ to $i = k$ **do**
14:         $c_{[N_i < label >]} = c_{[N_i < label >]} + 1$
15:     **end for**
16:     **Exit** with $\text{Max}(C)$
17: **end procedure**

---

7 Experimental Evaluation

The evaluation of the SkNN system, including the SCDM, the binding process and the SQC protocol, is presented in this section. For the evaluation both synthetic data and fifteen datasets from the UCI data repository [14] were used, the latter listed in Table 2. The objectives were to consider the proposed solution in terms of: (i) computation and communication costs on behalf of the DO, (ii) computation and communication costs on behalf of QUs, (iii) performance in terms of runtime, (iv) classification accuracy, (v) the security of the proposed approach and (vi) scalability; each discussed in detail in Subsects. 7.1 to 7.6.

7.1 DO Cost Analysis

The DO will participate in preparing data for the TPDM, running the SQC protocol and authorising QU queries. As noted earlier, there is no DO involvement in the processing of QU queries once authorisation has taken place. The data preparation encompasses: (i) the generation of secret keys, (ii) data encryption, (iii) CDM calculation and (iv) CDM encryption to produce a SCDM.

Key generation is a one time process that does not add any overhead on behalf of the DO. Experiments demonstrated that the average time required to generate the FDH-OPE encryption keys was 80.32 ms, whilst the Liu's HE scheme keys were generated in 1.39 ms. The magnitude of the remaining DO participation is dependant on the size of the DO's dataset. Therefore, twenty synthetic dataset of differing size where used; ten synthetic datasets were directed at evaluating the effect of the number of data records (r) and the remaining ten were directed at evaluating the effect of the number of data attributes (a). The size of the targeted dimension (r or a) was increasing from $1K$ to $10K$ in steps of $1K$, while the other dimension was kept constant at 100. The results are shown in Fig. 3. As expected, the average runtime required to encrypt D, generate the CDM and encrypt the CDM increases linearly as the size of r and a increases. For example, when $r = 1K$ the data was encrypted in 6.88 ms; the CDM was generated in 63.73 ms and encrypted in 168.04 ms, when $r = 10K$ the corresponding runtimes are 19.00 ms, 468.31 ms and 1101.37 ms. The recorded runtimes when $a = 1K$ were 3.81 ms, 60.7 ms and 158.57 ms, compared to 18.24 ms, 569.99 ms and 1225.79 ms when $a = 10K$. These results shown that regardless of dataset size, at least in the context of the conducted experiments, the runtime associated with DO participation was not significant and therefore does not introduce any limiting overhead with respect to the DO.

The SQC protocol requires DO participation in determining and encrypting the scale *scale* and e values required by FDH-OPE scheme so as to allow QUs to encrypt their queries. The runtimes for calculating *scale* and encrypting e were 0.16 ms and 0.11 ms respectively, which means that no significant computational overhead is encountered by the DO. The DO also participates in the generation and encryption of the binding record *BindRec*$_2$, this also does not introduces any significant overhead. Table 1 shows the recorded runtimes (ms) for different dimension of *BindRec*$_2$ records.

7.2   QU Cost Analysis

The QU participates in the SQC protocol to encrypt their query records and compute the binding record, $BindRec_1$, that is compared to the DO's binding record, $BindRec_2$, to produce the *Pivot* record to be included in the SCDM held by the TPDM. This novel approach allows the TPDM to securely resolve the QU's query without involving the DO or QU. Table 1 shows the time required to encrypt a range of query records of increasing length (number of attributes) and the time required by a QU to calculate a binding record $BindRec_1$. Inspection of the table indicates that the runtimes are negligible.

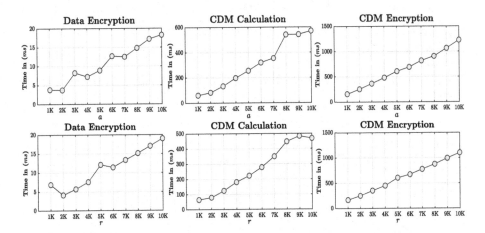

Fig. 3. Average runtimes (ms) for data encryption, CDM generation and CDM encryption using a range of values for r (number of records) and a (number of attributes).

7.3   Performance of SkNN

The runtime required to classify data using the proposed S*k*NN approach was compared with the runtime required for the standard *k*NN algorithm operating over un-encrypted data. Figure 4 shows the average recorded runtimes required to classify the datasets for the two stages of the *k*NN algorithm: secure NN retrieval (Stage 1) and determination of the major class label (Stage 2). The x-axis gives the evaluation dataset ID number from Table 2. The reported runtime were measured in terms of average runtime obtained using Ten-fold Cross Validation (TCV). As expected, the overall time required for S*k*NN Stage 1 was longer than in the case of standard approach. Note that runtimes for (standard) *k*NN Stage 1 are reported in millisecond (ms), while runtimes for S*k*NN Stage 1 are reported in second (sec). The experiment shows that, the bigger the dataset the larger the SCDM, and consequently the greater the time required to interact with the SCDM to classify a record. However, inspection of the recorded results indicates that this did not present a significant overhead. The Stage 2 runtimes were almost the same since the major class was determined over non-encrypted class labels in both cases. The effect of the size of a query record, measured in terms of a (number of attribute values) and the selected value for k was also evaluated. A range of values for a was considered from 1K to 10K increasing in steps of 1K, coupled with $k = 1$, $k = 5$ and $k = 9$. The required classification runtime in each case is plotted in Fig. 5. As expected, the runtime increases as the size of the query record increases, whilst the value of k does not introduce any significant overhead.

Table 1. Average runtimes (ms) for DO and QU participation when generating binding records and encrypting the query in the context of different values of a (number of attribute values).

	a									
	$1K$	$2K$	$3K$	$4K$	$5K$	$6K$	$7K$	$8K$	$9K$	$10K$
Encrypt query record (DO and QU)	4.42	6.11	10.77	11.28	11.58	13.41	14.24	15.5	17.76	18.89
Generate and encrypt the $BindRec_1$ (QU)	2.32	5.02	6.33	6.94	8.75	9.27	9.37	11.4	11.61	13.77
Generate and encrypt the $BindRec_2$ (DO)	2.38	4.23	9.47	7.03	8.9	9.85	12.04	13.94	15.62	16.38

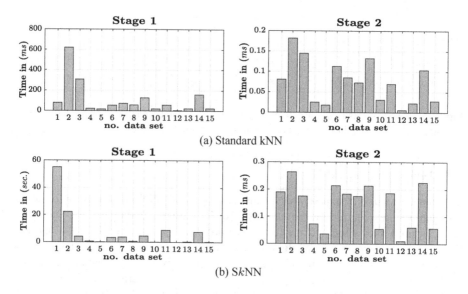

(a) Standard kNN

(b) SkNN

Fig. 4. Comparison of runtimes using standard kNN and SkNN classification.

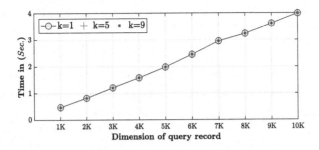

Fig. 5. Average computation costs of SkNN for varying number of k and number of attributes in query record.

7.4   Classification Accuracy

The classification accuracy obtained using the proposed SkNN was compared with the accuracy obtained using standard kNN. The aim was to evidence that SkNN operated correctly; the accuracy values obtained should be comparable. The UCI evaluation datasets were split into training (the outsourced dataset D) and testing (the query set Q). Average Precision, Recall and F1 measure [21] were used as the evaluation metrics obtained using TCV. So as to conduct a fair comparison the same value for k was used in all cases. The results are presented in Table 2. From the table it can be seen that from the fifteen datasets considered, in six cases the results obtained were different (highlighted in bold font); interestingly in five of the cases SkNN produced a better performance. In the remaining cases the performance was not as good (lower F1 value recorded in the context of Arrhythmia). The difference, it was conjectured, was because the FDH-OPE scheme does not support equality matching in that two identical plain text values will have different encrypted equivalents because of the δ random noise added. Sometimes this operated in favour of SkNN by preventing overfitting. The overall average Precision, Recall and F1 values were 0.71, 0.72 and 0.71 for Standard kNN and 0.72, 0.73 and 0.72 for SkNN, indicating that both approaches produced similar results and therefor the proposed SkNN operated correctly.

7.5   Security Under the Semi-honest Model

Using the SkNN approach, the TPDM and QUs are assumed to be non-colluding parties and the TPDM is considered to be a "passive adversary" who follows the semi-honest model where the proposed solution (algorithms and protocols) are honestly executed. This assumption is reasonable since the primary objective of CSPs, acting as TPDMs offering DMaaS, is to deliver a high quality services to clients (DOs). The privet data of a DO and the privet queries of a QU are not shared with any other parties in the proposed system. The TPDM is the only party who gains access to the encrypted dataset D', SCDM and the query binding records. No decryption takes place at the TPDM side which implies even more security.

Table 2. Comparison of prediction accuracies using Standard kNN and S*k*NN (differing results highlighted in bold font).

No. UCI dataset	Standard kNN			SkNN		
	Precision	Recall	F1	Precision	Recall	F1
1. Arrhythmia	0.25	0.22	**0.24**	0.25	0.22	**0.23**
2. Banknote authent.	1.00	1.00	1.00	1.00	1.00	1.00
3. Blood transfusion	**0.60**	**0.59**	**0.60**	**0.61**	**0.61**	**0.61**
4. Breast cancer	0.64	0.63	0.63	0.64	0.63	0.63
5. Breast tissue	0.57	0.57	0.57	0.57	0.57	0.57
6. Chronic kidney	0.82	**0.84**	0.82	0.82	**0.85**	0.82
7. Dermatology	**0.90**	**0.90**	**0.90**	**0.92**	**0.92**	**0.92**
8. Ecoli	**0.58**	**0.61**	**0.59**	**0.65**	**0.69**	**0.67**
9. Indian liver patient	0.58	0.58	0.58	0.58	0.58	0.58
10. Iris	0.96	0.96	0.96	0.96	0.96	0.96
11. Libras movement	0.88	0.87	0.87	0.88	0.87	0.87
12. Lung cancer	**0.45**	**0.51**	**0.47**	**0.50**	**0.58**	**0.52**
13. Parkinsons	0.81	0.82	0.81	0.81	0.82	0.81
14. Pima disease	0.67	0.66	0.66	0.67	0.66	0.66
15. Seeds	0.90	0.90	0.90	0.90	0.90	0.90
Average	**0.71**	**0.72**	**0.71**	**0.72**	**0.73**	**0.72**

To better evaluate the strength of the proposed scheme, potential attacks were divided into two categories according to the knowledge H that the attacker possess:

Low-level: The attacker only has access to cyphertexts; the encrypted dataset (D'), the encrypted CDM (SCDM) and the encrypted binding records; thus $H = <D', SCDM, BindRec_1'', BindRec_2'>$. In terms of cryptography a Low-Level attack therefore corresponds to a Cyphertext Only Attack (COA) [24].

High-level: Apart from cyphertexts, the attacker also has access to at least one plaintext record $d \in D$ (but not the corresponding cyphertext for d in D'); thus $H = <D', d>$. The attacker may then be able to obtain knowledge concerning the distribution and/or frequency of records in D. In terms of cryptography a High-Level attack corresponds to a Known Plaintext Attack (KPA).

High-Level attacks present a greater threat than Low-Level attacks.

Liu's HE scheme, used to encrypt D (and the second level encryption for binding record $BindRec_1$), has been shown to be semantically secure [17], which in turn means that the S*k*NN approach is secure against Low-Level attacks (COAs). Deriving any information from accessing cyphertexts generated using Liu's HE scheme will be computationally expensive due to the semantically secure features incorporated into the scheme, the likely success of a High-Level attacks is therefore negligible. In the context of the proposed FDH-OPE scheme, used to encrypt CDMs and binding records (the first level of encryption in the case of binding record *BindRec*$_1$), a feature of the scheme is that different cyphers are generated given plaintext values (by adding noise). The likelihood of an adversary being able to determine any information given an encrypted record d' is therefore negligible, hence the threat of a successful Low-Level attack is minimal. High-Level attacks directed at the FDH-OPE scheme, where the attacker attempts to obtain knowledge of the statistical make-up of the dataset (the data distribution and/or data frequency), are of greater concern. However, the proposed FDH-OPE scheme utilises the concept of "message space splitting" and "non-linear cypher space expansion" to obscure the data distribution in the generated cyphertexts, and a one-to-many encryption function to obscure the data frequency, thus protecting against the threat of High-Level attacks.

7.6 Scalability

The scalability of the proposed SkNN approach was measured in terms of: (i) the resource required to generate SCDMs compared to other comparable approaches from the literature, namely the Updatable Distance Matrices (UDMs) mechanism presented in [2]; (ii) the potential for extending the SkNN approach to support different data mining algorithms; and (iii) the potential of extending the approach in the context of collaborative data mining involving a number of DOs. In terms of the required memory resources the linear chain feature of SCDMs reduces the number of elements in a SCDM compared to a UDM. This is illustrated in Fig. 6 which shows the number of SCDM and UDM elements with respect to a sequence of datasets increasing in size from $r = 1$K to $r = 10$K in steps of 1K (a kept constant throughout at $a = 100$). As shown in the figure, the number of UDM elements grows exponentially with the dataset size. More formally the number of elements in a UDM equates to $\frac{r(r+1) \times a}{2}$, while the number of elements in a SCDM equates to $(r - 1) \times a$. The reduced memory requirement associated with SCDMs, compared to UDMs, facilitates the scalability of the proposed SkNN approach. The small number of elements in a SCDM also means that the time required to calculate the SCDM is less than that required for the UDM. In terms of extending the proposed SkNN approach to address alternative data mining algorithms, the SCDM concept can support any data mining algorithm that involve distance comparison. For example three different clustering algorithms, founded on the idea of SCDMs, were presented in [3]: Secure k-Means (Sk-Means), Secure DBSCAN

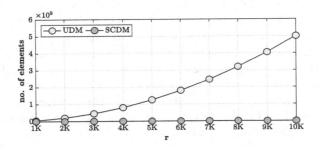

Fig. 6. Number of elements in UDM and SCDM for different number of records in dataset ($a = 100$).

(SDBSCAN) and Secure Nearest Neighbour clustering (SNNC). With respect to the concept of collaborative data mining, where a number of DOs pool their data for analysis so as to gain some mutual advantage, the proposed SkNN approach can be adapted so that the idea of Super SCDMs (SSCDMs), as presented in [4], is supported. Note that in [4] a mechanism was presented whereby SCDMs belonging to a number of DOs could be "bind" to produce a Super SCDM (SSCDM) which could then be used in the context of collaborative data clustering.

8 Conclusion and Future Work

In this paper the SkNN approach to secure kNN querying (classification) has been presented that features a novel cryptographic approach. The approach delegates the required data analysis to a Third Party Data Miner (TPDM), the assumption is that this will typically be a Cloud Service Provider. SkNN operates in such a way that the data confidentiality of the Data Owner's (DO's) dataset D and the Query User's (QU's) query set Q is maintained; the dataset D belonging to the DO and the query set Q belonging to a QU are never shared. The mechanism operates using the concept of Secure Chain Distance Matrices (SCDMs), encrypted using a proposed Frequency and Distribution Hiding Order Preserving Encryption (FDH-OPE) scheme, which are generated by the DO and sent to the TPDM. For a query $q \in Q$ to be resolved by the TPDM using the SCDM received from the DO the distance information concerning q needs to be incorporated into the SCDM. To do this q first needs to be encrypted using the same FDH-OPE encryption as used by the DO to encrypt the SCDM. However, given that the FDH-OPE scheme is a symmetric scheme, it is not appropriate for the DO to share the FDH-OPE key with the QU. Instead the relevant FDH-OPE encryption parameters, encrypted using Liu's Scheme, are sent to the QU who can then encrypt q without decrypting the received parameters. The effect is that q is double encrypted (using Liu's scheme and the FDH-OPE scheme) to give q''. This is facilitated through a proposed Secure Query Cyphering (SQC) protocol. However, q'' is never shared with the TPDM. What the TPDM needs to resolve the query is to include the difference between the query record and the first record in D into the SCDM, essentially adding an additional row at the start of the SCDM. This is achieved by both the DO and the QU each generating an encrypted "binding" record, the DO with respect to the first record in D and the QU with respect to q'', and sending them to the TPDM who creates a "pivot" record to add to the SCDM. The process of the DO generating a binding record and sending it to the TPDM indicates authorisation for the resolution of the query. The TPDM then resolves the query, using a Nearest Neighbour (NN) search facilitated by the contents of the SCDM and returns the major class label to the QU. The proposed SkNN approach was evaluated by: comparing its operation with standard kNN, considering the security level provided by the approach and analysing the potential for scalability. The evaluation indicated that: (i) the SkNN approach operated in a manner comparable to Standard kNN (sometimes better) without entailing a significant runtime overhead; (ii) was robust against Low-Level (Cyphertext Only) and High-Level (Known Plaintext) attacks; (iii) had the potential to operate using "Big Data" datasets; and (iv) be applicable to other data mining activities that entail distance comparison and alternative forms of collaborative data mining.

References

1. Agrawal, R., Srikant, R.: Privacy-preserving data mining. In: Proceedings of the 2000 SIG-MOD International Conference on Management of Data, pp. 439–450. ACM (2000)
2. Almutairi, N., Coenen, F., Dures, K.: K-means clustering using homomorphic encryption and an updatable distance matrix: secure third party data clustering with limited data owner interaction. In: Bellatreche, L., Chakravarthy, S. (eds.) DaWaK 2017. LNCS, vol. 10440, pp. 274–285. Springer, Cham (2017). https://doi.org/10.1007/978-3-319-64283-3_20
3. Almutairi, N., Coenen, F., Dures, K.: Data clustering using homomorphic encryption and secure chain distance matrices. SciTePress (2018). https://liverpool.idm.oclc.org/login?url=search.ebscohost.com/login.aspx?direct=true&db=ir00019a&AN=uol.3023624&site=eds-live&scope=site
4. Almutairi, N., Coenen, F., Dures, K.: Secure third party data clustering using Φ data: multi-user order preserving encryption and super secure chain distance matrices (best technical paper). In: Bramer, M., Petridis, M. (eds.) SGAI 2018. LNCS (LNAI), vol. 11311, pp. 3–17. Springer, Cham (2018). https://doi.org/10.1007/978-3-030-04191-5_1
5. Chen, T., Chen, J., Zhou, B.: A system for parallel data mining service on cloud. In: Second International Conference on Cloud and Green Computing, pp. 329–330 (2012)
6. Das, A.K.: European Union's general data protection regulation, 2018: a brief overview. Ann. Libr. Inf. Stud. (ALIS) **65**(2), 139–140 (2018)
7. Dasarathy, B.V.: Nearest neighbor (NN) norms: NN pattern classification techniques. IEEE Computer Society Press (1991)
8. Domingo-Ferrer, J.: A provably secure additive and multiplicative privacy homomorphism*. In: Chan, A.H., Gligor, V. (eds.) ISC 2002. LNCS, vol. 2433, pp. 471–483. Springer, Heidelberg (2002). https://doi.org/10.1007/3-540-45811-5_37
9. Elmehdwi, Y., Samanthula, B.K., Jiang, W.: Secure k-nearest neighbor query over encrypted data in outsourced environments. In: 2014 IEEE 30th International Conference on Data Engineering, pp. 664–675, March 2014
10. Goldreich, O.: Secure multi-party computation. Manuscript. Preliminary Version **78** (1998)
11. Gostin, L.O.: National health information privacy: regulations under the Health Insurance Portability and Accountability Act. J. Am. Med. Assoc. (JAMA) **285**(23), 3015–3021 (2001)
12. Hu, H., Xu, J., Ren, C., Choi, B.: Processing private queries over untrusted data cloud through privacy homomorphism. In: 27th International Conference on Data Engineering (ICDE), pp. 601–612 (2011). https://liverpool.idm.oclc.org/login?url=search.ebscohost.com/login.aspx?direct=true&db=edseee&AN=edseee.5767862&site=eds-live&scope=site
13. Huang, Z., Du, W., Chen, B.: Deriving private information from randomized data. In: Proceedings of the 2005 SIGMOD International Conference on Management of Data, pp. 37–48. ACM (2005)
14. Lichman, M.: UCI machine learning repository (2013). http://archive.ics.uci.edu/ml
15. Lindell, Y., Pinkas, B.: Privacy preserving data mining. J. Cryptol. **15**(3), 177–206 (2002)
16. Liu, D., Wang, S.: Nonlinear order preserving index for encrypted database query in service cloud environments. Concurr. Comput. Pract. Exp. **25**(13), 1967–1984 (2013)
17. Liu, D.: Homomorphic encryption for database querying. Patent **27**(PCT/AU2013/000674), December 2013. iPC_class = H04L 9/00 (2006.01), H04L 9/28 (2006.01), H04L 9/30 (2006.01)
18. Liu, J., Xiong, L., Luo, J., Huang, J.Z.: Privacy preserving distributed DBSCAN clustering. Trans. Data Priv. **6**(1), 69–85 (2013)
19. Liu, L., Kantarcioglu, M., Thuraisingham, B.: The applicability of the perturbation based privacy preserving data mining for real-world data. Data Knowl. Eng. **65**(1), 5–21 (2008)

20. Liu, Z., Chen, X., Yang, J., Jia, C., You, I.: New order preserving encryption model for outsourced databases in cloud environments. J. Netw. Comput. Appl. **59**, 198–207 (2016)
21. Makhoul, J., Kubala, F., Schwartz, R., Weischedel, R.: Performance measures for information extraction. In: Proceedings of DARPA Broadcast News Workshop, Herndon, VA, Morgan Kaufmann, pp. 249–252 (1999)
22. Narayanan, A., Shmatikov, V.: Robust De-anonymization of large sparse datasets. In: Proceedings of the 2008 Symposium on Security and Privacy, pp. 111–125. IEEE (2008)
23. Rahman, M.S., Basu, A., Kiyomoto, S.: Towards outsourced privacy-preserving multiparty DBSCAN. In: 22nd Pacific Rim International Symposium on Dependable Computing, pp. 225–226. IEEE (2017)
24. Robling Denning, D.E.: Cryptography and Data Security. Addison-Wesley Longman Publishing Co., Inc., Boston (1982)
25. Samanthula, B.K., Elmehdwi, Y., Jiang, W.: k-Nearest Neighbor classification over semantically secure encrypted relational data. IEEE Trans. Knowl. Data Eng. **27**(5), 1261–1273 (2015)
26. Samarati, P.: Protecting respondents identities in microdata release. IEEE Trans. Knowl. Data Eng. **13**(6), 1010–1027 (2001)
27. Sun, X., Wang, H., Li, J., Pei, J.: Publishing anonymous survey rating data. Data Min. Knowl. Discov. **23**(3), 379–406 (2011)
28. Sweeney, L.: Matching known patients to health records in Washington state data. 01 June 2013. http://thedatamap.org/risks.html, http://thedatamap.org/risks.html. Accessed 3 May 2019
29. Sweeney, L., Abu, A., Winn, J.: Identifying participants in the personal genome project by name, 24 April 2013. http://dataprivacylab.org/projects/pgp/. Accessed 3 May 2019
30. Takabi, H., Joshi, J.B., Ahn, G.J.: Security and privacy challenges in cloud computing environments. IEEE Secur. Priv. **8**(6), 24–31 (2010)
31. Wong, W.K., Cheung, D.W.l., Kao, B., Mamoulis, N.: Secure KNN computation on encrypted databases. In: Proceedings of the 2009 ACM SIGMOD International Conference on Management of data, SIGMOD 2009, pp. 139–152. ACM, New York (2009)
32. Xu, H., Guo, S., Chen, K.: Building confidential and efficient query services in the cloud with RASP data perturbation. IEEE Trans. Knowl. Data Eng. **26**(2), 322–335 (2014). https://doi.org/10.1109/TKDE.2012.251
33. Xu, S., Cheng, X., Su, S., Xiao, K., Xiong, L.: Differentially private frequent sequence mining. IEEE Trans. Knowl. Data Eng. **28**(11), 2910–2926 (2016)
34. Yao, B., Li, F., Xiao, X.: Secure nearest neighbor revisited. In: 2013 IEEE 29th International Conference on Data Engineering (ICDE), pp. 733–744, April 2013. https://doi.org/10.1109/ICDE.2013.6544870
35. Yiu, M.L., Assent, I., Jensen, C.S., Kalnis, P.: Outsourced similarity search on metric data assets. IEEE Trans. Knowl. Data Eng. **24**(2), 338–352 (2012)
36. Yuan, J., Yu, S.: Efficient privacy-preserving biometric identification in cloud computing. In: 2013 Proceedings IEEE INFOCOM, pp. 2652–2660. IEEE (2013)
37. Zhu, Y., Takagi, T., Hu, R.: Security analysis of collusion-resistant nearest neighbor query scheme on encrypted cloud data. IEICE Trans. Inf. Syst. **97**(2), 326–330 (2014)
38. Zhu, Y., Wang, Z., Zhang, Y.: Secure k-NN query on encrypted cloud data with limited key-disclosure and offline data owner. In: Bailey, J., Khan, L., Washio, T., Dobbie, G., Huang, J.Z., Wang, R. (eds.) PAKDD 2016. LNCS (LNAI), vol. 9652, pp. 401–414. Springer, Cham (2016). https://doi.org/10.1007/978-3-319-31750-2_32
39. Zhu, Y., Xu, R., Takagi, T.: Secure k-NN query on encrypted cloud database without key-sharing. Int. J. Electron. Secur. Digit. Forensics **5**(3–4), 201–217 (2013)

HCC-Learn Framework for Hybrid Learning in Recommender Systems

Rabaa Alabdulrahman[1(✉)], Herna Viktor[1(✉)], and Eric Paquet[1,2(✉)]

[1] School of Electrical Engineering and Computer Science, University of Ottawa, Ottawa, Canada
{ralab054,hviktor}@uottawa.ca, eric.paquet@nrc-cnrc.gv.ca
[2] National Research Council of Canada, Ottawa, Canada

Abstract. In e-business, recommender systems have been instrumental in guiding users through their online experiences. However, these systems are often limited by the lack of labels data and data sparsity. Increasingly, data-mining techniques are utilized to address this issue. In most research, recommendations to be made are achieved via supervised learning that typically employs the k-nearest neighbor learner. However, supervised learning relies on labeled data, which may not be available at the time of learning. Data sparsity, which refers to situations where the number of items that have been recommended represents only a small subset of all available items, further affects model performance. One suggested solution is to apply cluster analysis as a preprocessing step and thus guide the learning process from natural grouping, typically using similar customer profiles, to improve predictive accuracy. In this paper, we study the benefits of applying cluster analysis as a preprocessing step prior to constructing classification models. Our HCC-Learn framework combines content-based analysis in the preprocessing stage and collaborative filtering in the final prediction stage. Our results show the value of our HCC-Learn framework applied to real-world data sets, especially when combining soft clustering and ensembles based on feature subspaces.

Keywords: Recommender systems · Hybrid model · Data sparsity · Cluster analysis · Classification learning

1 Introduction

The design of recommender systems is an important area of research because of the added value they offer to online businesses. To meet the increasing demand for 24/7 online shopping, many organizations need more accurate and targeted recommendations. To achieve this goal, data-mining techniques, and notably lazy learning methods such as the k-nearest-neighbor (k-NN) supervised learning method, have been adopted [1, 2].

A major problem associated with the current solutions is that the number of items within customers' shopping carts typically constitutes only a tiny subset of those for sale. For instance, a customer of an online bookstore usually selects only a small number of books from those available to add to his or her shopping cart. This data sparsity problem may lead to inaccurate recommendations, since data-mining algorithms may

© Springer Nature Switzerland AG 2020
A. Fred et al. (Eds.): IC3K 2018, CCIS 1222, pp. 25–49, 2020.
https://doi.org/10.1007/978-3-030-49559-6_2

not generalize well when a large dimensionality is involved. Further, classification algorithms require class labels, which are frequently unavailable or late-arriving, as well as expensive to obtain. Specifically, resorting to manual labelling by domain experts is time-consuming and expensive, and consequently not realistic in an online business environment, where the numbers of customers and items are huge.

In general, recommender systems are divided into three categories: content-based (CB), collaborative-filtering (CF), and hybrid system. In a CB system, the focus is on the item matric and the assumption that users who were interested in certain items in the past will be interested in the same or similar items in the future [3, 4]. Hence, these systems rely on the attributes and categories associated with the items [5]. On the other hand, CF systems focus on user-rating matrices, where a similarity among users, bases on their preferences, is identified. Therefore, items that have been rated by users with similar interests are presented to the target user [6]. Consequently, historic data of user ratings and similarities among users across the system generally affect the overall performance of the system [3]. According to Elahi, Ricci, and Rubens [7], the prediction algorithm characteristics, as well as the number and the quality of the ratings stored in the system, highly influence the performance of a CF system. Both CB and CF systems have disadvantages. As a result, hybrid models were introduced to enhance performance. These systems consider both items based on users' preferences and similarity among the items' attributes and categories [4].

All recommender systems face the challenge of collecting relevant information about users or items. Recall, for example, the above-mentioned data sparsity problem where the number of items customers purchase is much smaller than the number of items for sale [1]. Further, there is a need to group customers who purchase similar items together without having to resort to manual labeling.

As mentioned above, data-mining techniques are used to enhance recommendations. In particular, ensemble learning is known for its ability to enhance the performance of a single classifier [8] by focusing on hard-to-learn examples through procedures such as instance weighting or instance resampling. In doing so, the ensemble combines the strengths of base-level classifiers to improve the overall performance [9]. Bagging and boosting are two known ensemble classification techniques that are widely used in machine learning, and the random subspace technique may be used to overcome disadvantages associated with bagging and boosting and thereby further improve the ensemble performance [10]. By focusing on a more informative feature subset, the computational complexity is reduced while also reducing the training time and addressing data sparsity.

Recall that data sparsity indicates that the number of recommended items is very small compared to the large number of items available in the system. In recommender system, the list of recommendations given to the user always contains a small number of items. Hence, the use of a subspace method reduces the features size [11] while guiding the learning process toward more informative samples [10]. To this end, this paper investigates the use of random subspace methods for recommendation systems.

We present an HCC-Learn framework that addresses the label and data-sparsity problem using data-mining techniques. Specifically, we introduce a hybrid cluster analysis and classification learning framework that combines unsupervised and supervised learning to obtain highly accurate classification models. We then study the impact of different cluster analysis techniques and report their impact on classification accuracy. In a previous work, we showed that combining diverse classification algorithms, such as k-NN and ensembles, with expectation maximization (EM) cluster analysis, hierarchical clustering, canopy, k-means, and cascade k-means methods generally produces high-quality results when applied to benchmark data sets [12]. This paper extends this work by introducing an ensemble-based algorithm that consider feature subsets. This approach constructs models based on a subset of available features [10] with the goal of making more accurate recommendation from a small subset of items to each user. For instance, the system's recommendation based on a customer's previous purchase history may be very "accurate" in this particular context but entirely irrelevant to a customer who has experienced a shift in preferences or who had made a series of purchases in order to address a temporary (not ongoing) need. In these cases, the system would not contribute to the online business improvement as it would neither enhance the sales, the revenues or the profits just to mention a few. The use of a random subspace method, where the learning process focuses on only a small subset of features should prove to be beneficial: our aim is to assess such a scenario.

In Sect. 2, we discuss related recommender system research. In Sect. 3, we present our HCC-Learn framework. In Sect. 4, we detail the data sets, experiment setup, and evaluation methodology, in Sect. 5, we discuss the results, and in Sect. 6, we conclude the paper.

2 Related Work

In many studies, cluster analysis and classification algorithms have been combined within the same framework. An examples is combining social network analysis with the study of human behavior to improve product marketing [2]. Moreover, several studies report that using cluster analysis as a preprocessing step, prior to classification, may lead to highly accurate models.

Recently, researchers have been studying human behavior in an effort to improve the simulations while increasing the accuracy of machine learning algorithms, for instance, customer habits and day-to-day activities affect marketing campaigns and revenues. Specifically, in e-business, recommender systems have been used to gain customer loyalty and increase company profits. For example, Liao and Lee [5], employ a self-clustering technique that addresses the high dimensionality challenge in the product matrix. By grouping similar products prior to the supervised learning, the classification algorithm produced accurate recommendations to the user while reducing the waiting time in order to provide an answer [5].

Another aspect that affects recommendation quality is the nature of the collected data. It follows that sparsity has a crucial impact on accuracy. Studies have addressed this problem using different solutions. For instance, Kanagal et al. [13] introduced the taxonomy-aware latent factor model that combines various taxonomies and latent factor models: the cluster analysis is used to categorize the item matrix with the aid of manual labeling. The objective of this research is to address the "cold-start" (i.e., incorporating unknown, anonymous users or new items) as well as the data-sparsity problems. Another solution presented by [14] used deep learning to address sparsity in the data set. Hierarchical Bayesian analysis is used to create a deep learning representation for both the items' information and users' rating.

However, privacy and users' unwillingness create another challenge. Users tend to care about their privacy from the unknown, so they prefer not to share any personal information—or information they perceive as personal. For this reason, Nikolaenko et al. employed a hybrid approach with matrix factorization that enables the system to collect additional information about the items while preserving users' privacy [15]. In another research project, Guo, Zhang, and Thalmann [16] created a simpler approach in which the system essentially borrows information from the targeted user's neighbors. These neighbors are chosen from the user's trusted social network. The model merges the collected information with those relative to the targeted user to find similar users in the system's network.

Furthermore, data are collected continuously in mobile applications. However, few users are interested in rating their experience or the services they received. However, some users keep returning to previously visited locations. The Rank-GeoFM algorithm was therefore developed, based on this observation, to collect check-in and check-out points that provide additional information to the system [17]. In a similar practice, Lian et al. created a location-based social network that groups items based on similar points of interest to solve data sparsity [18].

2.1 Ensemble Learning

Ensembles of classifiers, consisting of individually trained classifiers [19] or so-called "base learners" are powerful and improve classification accuracy compared to a single base learners [8]. However, the performance of an ensemble is highly influenced by the diversity of the base learners included and the characteristics of the data [20].

Created by Breiman in the early 1990s, bagging ensemble learning is one of the earliest ensemble learning methods [21]. It is widely used due to its many appealing qualities, as discussed below. Bagging aims to maximize prediction accuracy through combining a group of base learners. Suppose we have a data set, D, and N learners. The bagging algorithm randomly resamples this data set to obtain k bootstrap subsets. That is, each of the N learners is trained on different, resampled subsets of D. A bagging ensemble typically predicts the class of an example using majority voting. One of this algorithm's strengths is its computational ability, since it does not store the entire data set while resampling. This is important in recommender systems where the data set size increases over time. Note that because of bootstrapping, bagging helps reduce variance and is affected by class imbalance [22]. This is important in recommender systems, where users tend to favor one item over another with the consequence that some items have a higher number of ratings than other items do (Fig. 1).

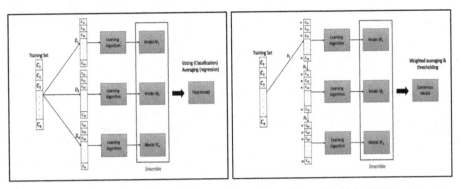

Fig. 1. Ensemble learning – Bagging (left) and Boosting (right) [23].

The second ensemble we employ is boosting, named for its ability to boost the performance of a weak learner to become a stronger one [24]. The goal is to build a series of models using a continuous number of iterations while focusing on hard-to-learn examples. This is done by putting more weight on the examples with high classification errors. In boosting, a new classifier is trained at each iteration to turn a weak learner into a strong one by emphasizing the examples that are misclassified. Each model aids to improve the performance of the previous one by reducing the weight error for each instance.

Bagging methods learn from a created subset of random examples, whereas boosting assigns a weight to each example that is readjusted during learning. However, neither method considers the importance of individual features when constructing a model. To this end, the random subspace method was introduced to guide the learning process [10]. Accordingly, the random subspace algorithm focuses on the attributes, or features, rather than the examples. With this approach, the subspace subsets are created from the feature selection, evaluation and reduction [11]. In random subspace methods, feature subsets are selected randomly with replacements from the training set. Subsequently, each individual classifier learns from the selected attributes in the subspace subsets while considering all training examples [10, 11].

Due to the numerous advantages of ensembles, studies have employed them in problems related to recommender systems and machine learning. For instance a recommender system for a human resources department, employs bagging and boosting [25]. In this prior study, the outputs from both models are combined to create a user-interest model to recommend certain employment opportunities to the target user. Furthermore, the Lili, C. (2015) uses a boosting ensemble approach to increase recommendation accuracy and recommender algorithm's ability to adapt to new data [26]. In the study by [8], bagging is used as a post-processing step in a random subspace algorithm (Fig. 2).

In this section, we introduced related work, with a focus on ensemble-based methods as used in our research. In the next section, we introduce the extended HCC-Learn multi-strategy learning framework in which multiple cluster analysis and classification techniques co-exists.

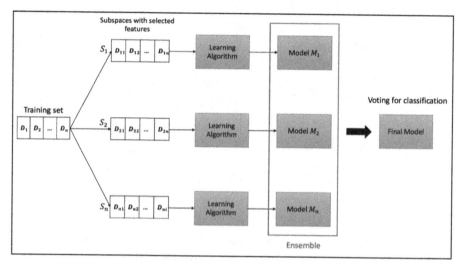

Fig. 2. Subspace method illustration by [23].

3 HCC-Learn Framework

This section presents our extended HCC-Learn framework where we address the label and data-sparsity problems through the combination of cluster analysis and classification algorithms. Note that the HCC-Learn framework was originally introduced in previous work [12]. In this paper, we extend our earlier work by introducing an ensemble method based on feature subspace sampling.

3.1 Framework Components

Figure 3 shows the UML diagram of the HCC-Learn framework, which consists of four stages. In stage one, the original data are merged to obtain integrated information about the items and users. In most rating systems, the items' and users' ratings information is stored in separate matrices. To this end, the rating matrix includes information about the users and an ID reference to the item. After exploring and understanding our data sets, we proceed with cleaning and categorizing the data sets. Data preprocessing is a crucial step, especially when considering the conversion of nominal data, the normalization of numeric data, and the determination of the best distance function, when applicable.

Unsupervised learning is done in stage two, where n cluster analysis techniques $(A_1 \ldots A_n)$ are applied to the pre-processed data sets. Cluster analysis algorithms group similar items into one cluster, attempting to minimize inter-cluster similarity. These algorithms include partitioning, hierarchical, density, and model-based algorithms [27].

In general, clustering may be divided into hard and soft clustering. In hard clustering, overlap between groups is not permitted, meaning that each example is assigned to one and only one group. In contrast, soft clustering allows group overlapping, implying that each example can belong to one or more than one cluster [28]. Soft clustering therefore allows recommender systems to better capture users' interests, since users may

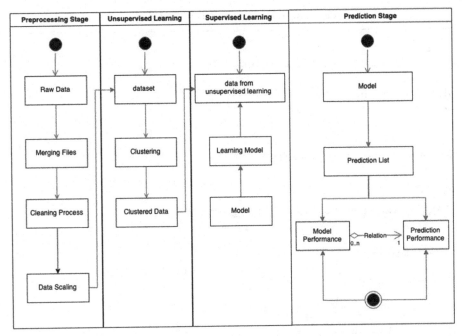

Fig. 3. UML diagram of the HCC-Learn framework.

be associated with more than one group, resulting in better recommendations accuracies, as noted by Mishra et al. [28], and confirmed in our experimental evaluation.

A strength of the HCC-Learn framework is that we employ multiple cluster analysis algorithms with different learning styles. Applying the algorithms $(A_1 \ldots A_n)$ to the data set results in n models being built, denoted by $(M_1 \ldots M_n)$. Next, we conduct a cluster-to-class evaluation for each M_i. That is, each pair of clustering and classification algorithms is considered in the evaluation.

The clustered data set resulting from stage two is then used as an input for step three. In this supervised learning stage, we use m classification algorithms $(C_1 \ldots C_m)$, once more employing techniques with diverse learning strategies. To this end, we employ probabilistic, eager, and lazy learners [29]. The data set is divided into training and test sets. The classifiers proceed to build models against the training set and test the models accordingly. Furthermore, we evaluate each clustering-classification combination using both a subspace and ensemble setting.

As a next step, a comparison between each classification model and each of the others is performed. We evaluate the accuracy and select the clustering algorithm demonstrating the highest improvement rate. It follows that this choice is domain-dependent. Finally, the clustering-classification pair with the highest predictive accuracy is selected to provide the user with a list of recommendations. Note that our framework is generic, in that it may incorporate many diverse cluster analysis and classification algorithms. The next section details our experimentation evaluation.

Algorithm 1: HCC-Learn Recommendation.

Input

D: a set of d class labelled training inputs,
C_i: Classifier;
A_j: Clustering algorithm;
k: Number of clusters;
Y: Class label of d;
x: Unknown sample;
p: size of each subset;
e: size of ensemble;
s_i: subspace;

Initialization for clustering stage:

  1- A_j discover k objects from D as initial cluster
     centre
  2- **Repeat:**
    - (re)assign each object to cluster according to
      A_j distance measure
    - Update A_j
    - Calculate new value
    Until no change
  3- Output models $(M_1, \ldots M_n)$
  4- Split dataset into train t_i and test t_j.

Initialization for Subspace method stage

  1- set size of p
  2- set size of e
  3- set base classifier as C_i
  4- create subspace as training set
  5- train the model for each individual s_i

prediction stage:

  1- Classify (t_i, Y, x)
  2- Output classification model n.
  3- Test model on t_j.

---

4 Experimental Setup

All our experiments were conducted on a desktop computer with an Intel i7 Core 2.7 GHz processor and 16 gigabytes of RAM. We implemented our framework using the WEKA data-mining environment [30].

4.1 Data Description

We used three data sets in our experimental evaluation. All data sets were generated using the customer rating for a specific product. Table 1 shows the data set descriptions.

Table 1. Datasets description.

Dataset	#Sample	#Attributes	#Classes
Restaurant-consumer rating (RC)	1161	14	3
Fuel-Consumption rating (FCR) 2017	1056	14	5
FCR 2016–2018	3225	14	5

The first data set is the restaurant and consumer (RC) data set, as obtained from [31]. The RC data set contains information about the users and restaurants together with a user-item rating matrix, as shown in Table 2. Based on their overall ratings, customers are divided into three classes. This data set was collected using a recommender system prototype to find the top N restaurants based on the customers' ratings.

Table 2. The restaurant and consumer (RC) dataset attributes.

User ID	Accessibility
Alcohol	Ambience
Area	Marital status
Place ID	Parking (Y/N)
Price ($)	Transport
Smoking area	Food rating
Service rating	Overall rating

The second data set, fuel consumption rating (FCR), was obtained from the Government of Canada Open Data Project[1]. Initially, we used the fuel-consumption collected data for only one year, 2017, denoted by FCR-1 and FCR-2, as reported in [11]. To extend our evaluation of the model's performance and prediction accuracy, we utilized an expanded version of this data set that includes data for three years, 2016 to 2018 [32]. The details of this data set are shown in Table 3. This data set contains information about the fuel consumption of different type of vehicle based on factors such as engine size, number of cylinders, transmission type, etc. In the original data set, the vehicle make attribute included 42 values. To reduce this number, attribute banding was performed, and based on the feedback from domain experts, two versions of the data set were created. In the first version (FCR-1), the vehicle makes were divided into three categories, North American, European, and Asian. For instance, records of vehicles of makes such as Honda, Kia, and Toyota are all assigned to the Asian category. In the second version (FCR-2), the vehicles were divided into seven categories based on the country where they were designed—the United States, Germany, Italy, Japan, Korea, the United Kingdom, and Sweden. For both versions, vehicles belong to five classes according to their smog rating.

---

[1] https://open.canada.ca/data/en/dataset/98f1a129-f628-4ce4-b24d-6f16bf24dd64.

Table 3. The fuel consumption rating (FCR) dataset attributes.

Vehicle make	Vehicle model
Engine size	Fuel consumption in city
Fuel type	Fuel consumption in highway
Vehicle class	Fuel consumption combined
Cylinders	Fuel consumption combined mpg
Transmission	CO_2 emissions
Rating CO2	Smog rating

As mentioned above, our earlier results against FCR-1 and FCR-2 were based on data from the year 2017 and included 1,056 samples. Adding the data for 2016 to 2018 to FCR-2 resulted in 3,225 examples.

4.2   Experimental Setup

In this experimental evaluation, the performance of four classifiers is evaluated individually. We consider the decision tree (DT) and Hoeffding tree (HT) algorithms, as well as the Naïve Bayes (NB) and k-NN learners. Theses classifiers belong to the probabilistic, lazy, and eager learning categories, respectively [29]. It is important to note that most recommender system frameworks employ the k-NN algorithm, which is therefore recognized as the benchmark in this field. Additionally, we employ the previously introduced bagging, boosting and random subspace ensemble methods. Note that in this work, we use a random subspace method implementation as available in WEKA. The original random subspace method developed by [10] uses a decision tree as the base learner. However, in WEKA, this method is a generic one that allows any classifier to be used as the base learner [30].

We employed five cluster analysis algorithms, namely hierarchical clustering (HC), k-means, the cascade k-means technique, the EM model-based method, and the canopy clustering technique. These methods were chosen because of their ability to handle numeric attributes, nominal attributes, and missing values, as well as for the diversity of learning strategies they represent [29]. The number of clusters is set to equal the number of classes in each data set.

For the k-NN algorithm, we determined that $k = 5$ is the optimal value for all our data sets. This value was set by experimentation. The number of base learners in ensemble learning is highly domain-dependent; this number was set to 25, in line with [33]. For the subspace size for the subspace method, we evaluate four sizes.

As discussed in Sect. 3 after stage two, cluster analysis, the data set is divided into a training set (70%) and a test set (30%). To validate our model performance, we use 10-fold cross-validation. Cross-validation provides a realistic performance and results in a valid statistical sample with a smaller variance [8].

4.3   Evaluation Criteria

The selection of algorithms and parameters, and the evaluation of cluster analysis results remain topics of significant debate [34, 35]. In this paper, since the ground truth in our data sets is always available, we evaluate the cluster analysis results using the well-known extrinsic cluster-to-class evaluation method. To evaluate the quality of the classification on the various data sets after clustering, we used the model accuracy as well as the F-score measures, which combines the precision and the recall rates.

However, since we are evaluating a recommender system framework, it is important to take the prediction rate into consideration as well. Most studies of recommender systems evaluate the overall performance of the system. In line with this approach, we evaluate the overall performance of the system in Sect. 5.2. In addition, we are interested in evaluating the effectiveness and usefulness of the system. To this end, Sect. 5.2 considers the prediction rate and evaluates the effectiveness of the system.

5   Results and Discussions

Our main goal is to address the data-sparsity problem in recommender systems. This focus is motivated by the observation that these systems intrinsically contain a large number of items while the requirement is to make a prediction based on a small number of items. As we mentioned above, k-NN is commonly used in traditional recommender systems [36, 37] and thus acts as a baseline in our evaluation.

5.1   Cluster-to-Class Evaluation – System Usefulness

In this section, our aim is to assess the impact of using cluster analysis via natural groupings in the data as a preprocessing step on classification accuracy. Each classifier was tested separately using one of the above-mentioned clustering methods. In addition, we used bagging, boosting, and random subspace ensemble learners. In total, 72 clustering-classification pairs were tested during this experimentation [12].

Our results from a previous study [12] confirmed that cluster analysis improves classification accuracy considerably, between 16.24% and 44.92%, compared to "no clustering." Across all experiments, accuracies improved by an average of 29.5%. Our previous results also indicated that EM, HC, and cascade k-means return the highest accuracies. The results for ensemble learning, bagging, and boosting, from our previous study [12] is presented in Table 4 and Table 5.

In this paper, we present additional results when using the subspace method on four subspace sizes—25%, 50%, 75%, and 90%—against the extended FCR data set. A total of 96 clustering-classification pairs was tested in this work using the four subspace sizes. In Table 6, the accuracies for the base learners are very similar to those depicted in Table 4 and Table 5 [12]. Again, the soft-clustering EM method resulted in better performance for almost all pairs. This method employs two steps: an assignment expectation step followed by a re-centering or maximization step. Similar to with the k-means algorithm, the covariance matrixes and the weight associated with the various Gaussian distributions (clusters) are evaluated [38]. Iteration will continue until convergence [38]. The advantage of this method is that it learns using soft clustering approach which provides an advantage in recommendation systems [28].

Table 4. Results, in term of accuracies, for bagging and boosting ensembles [12].

Classifier	No-clustering	HC	k-means	Cascade k-means	EM	Canopy	Increase over no-clustering	Dataset
Bagging-kNN	68.74	86.74	86.20	89.18	87.28	82.14	*20.43*	FCR-1
	70.23	87.42	88.23	86.06	87.42	79.84	*17.19*	FCR-2
	70.44	92.98	88.55	93.60	90.39	94.21	*23.77*	RC
Bagging-HT	58.46	89.45	86.20	88.50	88.63	78.62	*30.99*	FCR-1
	58.86	84.98	86.06	81.60	90.66	77.00	*31.80*	FCR-2
	60.47	90.39	77.09	90.52	98.28	73.15	*37.81*	RC
Bagging-DT	56.97	98.11	96.35	97.70	92.96	90.80	*41.14*	FCR-1
	57.92	96.75	94.59	95.13	92.56	91.20	*38.84*	FCR-2
	72.54	92.49	94.21	96.31	99.38	96.06	*26.85*	RC
Bagging-NB	59.00	89.31	86.20	88.36	88.63	79.16	*30.31*	FCR-1
	59.00	84.98	86.06	81.19	90.66	80.51	*31.66*	FCR-2
	74.51	92.12	90.03	92.00	98.89	91.38	*24.39*	RC
Boosting-kNN	67.12	83.36	87.01	87.69	87.69	79.43	*20.57*	FCR-1
	69.82	84.84	84.98	84.84	86.06	79.57	*16.24*	FCR-2
	68.84	93.10	88.18	93.23	88.42	92.37	*24.39*	RC
Boosting-HT	59.00	88.63	90.93	92.83	92.02	82.54	*33.83*	FCR-1
	59.95	88.23	88.77	87.01	94.18	84.17	*34.24*	FCR-2
	60.22	88.92	77.46	89.41	98.52	70.07	*38.30*	RC
Boosting-DT	54.53	97.84	96.08	97.16	95.54	94.86	*43.30*	FCR-1
	51.56	96.48	94.72	95.54	95.54	90.80	*44.93*	FCR-2
	70.81	92.61	92.61	96.31	99.02	96.68	*28.20*	RC
Boosting-NB	60.35	94.72	92.96	93.91	91.75	85.52	*34.37*	FCR-1
	60.76	87.82	91.07	89.99	93.10	83.76	*32.34*	FCR-2
	65.03	89.29	91.13	93.97	98.15	91.38	*33.13*	RC

In the other hand, the HC method follows an agglomerative approach when creating the clusters. That is, it is a bottom-up approach that initiates each cluster with its own observation. Subsequently, pairs of clusters are merged as one progresses through the hierarchy. In our experimental evaluation, following the work of Witten et al. [33], we used the mean distance to merge these clusters. The cascade k-means is a dendrite-based method based on the Calinski-Harabasz criterion [39] that extends the simple k-means algorithm by creating several partitions. The algorithm starts with a small k, which is then cascaded from a small to a large number of groups. In contrast with the HC method, this is a top-down method. In the k-means algorithm, the k value is set by an expert. The cascade k-means algorithm iterates until it finds the right number of classes, an advantage over the k-means algorithm, a fact confirmed by our experiment.

A closer look at the subspace results reveals that the best subspace size used in the experiments depends highly on the domain as well as the base learners, as expected.

Table 5. F-score results, for bagging and boosting ensembles [12].

Classifier	No-clustering	HC	k-means	Cascade k-means	EM	Canopy	Increase over no-clustering	Dataset
Bagging-kNN	0.69	0.98	0.96	0.97	0.87	0.93	_0.30_	FCR-1
	0.71	0.85	0.83	0.82	0.86	0.76	_0.14_	FCR-2
	0.71	0.93	0.89	0.94	0.91	0.94	_0.23_	RC
Bagging-HT	0.60	0.90	0.96	0.97	0.97	0.86	_0.37_	FCR-1
	0.62	0.84	0.80	0.79	0.89	0.74	_0.27_	FCR-2
	0.61	0.90	0.77	0.91	0.98	0.74	_0.37_	RC
Bagging-DT	0.57	0.92	0.98	0.98	0.96	0.96	_0.41_	FCR-1
	0.57	0.98	0.94	0.95	0.92	0.88	_0.41_	FCR-2
	0.74	0.93	0.95	0.96	0.99	0.96	_0.25_	RC
Bagging-NB	0.60	0.87	0.80	0.85	0.92	0.75	_0.32_	FCR-1
	0.61	0.84	0.82	0.82	0.89	0.74	_0.27_	FCR-2
	0.75	0.93	0.91	0.92	0.99	0.91	_0.25_	RC
Boosting-kNN	0.00	0.97	0.96	0.97	0.87	0.93	_0.97_	FCR-1
	0.00	0.82	0.80	0.78	0.83	0.75	_0.83_	FCR-2
	0.69	0.93	0.88	0.93	0.89	0.92	_0.24_	RC
Boosting-HT	0.61	0.96	0.95	0.97	0.96	0.87	_0.37_	FCR-1
	0.62	0.88	0.73	0.71	0.91	0.75	_0.29_	FCR-2
	0.60	0.89	0.77	0.89	0.99	0.70	_0.38_	RC
Boosting-DT	0.55	0.99	0.98	0.98	0.97	0.97	_0.45_	FCR-1
	0.52	0.98	0.92	0.93	0.94	0.88	_0.46_	FCR-2
	0.71	0.93	0.93	0.96	0.99	0.97	_0.28_	RC
Boosting-NB	0.62	0.97	0.86	0.93	0.97	0.90	_0.35_	FCR-1
	0.63	0.90	0.90	0.89	0.89	0.80	_0.27_	FCR-2
	0.65	0.89	0.91	0.94	0.98	0.91	_0.33_	RC

For instance, the EM and HC cluster analysis algorithms generally perform best when the subspace size is 50%, irrespective of the classification algorithm, while a subspace size of 25% resulted in a higher accuracy for canopy analysis than for the other sizes, and better results were achieved for k-means at a subspace size of 75%, meaning that some domains and learners need more or less features to construct accurate models against these data sets. If the feature subspace is too small, many useful features go unconsidered, while larger subspaces of 75% and 90% features may lead to a lower accuracy, as the algorithms are considering too many redundant features.

Evaluating recommender systems is performed generally via recall and precision, where these two measures are used to evaluate the truthfulness level of the model. Recall gives the ratio of the retrieved items considered notable by the user relative to the total number of relevant items, whereas precision provides the ratio of items retrieved by the

Table 6. Results, in term of accuracies, for all experiments.

Classifier	No-clustering	HC	k-means	Cascade k-means	EM	Canopy	Increase over no-clustering	Dataset
	Subspace of 25%							
kNN	64.04	89.27	80.13	85.49	**94.64**	84.23	*22.71*	FCR-1
	60.88	92.74	83.60	88.01	**94.95**	82.97	*27.57*	FCR-2
	64.08	92.24	87.93	88.22	**94.83**	89.37	*26.44*	RC
HT	63.09	87.38	68.14	77.92	**93.69**	74.45	*17.22*	FCR-1
	60.25	88.96	74.45	76.03	**95.27**	78.55	*22.40*	FCR-2
	75.57	87.64	79.31	85.92	**91.95**	78.16	*9.02*	RC
DT	62.46	89.91	73.82	80.44	**91.48**	74.76	*19.62*	FCR-1
	54.57	90.54	79.18	80.44	**96.53**	77.92	*30.35*	FCR-2
	72.41	83.62	75.86	84.77	**93.10**	81.90	*11.44*	RC
NB	61.51	86.75	76.03	80.13	**94.01**	81.39	*22.15*	FCR-1
	58.99	93.69	77.60	82.33	**97.79**	81.07	*27.51*	FCR-2
	73.28	93.97	82.76	88.22	**95.98**	82.47	*15.40*	RC
	Subspace of 50%							
kNN	66.25	90.22	82.33	85.49	**95.90**	88.01	*22.15*	FCR-1
	68.45	**94.64**	85.17	88.01	94.32	84.86	*20.95*	FCR-2
	74.71	94.25	91.09	92.24	**95.40**	92.53	*18.39*	RC
HT	64.04	87.70	74.13	79.18	**97.48**	74.76	*18.61*	FCR-1
	61.83	93.38	71.61	76.97	**98.74**	75.71	*21.45*	FCR-2
	61.78	91.95	70.98	84.48	**95.69**	74.43	*21.72*	RC
DT	67.51	90.85	81.39	79.50	**94.95**	78.86	*17.60*	FCR-1
	65.93	92.43	79.50	82.65	**94.32**	75.08	*18.86*	FCR-2
	77.59	93.39	75.29	85.63	**95.69**	91.95	*10.80*	RC
NB	60.88	88.01	78.86	80.13	**98.74**	82.33	*24.73*	FCR-1
	60.57	94.01	78.55	81.70	**98.42**	80.44	*26.06*	FCR-2
	77.59	**94.83**	86.21	89.66	97.41	89.37	*13.91*	RC
	Subspace of 75%							
kNN	67.19	91.17	84.54	83.28	**95.90**	84.54	*20.69*	FCR-1
	66.88	93.69	84.54	86.44	**95.58**	84.86	*22.15*	FCR-2
	72.13	**95.69**	91.95	90.80	94.83	92.53	*21.03*	RC

(*continued*)

Table 6. (*continued*)

Classifier	No-clustering	HC	k-means	Cascade k-means	EM	Canopy	Increase over no-clustering	Dataset
HT	62.46	87.07	76.34	72.87	**99.05**	70.35	*18.68*	FCR-1
	59.31	92.74	62.46	72.24	**99.05**	70.66	*20.13*	FCR-2
	58.33	94.54	58.91	89.08	**96.84**	65.52	*22.64*	RC
DT	70.35	87.70	81.07	81.39	**94.01**	80.76	*14.64*	FCR-1
	70.66	91.48	79.50	82.97	**92.74**	78.55	*14.38*	FCR-2
	72.41	92.82	77.30	85.63	**95.11**	93.10	*16.38*	RC
NB	61.51	87.07	79.50	78.55	**99.05**	79.81	*23.28*	FCR-1
	58.68	92.74	76.97	79.81	**99.05**	80.13	*27.07*	FCR-2
	76.15	93.68	85.34	89.08	**97.41**	87.64	*14.48*	RC
	Subspace of 90%							
kNN	65.62	90.54	84.86	83.28	**96.53**	83.91	*22.21*	FCR-1
	67.82	**93.06**	83.28	86.75	92.74	83.28	*20.00*	FCR-2
	73.56	**95.11**	90.52	91.38	94.54	89.08	*18.56*	RC
HT	59.94	87.38	78.86	62.15	**98.74**	66.25	*18.74*	FCR-1
	59.62	92.43	54.26	69.72	**99.05**	67.19	*16.91*	FCR-2
	58.33	93.68	57.76	89.94	**97.99**	62.93	*22.13*	RC
DT	69.72	87.70	79.81	80.13	**94.01**	77.60	*14.13*	FCR-1
	69.72	93.06	78.86	82.97	**93.38**	80.13	*15.96*	FCR-2
	73.56	93.39	75.86	79.31	95.69	**96.55**	*14.60*	RC
NB	58.68	87.38	78.55	78.86	**98.74**	79.81	*25.99*	FCR-1
	59.62	92.43	75.39	79.81	**99.05**	79.81	*25.68*	FCR-2
	77.01	93.68	86.21	89.66	**97.99**	89.08	*14.31*	RC

used method relative to the total number of recommendations [29, 37]. We combine these two metrics into an F-score measure in our evaluation. This measure combines recall and precision into a single measure [8].

$$F - score = 2 * \frac{Precision * Recall}{Precision + Recall} \tag{1}$$

The results, shown in Table 6 and Table 7, confirm the benefit of adding cluster analysis as a preprocessing step. Also, by considering Table 6 which shows the accuracies results for all experiments, we can see the model perform poorly in most cases where cluster analysis was not used.

Table 7. F-score results for all experiments.

Classifier	No-clustering	HC	k-means	Cascade k-means	EM	Canopy	Increase over no-clustering	Dataset
	Subspace of 25%							
kNN	0.00	0.89	0.79	0.85	0.95	0.84	*0.86*	FCR-1
	0.00	0.93	0.83	0.88	0.95	0.82	*0.88*	FCR-2
	0.63	0.92	0.88	0.88	0.95	0.89	*0.27*	RC
HT	0.00	0.87	0.68	0.78	0.94	0.74	*0.80*	FCR-1
	0.00	0.89	0.19	0.76	0.95	0.78	*0.72*	FCR-2
	0.76	0.87	0.79	0.86	0.92	0.78	*0.09*	RC
DT	0.00	0.90	0.73	0.81	0.94	0.75	*0.82*	FCR-1
	0.00	0.90	0.79	0.80	0.97	0.78	*0.85*	FCR-2
	0.72	0.81	0.75	0.83	0.93	0.82	*0.10*	RC
NB	0.00	0.87	0.76	0.81	0.94	0.81	*0.84*	FCR-1
	0.00	0.94	0.78	0.82	0.98	0.81	*0.87*	FCR-2
	0.73	0.94	0.82	0.88	0.96	0.82	*0.15*	RC
	Subspace of 50%							
kNN	0.00	0.90	0.82	0.86	0.96	0.88	*0.88*	FCR-1
	0.00	0.95	0.85	0.88	0.94	0.85	*0.89*	FCR-2
	0.72	0.94	0.91	0.92	0.95	0.93	*0.21*	RC
HT	0.00	0.88	0.74	0.80	0.97	0.75	*0.83*	FCR-1
	0.00	0.93	0.72	0.77	0.99	0.76	*0.83*	FCR-2
	0.62	0.92	0.71	0.84	0.96	0.75	*0.22*	RC
DT	0.00	0.91	0.81	0.80	0.94	0.79	*0.85*	FCR-1
	0.00	0.92	0.80	0.83	0.94	0.75	*0.85*	FCR-2
	0.78	0.93	0.75	0.85	0.96	0.92	*0.10*	RC
NB	0.00	0.88	0.79	0.81	0.99	0.82	*0.86*	FCR-1
	0.00	0.94	0.79	0.82	0.98	0.80	*0.87*	FCR-2
	0.78	0.95	0.86	0.90	0.97	0.89	*0.14*	RC
	Subspace of 75%							
kNN	0.00	0.91	0.85	0.83	0.96	0.84	*0.88*	FCR-1
	0.00	0.94	0.85	0.87	0.96	0.85	*0.89*	FCR-2
	0.72	0.96	0.92	0.91	0.95	0.93	*0.21*	RC
HT	0.62	0.87	0.77	0.73	0.99	0.70	*0.19*	FCR-1

(continued)

Table 7. (*continued*)

Classifier	No-clustering	HC	k-means	Cascade k-means	EM	Canopy	Increase over no-clustering	Dataset
	0.00	0.93	0.63	0.72	0.99	0.71	*0.80*	FCR-2
	0.58	0.95	0.59	0.89	0.97	0.66	*0.23*	RC
DT	0.00	0.88	0.81	0.81	0.95	0.81	*0.85*	FCR-1
	0.00	0.91	0.80	0.83	0.93	0.78	*0.85*	FCR-2
	0.73	0.93	0.77	0.85	0.95	0.93	*0.16*	RC
NB	0.61	0.87	0.79	0.79	0.99	0.80	*0.24*	FCR-1
	0.00	0.93	0.77	0.80	0.99	0.80	*0.86*	FCR-2
	0.76	0.94	0.85	0.89	0.97	0.88	*0.14*	RC
	Subspace of 90%							
kNN	0.00	0.91	0.85	0.84	0.97	0.84	*0.88*	FCR-1
	0.00	0.93	0.83	0.87	0.93	0.83	*0.88*	FCR-2
	0.74	0.95	0.91	0.91	0.95	0.89	*0.19*	RC
HT	0.60	0.88	0.79	0.62	0.99	0.66	*0.19*	FCR-1
	0.00	0.93	0.55	0.70	0.99	0.67	*0.77*	FCR-2
	0.58	0.94	0.58	0.15	0.98	0.63	*0.07*	RC
DT	0.00	0.88	0.80	0.81	0.91	0.77	*0.83*	FCR-1
	0.00	0.93	0.79	0.83	0.93	0.80	*0.86*	FCR-2
	0.74	0.93	0.76	0.80	0.96	0.97	*0.14*	RC
NB	0.58	0.88	0.79	0.79	0.99	0.80	*0.27*	FCR-1
	0.00	0.93	0.76	0.80	0.99	0.80	*0.85*	FCR-2
	0.77	0.94	0.86	0.90	0.98	0.89	*0.14*	RC

5.2 Predicting User Responses – System Effectiveness

By considering our previous results [12] and the additional evaluation presented in Sect. 5.2, we evaluate the effectiveness of the system by using the three cluster analysis algorithms with the highest overall results, namely EM, HC, and cascade k-means. That is, these three clustering methods were chosen based on their good performance as shown in the previous section.

In this section, we used the FCR-2 data from 2016 to 2018. Table 8 shows the number and percentage of ratings taken for each test subject to evaluate the systems effectives, by predicting each user's choice based on the resulted classification model. In Table 9, we depict the overall classification accuracy, whereas in Table 11 through Table 14, we illustrate the prediction rate for each test subject (user). Note that based on our results depicted in Sect. 5.2, the subspace size was set to 50% (Fig. 4).

Table 8. Number and percentage of each test subject rating records.

	Total # in original set	% from the original set	# in training set	% from training set	# in test set	% from test set
Ford	304	9%	218	72%	86	28%
Hyundai	80	2%	56	70%	24	30%
Jaguar	65	2%	38	58%	27	42%
Lincoln	47	1%	29	62%	18	38%
Mini	86	3%	49	57%	37	43%
Audi	113	4%	76	67%	37	33%

Table 9. Accuracies for user predicting models.

Cluster	Method			
	kNN	Subspace	Bagging	Boosting
No cluster	64.60	72.53	68.19	64.82
EM	93.62	95.57	94.42	93.62
HC	90.65	90.08	90.92	90.65
Cascade	77.98	81.48	79.44	77.98

Table 10. F-score for user predicting models.

Cluster	Method			
	kNN	Subspace	Bagging	Boosting
No cluster	0.63	0.71	0.67	0.63
EM	0.94	0.96	0.94	0.94
HC	0.91	0.90	0.91	0.91
Cascade	0.78	0.81	0.79	0.78

As mentioned earlier, in this section we further evaluate our models based on the prediction accuracies per user. To this end, six users were selected at random. Since this data set is about fuel consumption rating, we consider different vehicle makes as our test subject, the goal is to predict their rating, namely Ford, Hyundai, Jaguar, Lincoln, Mini, and Audi.

Table 11 depicts the prediction rate without using cluster analysis as a preprocessing step. The results in Table 12 through Table 14 show the prediction rate for each type of cluster analysis against each user. In this section, we focus on the performance of the ensemble learning method. We investigate the subspace ensemble method, and therefore test bagging, boosting, and the subspace algorithms.

Table 11. Predictions rate for users without using cluster analysis.

	kNN	Subspace	Bagging	Boosting
Ford	69.00	71.00	72.00	69.00
Hyundai	68.00	80.00	72.00	68.00
Jaguar	20.00	20.00	26.67	20.00
Lincoln	73.33	73.33	73.33	73.33
Mini	50.00	43.33	46.67	50.00
Audi	74.29	68.57	74.29	74.29
Average	*59.10*	*72.90*	*60.83*	*59.10*

Table 12. Predictions rate for users using EM analysis.

	kNN	Subspace	Bagging	Boosting
Ford	93.00	95.00	93.00	93.00
Hyundai	87.50	87.50	87.50	87.50
Jaguar	93.33	93.33	86.67	93.33
Lincoln	100.00	100.00	100.00	100.00
Mini	100.00	96.67	100.00	100.00
Audi	97.14	100.00	100.00	97.14
Average	*95.16*	*95.42*	*94.53*	*95.16*

Table 13. Predictions rate for users using HC analysis.

	kNN	Subspace	Bagging	Boosting
Ford	86.00	82.00	82.00	86.00
Hyundai	88.00	84.00	84.00	88.00
Jaguar	93.33	84.00	93.33	93.33
Lincoln	80.00	80.00	80.00	80.00
Mini	100.00	100.00	100.00	100.00
Audi	85.71	88.57	88.57	85.71
Average	*88.84*	*86.43*	*87.98*	*88.84*

Table 14. Predictions rate for users using Cascade analysis.

	kNN	Subspace	Bagging	Boosting
Ford	70.00	73.00	67.00	70.00
Hyundai	80.00	84.00	80.00	80.00
Jaguar	86.67	93.33	86.67	86.67
Lincoln	80.00	86.67	73.33	80.00
Mini	80.27	82.54	81.20	80.27
Audi	82.86	77.14	82.86	82.86
Average	*79.97*	*82.78*	*78.51*	*79.97*

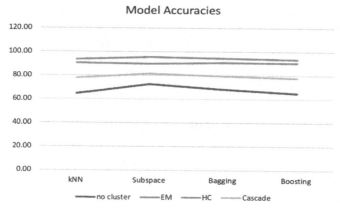

Fig. 4. Model accuracies for user predictions.

A review of Table 9 and Table 10 shows that using cluster analysis resulted in better performance for all ensemble methods used in this experimental evaluation. We also notice that for this data set, HC improved the performance for all ensemble methods over the use of no clustering. However, the performance is similar for all ensembles, while employing EM resulted in better performance for all ensembles. From the results shown in Table 9, we can conclude that for this data set, the best performance is achieved when utilizing the EM-subspace pair.

The following four tables show the results of the prediction rate for individual users. In these tables, we notice that clustering improves the prediction rate for individual users. Furthermore, we observe that subspace methods improve the prediction rate for both EM and cascade cluster analysis as a pre-processing step. In contrast, the results shown in Table 13 suggest that the prediction rate is lower when the subspace method is used together with the HC algorithm (Fig. 5).

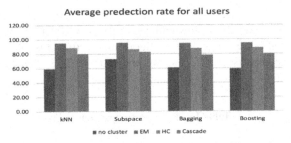

Fig. 5. We summarize the average prediction rate with and without cluster analysis, when considering the classification algorithms used.

5.3   Statistical Validation

To further validate our results, we perform a Friedman test, a non-parametric statistical test used to measure the difference between the EM, HC, and cascade k-means cluster analysis algorithms, when used in collaboration with bagging, boosting, or feature subset ensembles. As described above, these three cluster analysis algorithms generally yielded the best performances across our domains. Note that we use a confidence level of $\alpha = 0.05$, following standard practice in the machine-learning community (Table 15).

Table 15.   Hypothesis test summary.

Null hypothesis	Sig.	Decision
The distribution of EM, HC, and Cascade are the same	0.007	Reject the null hypothesis

This resultant p-value is 0.007383 which indicates that there is a significant difference between the three cluster analysis algorithms. The related-samples Friedman's two-way analysis of variance by ranks, as shown in Fig. 6, shows the mean ranks for each cluster analysis.

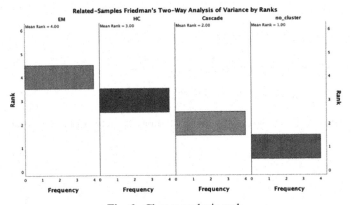

Fig. 6. Cluster analysis rank.

The p value is used to reject the null hypothesis, which states that all groups are from the same distribution and there is no significant difference among them. Subsequently, the alternative hypothesis that one or more algorithm is different is evaluated by using a post-hoc pairwise comparison test. First, we perform a pairwise comparison as shown in Table 16.

Table 16. Pairwise comparisons.

Method 1–Method 2	Test statistic	Std. error	Std. test statistic	Sig.
No cluster-Cascade	1.000	0.913	1.095	0.273
No cluster-HC	2.000	0.913	2.191	0.028
No cluster-EM	3.000	0.913	2.286	0.001
Cascade-HC	1.000	0.913	1.095	0.273
Cascade-EM	2.000	0.913	2.191	0.028
HC-EM	1.000	0.913	1.095	0.273

In this table, each row tests the null hypothesis that cluster method 1 and method 2 distribution are the same using a significance level of 0.05. Hence, we notice that the pairs *no cluster-HC, no cluster-EM,* and *Cascade-EM* have significant differences (Fig. 7).

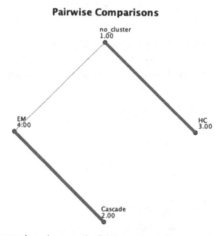

Fig. 7. Pairwise comparison in regard of the number of successes shown at each node.

Next, we conduct Nemenyi post-hoc tests to determine the critical difference (CD) of where the pairs significantly differ from one another, as shown in (Eq. 2) [40]. Our results show that there is a significant difference between EM and Cascade analysis as shown in Table 17.

$$CD = q_a \sqrt{\frac{k(k+1)}{6n}} \tag{2}$$

Table 17. Nemenyi p-values.

	No cluster	EM	HC
EM	0.005602		
HC	0.125707	0.692333	
Cascade	0.692333	0.125707	0.692333

Our results indicate that pairs using the EM, HC, or Cascade cluster analysis algorithms resulted in superior performance compared to other methods when considering all ensemble types. In addition, the statistical test confirms that there is no significant difference between EM and HC when used in collaboration with bagging, boosting, or feature subspace ensembles.

6 Conclusions and Future Work

In this paper, we introduce the Extended HCC-Learn, a multi-strategy framework that combines multiple cluster analysis and classification algorithms for recommender systems. Recommender systems are challenged by labeling and data sparsity, and the framework was created to address these challenges. Specifically, we focus on ensemble-based learning through the employment of bagging, boosting, and feature subspace methods. Our results confirm that a combination of cluster analysis and classification algorithms generally benefits the learning process. In addition, combining soft clustering with an ensemble based on feature subsets produces superior results when applied to our data sets. Further, when considering all type of ensembles, we used in this experiment, we can conclude that both soft and hierarchical clustering results in high performance. We conclude that cluster analysis clearly benefits learning, leading to high predictive accuracies for existing users.

In this work, the test subjects taken into evaluation were existing users in the system. In our future work, we plan on applying this framework to cold starts and to alleviate the so-called "grey sheep problem," which refers to recommending items to atypical users. In our current work, we assume that all the class labels are known. Our future work will focus on scenarios where this is not the case. Specifically, we plan to employ active learning, or so-called "user in the loop," and semi-supervised techniques, where few labels exist.

References

1. Su, X., Khoshgoftaar, T.M.: A survey of collaborative filtering techniques. Adv. Artif. Intell. (2009). Article no. 4
2. Wei, K., Huang, J., Fu, S.: A survey of e-commerce recommender systems. In: 2007 International Conference on Service Systems and Service Management, pp. 1–5. IEEE (2007)
3. Minkov, E., Charrow, B., Ledlie, J., Teller, S., Jaakkola, T.: Collaborative future event recommendation. In: Proceedings of the 19th ACM International Conference on Information and Knowledge Management, pp. 819–828. ACM (2010)
4. Acosta, O.C., Behar, P.A., Reategui, E.B.: Content recommendation in an inquiry-based learning environment. In: Frontiers in Education Conference (FIE), pp. 1–6. IEEE (2014)
5. Liao, C.-L., Lee, S.-J.: A clustering based approach to improving the efficiency of collaborative filtering recommendation. Electron. Commer. Res. Appl. **18**, 1–9 (2016)
6. Saha, T., Rangwala, H., Domeniconi, C.: Predicting preference tags to improve item recommendation. In: Proceedings of the 2015 SIAM International Conference on Data Mining, pp. 864–872. SIAM (2015)
7. Elahi, M., Ricci, F., Rubens, N.: Active learning strategies for rating elicitation in collaborative filtering: a system-wide perspective. ACM Trans. Intell. Syst. Technol. (TIST) **5**(1), 13 (2013)
8. Witten, I.H., Frank, E., Hall, M.A., Pal, C.J.: Data Mining: Practical Machine Learning Tools and Techniques. Morgan Kaufmann, Burlington (2016)
9. Panov, P., Džeroski, S.: Combining bagging and random subspaces to create better ensembles. In: RB, M., Shawe-Taylor, J., Lavrač, N. (eds.) IDA 2007. LNCS, vol. 4723, pp. 118–129. Springer, Heidelberg (2007). https://doi.org/10.1007/978-3-540-74825-0_11
10. Ho, T.K.: The random subspace method for constructing decision forests. IEEE Trans. Pattern Anal. Mach. Intell. **20**(8), 832–844 (1998)
11. Sun, S.: An improved random subspace method and its application to EEG signal classification. In: Haindl, M., Kittler, J., Roli, F. (eds.) MCS 2007. LNCS, vol. 4472, pp. 103–112. Springer, Heidelberg (2007). https://doi.org/10.1007/978-3-540-72523-7_11
12. Alabdulrahman, R., Viktor, H., Paquet, E.: Beyond k-NN: combining cluster analysis and classification for recommender systems. In: The 10th International Joint Conference on Knowledge Discovery, Knowledge Engineering and Knowledge Management (IC3K 2018), Seville, Spain, KDIR 2018, pp. 82–91 (2018)
13. Kanagal, B., Ahmed, A., Pandey, S., Josifovski, V., Yuan, J., Garcia-Pueyo, L.: Supercharging recommender systems using taxonomies for learning user purchase behavior. Proc. VLDB Endow. **5**(10), 956–967 (2012)
14. Wang, H., Wang, N., Yeung, D.-Y.: Collaborative deep learning for recommender systems. In: Proceedings of the 21th ACM SIGKDD International Conference on Knowledge Discovery and Data Mining, pp. 1235–1244. ACM (2015)
15. Nikolaenko, V., Ioannidis, S., Weinsberg, U., Joye, M., Taft, N., Boneh, D.: Privacy-preserving matrix factorization. In: Proceedings of the 2013 ACM SIGSAC Conference on Computer & Communications Security, pp. 801–812. ACM (2013)
16. Guo, G., Zhang, J., Thalmann, D.: A simple but effective method to incorporate trusted neighbors in recommender systems. In: Masthoff, J., Mobasher, B., Desmarais, M.C., Nkambou, R. (eds.) UMAP 2012. LNCS, vol. 7379, pp. 114–125. Springer, Heidelberg (2012). https://doi.org/10.1007/978-3-642-31454-4_10
17. Li, X., Cong, G., Li, X.-L., Pham, T.-A.N., Krishnaswamy, S.: Rank-GeoFM: a ranking based geographical factorization method for point of interest recommendation. In: Proceedings of the 38th International ACM SIGIR Conference on Research and Development in Information Retrieval, pp. 433–442. ACM (2015)

18. Lian, D., Zhao, C., Xie, X., Sun, G., Chen, E., Rui, Y.: GeoMF: joint geographical modeling and matrix factorization for point-of-interest recommendation. In: Proceedings of the 20th ACM SIGKDD International Conference on Knowledge Discovery and Data Mining, pp. 831–840. ACM (2014)

19. Guo, H., Viktor, H.L.: Learning from imbalanced data sets with boosting and data generation: the DataBoost-IM approach. ACM SIGKDD Explor. Newsl. **6**(1), 30–39 (2004)

20. Jayasree, S., Gavya, A.A.: Addressing imbalance problem in the class–a survey (2014)

21. Breiman, L.: Bagging predictors. Mach. Learn. **24**(2), 123–140 (1996)

22. Giovanni, S., John, E.: Ensemble Methods in Data Mining: Improving Accuracy Through Combining Predictions. Morgan Claypool (2010). https://doi.org/10.2200/S00240ED1V01Y200912DMK002

23. Dilon, B.: Short overview of weka. University De Strasbourg (2016). https://slideplayer.com/slide/3312931/

24. Freund, Y., Schapire, R.E.: A decision-theoretic generalization of on-line learning and an application to boosting. J. Comput. Syst. Sci. **55**(1), 119–139 (1997)

25. Cong, Z., Zhang, X., Wang, H., Xu, H.: Human resource recommendation algorithm based on ensemble learning and Spark. J. Phys. Conf. Ser. **887**, 012048 (2017)

26. Lili, C.: Recommender algorithms based on boosting ensemble learning. Int. J. Smart Sens. Intell. Syst. **8**(1), 368–386 (2015)

27. Pande, S.R., Sambare, S.S., Thakre, V.M.: Data clustering using data mining techniques. Int. J. Adv. Res. Comput. Commun. Eng. **1**(8), 494–499 (2012)

28. Mishra, R., Kumar, P., Bhasker, B.: A web recommendation system considering sequential information. Decis. Support Syst. **75**, 1–10 (2015)

29. Han, J., Pei, J., Kamber, M.: Data mining: concepts and techniques (2011)

30. Frank, E., Hall, M.A., Witten, I.H.: The WEKA workbench. In: Data Mining: Practical Machine Learning Tools and Techniques (2016)

31. Vargas-Govea, B., González-Serna, G., Ponce-Medellın, R.: Effects of relevant contextual features in the performance of a restaurant recommender system. ACM RecSys **11**(592), 56 (2011)

32. Canada, N.R.: Fuel Consumption Ratings. Open Government Canada (2018)

33. Alabdulrahman, R., Viktor, H., Paquet, E.: An active learning approach for ensemble-based data stream mining. In: Proceedings of the International Joint Conference on Knowledge Discovery, Knowledge Engineering and Knowledge Management, Porto, Portugal, pp. 275–282. SCITEPRESS-Science and Technology Publications, Lda (2016)

34. Mythili, S., Madhiya, E.: An analysis on clustering algorithms in data mining. J. IJCSMC **3**(1), 334–340 (2014)

35. Zhang, Y., Li, T.: Dclustere: a framework for evaluating and understanding document clustering using visualization. ACM Trans. Intell. Syst. Technol. (TIST) **3**(2), 24 (2012)

36. Sridevi, M., Rao, R.R., Rao, M.V.: A survey on recommender system. Int. J. Comput. Sci. Inf. Secur. **14**(5), 265 (2016)

37. Katarya, R., Verma, O.P.: A collaborative recommender system enhanced with particle swarm optimization technique. Multimed. Tools Appl. **75**(15), 9225–9239 (2016). https://doi.org/10.1007/s11042-016-3481-4

38. Bifet, A., Kirkby, R.: Data Stream Mining a Practical Approach (2009)

39. Caliński, T., Harabasz, J.: A dendrite method for cluster analysis. Commun. Stat. Theory Methods **3**(1), 1–27 (1974)

40. Flach, P.: Machine Learning: The Art and Science of Algorithms that Make Sense of Data. Cambridge University Press, Cambridge (2012)

Analysis and Detection of Unreliable Users in Twitter: Two Case Studies

Nuno Guimaraes[1]([⊠]) [iD], Alvaro Figueira[1] [iD], and Luis Torgo[2] [iD]

[1] CRACS/INESCTEC, University of Porto,
Rua do Campo Alegre 1021/1055, Porto, Portugal
nuno.r.guimaraes@inesctec.pt
[2] Faculty of Computer Science, Dalhousie University, Halifax, Canada

Abstract. The emergence of online social networks provided users with an easy way to publish and disseminate content, reaching broader audiences than previous platforms (such as blogs or personal websites) allowed. However, malicious users started to take advantage of these features to disseminate unreliable content through the network like false information, extremely biased opinions, or hate speech. Consequently, it becomes crucial to try to detect these users at an early stage to avoid the propagation of unreliable content in social networks' ecosystems. In this work, we introduce a methodology to extract large corpus of unreliable posts using Twitter and two databases of unreliable websites (Open-Sources and Media Bias Fact Check). In addition, we present an analysis of the content and users that publish and share several types of unreliable content. Finally, we develop supervised models to classify a twitter account according to its reliability. The experiments conducted using two different data sets show performance above 94% using Decision Trees as the learning algorithm. These experiments, although with some limitations, provide some encouraging results for future research on detecting unreliable accounts on social networks.

Keywords: Unreliable information · Machine learning · Data mining

1 Introduction

The exponential growth of users in social networks such as Twitter and Facebook has contributed to their rise as the number one medium for information diffusion and propagation. A recent study showed that, in 2017, 67% of adults consume some type of news in social media, with 20% of the respondents recurring often to this medium for news consumption [10].

The effortless way of sharing content via social networks combined with malicious users' intents, created conditions for the spread of misreported information

Nuno Guimaraes thanks the Fundação para a Ciência e Tecnologia (FCT), Portugal for the Ph.D. Grant (SFRH/BD/129708/2017).

© Springer Nature Switzerland AG 2020
A. Fred et al. (Eds.): IC3K 2018, CCIS 1222, pp. 50–73, 2020.
https://doi.org/10.1007/978-3-030-49559-6_3

and rumors. However, it was not until 2016, during the United States Presidential Elections that the term "fake news" became trending and a recurrent topic. In addition, it had provided a huge impact on the campaign, with several social media accounts deliberately disseminating false information via original posts or by sharing links to false news sites [19].

Due to the major impact that fake news had, high reputation companies such as Google and Facebook started working to tackle the problem [15,16]. The scientific community has also been active on the topic. As a matter of fact, Fig. 1 shows the number of hits per year in Google Scholar regarding the term "fake news" where we can observe a constant growth on the number of publications on the topic (there is a slight decay in 2019 but this is probably due to a large number of works that are still being published). Particularly, in 2017, there was an increase of approximately 7000 publications in comparison with the previous year.

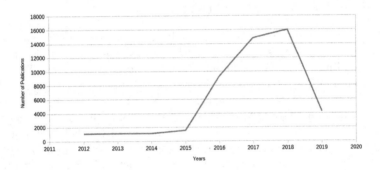

Fig. 1. Number of hits per year in Google Scholar for the term "fake news".

Although "fake news" has become a familiar term after the 2016 elections and is normally associated with political news, there are other domains of unreliable content that affect social media. Unreliable content on health conditions or miraculous cures is also a concerning problem, since this type of "information" is shared more extensively than reliable information [9]. Another example is extreme bias content which relies on out-of-context information or opinions distorted as facts [24]. All these types of unreliable information are disseminated through social networks, influencing users' beliefs and their perception of the truth. Therefore, not only it is important to determine which content is unreliable but also which accounts/sources to trust on social networks with respect to the large set of misinformation that exists.

In this study, we extend the work presented in [11] and apply the methodology to extract misinformation content from Twitter using two different unreliable websites databases. Next, we perform an analysis and comparison on the extracted data to determine possible indicators that can lead to the detection of unreliable users. Finally, we build models to determine this type of users using the different sources of data.

In the next section, we cover the related work on fake news and misinformation. In Sect. 3, we present the methodology to extract unreliable posts using as ground truth two of the most well-know databases of unreliable sources. In Sect. 4 we perform a study on the content of unreliable posts and users that propagate them. In addition, we also highlight the main differences on the two extracted data sets. Then, we create, compare, and evaluate models to detect unreliable accounts. Finally, we draw some conclusions and describe some paths for future work.

2　Related Work

We divided the literature review into three subgroups: propagation of unreliable content, detection of unreliable content and spam/bot accounts detection.

2.1　Propagation of Unreliable Content

We start by analyzing Shao's paper that describes a platform to track online misinformation [26]. In this paper, the authors crawl posts from social networks that includes links from fake content and fact-checking websites. Then, they proceed to an analysis of the popularity and activity of users that spread these URLs. One of the preliminary results achieved is that users who disseminate fake news are much more active and committed than the ones that spread the articles to refute them. In other words, there is a small set of top fake news accounts that generate a large number of tweets regarding the topic, while in the case of fact-checking it is more distributed across the network. This work presents some similarities with our approach. However, our goal is to detect unreliable accounts and not to analyse fact-checkers and users who disseminate fake news.

Another work, which presents an approach to the network propagation of fake news, is described in [31] where the interplay between believers of fake news and fact-checkers is analyzed. The presented model can be seen as a set of states and transitions similar to the spreading of a disease, where hoaxes (or fake news) are virus. The same model characterizes the users disseminating fake news as the infected patients, although they can "recover" when confronted with a fact-checking action. The main difference between the proposed approach and traditional SIS (Susceptible-Infected-Susceptible) and SIR (Susceptible-Infected-Recover) models is the existence of two sub-states in infected nodes: believers (the users that believe the hoax) and fact-checkers (the users who debunk the hoax). The authors test their approach in 3 different scenarios: a random network, a scale-free network, and a real social network (using Facebook). According to the authors, one of the main results of this work is that a minor activity regarding fact-checking can cancel a hoax, even when users believe it with a high probability.

2.2 Detection of Unreliable Content

In the study by Antoniadis [2] the authors try to identify misinformation on Twitter during an event (hurricane Sandy). For that purpose, they labelled a set of tweets into credible and misinformation. Then, a set of features were extracted from the text and social feedback. The best result was achieved (F-measure = 78%) using a Bootstrap Aggregating Method. Two experiments are described in this paper. In the first, social feedback features (number of retweets, number of favourites, etc.) were included. In the second, by removing these features, the results decay approximately 3%. Thus, authors claim that the method is efficient in real time.

In the work of Tacchini et al. [30] the authors state that "users who liked a post" is a feature of major importance for fake content detection and test their approach with two different models: Logistic Regression and an adaptation of a Boolean Label Crowdsourcing (BLC) algorithm to work with a training set. Using a small set of posts (15) as training set, the authors achieved an accuracy near 80%. In addition, even with users liking fake (hoax) and true posts, the accuracy achieved can be higher than 90% using only 10% of the data set for training.

2.3 Spammers/Bots Accounts Detection

The majority of existing works have tried to detect spammers or bots in Twitter. The study in [4] presents a model to detect spammers in Twitter. The authors relied on manual annotation to build a dataset of approximately 1000 entries of spammer and non-spammer users. Then, they developed attributes regarding content and user behaviour. The obtained model achieved 70% accuracy in detecting spammers and 96% in detecting non-spammers. Although spammer detection studies present a similar problem to the detection of unreliable accounts, spammers are more easily determined than unreliable accounts. According to the authors "Tweet spammers are driven by several goals, such as to spread advertise to generate sales, disseminate pornography, viruses, phishing, or simply just to compromise system reputation". Therefore, spammer accounts represent a subgroup of all unreliable accounts that we are trying to detect.

A similar work [5] provides a model to detect credibility in Twitter events. The authors start by building and annotating a data set of tweets (via Crowdsourcing) regarding specific trending topics. Then, they use 4 different sets of features (Message, User, Topic, and Propagation) and a Decision Tree model to achieve an accuracy of 86% in a balanced data set. Despite the fact this paper has tackled a different problem, some features presented may also have an impact on the detection of unreliable accounts.

Other works have also analyzed and tried to detect bot accounts. For example, the work in [6] presents an analysis of three different types of accounts: humans, bots, and cyborgs. The authors built a balanced data set of 6000 users manually annotated. Next, they created a system for user classification with 4 different components (entropy measures, spam detection, account properties, and decision maker). This system achieves an average accuracy of 96% with the "Human" class being the more correctly classified. In another work, [7] the authors present a framework to distinguish between human and bot accounts. In addition, the paper highlights the importance of sentiment features in such task.

Although the presented studies provide accurate systems to distinguish human accounts from bots and spammers, unreliable accounts are not guaranteed to be composed, in totality, of these two classes. In fact, human accounts may also spread unreliable posts due to their strong political beliefs or incapacity to distinguish reliable and unreliable content since that, on average, 50% of users who have seen a piece of fake content, prior to the U.S. 2016 election, believed it [1].

3   Methodology

Different definitions of misinformation, fake news, and rumors can be found in the literature. Our main goal in this work is to explore characteristics that are common to unreliable content in general. We define unreliable content more loosely than the current literature, which focuses on specific problems such as fake news or clickbait.

In this work, we will focus on unreliable content on Twitter. This type of content includes false information, clickbait, extremely bias content, hate speech, conspiracy theories, and rumors. To automatically retrieved tweets that contain this type of content, our methodology relies on the extraction of posts that contain links to websites outside the Twitter ecosystem. If the websites that these tweets are pointing to are unreliable, then the tweet is spreading unreliable content.

There are several articles that are collecting and exposing websites that spread false and unreliable information, such as Buzzfeed[1] and USNews[2]. However, in this work, we used two well-established resources for this type of data: OpenSources [24] and MediaBiasFactCheck.com (MBFC) [23].

OpenSources is a resource for assessing online information sources. Users can submit suggestions of websites to be inserted. However, submissions are carefully revised by the project researchers before inclusion. The classification for each site ranges from credible news sources to misleading and outright fake websites. For this study, we are interested in sites that are labelled as "bias", "fake", "fake news", "hate","junksci"[3], "rumour", "conspiracy", "clickbait", or "unreliable".

In MBFC the sources are annotated by professionals, though users can vote on the classification. This action does not change the annotation but it provides the annotators with information that may lead them to re-evaluate sources where discrepancy from the two classifications is high. MBFC also presents a large set

---

[1] https://www.buzzfeednews.com/article/craigsilverman/top-fake-news-of-2016.

[2] https://www.usnews.com/news/national-news/articles/2016-11-14/avoid-these-fake-news-sites-at-all-costs.

[3] "junksci" is an acronym for "junk science".

of labels in which sources are annotated as well as a factuality score. The labels provided by this resource are leftBias, lefCenterBias, leastBias, rightCenterBias, rightBias, conspiracy, fake and proScience. However, since we want to target tweets that are spreading unreliable information, the leftCenteBias, rightCenterBias, leastBias, and proScience sources were discarded. The first 3 because they only show a moderated level of bias (or no bias at all) and the last because their sources are trustworthy and always back-up their articles with trustworthy references.

Table 1 presents the number of websites in OpenSources distributed by the selected categories at the time of the analysis. Table 2 presents similar data for MediaBiasFactCheck.

Table 1. Distribution of websites per dubious class in OpenSources.

Classification	Number of websites
Bias	133
Hate	29
JunkSci	32
Fake	237
Clickbait	32
Unreliable	56
Total	**522**

Table 2. Distribution of websites per dubious class in MBFC.

Classification	Number of websites
Conspiracy	258
Fake	413
Left Bias	277
Right Bias	243
Total	**1191**

For each web page on the previously mentioned categories, we convert the URL to a query for the Twitter Search API. Consequently, the tweets returned include the queried URL (or sub-domains/pages). For each URL, a maximum of 100 tweets was extracted. This limit was established considering the API rate limit and the number of websites in OpenSources and MBFC. However, for some websites, we have observed that this limit was not reached.

The extraction procedure was executed daily and the retrieved information was stored in a non-relational database built for the effect. All the extra fields provided by the Search API were stored. In addition, sentiment analysis and named entity recognition (NER) were computed for each tweet. For sentiment analysis, we used Vader [17] rule-based approach to determine the negative and positive sentiment values for each tweet. Regarding the NER component, we used NLTK [20] to detect 3 types of entities: location, organization, and persons.

In order to understand and identify common properties on tweets propagating unreliable content, an analysis of the retrieved data was conducted and is presented in the following section.

4   Exploratory Analysis

In this section, we describe the exploratory analysis of two data sets retrieved using the methodology described previously.

- The OpenSources data set has a time window of approximately two months of tweets ranging from March, 15 to May, 4 of 2018 combining the methodology described in Sect. 3 with the OpenSources website database. The total number of tweets retrieved in this period of time was 499530.
- The Media Bias Fact Check data set was extracted during a 53 day period (from 30 of June 2018 to 22 August 2018). The total number of extracted tweets was 34461.

We formulate three research questions (RQ) that are important in order to establish useful indicators on unreliable tweets.

- **RQ 1: Do Unreliable Tweets Follow Traditional Media Outlets in Terms of the Entities That They Mention?** The authors in [34] have concluded that traditional online media outlets appear to be responsible for fake news agenda since the content of traditional media news make users more attentive to all content regarding that subject online. With this RQ we want to analyze if that is also the case on tweets. In addition, we also inspect the frequency of entities per post on both unreliable and traditional news media outlet tweets.
- **RQ 2: Which Hashtags Are Commonly Used by Unreliable Users?** Hashtags are frequently used by users to aggregate tweets regarding the same topic. We study which are the most common hashtags on unreliable tweets and how they differ from traditional news media.
- **RQ 3: Does the Sentiment Differ between Unreliable Tweets and Tweets From Reputed Sources?** One important factor suggested by the authors in [25] is that a news headlines are more attractive if their sentiment is extreme. The same analysis was later conducted with "fake news" [27] with the conclusion that this type of content presents more negative sentiment than mainstream news outlets. Therefore, it is important to analyze if such behaviour is also noticed in unreliable tweets.

In addition, we also formulate an extra question regarding characteristics of unreliable accounts:

– **RQ 4: Can We Trust Verified Accounts?** Twitter has signalled with verified badges that a certain account of public interest is authentic [14]. However, this does not directly imply that we can trust the content posted. In fact, there have been cases of verified accounts that propagated misinformation [35]. Therefore, it is important to analyze the percentage of verified accounts that spread unreliable news content, since they are likely to have more engagement and retweets.

The majority of our research questions requires complementary data from news media outlets. Thus, we extract a collection of tweets from the same interval used on OpenSources and MBFC data sets.

We started by manually selecting a set of mainstream news outlets. We restrained our research to those which are written in the English language and whose impact and popularity are relevant in the United States and the United Kingdom (since they are two of the most influential countries in the world [13]). Therefore, we weighed on the number of followers of news accounts as well as how trustworthy they are for the general audience in the US [22] and UK [3]. The news media outlets selected are presented in Table 3:

Table 3. Selected News Media Outlets (based from [11]).

The Guardian	CNN	BBC
The Economist	Wall Street Journal	ABC
CBS News	Washington Post	NBC News
Reuters	Sky News	Fox News

Next, we describe an exploratory analysis on both data sets retrieved (OpenSources and MBFC) as well as their reputation tweets datasets counterparts. We assign the name "Rep-1" to the dataset composed of tweets from mainstream news media outlets extracted in the same interval as OpenSources and "Rep-2" to the one extracted in the same interval as MBFC.

4.1 Content Analysis

OpenSources Data Set Analysis. To answer **RQ 1**, we compare the most mentioned entities in OpenSources and Rep-1. Next, we extracted the top 50 entities for each category (persons, locations and organizations) for each data set (reliable and unreliable tweets). The results show that 36% of locations and persons identified, and 42% of the organizations, are the same in both data sets. This means that not only there are a lot of similar entities but also that these occur frequently on both data sets (since we are restraining our analysis to the top 50 entities of each category). In addition, the number of entities of unreliable tweets is, on average, far superior than the ones on news media outlets accounts. Table 4 illustrates the average entities per tweet on both data sets.

Table 4. Entities per tweet on unreliable and reliable data in OpenSources and Rep-1 data sets (based from [11]).

Entities	Locations (per tweet)	Persons (per tweet)	Organizations (per tweet)
Unreliable	**0.007**	**0.90**	**1.20**
Reliable	0.002	0.16	0.60
Difference	+0.005	+0.74	+0.6

Therefore, the constant presence of entities in tweets must provide useful information regarding its reliability. However, it is also important to point out some limitations of these results. First, the current state of the art systems have some difficulty to detect entities on short and unstructured texts (such as the case of tweets). Therefore, although posts from credible sources tend to be syntactically well written, tweets from common users are more free-form. Consequently, the detection of entities can result in a low accuracy when compared to larger text corpus.

Regarding **RQ2** we inspected the 50 most used hashtags for each data set (news media outlet tweets and unreliable tweets). Figure 2 represents each data set word cloud where the font size corresponds to the number of occurrences of the hashtag in the data (the larger the font, the larger the number of occurrences). Some interesting information can be observed. First, in unreliable tweets, the majority of words can be associated with the political domain. Some examples include MAGA (an acronym for the slogan "Make America Great Again"), TeaParty and Trump. Another interesting word is PJNET which stands for Patriot Journalist Network, a Twitter group which was responsible for coordinating tweets and propagating false information through the network [18]. There is also the mention of other groups such as TCOT and Red Nation Rising. In addition (and as expected) some hashtags refer to some topics that were trending in the news such as Trump, Syria, Skripal, Israel and Russia. Therefore, we can conclude that there is a mixture of hashtags regarding relevant topics, with Twitter-specific groups and propaganda. We can hypothesize that, in one hand, these hashtags lead to user engagement by using interesting and relevant topics and in another hand, try to associate the content with a specific group or page in an attempt to achieve a larger audience for those specific accounts.

The hashtag word cloud for the news media outlet accounts has more emphasis on words corresponding to entities (such as Trump, Hannity, Syria and Comey) and topics associated with events or movements (MeToo, NationalWalkoutDay, MarchForOurLives). However, there is also the presence of self-reference hashtags (i.e. that promote the news media outlet where the tweets were extracted). For example CNNSOTU (a news program from CNN), TheFive, and The Story (both FoxNews shows). Hence, and similar to the unreliable tweets word cloud, there is a mixture of news events related hashtags and self-promotion for news media outlets accounts.

(a) Hashtag word cloud from unreliable tweets

(b) Hashtag word cloud from news media outlet tweets

Fig. 2. Hashtag word cloud for reliable and unreliable tweets in OpenSources and Rep-1 data sets (based from [11]).

However, when comparing the frequency of hashtags per post, they largely differ. The average hashtag per tweet is 0.05 for the traditional news media outlets. This means that this type of tweets does not often contain hashtags. In another hand, the average hashtag per tweet in unreliable posts is 0.42 which means that, on average, there is a hashtag for every two tweets. This difference can provide effective indicators on the task of identifying unreliable accounts.

To answer **RQ3** once again we reuse Rep-1 dataset.

Figure 3 presents the average sentiment strength of tweets by day on both reliable and unreliable sources. It is clear that negative sentiment is predominant across all the interval of time studied. Positive sentiment varies between 0.06 and 0.085, whether negative sentiment has its lowest value at approximately 0.105. In addition, the negative sentiment is stronger on unreliable tweets than on tweets from reliable sources. This pattern is observable across the majority of the days from the selected time period. Hence, sentiment analysis provides clear indicators that the text of tweets that share unreliable links follow the same principle for appealing users. Furthermore, in agreement with what was concluded in [27], the negative sentiment seems to have a small decay with time. This provides some enlightenment on the behavior of this content. However, further analysis must be conducted to gain more confidence in these results.

Finally, **RQ 4** refers to the verification of accounts. More specifically to understand the ratio of verified accounts that spread unreliable content. In order to do it, we sampled 72000 user accounts from the dataset and extracted their

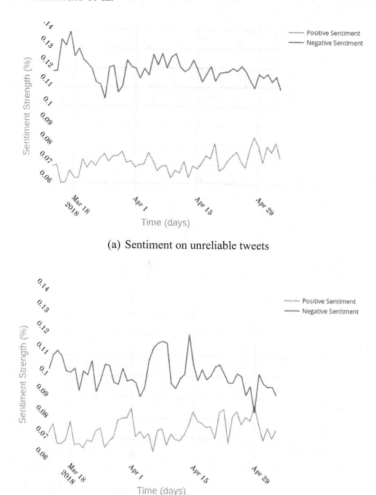

(a) Sentiment on unreliable tweets

(b) Sentiment on reliable tweets

Fig. 3. Comparison of sentiment through time in reliable and unreliable tweets in OpenSources and Rep-1 datasets (based from [11]).

verified status. The number of accounts that had tweeted unreliable links in this sample is 407 (0.6%) which is a significantly low percentage. This provides important insight that verified accounts are much less likely to diffuse unreliable information. Nevertheless, it is important to highlight that these type of accounts also represent a small percentage of all Twitter users, since only 226K of 330 million users [28] are verified (according to the official "Verified" account which follows all verified users [33]).

MBFC Dataset Analysis. Using the MBFC dataset and the Rep-2, we conducted a similar analysis to the one presented in the previous section and highlight the main differences in the unreliable datasets.

We started by analyzing **RQ 1** and present the frequency of entities on the tweets extracted from the MBFC and Rep-2 datasets. Table 5 illustrates the differences in the average number of entities between reliable and unreliable tweets from MBFC. The first observation is that unreliable tweets still are predominant regarding the presence of entities comparing to tweets from reputable sources. Furthermore, the difference in the frequency of entities is lower in locations and persons but twice larger in organizations when comparing to OpenSources and Rep-1 datasets.

With respect to the similarity of the top 50 entities, the percentage is smaller on the MBFC/Rep-2 group. The number of similar entities of the type person is 14% (approximately 22% less than in OpenSource/Rep-1). Locations and organizations have a slight increase with 20% and 26% respectively (thus, these values are still 16% smaller with respect to OpenSource/Rep-1).

Table 5. Entities per tweet on unreliable and reliable data in MBFC and Rep-2 datasets.

Entities	Locations (per tweet)	Persons (per tweet)	Organizations (per tweet)
Unreliable	**0.0048**	**0.7688**	**1.5341**
Reliable	0.0017	0.1414	0.2423
Difference	+0.0031	+0.6274	+1.2918

We proceed to analyse the hashtags of each of the datasets to understand if there is similarity on the words used or, similar to the OpenSources/Rep-1 group, a mixture of *self-propaganda* hashtags and trending keywords and topics. Figure 4 shows both hashtags word clouds for the MBFC and Rep-2 datasets.

Since we used the same reputation sources, the type of propaganda hashtags such as The Story, SpecialReport and OpenFuture are similar to Rep-1. In addition, there are also topics from Rep-1 that occur, thus less frequently (for example Brexit and Trump). There is also the rise of new hashtags (such as WorldCup) due to the different time intervals of both groups of datasets.

With respect to the word cloud built with hashtags from unreliable tweets, the change from OpenSources to MBFC has influenced the self-propaganda hashtags that appear. Nevertheless, there are still references to newsworthy topics (such as "Trump" and "WorldCup").

One of the most frequent hashtag is BB4SP which refers to a website of questionable extreme right-wing content[4]. Curiously, other frequent hashtags are religion-related words such as "catholic", "catholicsaint" and "catholicfaith".

---

[4] https://mediabiasfactcheck.com/bb4sp/.

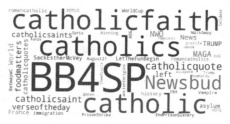

(a) Hashtag wordcloud from unreliable tweets

(b) Hashtag wordcloud from news media outlet tweets

Fig. 4. Hashtag Wordcloud for reliable and unreliable tweets in MBFC and Rep-2 datasets.

These hashtags belong to a website also labelled right wing by MBFC, with mixed content of true and false stories.

To sum up, in both groups (OpenSources/Rep-1 and MBFC/Rep-2) there is a predominance of *self-propaganda* hashtags (i.e. self mentioned twitter accounts or related content) and newsworthy topics. Modifying the unreliable data sources, the tendency is still the same, changing only the type of groups that are mentioned.

To answer **RQ 3** the sentiment of both MBFC and Rep-2 datasets was aggregated and analyzed. Although the same methodology was applied in the analysis of OpenSources/Rep-1 data, the sentiment strength patterns are significantly different. In the previous analysis, it was clear the difference of strength in both datasets, with the negative sentiment always achieving higher values than the positive. However, Fig. 5 shows a different scenario where in unreliable tweets the positive sentiment overcomes the negative. It is also interesting to highlight that this tendency is not maintained in reliable tweets, where is a predominance of negative sentiment.

We proceed to analyze a sample of accounts to answer **RQ 4**. Due to the different size of MBFC dataset, we retrieve the same percentage of users that was used to answer this RQ in OpenSources. Hence, we extract 4968 random users from the dataset and check their verified status. The percentage of users that were verified in this sample is 1.15%. This value is superior to the one obtained from the OpenSources dataset although it is still a small percentage of the users

Sentiment Strength Through MediaBias Tweet Posts

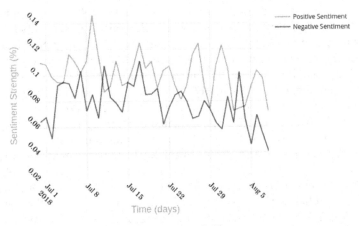

(a) Sentiment on unreliable tweets

Sentiment Strength Through MediaBias Tweet Posts

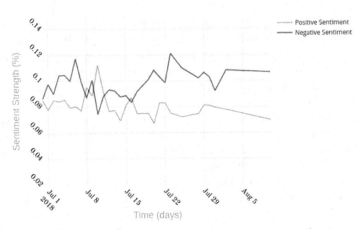

(b) Sentiment on reliable tweets

Fig. 5. Comparison of sentiment through time in reliable and unreliable tweets in MBFC and Rep-2 datasets.

that spread unreliable content regarding the total size of the sample. Therefore, we can hypothesize that the number of verified users that spread unreliable content is a small fraction of the total users retrieved using the methodology described in Sect. 3.

4.2   Unreliable Users Analysis

Not only it is important to have an overview analysis of tweets that propagate unreliable content, but also to make an in-depth analysis of accounts that more frequently propagate it. Thus, we plot the number of tweets that propagate dubious content per account. However, to avoid a very long tail plot, we only included accounts that posted more than 200 dubious tweets in the OpenSources dataset and 100 unreliable tweets in the MBFC dataset. The reason for this disparity is the difference in the number of posts for the most frequent users in each dataset. In Fig. 6, we begin by presenting the accounts ordered by the number of tweets in the OpenSources and MBFC dataset. There is some important information to retain from this analysis. First, with respect to the OpenSources dataset, in the course of 50 days there were accounts that have posted more than 1500 tweets with unreliable websites that were captured by our extraction methodology. It is important to emphasize that this number can be higher since the Twitter Search API only captures a small percentage of the total number of tweets matching the query parameters [32]. This means that, on average, there are accounts that post over 30 tweets a day containing unreliable links. In addition, there are 28 accounts that tweeted more than 500 times with the most frequent account to post a total of (at least) 2154 tweets.

In the MBFC dataset, the numbers are slightly different. First, the most frequent account has 1750 tweets captured which is approximately 400 tweets less than its OpenSources counterpart. In addition, there is approximately a 1000 tweets decay between the first and second most frequent user. Furthermore, when looking at the tail of each plot, OpenSource users tend to have a higher volume of tweets than MBFC users.

To make a more detailed study of the users that are continuously propagating unreliable content, we proceed to extract the last tweets for each one of the ten more frequent accounts of both datasets. Consequently, for each user, we extracted the most recent tweets from their timeline. It is important to mention that the tweets from the top users in OpenSources and MBFC were extracted at different times. The first was collected in June 2018 and the second in April 2019.

For each account, at least 3200 tweets were retrieved (the maximum allowed by the API). However, before the extraction procedure began, one user account from OpenSources dataset has been suspended, which restrain our analysis to 9 users.

First, we conducted an analysis of the post frequency of the top users to understand if there is a common pattern. Figure 7 presents the "tweeting" distribution of the last 3200 tweets for each account per day in both datasets. In other words, for each day, we divide the total number of posts for each account by the total number of posts for that day regarding all the top accounts analyzed.

The main conclusion is that post frequency is not similar in all accounts. For example, in the OpenSources dataset, account 7 posted the last 3200 tweets at a low rate across 5 months. This is illustrated by the 100% presence on the most distant dates. On another hand, the 3241 more recent tweets from account 3 were

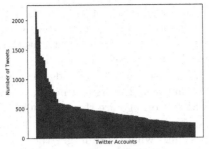

(a) Number of dubious tweets per account in OpenSources dataset (based from [11]).

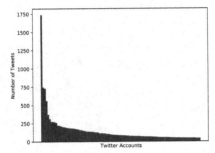

(b) Number of dubious tweets per account in MBFC dataset

Fig. 6. Comparison on the volume of tweets on the most frequent accounts.

posted in a 2 day period (consequently, it appears with a large volume at the end of the plot). Thus, pattern frequency is on both ends of the spectrum, with accounts presenting a constant number of posts per day and others presenting a difference of approximately 500 tweets between two days (account 3). In addition, through a more detail analysis, we conclude that account 4,5, and 7 are with a great probability associated with websites used for the extraction methodology since they share very similar names.

Although with a few exceptions, it is possible to perceive some similarities between the top users' distributions from both datasets. Like OpenSources, the top users from MBFC also are incoherent on propagation patterns. More specifically, account 6 from MBFC has a similar pattern to account 7 on OpenSources as well as account 5 from MBFC and account 6 from OpenSources. In conclusion, the patterns observed in OpenSources (i.e. low posting frequency throughout a wide interval of time and high posting frequency in a small interval of time) are also visible in MBFC dataset. Thus, the origin of the unreliable content, as well as the extraction time, do not seem to affect the behaviour of the top accounts.

The second analysis refers to the extended network of mentions in each tweet. By analyzing each mentioned user (on the latest tweets for the top accounts) we can figure out if they had already spread dubious content (by performing a query in our database). Unlike the current state of the art, the goal is not to study the neighbour accounts by the following/follow metric but according to the number of "mentions" of unreliable accounts. Figure 8 illustrates the connection between top users and other users through tweet mentions in OpenSources and MBFC dataset. Duplicate mentions are removed. The nodes represented in blue are the top users (in OpenSources dataset, 2 users did not have any mention to other users on their tweets). Nodes in orange are the accounts with no information in the database and whose accounts are not verified. Nodes in red are users that have already post dubious links where, the larger the node, the more dubious tweets were found on the database. The verified accounts were excluded since they are not likely to disseminate dubious content (as it was analyzed in RQ4).

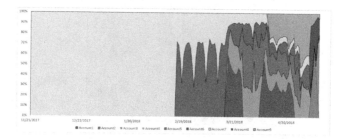

(a) Last tweets of the most frequent accounts in OpenSources dataset (based from [11]).

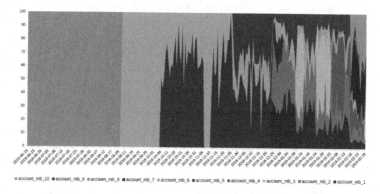

(b) Last tweets of the most frequent accounts in MBFC dataset

Fig. 7. Comparison on the distribution of tweets through time on the most frequent accounts.

In OpenSources dataset, two of the accounts mention a slightly larger number of unknown users while the others mention, in their majority, users already flagged in our database. The number of mentions also differs significantly. In the last 3200 tweets, a few top users had over 200 mentions while others only 2.

Curiously, the accounts that are associated with websites from OpenSources also behave differently since one of the accounts does not have user mentions in the latest tweets while the other is the one that has the most. However, almost all nodes (except one which only mentions two users) are linked to dubious users.

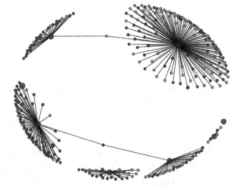

(a) Graph representing mentions from the top accounts of the Open-Sources dataset (based from [11]).

(b) Graph representing mentions from the top accounts of MBFC dataset

Fig. 8. Mentions graph for the most frequent accounts on both datasets.

In the MBFC dataset, the volume of mentions is significantly higher. However, in the top 9 users (similar to OpenSources, one of the users did not have any mentions) it is also possible to visualize some similarities with the previous graph in terms of the diversity of the unreliable accounts mentioned. In other words, from the 9 accounts analyzed there is an account who clearly mentions a larger number of unreliable users (that were already captured by our methodology) than unknown users. Other accounts display a more balanced number between unknown accounts and unreliable accounts or an imbalanced number of mentions towards unknown accounts. Summarizing, it is possible to detect some similarities (in MBFC and OpenSource graphs) regarding the inconsistency on the type of mentions and the different number of mentions between the top users of the same graph.

5   Model Creation

There are two components which play an important role in building a high accuracy model in machine learning: the learning data (i.e. ground-truth) and features extracted from it. Regarding the assessment of establishing a ground truth and build a scalable dataset without human annotation, we consider the top 200 accounts who spread unreliable links from OpenSources. Regarding the MBFC dataset, we increase this number to 1412. It is important to mention that we are no longer restricted to the subset used for data analysis but to all the tweets in the database. Regarding the reliable class and considering the negligible percentage of verified accounts that was captured in our analysis (RQ 4), we can assume with a certain degree of confidence that these accounts are reliable. In addition, since our main goal is to detect reliable and unreliable accounts, only using news media outlet accounts (like the ones in Sect. 3) would probably skew the learning step of our models. Thus, we argue that verified accounts capture a larger set of different accounts, ranging from celebrities, companies to news media outlets. Consequently, this would allow the model to better discriminate unreliable accounts from all others.

Therefore, we extract 200 verified accounts randomly selected from the Twitter Verified account [33] to complement the OpenSources users and 1484 to complement the MBFC users.

With respect to the features, there were some constraints due to the limitations of our dataset. First, since the goal of our model is not being able to distinguish between unreliable and verified accounts, this type of meta-data can't be used. In addition, the number of followers and following is also an important discriminating characteristic between verified accounts and others since verified accounts are normally accounts of public interest [14]. Hence, we focus on determining posting patterns and the characteristics of the content of the posts where verified accounts behaviour is more likely to the common user. The set of features extracted were:

- **Posting Patterns:** we extracted features based on the frequency of tweets posted by day. Due to the analysis conducted, unreliable accounts post in a higher frequency and unusual patterns, while the majority of users "tweet" less than one time a day [29]. Thus we computed the average and standard deviation of posts by day for each user.
- **Sentiment Patterns:** The difference of sentiment between unreliable and news media accounts (studied in the previous section) is the basis for these features. In addition, sentiment features have also provided significant importance in related tasks [7]. Therefore, we extracted the average positive and

negative sentiment for the tweets of each account using Vader sentiment system [17].

- **Hashtags and Mentions Patterns:** The number of hashtags and mentions have already been pointed out as a differentiating factor from normal user accounts and spammers [4,21]. Accordingly, we complemented our feature set with this indicator since spammers are a subgroup and fit our definition of unreliable accounts. We also do not differentiate mentions that have been verified and that are present in our database (unreliable) since we are using this principle to determine our ground-truth. For this reason, the inclusion of such features would skew our analysis.
- **Entities Pattern:** It is our assumption that entities are an important factor for building a model capable of detecting unreliable accounts, since a large portion of posts on social media are regarding irrelevant information and chat between users [5,8]. In addition, the analysis conducted in RQ1 provided evidence on the different number of entities in traditional news outlets and unreliable tweets. Consequently, the frequency of the different type of entities may present decisive indicators for differentiating unreliable accounts from all others. Thus, we built 3 numeric features regarding the average of entities detected by tweet in 3 different categories: persons, locations and organizations.

To extract the set of features we repeated the process from Sect. 4.2 and extract the most recent tweets for each account of our dataset.

5.1   Evaluation

We set two experiments considering the origin of the data (OpenSources or MBFC). We split our data into train and test sets in an 80% and 20% ratio, respectively. We used three machine learning algorithms to perform our experimental evaluation: Decision Trees (J48), Naive-Bayes and Support Vector Machines (SVM). Decision Trees used a confidence factor of 25%. The kernel chosen for the SVM was a radial basis function (RBF) with a gamma value of 0.083 and a cost of 1.0. The tests were conducted using WEKA [12]. Regarding the evaluation metrics, we focused on weighted precision, recall, and F1-measure. The results are presented in Table 6.

The results achieved in the evaluation procedure provide some reliability on our approach to the problem. In addition, the origin of unreliable users (OpenSources or MBFC) or the difference in the dataset sizes does not seem to affect the performance of the models. Decision trees accomplish the best result (96.2% and 94.0% in F1-measure in OpenSources and MBFC users, respectively) while Naive Bayes has the lowest performance of the three models tested. When analyzing the performance on individual classes, Decision Trees maintain the highest F1-measure score (96.4 % in the reliable accounts class and 96.0% in the unreliable for OpenSources and in MBFC 94.0% in the reliable class and 93.9% in the unreliable).

Table 6. Model performance on OpenSources and MBFC users.

Model	Precision (%)	Recall (%)	F1-Measure (%)
OpenSources users			
Naive Bayes	91.2	91.1	91.1
Decision Trees	**96.2**	**96.2**	**96.2**
SVM	93.5	92.4	92.4
MBFC users			
Naive Bayes	87.9	85.8	85.6
Decision Trees	**94.0**	**94.0**	**94.0**
SVM	90.4	90.3	90.3

There are some limitations that must be mentioned. First, the automatic annotation may not represent the totality of Twitter users. However, due to the analysis conducted in Sect. 3 and the information provided in [14], this type of accounts seems like a good ground-truth data for users that do not spread unreliable content and has the advantage of scaling the dataset without human intervention. In addition, the manual annotation of Twitter accounts would be an exhaustive and enduring task, since annotators would have to analyze content post by post and verify its veracity. Second, the size of the dataset is also not ideal. However, we wanted at a first stage to capture characteristics of accounts which are frequently spreading unreliable content. Nonetheless, since our methodology is constantly updating and populating our database, the number of users with significantly large tweets will increase and in future work, we will explore how a large number of entries influence these results.

6   Conclusion and Future Work

In this paper, we analyze and characterize unreliable content in Twitter, combining the methodology proposed in [11] with two different databases (OpenSources and Media Bias Fact Check). In addition, we used the data extracted to tackle the problem of detecting unreliable users in social networks.

We started by conducting an analysis on the content of unreliable tweets as well as on users who frequently published it. Some of the main findings are 1) the difference on the number of entities and hashtags between unreliable and reliable tweets, 2) the negligible number of verified accounts that spread unreliable content, 3) the high variation on the number of posts per day in the top unreliable accounts and 4) the variation on the number of mentions from the top accounts in both datasets.

Based on these analyses, we built models and determine their effectiveness in distinguishing unreliable and reliable social media accounts. We used the top accounts from OpenSources and MBFC data as "unreliable" accounts and verified Twitter accounts as "reliable" since 1) the vast majority does not spread unreliable content and 2) they represent a broader diversification of entities (celebrities, companies, politicians) than news outlets do.

We extract features based on the analysis conducted in Sect. 4 and related literature. Then, we built three different models for each dataset. Using F1-measure, the performance achieved is above 85% in all models from both datasets, with Decision Trees obtaining the best results. These results on datasets built from two different sources of data (OpenSources and MBFC), provide confidence on the methods proposed and that unreliable accounts can be distinguished based on publication patterns and on the history of the content posted.

Nevertheless, the current study presents some limitations that we intend to tackle in future work. Thus, we intend to use Crowdsourcing platforms to build a dataset that is not restrained to verified accounts (as reliable accounts) and automatically labeled unreliable accounts. This dataset will be used to validate our current models in human-annotated data and verify if our models generalized well outside the limitations imposed by the automatic labeling. With a new dataset, we can also include features derived from our database without incurring into building a skewed model (for example, if the account has tweets with unreliable content captured by our methodology).

Finally, we also wish to study the importance of the features extracted over time. More concretely, if the features used in the current models are still relevant as the database size grows and with more recent unreliable accounts.

References

1. Allcott, H., Gentzkow, M.: Social media and fake news in the 2016 election. Working Paper 23089, National Bureau of Economic Research, January 2017. https://doi.org/10.3386/w23089. http://www.nber.org/papers/w23089
2. Antoniadis, S., Litou, I., Kalogeraki, V.: A model for identifying misinformation in online social networks. In: Proceedings of the Confederated International Conferences: CoopIS, ODBASE, and C&TC 2015, Rhodes, Greece, 26–30 October 2015, vol. 9415, pp. 473–482 (2015). https://doi.org/10.1007/978-3-319-26148-5. http://link.springer.com/10.1007/978-3-319-26148-5
3. BBC: Public perceptions of the impartiality and trustworthiness of the BBC (2015). Accessed 31 May 2017
4. Benevenuto, F., Magno, G., Rodrigues, T., Almeida, V.: Detecting spammers on Twitter. In: Collaboration, Electronic Messaging, Anti-Abuse and Spam Conference (CEAS), vol. 6, p. 12 (2010). http://citeseerx.ist.psu.edu/viewdoc/summary?doi=10.1.1.297.5340
5. Castillo, C., Mendoza, M., Poblete, B.: Information credibility on Twitter. In: Proceedings of the 20th International Conference on World Wide Web (2011)
6. Chu, Z., Gianvecchio, S., Wang, H., Jajodia, S.: Detecting automation of Twitter accounts: are you a human, bot, or cyborg? IEEE Trans. Dependable Secur. Comput. 9(6), 811–824 (2012). https://doi.org/10.1109/TDSC.2012.75
7. Dickerson, J.P., Kagan, V., Subrahmanian, V.S.: Using sentiment to detect bots on Twitter: are humans more opinionated than bots? In: ASONAM 2014 - Proceedings of the 2014 IEEE/ACM International Conference on Advances in Social Networks Analysis and Mining, pp. 620–627 (2014). https://doi.org/10.1109/ASONAM.2014.6921650

8. Figueira, A., Sandim, M., Fortuna, P.: An approach to relevancy detection: contributions to the automatic detection of relevance in social networks. In: Rocha, Á., Correia, A., Adeli, H., Reis, L., Mendonça Teixeira, M. (eds.) New Advances in Information Systems and Technologies. AISC, vol. 444, pp. 89–99. Springer, Cham (2016). https://doi.org/10.1007/978-3-319-31232-3_9

9. Forster, K.: Revealed: How dangerous fake health news conquered facebook (2018). https://www.independent.co.uk/life-style/health-and-families/health-news/fake-news-health-facebook-cruel-damaging-social-media-mike-adams-natural-health-ranger-conspiracy-a7498201.html. Accessed 22 May 2018

10. Gottfried, B.Y.J., Shearer, E.: News Use Across Social Media Platforms 2017. Pew Research Center, September 2017 (News Use Across Social Media Platforms 2017), 17 (2017). http://www.journalism.org/2017/09/07/news-use-across-social-media-platforms-2017/

11. Guimarães., N., Álvaro Figueira., Torgo., L.: Contributions to the detection of unreliable Twitter accounts through analysis of content and behaviour. In: Proceedings of the 10th International Joint Conference on Knowledge Discovery, Knowledge Engineering and Knowledge Management - Volume 1, KDIR, pp. 92–101. INSTICC, SciTePress (2018). https://doi.org/10.5220/0006932800920101

12. Hall, M., Frank, E., Holmes, G., Pfahringer, B., Reutemann, P., Witten, I.H.: The WEKA data mining software: an update. SIGKDD Explor. Newsl. **11**(1), 10–18 (2009). https://doi.org/10.1145/1656274.1656278. http://doi.acm.org/10.1145/1656274.1656278

13. Haynie, D.: The U.S. and U.K. are the world's most influential countries, survey finds (2015). www.usnews.com/news/best-countries/best-international-influence. Accessed 23 May 2016

14. Help, T.: About verified accounts (2018). https://help.twitter.com/en/managing-your-account/about-twitter-verified-accounts. Accessed 14 May 2018

15. Hern, A.: Google acts against fake news on search engine (2017). https://www.theguardian.com/technology/2017/apr/25/google-launches-major-offensive-against-fake-news. Accessed 13 Apr 2018

16. Hern, A.: New facebook controls aim to regulate political ads and fight fake news (2018). https://www.theguardian.com/technology/2018/apr/06/facebook-launches-controls-regulate-ads-publishers. Accessed 13 Apr 2018

17. Hutto, C.J., Gilbert, E.: Vader: A parsimonious rule-based model for sentiment analysis of social media text. In: Adar, E., Resnick, P., Choudhury, M.D., Hogan, B., Oh, A.H. (eds.) ICWSM. The AAAI Press (2014). http://dblp.uni-trier.de/db/conf/icwsm/icwsm2014.html#HuttoG14

18. Klein, R.: An army of sophisticated bots is influencing the debate around education (2017). https://www.huffingtonpost.com/entry/common-core-debate-bots_us_58bc8bf3e4b0d2821b4ee059. Accessed 07 May 2018

19. Lazer, D.M.J., et al.: The science of fake news. Science **359**(6380), 1094–1096 (2018). https://doi.org/10.1126/science.aao2998. http://science.sciencemag.org/content/359/6380/1094

20. Loper, E., Bird, S.: NLTK: the natural language toolkit. In: Proceedings of the ACL-02 Workshop on Effective Tools and Methodologies for Teaching Natural Language Processing and Computational Linguistics - Volume 1, ETMTNLP 2002, pp. 63–70. Association for Computational Linguistics, Stroudsburg (2002). https://doi.org/10.3115/1118108.1118117

21. McCord, M., Chuah, M.: Spam detection on twitter using traditional classifiers. In: Calero, J.M.A., Yang, L.T., Mármol, F.G., García Villalba, L.J., Li, A.X., Wang, Y. (eds.) ATC 2011. LNCS, vol. 6906, pp. 175–186. Springer, Heidelberg (2011). https://doi.org/10.1007/978-3-642-23496-5_13

22. Nichols, L.: Poll: Majority find major media outlets credible (2016). https://morningconsult.com/2016/12/07/poll-majority-find-major-media-outlets-credible/. Accessed 31 May 2017

23. OpenSources: Media bias/fact check -the most comprehensive media bias resources. https://mediabiasfactcheck.com/. Accessed 03 May 2018

24. OpenSources: Opensources - professionally curated lists of online sources, available free for public use. http://www.opensources.co/. Accessed 03 May 2018

25. dos Reis, J.C., Benevenuto, F., de Melo, P.O.S.V., Prates, R.O., Kwak, H., An, J.: Breaking the news: first impressions matter on online news. CoRR abs/1503.07921 (2015). http://arxiv.org/abs/1503.07921

26. Shao, C., Ciampaglia, G.L., Flammini, A., Menczer, F.: Hoaxy: a platform for tracking online misinformation. In: Proceedings of the 25th International Conference Companion on World Wide Web, pp. 745–750 (2016). https://dl.acm.org/doi/10.1145/2872518.2890098

27. Souppouris, A.: Clickbait, fake news and the power of feeling (2016). https://www.engadget.com/2016/11/21/clickbait-fake-news-and-the-power-of-feeling/. Accessed 07 May 2018

28. Statista: Most popular social networks worldwide as of April 2018, ranked by number of active users (2018). (in millions). https://www.statista.com/statistics/272014/global-social-networks-ranked-by-number-of-users/. Accessed 17 May 2018

29. Sysmonos: An in-depth look at the most active Twitter user data (2009). https://sysomos.com/inside-twitter/most-active-twitter-user-data/. Accessed 17 May 2018

30. Tacchini, E., Ballarin, G., Della Vedova, M.L., Moret, S., de Alfaro, L.: Some Like it Hoax: automated fake news detection in social networks. arXiv e-prints, April 2017

31. Tambuscio, M., Ruffo, G., Flammini, A., Menczer, F.: Fact-checking effect on viral hoaxes: a model of misinformation spread in social networks. In: Proceedings of the 24th International Conference on World Wide Web, WWW 2015, Companion, pp. 977–982. ACM, New York (2015). https://doi.org/10.1145/2740908.2742572

32. Twitter: Twitter - search api (2018). https://developer.twitter.com/en/docs/tweets/search/api-reference/get-search-tweets. Accessed 07 Mar 2018

33. Twitter: Twitter verified (2018). https://twitter.com/verified. Accessed 17 Mar 2018

34. Vargo, C.J., Guo, L., Amazeen, M.A.: The agenda-setting power of fake news: a big data analysis of the online media landscape from 2014 to 2016. New Media Soc., 146144481771208 (2017). https://doi.org/10.1177/1461444817712086

35. Weisman, J.: Anti-semitism is rising. why aren't American jews speaking up? (2018). https://www.nytimes.com/2018/03/17/sunday-review/anti-semitism-american-jews.html. Accessed 07 May 2018

An Environment to Model Massive Open Online Course Dynamics

Maria De Marsico[1], Filippo Sciarrone[2(✉)], Andrea Sterbini[1], and Marco Temperini[3]

[1] Department of Computer Science, Sapienza University of Rome, Via Salaria, 113, Rome, Italy
{demarsico,sterbini}@di.uniroma1.it
[2] Department of Engineering, ROMA TRE University, Via della Vasca Navale 79, Rome, Italy
sciarro@ing.uniroma3.it
[3] Department of Computer, Control and Management Engineering, Sapienza University of Rome, Via Ariosto 25, Rome, Italy
marte@diag.uniroma1.it

Abstract. Learning at every time and in every place is nowadays possible thanks to the exponential growth of the Internet and of services deployed through it. Due to its undeniable advantages, Distance Education is becoming strategic in many fields of daily life, and encompasses both educational as well as training applications. Present platforms suitable for the former include Moodle, ATutor and others. Coursera is a popular example of a MOOC-type (Massive Open Online Courses) platform that offers different courses to thousands of enrolled students. Like happens for other technological advancements, there is also a reverse of the medal. As a matter of fact, new problems arise, such as the reliable assessment of the learning status of the learner. This is a critical point especially when the assessment has an academic/legal value, and becomes dramatic when thousands of students attend a course, as is in MOOCs. In these cases, Peer Assessment, possibly mediated by a light teacher's activity, can represent a valuable solution. The evaluation mostly involves peers, and further creates a kind of dynamics in the community of learners that evolves autonomously. Such evolution can provide further information on both individual and group learning progress. This paper proposes a first step along this line, which entails a peer assessment mechanism led by the teacher. However, the latter only enters the process by evaluating a very small portion of the students. The proposed mechanism relies on machine learning, and in particular on a modified form of K-NN. Given the set of teacher's grades, the system is designed to converge towards an evaluation for the remaining students, that is as similar as possible to the one that the teacher would have given. The results of the presented experiment are encouraging and suggest more research on the topic.

Keywords: Peer Assessment · Machine learning · MOOC

© Springer Nature Switzerland AG 2020
A. Fred et al. (Eds.): IC3K 2018, CCIS 1222, pp. 74–89, 2020.
https://doi.org/10.1007/978-3-030-49559-6_4

1   Introduction

The tremendous growth of Internet network and services has lead to dramatic changes in many fields of everyday life. Among them, distance education and training both provide new possibilities of ubiquitous fruition, and pose new problems. An evolving technology supports platforms available 24 h a day, allowing to offer many distance courses, such as those included in *Coursera*[1] and *Khan Academy*[2]. Such courses often belong to the category of MOOCs (Massive Open Online Courses). On the training side, Communities of Practice (CoPs) [20] allow socially driven acquisition and enforcement of professional skills, and take advantage of mentoring of more expert participants. Both for education and continuous professional training, the lack of restrictions in space and time, and the new interactive features available for advanced teaching material, create a powerful framework for better personal as well as social achievements. In this context, the number of participants (from "local" courses to MOOC) and the need for a "formal" assessment (from self-assessment to official assessment) represent critical elements. The new scenarios closely relate to "traditional" social constructivism, in which students also learn through peer interactions [19]. However the aspect of student assessment, especially with big numbers, requires a re-thinking of the approach. It is hardly expected that a single teacher can review thousands of assignments. On one hand, multiple-choice tests seem to provide a viable solution. However, their many flaws represent an obstacle for their exclusive use [5]. On the other hand, recent software tools developed for the automatic correction of open answer assignments still need sufficient generalization abilities. In order to address this problem, and also to provide a further meta-cognitive training to students, this paper presents a novel semi-automatic method that helps the teacher to evaluate a community of students for open answers assignments. In some previous works, we have already addressed this problem with the OpenAnswer system, entailing a peer evaluation of open-ended questions, with the support of the teacher. The underlying strategy was based on Bayesian Networks [8] while in [9] a first version of a modified K-NN technique was presented. Subsequently, in [7], the previous environment was enriched with some statistical features to simulate a MOOC dynamic through K-NN. In the present work we build some preliminary results in order to address the same problem but with different variations in the learning algorithms and in the student models. The Student Model (SM) is enriched by adding a stochastic variable, the *Dev* variable, representing the credibility of the *Knowledge Level K*. Furthermore we propose a more complete version of the learning algorithms partially modifying K-NN [15]. Finally, a novel environment is used in order to simulate communities of learners. In Sect. 2 we present a brief review of the literature relevant to the work; in Sect. 3 the Student Model is introduced, while Sect. 4 presents its initialization and evolution. Section 5 describes algorithms for network update.

---

[1] https://www.coursera.org.
[2] https://it.khanacademy.org/.

In Sect. 6 we illustrate an experimental evaluation in a simulated environment and finally in Sect. 7 some conclusions and future developments are drown.

2 Related Work

Many proposals in literature tackle the dynamics of both individuals and of communities of students using Artificial Intelligence strategies, especially entailing Machine Learning techniques [12–14]. Some works worth of mention for peer assessment are shortly discussed in the following.

A student (or a group) involved in peer assessment [11] is allowed/asked (possibly as a further educational activity) to evaluate other students' assignments. In addition, it is also possible to take into account self-assessment. This activity entails meta-cognitive skills [3], that can be further spurred by computer-based activities [4]. Though possibly organized in several ways, a basic aspect characterizing peer-assessment is the possibility to trigger social interaction and collaboration among students. It is also a way to verify if the teacher and the students actually share the same evaluation criteria, i.e., if the teacher has been able to transmit a robust scale of values related to a specific learning topic: if this happens, assessments from peers can be considered as a reliable estimate of the teacher's one [17]. Actually, consolidated evaluation criteria and standards are the basis for individual judgment in both peer and self-assessment [10].

Peer assessment is grounded in philosophies of active learning [16] and andragogy [6], and may also be seen as being a manifestation of social constructionism [19], as it often involves the joint construction of knowledge through discourse.

The proposal in [8] is based on the *OpenAnswer* peer assessment system. The underlying engine is based on Bayesian networks. It is trained for the evaluation of open ended questions. The system is based on the Student Model (SM), that is instantiated through some stochastic variables. Among them, the variable K representing the learner's estimated *Knowledge Level*, and the variable J representing the learner's estimated ability to judge the answers of her peers. Each student initially grades n open-ended exercises of peers. Subsequently, the teacher grades m students. Each student has therefore associated a *Conditional Probability Table* that evolves with time according to the "possible" evaluation resulting from the assessment of peers, and the "certain" evaluation possibly given by the teacher. This system has the same goal of the system proposed in this paper, but is based on a different learning/information propagation mechanisms. The limit of the approach is that Bayesian networks presents aspects of complexity that make the whole system little treatable for large numbers of students, as in the case of MOOCs. On the contrary, the present proposal has a much lower complexity and does not present problems of intractability. The work in [1] proposes peer assessment to improve Student Team Experiences. The authors discuss an online peer assessment system and team improvement process based on three design criteria: efficient administration of the assessment, promotion of quality feedback, and fostering effective team processes. In [18] the authors propose an approach to open answers grading. It is based on Constraint

Logic Programming (CLP) and peer assessment, where students are modeled as triples of finite domain variables. A CLP Prolog module supports the generation of hypotheses of correctness for answers (grounded on students peer-evaluation), and the assessment of such hypotheses (also based on the answers already graded by the teacher).

3 The Core of the Peer Assessment Engine: The Student Model

The proposed peer assessment strategy improves the performance of the underlying engine presented in [9]. A new simulation environment is generated and, most importantly, the evolution policy of the student model is enriched by taking into account some community aspects. The inference engine is based on the well known K-NN *learning* algorithm. In particular, the engine implements a *Lazy Learning* approach (see, e.g., [15]) (*Instance Based* learning). Explicit generalization is substituted by the comparison of new problem instances with stored training ones. The best elements for a good classification are *learned* by adapting the classification to each further instance, that becomes on its turn a part of the training set. Of course, the latter "grows" in time, increasing the complexity of the hypothesis. This complexity growth can be avoided by substituting older, less relevant training instances. The positive aspect is that this method better adapts to the "unseen". As usual, each training instance is represented as a point in the n-dimensional space built by the feature vector storing the instance attributes.

In the present case, such feature vectors are instances of the Student Model, each univocally associated with a specific student. Each vector, denoted as $SM \equiv \{K, J, Dev, St\}$, is composed by the following variables:

- $[K \equiv [1, 10]]$: when the student is actually assessed by the teacher, it is the actual grade assigned by the teacher through the correction of one or more structured open-ended exercises; otherwise, when only peer-assigned values exist for K, it is the average of marks received by peers; from a learning point of view, it represents the assessed learner's competence (*Knowledge level*) about the exercise domain; in the following, $k_{p,q}$ will denote the grade assigned by student s_p (or by the teacher if $p = teacher$) to student s_q;
- $[J \equiv [0, 1]]$: it measures the learner's (meta-cognitive) assessing capability (*Judgement*) and depends on K;
- **Standard Deviation.** Dev: it represents the "reliability" or "trustworthiness" of the value achieved by K; the higher this value, the less the value of K of the student is credible; Dev is calculated as the standard deviation generated, for each i-th learner, as follows:

$$Dev_i = \sqrt{\frac{\sum_{l=1}^{n}(K_{\bar{l},i} - K_i)^2}{n}} \tag{1}$$

being $K_{\bar{l},i}$ the $l-th$ out of the group of students that graded s_i; it is worth anticipating that, at the beginning, K_i is the average of the received peer grades, and in the following it gets modified by the rules of teacher's grade propagation (see below). Of course, when the student gets graded by the teacher, K_i will take the value of the teacher's grade and neither it nor Dev_i will change anymore.

- $State \equiv \{CORE, NO\_CORE\}$: each student can be in one of two states: CORE and NO_CORE; when the assessment starts, all the students are NO_CORE; if and when a the student is assessed by the teacher then her state switches to CORE; the students in this latter state, as we will see later, determine the dynamics of the network; when a distinction is not obvious and important for the discussion, a NO_CORE student s_i will be denoted with s_i^- while a CORE student s_i will be denoted as s_i^+. The same superscripts will be used when necessary for the variables in the SM to distinguish a pre-grading value form a post-grading one. In practice, at any given moment, the community of students is dynamically partitioned into two groups: the *Core Group* (CG), and its complement $\overline{CG}$. CG is composed by the students whose answers have been graded directly by the teacher: for these students the value for K is fixed. In the following we also denote this set as S^+. On the contrary, S^- is the set of students whose grade is to be inferred (so, they have been graded only by peers).

From this SM, variables K ad J are used to represent each learner as a point in a 2-dimensional space (K, J).

4 Formal Definitions of Steps in the Student Model Lifecycle

In the present proposal, the Student Model is initialized for each assessment session. In the future, we plan to add a history feature, tracking the variables K and J across sections, in order to have a starting point that more accurately describes the student's skills. Initialization is carried out during the peer assessment activity. In the following steps, when a teaches evaluates a student s_i, this action "freezes" the K_i value for the assessed student, that moves from S^- to S^+, and triggers the evolution of the models of the students that provided an assessment for s_i. The following subsections provide the formal details of the operations involved in the process.

4.1 Student's Model Initialization

As a starting step in the assessment session, the teacher assigns an open-ended question to all the students; each student provides an answer, grades the answers of n different peers, and receives n peer grades. Once the whole peer-evaluation has been completed, and no teacher's grading has yet been performed, each s_i^- Student Model, $SM_i = \{K_i, J_i, Dev_i, St_i\}$, is initialized basing only on the peer-evaluation data. Let's remind that $k_{p,q}$ denotes the grade assigned by student

s_p (or by the teacher if $p = teacher$) to student s_q. The initialization step works as follows:

– K_i:

$$K_i^- = \frac{\sum_{l=1}^n K_{\bar{l},i}^-}{n} \qquad (2)$$

where $K_{\bar{l},i}^-$ is the grade assigned by the $l-th$ of the n peers who graded the s_i^- student; therefore, the K_i^- value is initialized with the mean of all received grades; the rationale is that in this step we do not know the differences among students' true assessment capabilities, and so we give to each of them the same weight.

– J_i:
for each s_i^- student, J_i^- is initialized as follows:

$$J_i^- = \frac{1}{1 + \sqrt{\sum_{l=1}^n \Delta_l^2}} \qquad (3)$$

with $\Delta_l^2 = (K_{i,\bar{l}} - K_{\bar{l}})^2$, being $K_{i,\bar{l}}$ the grade assigned by the student s_i to the $l-th$ peer out of the graded n (that can be denoted as $s_{\bar{l}}$), and $K_{\bar{l}}$ is the arithmetic mean or grades received by such $l-th$ peer, i.e., the initial value of K^- of the student $s_{\bar{l}}$, computed by Eq. 2; therefore, if a student s_i grades the assigned n peers with values always equal to their K^- values, the value for J_i^- gets maximal: $J = 1$ (here no teacher's grades are available, but peer evaluations only);

– Dev_i:
each value is initialized according to Eq. 1;

– St_i:
all students are initialized to $St_i = NO\_CORE$;

After this initialization, the learning process continues: at each following step, some answers from the S^- students are graded by the teacher, and consequently some students move from S^- to S^+, and the SMs are recomputed. At each step the positions of the points representing S^- students change, implying a new classification for them, which depends on their distance from points in S^+, according to the K-NN protocol.

In practice, as it will be described in the next section, at each step the module *learns* to (hopefully) better classifies the students still in S^-, until a termination condition suggests to stop cycling, and the values from SM for S^- students become their final assessment (K will be the grade) inferred by the module.

4.2   Student's Model Evolution

After the SM initialization is completed, all learners belong to the S^- set. Each learner evolves in the (K, J) space according to a process that entails that the teacher directly grades (a small subset of) students. Each direct teacher's grading triggers an evolution step involving a set of SMs.

In order to make the teacher's action more effective from a learning convergence point of view, the system supports the teacher in the choice of the students to grade first. In more detail, the system suggests a ranked list of students/answers to grade, sorted by the Dev^- values (only students that have not been graded yet are taken into account, i.e., those in S^-). It is worth reminding that the variable Dev_i is very important because, after each evolution step, it is an aggregate measure of how much the estimated knowledge level K_i of a student s_i differs from the individual evaluations given to s_i by the peers. A very high Dev value means having a K that is not very reliable since the n peers grading s_i do not sufficiently agree on the evaluation. In this case the teacher's definition of the "true" value for K is expected to be beneficial, also to update the models of involved students.

Given the list suggested by the system, the teacher selects a group of students/answers to grade. As already described, such grades will be the new, final, K^+ values for such students, that become s^+ students changing their position in the (K, J) space. Then the system automatically updates the SMs of all peers who had graded these students. The model updating algorithm follows recursively a graph path starting from the graded students and proceeding backwards. For each student s_l influenced by the new teacher's grades, first K_l and J_l are updated, and then the system updates the Dev_l values.

In the following $KMIN$ and $KMAX$ will denote the minimum and maximum values for K (here they are set to 1 and 10 respectively). $IMAX$ will denote the maximum difference between two values of K, i.e. here 9. Moreover $JMIN$ and $JMAX$ will denote the minimum and maximum values for J (here they are set to 0 and 1 respectively).

The SM updating is explained in detail in the next paragraphs.

Updating the SM of a Graded Student. The SM of a graded student s_i is updated as soon as the teacher assigns a mark. The K_i value is updated first:

$$K_i = K_{teacher,i} \tag{4}$$

being $K_{teacher,i}$ the grade assigned by the teacher.

As a consequence of grading, the student moves to S^+, the value for K_i will not change further during the session (when necessary, it will be denoted with K_i^+), and the status St_i is set to $CORE$.

The value of J_i is updated afterwards. Two considerations are worth before presenting the corresponding formula. First of all, while the K_i^+ value for graded students s_i (now in S^+) remains fixed after teacher's grading, the value for J_i continues changing even after, according to the next teacher's grading of students that s_i had assessed. Second, one of the assumptions underlying the presented model is that the assessment skill of a student, represented by the value of J, depends on the value of *Knowledge Level K* for the same student. Therefore it may increase or decrease accordingly as a function of K. In the case

$K_{teacher,i} = K_{i_{old}}^-$, no change is implied for J. In order to take this into account we introduce a parameter α defined as follows:

$$\alpha = \frac{K_{teacher,i} - K_{i_{old}}^-}{IMAX} \tag{5}$$

A function determines the update of J, that takes into account two cases according to the possible value of α. If the student receives a grade higher than her current one, the *Judgement Level* increases accordingly. Otherwise K had been overestimated by peers, and J decreases too. The difference $K_{teacher,i} - K_{old}^-$ in α is normalized with respect to I_{max} so that the Eq. 6 increases or decreases J such that its value always remains in the range $[0,1]$. The update formula for J is therefore:

$$J_{i_{new}}^+ = J_{i_{old}} + \alpha(JMAX - J_{i_{old}}) \ (0 \leq \alpha \leq 1)$$
$$J_{i_{new}}^+ = J_{i_{old}} + \alpha J_{i_{old}} \ (\alpha < 0) \tag{6}$$

It is worth noticing that the above formula will be also used in the future for the already graded students when the teacher will grade peers that they have assessed (of course in that case α would not have changed in the meanwhile). Therefore J_{old} could stand either for J_{old}^+ or J_{old}^-, depending on whether the student is already in S^+ (case J_{old}^+) or being just entering in S^+ (case J_{old}^-). The case of a student remaining in S^- will be taken into account in the next subsection.

This evolutionary form was used because it is easiest to treat in a preliminary approach and also because it is very often used to update statistical variables in a machine learning context (see for example [2]).

Subsequently the value of Dev_i is modified recalculating it using the teacher's grade, then according to the same rule used in Eq. 1:

$$Dev_{new}^+ = \sqrt{\frac{\sum_{l=1}^n (K_{teacher,i} - K_{\bar{l}})^2}{n}} \tag{7}$$

where $K_{\bar{l}}$ is the grade received by the $l - th$ peer. This value may suggest how "controversial" is the student's answer, or, in other words, how much it "confused" the peers with respect to a correct evaluation. Being based on the static (once given) teacher's grade and on the static peers' grades, this value will not change anymore after the teacher's evaluation, and, as mentioned above, the values Dev^+ of students in S^+ will not be taken into further account in the process of suggesting to the teacher the answers to grade.

In summary, once a student s_i^+ has been graded, only J_i^+ can further change, while the other elements in the SM remain fixed.

Updating the SMs of the Other (not Graded) Students Involved in the Process. Once the SM of the student s_i, who has been graded by the teacher, has changed, the algorithm recursively changes the models of all the students that had a direct (grading) or indirect relation with s_i. In fact, the assessing students community can be represented by a weighted oriented graph, where each node is a student and the following rules apply:

- Two nodes s_i and s_j are connected by a weighed edge iff either s_i graded s_j ($s_i \longrightarrow s_j$) or s_j graded s_i ($s_j \longrightarrow s_i$);
- each edge is labelled by a weight w_{ij} (resp w_{ji}), representing the grade that the student s_i gave s_j (resp s_j gave s_i);

Figure 1 shows a fragment of such a graph. The update algorithm recursively works on the adjacency matrix corresponding to the graph, starting from the just graded student and navigating backwards along the edges: if s_p graded s_q (a directed arc connects s_p to s_q) and then s_q gets graded by the teacher, then the model for s_p is updated afterwards. The algorithm updates the SM of each student (i.e. a node) in S^- (not a CORE student), who is influenced by the graded student. As mentioned above, regarding the students in S^+ (the graded ones), only the J^+ values can still change. Regarding the update of K^-, some notation is defined before presenting the corresponding equation. First of all, a parameter β is defined in the following way:

$$\beta = \frac{1}{IMAX}(K^-_{grading,graded} - K^-_{graded})\frac{Dev_{grading}}{IMAX} \tag{8}$$

where $K_{grading,graded}$ is the grade given by the student being updated (the head of the graph arch) to the already graded/updated student (K_{graded}) (the tail of the graph arch). For the teacher's graded student, of course we have K^+_{graded}. In fact, it is to remind that the update proceeds backwards. At the beginning of the propagation, the student graded by the teacher is the tail node and K_{graded} is the grade just assigned by the teacher. $IMAX$ is a normalization factor to maintain the final value of the formula for the update of K in the correct range. The update is influenced by difference of the grade given by $s_{grading}$ to s_{graded} and the already updated value of the latter (the final value, if the student has been evaluated by the teacher). This difference determines the sign of β and therefore the final either increase or decrease of K for the head node.

Furthermore, the $\frac{Dev_{grading}}{IMAX}$ factor expresses a kind of inverse of the inertia of the value of K to change: the higher this value is, the more the value of K changes. The rationale behind this choice is that a student with a high value for Dev has received very different grades from the grading peers and therefore is a candidate for a larger change. When updating s_i due to the previous update of s_j we have $K_{grading,graded} = K_{i,j}$ and either $K_{graded} = K^-_j$ or $K_{graded} = K^+_{teacher,j}$. In order to simplify the notation, we will use K_j in the following formula:

$$K^-_{i_{new}} = K^-_{i_{old}} + \beta(KMAX - K_j) \quad (0 \le \beta \le 1)$$
$$K^-_{i_{new}} = K^-_{i_{old}} + \beta K_j \quad (\beta < 0) \tag{9}$$

where: $K_{i_{new}}$ is the new value of K of the intermediate student (in Fig. 1 it is the $s1$ node).

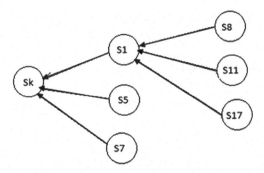

Fig. 1. A fragment of the assessment graph. The teacher has graded the student s_k. Starting from this student, the algorithm first updates the models of the students who graded s_k, and then the models of the students that are connected to them. In the example in the figure, the model for s_1, is updated, and as a consequence also the models of s_8, s_{11}, s_{17} (and the update is further propagated to their connections). Then the algorithm passes to s_5 and s_7.

Each J value is changed considering the parameter γ defined as follows:

$$\gamma = \frac{1}{IMAX}(K^-_{grading_{new}} - K^-_{grading_{old}})|J_{grading} - J_{graded}|\frac{Dev_{grading}}{IMAX} \quad (10)$$

Using the same convention as above, with s_i being the grading student to update and s_j the already graded/updated student, we have:

$$J^-_{i_{new}} = J^-_{i_{old}} + \gamma(JMAX - J^-_{i_{old}}) \ (0 \leq \gamma \leq 1)$$
$$J^-_{i_{new}} = J^-_{i_{old}} + \gamma J^-_{i_{old}} \ (\gamma < 0) \quad (11)$$
$$J^-_{i_{new}} = J^-_{i_{old}} + (K^-_{i_{new}} - K^-_{graded})$$
$$(\gamma = 0 \wedge J^-_{i_{old}} = J^-_j)$$

After that, in order to complete the SMs, all the *Dev* variables are updated.

5   K-NN Network Evolution

The propagation of the effect of teacher's grades (some s^- students, which become s^+ students and a set of SMs has been updated) causes to trigger the modified K-NN algorithm. The learning process is influenced by the value of parameter δ determined by the following equation:

$$\delta = \frac{1}{IMAX}\frac{\sum_{i=1}^k \frac{1}{d_i}(K^+_i - K^-_{i_{old}})}{\sum_{j=1}^k \frac{1}{d_i}}\frac{Dev_i}{IMAX} \quad (12)$$

where:

1. the acronym K-NN features a K, possibly misleading here, so we are using k for the number of nearest neighbors (in the CORE group) to be used in the learning algorithm;
2. d_i is the Euclidean distance between the $s_{i_{old}}^-$ student under update, and the $j - th$ student in the Core Group ($s_{\overline{j}}^+$);
3. The $\frac{Dev_i}{IMAX}$ factor has the same meaning as in the definition of the other parameters above.

$$K_{i_{new}}^- = K_{i_{old}}^- + \delta(KMAX - K_{i_{old}}^-) \ (0 \le \delta \le 1)$$
$$K_{i_{new}}^- = K_{i_{old}}^- + \delta(1 - K_{old}^-) \ (\delta < 0)$$

(13)

The K_{new}^- value is given as a function to keep K in $[1, 10]$.

Regarding J, a reference parameter θ is defined in a way similar to the above:

$$\theta = \frac{(K_{new}^- - K_{old}) \sum_{i=1}^{k} \frac{1}{d_i} |J_i^+ - J_{old}^-|}{IMAX} \frac{Dev_i}{\sum_{i=1}^{k} \frac{1}{d_i}} \frac{Dev_i}{IMAX}.$$

(14)

where:

1. As mentioned earlier, we assume J depending on K: this is expressed through the difference between the K_{new}^- value, obtained by Eq. 13, and the K_{old}^- value.
2. d_i is the Euclidean distance between the s_{old}^- student under update, and the $i - th$ student in the Core Group (s_i^+);

Some notices are worth, regarding the cases when the $\theta = 0$. On the one hand, when the J^+ of the k nearest neighbors is equal to the J_{old}^- value of the s_i^- student under update, J_{new}^- is computed by the difference between K_{new}^- and K_{old}^- only. The rationale is that when the K^- value for student s^- changes, this student's assessment skill should change as well (by the assumption of dependence of J on K). However, when the K^- value for the student under update is not changed, the assessment skill stays unchanged as well.

The formula for updating J is the following:

$$J_{new}^- = J_{old}^- + \frac{(K_{new}^- - K_{old}^-)}{IMAX} J_{old}^- \ (\theta = 0 \ \wedge \ J_i^+ = J_{old}^-, i = 1 \dots k)$$
$$J_{new}^- = J_{old}^- + \theta(JMAX - J_{old}^-) \ (0 \le \theta \le 1)$$
$$J_{new}^- = J_{old}^- + \theta J_{old}^- \ (\theta < 0)$$

(15)

The J_{new} value is given as a function to keep J in its normal range $[0, 1]$. The parameter K has the same meaning as above.

6 Experimental Evaluation

In this section we illustrate a first experiment concerning the verification of network dynamics. In particular the goal is to verify if, thanks to the evolutionary rules expressed in Sects. 3–5 and, the network, after a certain number of iterations converges towards a configuration where the grades of each student are close enough to those that the teacher would have given. This evaluation is a step forward with respect to the previous one presented in [7], where a network composed by 1, 000 students was studied with different sample generation rules. As previously stated, the evolutionary process is based on peer assessment, that is, on the fact that students judge other students. The teacher intervenes by grading only a small part of assignments. In this way, the teacher pushes the dynamics of the whole network towards the grades that she would have given to all the students, with a great time saving. To make this experimentation an environment developed in C language has been implemented. It allows to simulate the dynamics of a community of students, also formed by a large number of learners. For this experimentation our system generated sets of students from some well-known and realistic statistical distributions. For the grades assigned both by the teacher and by the learners, we referred to the *Gaussian* distribution, generated with the statistical environment R^3. These assumptions are consistent with the literature, where the Gaussian distribution is an acceptable hypothesis.

Here we report our main experiment performed with a sample of $n = 7,000$ students. In Fig. 2 the sample distribution is shown in the (K, J) space while in Fig. 3 the teacher grading distribution shows the Gaussian's shape of the sample. Finally, in Fig. 4, the initial distribution of the *Dev* variable is shown. The experimental plan consists of several runs of the learning algorithms until a final condition is met. The final condition is that the difference between two consecutive variations of the network is below a small pre-set quantity ϵ. Consequently we run the following steps:

1. A sample of $n = 7,000$ students is generated with a Gaussian distribution in peer assessments.The R statistical environment has been used;
2. The teacher selects n (in our case n = 5) students to grade from the ranked list;
3. All the SMs are updated according to the algorithms shown in Sect. 3;
4. The K-NN algorithm is launched;
5. The new statistical general parameter are computed.

The steps 2–4 are launched several times, until the final condition is met.

After 6 K-NN runs and 12 teacher grades, we obtained the results shown in Table 1. The teacher gave a $\mu = 5.88$ mean grade, with $\sigma = 1.3$ while the peers a more generous $\mu = 6.28$ with $\sigma = 1.71$. The initialization of the system started from a mean $\mu = 6.83$, and ended to $\mu = 6.28$ after the k-NN steps. One key point, in our opinion, is in the standard deviation of the assessments, which is diminishing with the k-NN step. This seems encouraging, as it suggests that the framework can improve on the pure peer-evaluation, and also produce more stable assessment distributions. This results confirm the previous ones in [7].

---

^{3} https://www.r-project.org/.

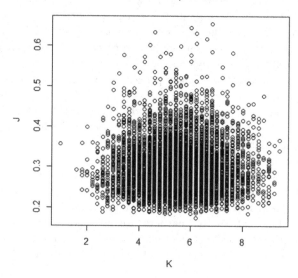

Fig. 2. The initial students distribution in the K-J space for n = 7,000 students.

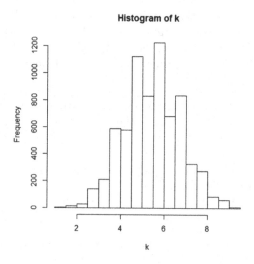

Fig. 3. The initial distribution of the K values coming from the peer assessments with 5 assessments each.

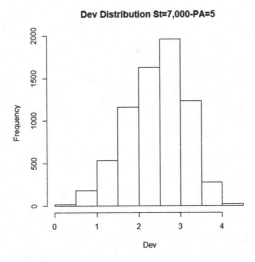

Fig. 4. The initial distribution of the *Dev* values among peers.

Table 1. A comparison between the final grades distributions after the last step.

	μ	σ
Teacher	5.88	1.3
Students	6.28	1.71

7 Conclusions and Future Work

Following the dynamics of a network of a huge number of learners, is not an easy task from the teacher's point of view. This article proposes an environment to study the dynamics of a network through a peer assessment action together with a minimal grading action performed by the teacher. The student is modeled according to his knowledge, her ability to judge other peers and the inertia she presents to changes. A machine learning engine is implemented, based on a modified version of the K-NN algorithm, which, through some working hypotheses, guides the network by a dynamic which, after several iterations, approaches the teacher's grading. The experiment was carried out with a high number of students with consistent results with previous work carried out with different numbers and hypotheses. In the future we plan to carry out a broader experimentation to verify the convergence of the network in more complex cases. Finally, another perspective regarding future developments concerns the possibility of making the student community evolve autonomously without the teacher's intervention, but based only on social network analysis.

References

1. Anson, R., Goodman, J.A.: A peer assessment system to improve student team experiences. J. Educ. Bus. **89**(1), 27–34 (2014)
2. Bishop, C.M.: Pattern Recognition and Machine Learning. Information Science and Statistics. Springer, Heidelberg (2006)
3. Carns, A.W., Carns, M.R.: Teaching study skills, cognitive strategies, and metacognitive skills through self-diagnosed learning styles. Sch. Couns. **38**(5), 341–346 (1991)
4. Conati, C., Vanlehn, K.: Toward computer-based support of meta-cognitive skills: a computational framework to coach self-explanation. Int. J. Artif. Intell. Educ. (IJAIED) **11**, 389–415 (2000)
5. Couch, B.A., Hubbard, J.K., Brassil, C.E.: Multiple-true-false questions reveal the limits of the multiple-choice format for detecting students with incomplete understandings. Bioscience **68**(6), 455–463 (2018)
6. Cross, K.P.: Adults as Learners. Jossey-Bass, San Francisco (1981)
7. De Marsico, M., Sciarrone, F., Sterbini, A., Temperini, M.: Peer assessment and knowledge discovering in a community of learners. In: Proceedings of the 10th International Joint Conference on Knowledge Discovery, Knowledge Engineering and Knowledge Management - Volume 1: KDIR, pp. 119–126. INSTICC, SciTePress (2018)
8. De Marsico, M., Sciarrone, F., Sterbini, A., Temperini, M.: The impact of self- and peer-grading on student learning. EURASIA J. Math. Sci. Technol. Educ. **13**(4), 1085–1106 (2017)
9. De Marsico, M., Sterbini, A., Sciarrone, F., Temperini, M.: Modeling a peer assessment framework by means of a lazy learning approach. In: Huang, T.-C., Lau, R., Huang, Y.-M., Spaniol, M., Yuen, C.-H. (eds.) SETE 2017. LNCS, vol. 10676, pp. 336–345. Springer, Cham (2017). https://doi.org/10.1007/978-3-319-71084-6_38
10. Falchikov, N., Goldfinch, J.: Student peer assessment in higher education: a meta-analysis comparing peer and teacher marks. Rev. Educ. Res. **70**(3), 287–322 (2000)
11. Kane, L.S., Lawler, E.E.: Methods of peer assessment. Psychol. Bull. **85**, 555–586 (1978)
12. Limongelli, C., Lombardi, M., Marani, A., Sciarrone, F.: A teacher model to speed up the process of building courses. In: Kurosu, M. (ed.) HCI 2013. LNCS, vol. 8005, pp. 434–443. Springer, Heidelberg (2013). https://doi.org/10.1007/978-3-642-39262-7_50
13. Limongelli, C., Sciarrone, F., Temperini, M.: A social network-based teacher model to support course construction. Comput. Hum. Behav. **51**, 1077–1085 (2015)
14. Limongelli, C., Sciarrone, F., Vaste, G.: LS-PLAN: an effective combination of dynamic courseware generation and learning styles in web-based education. In: Nejdl, W., Kay, J., Pu, P., Herder, E. (eds.) AH 2008. LNCS, vol. 5149, pp. 133–142. Springer, Heidelberg (2008). https://doi.org/10.1007/978-3-540-70987-9_16
15. Mitchell, T.M.: Machine Learning, 1st edn. David McKay, New York (1997)

16. Piaget, J.: Science of Education and the Psychology of the Child. Longman, London (1971)
17. Sadler, P., Good, E.: The impact of self- and peer-grading on student learning. Educ. Assess. **11**(1), 1–31 (2006)
18. Sterbini, A., Temperini, M.: Dealing with open-answer questions in a peer-assessment environment. In: Popescu, E., Li, Q., Klamma, R., Leung, H., Specht, M. (eds.) ICWL 2012. LNCS, vol. 7558, pp. 240–248. Springer, Heidelberg (2012). https://doi.org/10.1007/978-3-642-33642-3_26
19. Vygotsky, L.S.: Thought and Language. MIT Press, Cambridge (1962)
20. Wenger, E.: Communities of Practice: A Brief Introduction (2011)

Knowledge Engineering and Ontology Development

An Advanced Driver Assistance Test Cases Generation Methodology Based on Highway Traffic Situation Description Ontologies

Wei Chen[1,2][✉] and Leïla Kloul[1]

[1] Laboratory DAVID, Versailles Saint-Quentin-en-Yvelines University,
45, Avenue des États-Unis, 78000 Versailles, France
`wei.chen@ens.uvsq.fr, leila.kloul@uvsq.fr`
[2] Institute of Technological Research SystemX,
8, Avenue de la Vauve, 91120 Palaiseau, France

Abstract. Autonomous cars mainly rely on an intelligent system pilot to achieve the purpose of self-driving. They combine a variety of sensors to perceive their surroundings, such as cameras, radars and lidars. The perception algorithms of the Advanced Driver-Assistance Systems (ADAS) provide observations on the environmental elements based on the data provided by the sensors, while decision algorithms generate the actions to be implemented by these vehicles. To ensure the safety of the autonomous vehicle, it is necessary to specify, validate and secure the dependability of the architecture and the behavioural logic of ADAS running on the vehicle for all the situations that will be met by the vehicle. These situations are described and generated as different test cases. In this work, we propose a methodology to generate automatically test cases of autonomous vehicle for highway. This methodology is based on a three layers hierarchy. The first layer exploits static and mobile concepts we have defined in the context of three ontologies: highway, weather and vehicle. The second layer exploits the relationships between these concepts while the third one exploits the method of test case generation based on the first two layers. Finally, we use the Performance Evaluation Process Algebra (PEPA) for modelling the transitions between the driving scenes. To apply our methodology, we consider a running example about a riding vehicle on the left of the autonomous vehicle to take a right exit lane of a highway.

Keywords: Autonomous vehicle · Ontology · Test cases · Formal method PEPA

1 Introduction

Since the 1970s, the research on autonomous vehicle became a tentancy in the industry. After years of exploration, certain progress has been made. In early

Supported by IRT SystemX.

© Springer Nature Switzerland AG 2020
A. Fred et al. (Eds.): IC3K 2018, CCIS 1222, pp. 93–113, 2020.
https://doi.org/10.1007/978-3-030-49559-6_5

2018, Audi expanded Traffic Light Information Vehicle-to-Infrastructure (V2I) system to Washington [12]. Nissan plans to continue the collaboration with NASA to adapt NASA technology for use in their Seamless Autonomous Mobility platform [3]. Not only is the traditional auto industry dedicated to this research domain, but other companies, such as Google and Intel, have also participated to the development of the autonomous vehicles. Waymo, which started as Google's self-driving car project, canceled the design of the steering wheel and pedals [7], which completely overturns the design of traditional cars.

Recently, the world's first driverless taxi was put into use in Dubai [4]. Tesla has made the first delivery of fifty (50) out of two hundreds (200) vehicles to Dubai. The goal is for the cars to evolve into a fully autonomous taxi service. Autonomous vehicles are no longer just in the scenes of science fiction movies. They come to real life and will become more commonplace as ordinary cars. They must evolve in an unpredictable environment and a wide context of dynamic execution, with strong interactions. But the autopilot is not smart enough to hold all the situations it meets. Human driver needs to be involved at critical moments, but its attention cannot be focused for a long time since most of the time the driver has nothing to do in such vehicles. Therefore, the issue of safety become one of the most important problems at present.

To ensure the safety of the autonomous vehicle, its occupants and the other road users, when it evolves in the dynamic environment, it is necessary to simulate all possible situations as much as possible to specify, validate and secure the dependability of the architecture and the behaviour logic of the Advanced Driver-Assistance Systems (ADAS) running on the vehicle. The functions of ADAS may encounter a very high number of situations that can be considered as infinite because of the nearly infinite number of parameters combinations. These situations are described and generated as different test cases of automated vehicles. Thus test cases generation faces the question of inherent combinatorial explosion. Clearly, it is not possible to test all situations. To reduce the sample components of parameters, we can choose the most representative and influential situations to make the test possible.

In this work, we propose a methodology to generate automatically test cases of autonomous vehicle for highway. This methodology is based on a three layers hierarchy, which exploits static and mobile concepts we have defined in the context of three ontologies: highway, weather and vehicle. We use Performance Evaluation Process Algebra (PEPA) [8] to model the transitions between the driving scenes. PEPA is a stochastic process algebra designed for modelling computer and communication systems and introduced by Jane Hillston in the 1990s [8]. PEPA is a simple language with a small set of operators. It is easy to reason about the language as it provides a great deal of flexibility to the modeller [8]. We consider a running example: *"Riding vehicle on the left track before the autonomous vehicle to take a right exit lane of a highway"*, to show the concepts and their relationships in the ontologies. We introduce the methodology of test cases generation with different scenarios constructed using several scenes and we show how to apply this methodology on the running example.

Structure of the paper: Section 2 is dedicated to Related Works. In Sect. 3, we describe our running example. Our methodology of test cases generation is presented in Sect. 4. Finally, we conclude our work in Sect. 5.

2   Related Works

Several researchers have used ontologies for the conceptualization of the ADAS or the control of the autonomous vehicle.

An ontology of recognition for the ADAS system is presented in [1]. The authors define an ontology composed of concepts and their instances. This ontology includes contextual concepts and context parameters. It is able to process human-like reasoning on global road contexts. Another ontology is proposed by Pollard et al. [16] for situation assessment for automated ground vehicles. It includes the sensors/actuators state, environmental conditions and driver's state. However, as the classes of both ontologies are highly generalized, they are not enough to describe test cases allowing to simulate and validate ADAS.

To build a knowledge base for smart vehicles and implement different types of ADAS, Zhao et al. [20] proposed three ontologies: map ontology, control ontology and car ontology. They focus on algorithms for rapid decision making for autonomous vehicle systems. They provide an ontology-based knowledge base and decision-making system that can make safe decisions about uncontrolled intersections and narrow roads. However, the authors did not consider the equipment of the road infrastructure in their map ontology, for example the traffic signs which are an important part for test cases construction.

Morignot et al. [15] propose an ontology to relax traffic regulation in unusual but practical situations, in order to assist drivers. Their ontology represents the vehicles, the infrastructure and the traffic regulation for the general road. It is based on the experience of the members of the lab with driving license, not based on a texts corpus. That may be useful for modelling the concepts involved in traffic regulation relaxation, but we need more rigorous ontologies for modelling the concepts involved in general situations.

In [2], the authors propose, using ontology, to create scenarios for development of automated driving functions. They propose a process for an ontology based scene creation and a model for knowledge representation with 5 layers: road-level, traffic infrastructure, temporary manipulation of the first two levels, objects and environment. A scene is created from first layer to fifth layer. This ontology has modelled German motorways with 284 classes, 762 logical axioms and 75 semantic web rules. A number of scenes could be automatically generated in natural language. However, the natural language is not a machine-understandable knowledge and the transformation of natural language based scenes to simulation data formats with such a huge ontology is a tremendous work.

In [9] and in [10] the authors use a description logic to describe the scenes. The first work provides a generic description of road intersections using the concepts *Car*, *Crossing*, *RoadConnection* and *SignAtCrossing*. They use description logic to reason about the relations between cars and describe how a traffic intersection situation is set up in this ontology and define its semantics. The results are presented for an intersection with 5 roads, 11 lanes and 6 cars driving towards the intersection. Hummel et al. [10] also propose an ontology to understand road infrastructures at intersections. This methodology focuses on the geometrical details related to the multilevel topological information. It presents scene comprehension frameworks based on the description logic, which can identify unreasonable sensor data by checking for consistency. All these ontologies are limited to the situation of intersection which is not enough to simulate an environment and validate the ADAS.

In the context of formal modelling techniques for concurrent systems, the authors in [5] use the Markovian process algebra PEPA [8] to describe quantitative aspects of driver behaviour to understand the relation between driver behaviour and transport systems. A three-way junction consisting of a two-way main road with a diverging one-way road is used as an example to illustrate their approach. They are interested in the probability of possible collisions, the average waiting time in a queue from arrival at the junction to finally passing the junction and the average number of cars waiting in a queue. They have modelled the effects of driver's experience in terms of state transitions associated with a finite number of pre-defined probability factors. The results show a trade-off between junction performance (reflected in number of cars in a queue and waiting time) and safety (reflected in probability of possible collision) under certain conditions on driver behaviour.

In this paper, we use the PEPA for modelling the transitions between the driving scenes.

3   Running Example

We consider the situation *"Riding vehicle on the left track before the autonomous vehicle Ego to take a right exit lane of a highway"* as the running example. It is daylight and the temperature is $c°C$. The humidity is $h\%$ and the pressure is p mPa. The wind speed is v_w km/h and its direction is $d_w^°$ (from 0 to 360°, 180° refers to a southerly wind).

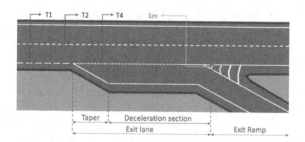

Fig. 1. Scenography of the running example.

The highway is separated into two carriageways by median. In the scenography of this running example (Fig. 1), a portion of one carriageway is selected. The left hard shoulder is located on the immediate outside of the median. The edge of the left hard shoulder is marked by two single solid white lines. This carriageway has two (2) main lanes and an exit lane. The main lane which near to the shoulder is $Lane_R$, and the other one is $Lane_L$. There is a chevrons marking placed between the outside lane and the exit lane. The exit lane is composed of a deceleration section and a taper. An exit ramp is connected with the exit lane at the point where the width of the chevrons increases to one meter (1 m). The right soft shoulder is located on the immediate outside of the right hard shoulder. In the beginning of the deceleration section, a speed limit sign is placed on the right soft shoulder. The types of dashed lines are provided in Fig. 1. Their definitions are those provided in the official French document for road symbols [13].

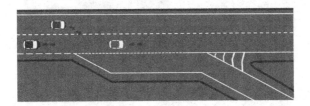

Fig. 2. Initial scene of the running example. (Color figure online)

In the initial scene (Fig. 2) of running example, the autonomous vehicle Ego (blue) rolls on the right lane of a separated lane road. The speed of Ego is given by 70 km/h on the portion which speed is limited to 130 km/h. The System Traffic Jam Chauffeur (TJC) is active and regulates the speed of Ego with respect to a target vehicle V_A (green) which is located 100 m in front of Ego. A third vehicle V_B (red) arrives on the left and exceeds the Ego, then it cuts the way in front of the Ego to take the way out.

From the initial scene (Fig. 2), we consider a scenario as presented in Fig. 3: V_B changes to the right lane before Ego, then it cuts the way in front of Ego. It follows that the radar of Ego detects this vehicle which becomes the new target vehicle. The TJC regulates the speed of the Ego to maintain a safe distance with V_B. Finally, V_B changes to the exit lane. The radar of Ego detects V_A which becomes the new target vehicle. The Ego takes over the regulation behind V_A.

4 Test Cases Generation

Simon Ulbrich et al. [17] present a definition of interfaces for the design and test of functional modules of an automated vehicle. Based on that, we define the *scene* as a snapshot of the vehicle environment including the static and mobile elements, and the relationships among those elements. A *scenario* describes the temporal development between several scenes in a sequence of scenes (Fig. 4).

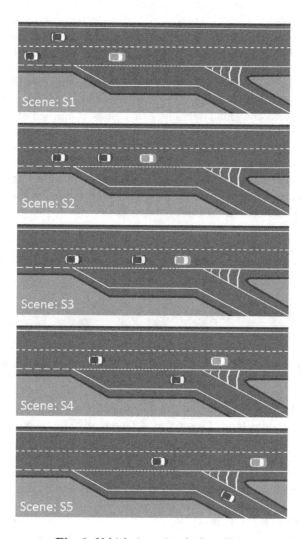

Fig. 3. Vehicle insertion before *Ego*.

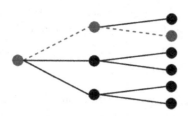

Fig. 4. A scenario (red dashed line) made by actions/events (edges) and scenes (nodes), extracted from [6]. (Color figure online)

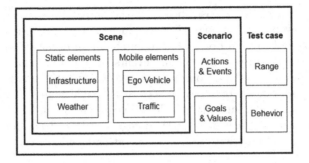

Fig. 5. Scene, scenario and test case.

These scenes are developed by the actions made by *Ego* or the events occurring due to the actions made by other vehicles, and this from the point of view of *Ego*. A *use case* describes one or several scenarios applied to some ranges and behaviours to simulate the ADAS (Fig. 5).

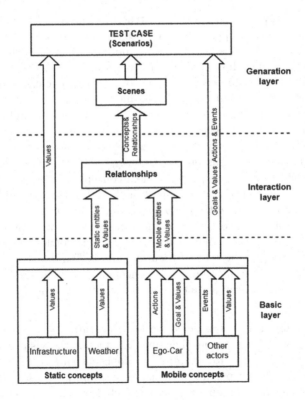

Fig. 6. Test cases generation methodology.

In order to generate test cases based on the ontologies we have defined, we define a three-layers methodology (Fig. 6) whichs is based on our last work [6]. This methodology follows a bottom-up hierarchy of an ontology with three layers for semantic expression of dynamic events in dynamic traffic scenes [19]. Our methodology is also based on ontologies. We define three ontologies: highway ontology and weather ontology to specify the environment in which evolves the autonomous vehicle, and the vehicle ontology which consists of the vehicle devices and control actions. Our methodology consists of the following three layers: basic layer, interaction layer and generation layer.

4.1   Basic Layer

The basic layer includes all static and mobile elements for the test cases. We represent them with ontologies as a structural framework. Ontology is often conceived as a set of concepts with their definitions and relationships [18]. This layer includes the static concepts and the mobile concepts of the highway, the weather and the vehicle ontologies.

In the following, we describe the concepts of the three (3) ontologies.

Highway Ontology: The highway infrastructure consists of the physical components of highway system providing facilities essential to allow the vehicle driving on the highway. We have built highway ontology based on the French official documents [13,14]. This ontology involves four main concepts: *RoadPart*, *Roadway*, *Zone* and *Equipment*. The concept *RoadPart* refers to the long profile of the highway. We consider that the highway is composed of connected segments and interchanges. There are two types of interchanges on highway: *Branch* and *Ramp*. The branch connects to another highway and the ramp connects to other types of roads. The concept *Roadway* refers to the longitudinal profile of the highway. The special areas on the highway (*Toll*, *SafetyArea*, *RestArea*, etc.) are classified in the concept *Zone*. The concept *Equipment* refers to the facilities that guarantee the normal operation of highways. It could be *Barrier*, *Fence*, *TrafficSymbol*, *Lighting* or *EmergencyTelephone*.

The concepts of this ontology are defined in terms of entity, sub-entities and properties. For example, the concept *EntranceLane* is defined as in the Table 1. In the running example, the ID of *EntranceLane* is $EnLane_1$.

Figure 7 shows all the fifty-four (54) concepts we have defined for highway ontology. The framed concepts are the concepts that can be used for the running example.

Weather Ontology: The weather describes the state of the atmosphere at a particular place and time. Some phenomena influence the visibility of captors on the autonomous vehicle, for example the concepts *Daylight*, *Precipitation*, *Fog* and *Haze*. As the properties of the concept *Daylight* presented in Table 2, the visibility of the autonomous vehicle is reflected by the distance at which an infrastructure or a vehicle can be clearly discerned. Some concepts have their properties to show the physical quantity, such as the concepts *Temperature*, *Pressure* and *Humidity*.

Table 1. Definition of the concept *EntranceLane*, extracted from [6].

Concept	*EntranceLane*
Entity	entrance_lane
Definition	A lane which allows vehicles wishing to leave the highway to slow down at the speed imposed by the bend encountered at the exit of the fast flow of traffic
Properties	ID, Alignment (Horizontal & Vertical), Length, Width, SpeedLimit
Sub-entities	Deceleration Section, Taper

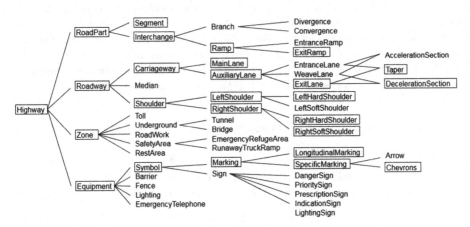

Fig. 7. Concepts of highway ontology (framed concepts for running example), based from [6].

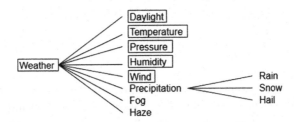

Fig. 8. Concepts of weather ontology (framed concepts for running example), based from [6].

We have defined twelve (12) concepts for the weather ontology (Fig. 8). The framed concepts are those that can be used for the running example.

Vehicle Ontology: This ontology describes the performance of a vehicle with nine (9) properties. Table 3 shows the properties of three vehicles in the initial scene of running example. All roles (*EgoCar*, *TargetCar* and *OtherCar*) of vehicles can be represented. There are five classes of vehicle category provided

Table 2. Definition of the concept *Daylight*, extracted from [6].

Concept	*Daylight*
Entity	Daylight
Definition	The combination of all direct and indirect sunlight during the daytime
Properties	Direction (from 0 to 360°, 180° refers to south light), Visibility (*m*)

in [14], where *Class*1 refers to light vehicles whose hight is less than or equal to $2m$ and GVWR (Gross Vehicle Weight Rating) is less than or equal to $3,5t$. The concept *Vehicle* consists of two main sub-entities: *Device* and *Action*. *Device* refers to the devices actionable during the performance of the vehicle, such as the *WindscreenWiper* and the *Light*. *Action* refers to the control actions that could be made by pilot, such as action *ChangeLane* defined in Table 4.

Table 3. Properties of concept *Vehicle*, extracted from [6].

ID	*Ego*	V_A	V_B
Role	*EgoCar*	*TargetCar*	*OtherCar*
Category	*Class*1	*Class*1	*Class*1
Height	H_e	H_1	H_2
Width	W_e	W_1	W_2
Length	L_e	L_1	L_2
Weight	m_e	m_1	m_2
Color	*Blue*	*Green*	*Red*
Speed	v_e	v_1	v_2

Figure 9 shows the twenty-six (26) concepts we have defined for vehicle ontology. The framed concepts are those that can be used for the running example.

The entities that do not change position are considered as static. The infrastructure and the weather are considered as the static concepts, whiles *Ego* and the traffic are considered as the mobile ones. Some of the static concepts, such as the lighting and the weather, can change state but not their position. We call them dynamic concepts, in order to distinguish them from the mobile ones. All the concepts that appear in the running example are framed in Fig. 7, Fig. 8 and Fig. 9.

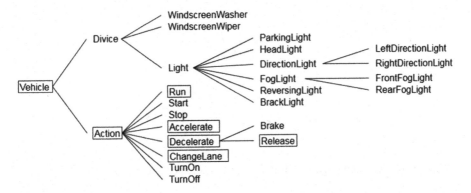

Fig. 9. Concepts of vehicle ontology (framed concepts for running example), based from [6].

Table 4. Definition of the concept *ChangeLane*, extracted from [6].

Concept	*ChangeLane*
Entity	change_lane
Definition	An action indicating a lane change to enter or exit the highway or overtaking another vehicle
Properties	Direction (Left/Right)

4.2 Interaction Layer

The interaction layer describes the interaction relationships, between on the one hand the static entities, and on the other hands the mobile entities. Moreover this layer describes the relationships between static and mobile entities.

In order to represent the complex and intricate relationships between the entities, we consider three kinds of relationships (Fig. 10): the relationships between the highway entities, the relationships between the vehicle entities, and the relationships between the entities of highway and vehicle. Moreover, the traffic regulation and the interactions between the concepts are written as rules to simulate the environment of autonomous vehicle. We use first-order logic to represent these relationships and rules. Note that we use the *ID* of concepts as the variables in the relationship formulas.

There are three types of relationships:

- the inheritance relationship, for example the relationship $isHighway(Roadpart_1, Highway_1)$ means that $Roadpart_1$ is a sub-entity of $Highway_1$.
- the composition relationship, for example $hasCarriageway(Roadway_1, Carriageway_1)$ means that $Roadway_1$ is composed of $Carriageway_1$.
- the position relationship which consists of the longitudinal position, the transverse position and the vertical position.

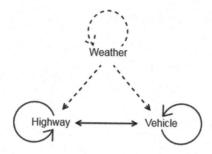

Fig. 10. Relationships (solid lines) and effects (dashed lines), extracted from [6].

Table 5 lists out all relationships between the entities of highway for running example. We note that the relationships $hasRightHardShoulder(Median_1,$ $Lefthardshoulder_1)$ means that there is $Lefthardshoulder_1$ at the right hand of $Median_1$. $Lefthardshoulder_1$ is the ID of entity $left\_hard\_shoulder$. This entity is different from $right\_hard\_shoulder$ which refers to the hard shoulder at the edges of the highway.

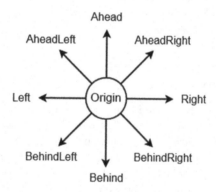

Fig. 11. Vehicles around the $EgoCar$, extracted from [6].

There are eight (8) relationships between $EgoCar$ and the other cars ($TargetCar$ and $OtherCar$) as showed in Fig. 11. The $EgoCar$ is in the origin and it can have a $TargetCar$ in front, which is conceptualised using relationship $hasAheadVehicle$. Each $OtherCar$ around $EgoCar$ is considered using the following relationships:

- hasAheadLeftVehicle
- hasLeftVehicle
- hasBehindLeftVehicle
- hasBehindVehicle
- hasBehindRightVehicle

- `hasRightVehicle`
- `hasAheadRightVehicle`

In the first scene of our running example, the relationship between $EgoCar$ and $TargetCar$ can be described using Formula (1), and the relationship between $EgoCar$ and $OtherCar$ can be described using Formula (2).

$$hasAheadVehicle(Ego,\ V_A) \tag{1}$$

$$hasAheadLeftVehicle(Ego,\ V_B) \tag{2}$$

Table 5. Relationships between highway entities for running example, extracted from [6].

Type	Relationship
Inheritance	$isHighway$, $isInterchange$, $isRamp$, $isShoulder$, $isEquipment$, $isSymbol$, $isMarking$, $isSpecificMarking$, $isSign$, $isPrioritySign$
Composition	$hasSegment$, $hasInterchange$, $hasRoadway$, $hasMedian$, $hasCarriageway$, $hasShoulder$, $hasLane$, $hasMainLane$, $hasAuxilaryLane$, $hasAccelerationSection$, $hasTaper$
Position	Longitudinal position:
	$connecteToSegment$, $connecteToAccelerationSection$, $connecteToTaper$
	Transverse position:
	$hasLeftMedian$, $hasLeftShoulder$, $hasRightShoulder$, $hasLeftLine$, $hasRightLine$, $hasLeftChevronMarking$, $hasRightChevronMarking$, $hasLeftSoftShoulder$, $hasRightSoftShoulder$
	Vertical position:
	$hasSignCedezlepassage$, $hasDeflectionArrowMarking$

In this study, we consider that all vehicles obey the traffic rules. Therefore, the relationships between vehicle and highway entities are the followings:

- `enters`
- `leaves`
- `on`

The formulas of these relationships have two variables, the ID of $Vehicle$ and the ID of a concept which can be any of $Lane$, $Shoulder$ or $SafetyArea$.

For example, in the first scene (Fig. 3), the relationships between the entities of vehicle and highway can be describe as:

$$on(Ego, \ Lane_R) \tag{3}$$

$$on(V_A, \ Lane_R) \tag{4}$$

$$on(V_B, \ Lane_L) \tag{5}$$

We consider the traffic regulation as rules to define the features and significance of highway infrastructure, and regulate the behaviour of vehicles. In the running example, the speed on $Carriageway_1$, which is the ID of $Carriageway$, is limited to 130 km/h. This rule limits the speed of Ego and it can be specified as:

$$Speed(Ego) \leq SpeedLimit(Carriageway_1) \tag{6}$$

where $Speed$ is a function to generate the speed of vehicles and $SpeedLimit$ is a function to show the speed limit on a portion of highway. Note that $v_e \leq$ 130 km/h can be derived from Formula (6).

The weather phenomena can have an effect on the highway, the vehicle and on itself (Fig. 10). These effects are also written as rules. For example, the $Snow$ phenomenon can only appear at very low temperatures, and it can make the vehicle make action $TurnOn$ the $FogLight$ to increase the visibility of Ego for the other cars. And the $Snow$ phenomenon can affect the visibility of $Equipment$ of highway. In this work, we assign values directly to the function $Visibility$ because there is not enough available data to build the model which simulates the effects of weather phenomena.

A scene can be defined using the concepts in the basic layer and the relationships in the interaction layer. With the first order logic, we describe the relationships between the entities using formulas such as those used for the running example. Then the scene generated is described as the logic formulas with the concepts in the basic layer and the relationships in the interaction layer. For example, in the first scene S_1 (Fig. 3) of running example, the part of vehicles can be described as follows:

$$on(Ego, \ Lane_R) \tag{7}$$

$$on(V_A, \ Lane_R) \tag{8}$$

$$on(V_B, \ Lane_L) \tag{9}$$

$$hasAheadVehicle(Ego, \ V_A) \tag{10}$$

$$Distance(Ego, \ V_A) = d_1 \tag{11}$$

$$hasAheadLeftVehicle(Ego,\ V_B) \tag{12}$$

$$Distance(Ego,\ V_B) = d_2 \tag{13}$$

4.3   Generation Layer

The task of the generation layer is to build test cases which include one or several scenarios. In this section, firstly we introduce how to generate scenarios based on the concepts and relationships of the first two layers. Then we show how we use PEPA for modelling the transitions between the driving scenes.

Generation Method. In the beginning of Sect. 4, the scenario is defined as a sequence of scenes, assailed with goals, values and actions of *Ego*, values and events from the other actors, and values of the static concepts. In the running example, the goal is that V_B takes the right exit lane of a highway. The actions which can possibly be made by *Ego* are *Detect*, *Decelerate*, *Accelerate* and *Run*. The actions possibly made by other vehicles, which are considered as events from *Ego*'s point of view, are *Decelerate*, *Accelerate*, *Run* and *ChangeLane* (Fig. 9). The change of states of the dynamic concepts also make events to *Ego* with the change of the values of their properties. These actions and events make a scene develop to another scene. So we use a formula to represent the relationship between the next scene (*NextScene*) and the current scene (*CurrentScene*):

$$NextScene = (CurrentScene,\ Action \lor Event)$$

where *CurrentScene* can be any scene built by our ontologies. In the running example, it can be any of S_1, S_2, S_3, S_4 or S_5. *Action* and *Event* are functions based on their actors and their properties. The actor of actions is *EgoCar* and the events are those occurring due to the actions made by *TargetCar* or *OtherCar*. So an event can be presented as

$$Event \equiv (Actor,\ Action)$$

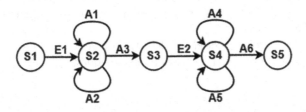

Fig. 12. Transition graph of the PEPA model.

With the same initial scene, it is evident that different actions or events lead to different scenes, and make different scenarios. In the running example, we describe one of several possibilities. Figure 12 shows the process of the scenarios which constitute a test case from the initial scene. It can be generated as:

$$S_1 = \{Concepts\} \vee \{Relationships\}$$
$$S_2 = (S_1, E_1)$$
$$S_2 = (S_2, A_1)$$
$$S_2 = (S_2, A_2)$$
$$S_3 = (S_2, A_3)$$
$$S_4 = (S_3, E_2)$$
$$S_4 = (S_4, A_4)$$
$$S_4 = (S_4, A_5)$$
$$S_5 = (S_4, A_6)$$

Where

$$E_1 \equiv (V_B, ChangeLane(Right))$$
$$A_1 \equiv (Ego, DetectCarIn)$$
$$A_2 \equiv (Ego, ChangeTaget)$$
$$A_3 \equiv (Ego, Decelerate)$$
$$E_2 \equiv (V_B, ChangeLane(Right))$$
$$A_4 \equiv (Ego, DetectCarOut)$$
$$A_5 \equiv (Ego, ChangeTarget)$$
$$A_6 \equiv (Ego, Accelerate)$$

PEPA Model. We use Performance Evaluation Process Algebra (PEPA) [8] to model the transitions between the driving scenes. PEPA is a stochastic process algebra designed for modelling computer and communication systems and introduced by Jane Hillston in the 1990s [8]. PEPA is a simple language with a small set of operators. It is easy to reason about the language as it provides a great deal of flexibility to the modeller [8].

A PEPA model is constructed by identifying components performing activities. The syntax for terms in PEPA is defined as follows:

$P ::= (\alpha, r).P$ Prefix: component P carries out activity (α, r) which has action type α and a
duration which is exponentially distributed with parameter r

$\quad | \ P + Q$ Choice: a system which may behave either as component P or as Q

$\quad | \ P \bowtie_L Q$ Cooperation: shared activity in the cooperation set L determines the interaction
between the components P and Q, replacing the individual activities of
the individual components P and Q with a rate reflecting the rate of the slower participant.

$\quad | \ P/L$ Hiding: P except that any activities of types within the set L are hidden, their
type is not witnessed upon completion. They appear as the unknown type τ
and can be regarded as an internal delay by the component

$\quad | \ A$ Constant: gives the constant A the behaviour of the component P to assign names to components

PEPA abstracts the activities performed by components into a continuous-time Markov process. The generation of this underlying Markov process is based on the derivation graph of the model. The derivation graph is a directed multigraph whose set of nodes is reachable states of model and whose arcs represent the possible transitions between them. These edges are labelled only by the rates of activities which become the corresponding entry in the infinitesimal generator matrix [11].

A PEPA model is constructed by identifying components performing activities. The components are the dynamic entities of ontologies and the activities are the actions and the events performed by these entities with their occurrence rates. In the running example, we identified the components and their actions as follows:

The Model Components: There are the vehicles and the scene, that is: Ego, V_A, V_B, S_1.

The Model Actions: There are the actions and events in the system. Figure 12 shows the process of the scenario from the initial scene, associated with the actions and events in Table 6. The actor of actions is $EgoCar$ and the events are those occurring due to the actions made by $TargetCar$ or $OtherCar$.

Table 6. Actions & Events.

Events	Actions
E1: ChangeLaneToLaneB	A1: DetectCarIn
E2: ChangeLaneToLaneE	A2: ChangeTargetIn
	A3: Decelerate
	A4: DetectCarOut
	A5: ChangeTargetOut
	A6: Accelerate

The behaviours of concepts described using the following equations: Component Ego:

$$Ego = (RunEgo, \lambda_1).Ego + (DetectCarIn, \lambda_2).Ego_1$$
$$+ (DetectCarOut, \lambda_3).Ego_2$$
$$Ego_1 = (ChangeTargetIn, \lambda_4).Ego_3$$
$$Ego_2 = (ChangeTargetOut, \lambda_5).Ego_4$$
$$Ego_3 = (Decelerate, \lambda_6).Ego$$
$$Ego_4 = (Accelerate, \lambda_7).Ego$$

Component V_A:

$$V_A = (RunV_A, \mu_1).V_A$$

Component V_B:

$$V_B = (RunV_B, \eta_1).V_B + (ChangeToLaneB, \eta_2).V_{B1}$$
$$V_{B1} = (ChangeToLaneE, \eta_3).V_B + (RunV_B, \eta_4).V_B$$

Component S_1:

$$S_1 = (ChangeToLaneB, \top).S_2$$
$$S_2 = (DetectCarIn, \top).S_2 + (ChangeTargetIn, \top).S_2$$
$$+ (Decelerate, \top).S_3$$
$$S_3 = (ChangeToLaneE, \top).S_4$$
$$S_4 = (DetectCarOut, \top).S_4 + (ChangeTargetOut, \top).S_4$$
$$+ (Accelerate, \top).S_5$$
$$S_5 = (RunEgo, \top).S_1$$

In the equations above, λ_i, μ_i and η_i are the rates of the corresponding actions, $\top$ is the rate of unspecified actions.

The equation of the complete model is the following:

$$Scenario \stackrel{\text{def}}{=} (V_B \underset{L}{\bowtie} S_1 \underset{M}{\bowtie} Ego) \parallel V_A$$

where L and M are the action sets on which V_B and S_1, on the one hand, and S_1 and Ego, on the other hand, must synchronise.

$$M = \{DetectCarIn, ChangeTargetIn, Decelerate,$$
$$DetectCarOut, ChangeTargetOut, Accelerate,$$
$$RunEgo\}$$
$$L = \{ChangeToLaneB, ChangeToLaneE\}$$

One scenario is one possibility of a test case (Fig. 5). A test case includes one or several scenarios. The test case of autonomous vehicle is the simulation of the driving environment, the traffic and the pilot. As the role of the pilot, system ADAS limits to a set of decisions that will be made by $EgoCar$. For example, the existence of a target vehicle is necessary for the $EgoCar$ to activate the system TJC. Therefore, the $EgoCar$ cannot make the action $ChangeLane$ to the left lane because there is no target vehicle. These ranges and behaviours are presented as rules to make sure that only reasonable test cases will be generated.

5   Conclusions

In this article, we present an ADAS test cases generation methodology based on highway traffic situation description ontologies. A highway ontology, a weather ontology and a vehicle ontology are built for the conceptualization and characterization of the components of test cases. The first two allow the specification of the environment in which evolves the autonomous vehicle, and the third one consists of the vehicle devices and the control actions. We use a first-order logic to express the relationships and rules, such as traffic regulation. Our methodology consists of three layers: a basic layer which exploits static and mobile concepts we have defined in the context of three ontologies, an interaction layer which exploits the relationships between these concepts and a generation layer which exploits the method of test case generation based on the first two layers. We use the semantically explicit formal modelling language PEPA to model the generation of scenarios. In the future, we plan to extend our work to include the highway infrastructure and weather impact.

Acknowledgements. This research work has been carried out in the framework of IRT SystemX, Paris-Saclay, France, and therefore granted with public funds within the scope of the French Program "Investissements d'Avenir".

References

1. Armand, A., Filliat, D., Guzman, J.I.: Ontology-based context awareness for driving assistance systems. In: 2014 IEEE Intelligent Vehicles Symposium Proceedings, Dearborn, MI, USA, 8–11 June 2014, pp. 227–233 (2014). https://doi.org/10.1109/IVS.2014.6856509

2. Bagschik, G., Menzel, T., Maurer, M.: Ontology based scene creation for the development of automated vehicles. CoRR Computing Research Repository abs/1704.01006 (2017). http://arxiv.org/abs/1704.01006

3. Bartosiak, D.: Nissan and NASA extend partnership on autonomous tech (2018).   http://www.thedrive.com/sheetmetal/17607/nissan-and-nasa-extend-partnership-on-autonomous-tech

4. Caughill, P.: Dubai jump starts autonomous taxi service with 50 tesla vehicles (2017). https://futurism.com/dubai-jump-starts-autonomous-taxi-service-with-50-tesla-vehicles/

5. Cerone, A., Zhao, Y.: Stochastic modelling and analysis of driver behaviour. ECE-ASST **69** (2013). https://doi.org/10.14279/tuj.eceasst.69.965

6. Chen, W., Kloul, L.: An ontology-based approach to generate the advanced driver assistance use cases of highway traffic. In: Proceedings of the 10th International Joint Conference on Knowledge Discovery, Knowledge Engineering and Knowledge Management, IC3K 2018, Volume 2: KEOD, Seville, Spain, 18–20 September 2018, pp. 73–81 (2018). https://doi.org/10.5220/0006931700730081

7. Gain, B.: Waymo patent shows plans to replace steering wheel & pedals with push buttons (2017). https://driverless.wonderhowto.com/news/waymo-patent-shows-plans-replace-steering-wheel-pedals-with-push-buttons-0179498/

8. Hillston, J.: A compositional approach to performance modelling. Ph.D. thesis, University of Edinburgh, UK (1994). http://hdl.handle.net/1842/15027

9. Hülsen, M., Zöllner, J.M., Weiss, C.: Traffic intersection situation description ontology for advanced driver assistance. In: IEEE Intelligent Vehicles Symposium (IV), 2011, Baden-Baden, Germany, 5–9 June 2011, pp. 993–999 (2011). https://doi.org/10.1109/IVS.2011.5940415

10. Hummel, B., Thiemann, W., Lulcheva, I.: Scene understanding of urban road intersections with description logic. In: Logic and Probability for Scene Interpretation, 24–29 February 2008 (2008). http://drops.dagstuhl.de/opus/volltexte/2008/1616/

11. Kloul, L.: From performance analysis to performance engineering: some ideas and experiments. Ph.D. thesis (2006)

12. Krok, A.: Audi expands traffic light information v2i to Washington (2018). https://www.cnet.com/roadshow/news/audi-v2i-traffic-light-information-washington-dc/

13. Ministère de l'écologie, E.d.r.e.d.r.: Arrêté du 16 Février 1988 relatif à l'approbation de modifications de l'instruction interministérielle sur la signalisation routiere, instruction interministerielle sur la signalisation routiere. Journal officiel du 12 mars 1988 (1988)

14. Ministère de l'équipement, des Transports, d.L.d.T.e.d.l.M.: Décret n°2000-1355 du 30/12/2000 paru au jorf n°0303 du 31/12/2000. JORF n°0303 du 31 décembre 2000 (2000)

15. Morignot, P., Nashashibi, F.: An ontology-based approach to relax traffic regulation for autonomous vehicle assistance. CoRR Computing Research Repository abs/1212.0768 (2012). http://arxiv.org/abs/1212.0768

16. Pollard, E., Morignot, P., Nashashibi, F.: An ontology-based model to determine the automation level of an automated vehicle for co-driving. In: Proceedings of the 16th International Conference on Information Fusion, FUSION 2013, Istanbul, Turkey, 9–12 July 2013, pp. 596–603 (2013). http://ieeexplore.ieee.org/document/6641334/

17. Ulbrich, S., Menzel, T., Reschka, A., Schuldt, F., Maurer, M.: Defining and substantiating the terms scene, situation, and scenario for automated driving. In: IEEE 18th International Conference on Intelligent Transportation Systems, ITSC 2015, Gran Canaria, Spain, 15–18 September 2015, pp. 982–988 (2015). https://doi.org/10.1109/ITSC.2015.164

18. Uschold, M., Gruninger, M.: Ontologies: principles, methods and applications. Knowl. Eng. Rev. **11**(2), 93–155 (1996)

19. Yun, Y., Kai, C.: A method for semantic representation of dynamic events in traffic scenes. Inf. Control **44**(1), 83–90 (2015). http://ic.sia.cn/CN/10.13976/j.cnki.xk.2015.0083

20. Zhao, L., Ichise, R., Mita, S., Sasaki, Y.: Core ontologies for safe autonomous driving. In: Proceedings of the ISWC 2015 Posters & Demonstrations Track co-located with the 14th International Semantic Web Conference (ISWC-2015), Bethlehem, PA, USA, 11 October 2015 (2015). http://ceur-ws.org/Vol-1486/paper_9.pdf

Reasoning over Ontologies with DLV

Carlo Allocca[3], Mario Alviano[1], Francesco Calimeri[1,2], Roberta Costabile[1],
Alessio Fiorentino[1], Davide Fuscà[1], Stefano Germano[1,2],
Giovanni Laboccetta[2], Nicola Leone[1]([⊠]), Marco Manna[1], Simona Perri[1],
Kristian Reale[2], Francesco Ricca[1], Pierfrancesco Veltri[2],
and Jessica Zangari[1,2]

[1] Department of Mathematics and Computer Science,
University of Calabria, Rende, Italy
{alviano,calimeri,r.costabile,fiorentino,fusca,
germano,leone,manna,perri,ricca,zangari}@mat.unical.it
[2] DLVSystem L.T.D., Polo Tecnologico Unical, Rende, Italy
{laboccetta,reale,veltri}@dlvsystem.com
[3] Samsung Research, Staines, UK
c.allocca@samsung.com

Abstract. The paper presents DLV, an advanced AI system from the area of
Answer Set Programming (ASP), showing its high potential for reasoning over
ontologies. Ontological reasoning services represent fundamental features in the
development of the Semantic Web. Among them, scientists are focusing their
attention on the so-called ontology-based query answering (OBQA) task where a
(conjunctive) query has to be evaluated over a logical theory (a.k.a. Knowledge
Base, or simply KB) consisting of an extensional database (a.k.a. ABox) paired
with an ontology (a.k.a. TBox). From a theoretical viewpoint, much has been
done. Indeed, Description logics and Datalog$^\pm$ have been recognized as the two
main families of formal ontology specification languages to specify KBs, while
OWL has been identified as the official W3C standard language to physically
represent and share them; moreover sophisticated algorithms and techniques have
been proposed. Conversely, from a practical point of view, only a few systems
for solving complex ontological reasoning services such as OBQA have been
developed, and no official standard has been identified yet. The aim of the present
paper is to illustrate the applicability of the well-known ASP system DLV for
powerful ontology-based reasoning.

Keywords: Ontology-based query answering · Ontological reasoning · Answer
Set Programming · DLV · Semantic Web

1 Introduction

Answer Set Programming (ASP for short) [12,21,23] is a declarative programming
paradigm evolved from logic programming, deductive databases, knowledge representation, and nonmonotonic reasoning, and serves as a flexible language for solving problems in a declarative way: the user does not need to provide an algorithm for solving

This work has been partially supported by Samsung under project "Enhancing the DLV system
for large-scale ontology reasoning" (Ref. EHQ180906_0004).

© Springer Nature Switzerland AG 2020
A. Fred et al. (Eds.): IC3K 2018, CCIS 1222, pp. 114–136, 2020.
https://doi.org/10.1007/978-3-030-49559-6_6

the problem; rather, it is sufficient that (s)he specifies the properties of the desired solution for its computation. ASP is highly expressive, and allows to solve problems even beyond the complexity class NP. The main representation feature of ASP are rules, which are interpreted according to common sense principles according to the classical *closed-world* assumption/semantics (CWA) of deductive databases. In ASP, one writes a program, that is, a collection of rules, which represent a problem to be solved. This program, together with some input, usually expressed using factual rules, possesses a collection of models (possibly also no model), called answer sets, which correspond to the solutions of the modeled problem. Efficient systems for computing answer sets are available and have stimulated the development of applications relying on ASP, both in academia and business.

The field of ASP is growing, and several extensions of the basic language have been proposed and used in applications. For example, it can be profitably applied in *ontology-based query answering*, for short OBQA [14,37], where a Boolean query q has to be evaluated against a *logical theory* (a.k.a. *knowledge base*) consisting of an extensional *database* (a.k.a. ABox) D paired with an *ontology* (a.k.a. TBox) Σ. This problem, usually stated as $D \cup \Sigma \models q$, is equivalent to checking whether q is satisfied by all models of $D \cup \Sigma$ according to the classical *open-world* semantics/assumption (OWA) of first-order logic [1].

During the last decade, OBQA is attracting the increasing attention of scientists in various fields of Computer Science, ranging from Artificial Intelligence [7,18,24] to Database Theory [9,10,25] and Logic [8,26,38]. As a result, Description Logics (DLs) [6] and Datalog$^\pm$ [14] have been recognized as the two main families of formal knowledge representation languages to specify Σ, while conjunctive queries (CQs) represent the most common and studied formalism to express q. For both these families, OBQA is generally undecidable [13,30,39]. Hence, syntactic decidable fragments of the above two languages have been singled out with the aim of offering a good balance between complexity and expressiveness.

The aim of the present paper is to illustrate the applicability of the well-known ASP system DLV [17,34] in the context of ontology-based reasoning. In what follows, after introducing the DLV-language in Sect. 2 and the main ontology specification languages in Sect. 3, we move to Sect. 4 to formally define OBQA and show how to deal with OBQA in DLV. In Sect. 5 we consider a number of real-life ontologies and discuss expressiveness issues, which evidentiate the need to go beyond the OWL 2 RL profile. In Sect. 6, we describe the architecture of the DLV system; moreover, we introduce the main query-oriented optimization technique implemented by DLV. In Sect. 7 we report on some experiments carried out to evaluate the efficiency and the effectiveness of DLV. Finally, we conclude with Sect. 8 to summarize our ongoing work.

2   DLV Language and CWA

In this section we introduce the reader to the DLV world: terminology, syntax, semantics, core language, extensions, knowledge representation capabilities, and expressive power.

2.1   Core Language

A *term* is either a *simple term* or a *functional term*. A *simple term* is either a constant or a variable. If $t_1 \ldots t_n$ are terms and f is a function symbol of arity n, then $f(t_1, \ldots, t_n)$ is a *functional term*. If $t_1, \ldots, t_k$ are terms and p is a *predicate symbol* of arity k, then $p(t_1, \ldots, t_k)$ is an *atom*. A *literal* l is of the form a or not a, where a is an atom; in the former case l is *positive*, otherwise *negative* A *rule* r is of the form $\alpha_1 \mid \cdots \mid \alpha_k \leftarrow \beta_1, \ldots, \beta_n$, not $\beta_{n+1}, \ldots$, not β_m. where $m \geq 0$, $k \geq 0$; $\alpha_1, \ldots, \alpha_k$ and $\beta_1, \ldots, \beta_m$ are atoms. We define $H(r) = \{\alpha_1, \ldots, \alpha_k\}$ (the *head* of r) and $B(r) = B^+(r) \cup B^-(r)$ (the *body* of r), where $B^+(r) = \{\beta_1, \ldots, \beta_n\}$ (the *positive body* of r) and $B^-(r) = \{$not $\beta_{n+1}, \ldots$, not $\beta_m\}$ (the *negative body* of r). If $H(r) = \emptyset$ then r is a *(strong) constraint*; if $B(r) = \emptyset$ and $|H(r)| = 1$ then r is a *fact*.

A rule r is safe if each variable of r has an occurrence in $B^+(r)$. A DLV program is a finite set P of safe rules. A program (a rule, a literal) is said to be *ground* if it contains no variables. A predicate is defined by a rule if the predicate occurs in the head of the rule. A predicate defined only by facts is an *EDB* predicate, the remaining predicates are *IDB* predicates. The set of all facts in P is denoted by $Facts(P)$; the set of instances of all EDB predicates in P is denoted by $EDB(P)$.

Given a program P, the *Herbrand universe* of P, denoted by U_P, consists of all (ground) terms that can be built combining constants and function symbols appearing in P. The *Herbrand base* of P, denoted by B_P, is the set of all ground atoms obtainable from the atoms of P by replacing variables with elements from U_P. A *substitution* for a rule $r \in P$ is a mapping from the set of variables of r to the set U_P of ground terms. A *ground instance* of a rule r is obtained applying a substitution to r. The *instantiation (grounding) $Ground(\mathcal{P})$* of P is defined as the set of all ground instances of its rules over U_P. An *interpretation* I for P is a subset of B_P. A positive literal a (resp., a negative literal not a) is true w.r.t. I if $a \in I$ (resp., $a \notin I$); it is false otherwise. Given a ground rule r, we say that r is satisfied w.r.t. I if some atom appearing in $H(r)$ is true w.r.t. I or some literal appearing in $B(r)$ is false w.r.t. I. Given a ground program P, we say that I is a *model* of P, iff all rules in $Ground(\mathcal{P})$ are satisfied w.r.t. I. A model M is *minimal* if there is no model N for P such that $N \subset M$. The *Gelfond-Lifschitz reduct* [23] of P, w.r.t. an interpretation I, is the positive ground program P^I obtained from $Ground(\mathcal{P})$ by: (i) deleting all rules having a negative literal false w.r.t. I; (ii) deleting all negative literals from the remaining rules. $I \subseteq B_P$ is an *answer set* for a program P iff I is a minimal model for P^I. The set of all answer sets for P is denoted by $AS(P)$.

Example 1. Let us consider the problem EXAM-SCHEDULING, which consists of scheduling examinations for courses. In particular, we want to assign exams to time slots such that no two exams are assigned for the same time slot if the respective courses have a student in common (we call such courses "incompatible"). Supposing that there are three time slots available, namely, ts_1, ts_2 and ts_3, we express the problem by the following program P_{sch}:

$$r_1 : \quad assign(X, ts_1) \mid assign(X, ts_2) \mid assign(X, ts_3) \leftarrow course(X).$$
$$s_1 : \quad \leftarrow assign(X, S), assign(Y, S), incompatible(X, Y).$$

Here we assume that the courses and the pair of incompatible courses are specified by a set F of input facts with predicate *course* and *incompatible*, respectively. Rule r_1 says that every course is assigned to one of the three time slots; strong constraint s_1 expresses that no two incompatible courses can be overlapped, that is, they cannot be assigned to the same time slot. There is a one-to-one correspondence between the solutions of the EXAM-SCHEDULING problem and the answer sets of $P_{sch} \cup F$.   □

2.2   Linguistic Extensions

An important feature of the DLV language are *weak constraints* [34], which allow for expressing optimization problems. A weak constraint is denoted like a strong constraint, but using the symbol $:\sim$ instead of $\leftarrow$. Intuitively, weak constraints allow for expressing conditions that *should* be satisfied, but not necessarily have to be. The informal meaning of a weak constraint $:\sim B.$ is "B should preferably be false". Additionally, a weight and a priority level for the weak constraint may be specified enclosed in square brackets (by means of positive integers or variables). When not specified, these values default to 1. Optimal answer sets are those minimizing the sum of weights of the violated weak constraints in the highest priority level and, among them, those which minimize the sum of weights of the violated weak constraints in the next lower level, and so on. Weak constraints allow us to express "desiderata" and are very useful in practice, since they allow for obtaining a solution (answer set) also when the usage of strong constraints would imply that there is no answer set.

Example 2. In specific instances of EXAM-SCHEDULING, there could be no way to assign courses to time slots without having some overlapping between incompatible courses. However, in real life, one is often satisfied with an approximate solution, that is, one in which constraints are satisfied as much as possible. In this light, the problem at hand can be restated as follows (APPROX-SCHEDULING): "assign exams to time slots trying to not overlap incompatible courses". This can be expressed by the program P_{asch} using weak constraints:

$$r_1: \qquad assign(X, ts_1) \mid assign(X, ts_2) \mid assign(X, ts_3) \leftarrow course(X).$$
$$w_1: \qquad :\sim assign(X, S), assign(Y, S), incompatible(X, Y).$$

An informal reading of the weak constraint w_1 is: "preferably, do not assign the exams X and Y to the same time slot if they are incompatible". Note that programs P_{sch} and P_{asch} have the same answer sets if all incompatible courses can be assigned to different time slots. However, when P_{sch} has no answer sets, P_{asch} provides answer sets corresponding to ways to satisfy the constraints "as much as possible".   □

The DLV language also supports *aggregate atoms* [4,22], allowing for representing in a simple and natural manner also properties that require the use of arithmetic operators on (multi-)sets, often arising in real-world applications. Aggregate atoms consist of an aggregation function (currently one of cardinality, sum, product, maximum, minimum), evaluated over a multiset of terms, the content of which depend on the truth of non-aggregate atoms. The syntax is $L \prec_1 \mathbf{F}\{Vars : Conj\} \prec_2 U$ where $\mathbf{F}$ is a function among #count, #min, #max, #sum, and #times, $\prec_1, \prec_2 \in \{=, <, \leq, >, \geq\}$, L and U are integers or variables, called guards, and $\{Vars : Conj\}$ is a symbolic set, which intuitively represents the set of values for $Vars$ for which the conjunction $Conj$ is true. For instance, the symbolic set $\{X, Y : a(X, Y, Z), \text{not } p(Y)\}$ stands for the set of pairs (X, Y) satisfying the conjunction $a(X, Y, Z), \text{not } p(Y)$, i.e., $S = \{(X, Y) \mid \exists Z : a(X, Y) \wedge \text{not } p(Y) \text{ is true}\}$. When evaluating an aggregate function over it, the projection on the first elements of the pairs is considered, which yields a multiset in general. The value yielded by the function evaluation is compared against the guards, determining the truth value of the aggregate.

Example 3. Let us consider a TEAM-BUILDING problem, where a project team has to be built according to the following specifications: (1) the team consists of a certain number of employees; (2) at least a given number of different skills must be present; (3) the sum of the salaries of the employees in the team must not exceed a given budget; (4) the salary of each individual employee is within a given limit; (5) the team must include at least a given number of women. Information on employees is provided by facts of the form $emp(EmpId, Sex, Skill, Salary)$. The size of the team, the minimum number of different skills in the team, the budget, the maximum salary, and the minimum number of female employees are given by facts $nEmp(N)$, $nSkill(N)$, $budget(B)$, $maxSal(M)$, and $women(W)$. We then encode each property p_i above by an aggregate atom A_i, and enforce it by an integrity constraint containing not A_i.

$$
\begin{aligned}
r_1: &\quad in(I) \mid out(I) \leftarrow emp(I, Sx, Sk, Sa). \\
s_1: &\quad \leftarrow nEmp(N), \text{not } \#\text{count}\{I : in(I)\} = N. \\
s_2: &\quad \leftarrow nSkill(M), \#\text{count}\{Sk : emp(I, Sx, Sk, Sa), in(I)\} < M. \\
s_3: &\quad \leftarrow budget(B), \#\text{sum}\{Sa, I : emp(I, Sx, Sk, Sa), in(I)\} > B. \\
s_4: &\quad \leftarrow maxSal(M), \#\text{max}\{Sa : emp(I, Sx, Sk, Sa), in(I)\} > M. \\
s_5: &\quad \leftarrow women(W), \#\text{count}\{I : emp(I, f, Sk, Sa), in(I)\} < W.
\end{aligned}
$$

Rule r_1 "guesses" whether an employee is included in the team or not, while each constraint s_1–s_5 corresponds one-to-one to a requirement p_1–p_5.   □

2.3 Expressive Power

The DLV input language can be seen as a "general purpose" formalism able to deal, with a reasonable degree of efficiency, with different kinds of applications, ranging from more "database-oriented" deductive database applications to NP search and optimization problems, up to harder problems whose complexity resides at the second layer of the Polynomial Hierarchy. Indeed, even disregarding the linguistic extensions, the DLV core language is quite expressive: its function-free fragment can express, in a precise mathematical sense, every property of finite structures over a function-free first-order structure that is decidable in nondeterministic polynomial time with an oracle in NP [20] (i.e., it captures the complexity class Σ_2^P). Thus, even this fragment allows to encode problems that cannot be translated to SAT in polynomial time. If weak constraints are added to the function-free fragment of the core language, one can express optimization problems of complexity up to Δ_3^P [34]. If uninterpreted function symbols of positive arities are permitted, the expressive power of the core language increases considerably, at the cost of undecidability in the general case; DLV allows to work with the class of Finitely-Ground programs, which allow to represent any computable function [16].

3   Ontology Languages

In this section we provide a formal definition of the two main formal ontology specification languages: Description Logics and Datalog$^\pm$. For the sake of presentation, we start with the latter one.

3.1   Datalog$^\pm$

Let **C** (*constants* or *individuals*) and **V** (*variables*) be pairwise disjoint discrete sets of *terms*. An *atom* α is a labeled tuple $p(\mathbf{t})$, where $p = pred(\alpha)$ is a predicate symbol, $\mathbf{t} = t_1, ..., t_m$ is a tuple of terms, $m = |p|$ is the arity of p or α, and $\alpha[i] = t_i$. A *substitution* is any map $\mu : \mathbf{V} \to \mathbf{C}$. For a set A of atoms, $\mu(A)$ is obtained from A by replacing each variable X by $\mu(X)$. A *database* (resp., *instance*) is any variable-free finite (resp., possibly infinite) set of atoms. A *rule* ρ is any logical implication of the form $\forall \mathbf{X} \forall \mathbf{Y} \, (\phi(\mathbf{X}, \mathbf{Y}) \to \exists \mathbf{Z} \, \psi(\mathbf{X}, \mathbf{Z}))$—with $\mathbf{X} \cup \mathbf{Y} \cup \mathbf{Z} \subseteq \mathbf{V}$—whose body (resp., head) $body(\rho) = \phi(\mathbf{X}, \mathbf{Y})$ (resp., $head(\rho) = \psi(\mathbf{X}, \mathbf{Z})$) is a conjunction of atoms, possibly with constants. If the head is empty (denoted by $\bot$), then the rule is a *negative constraint*. Universal and existential variables are respectively denoted by $\mathbf{UV}(\rho)$ and $\mathbf{EV}(\rho)$. The set $\mathbf{X}$ is the *frontier* of ρ. An ontology Σ is any finite set of rules. A *conjunctive query* is any first-order expression of the form $q(\mathbf{X}) \equiv \exists \mathbf{Y} \, \phi(\mathbf{X}, \mathbf{Y})$, where ϕ is defined as in the body of rules. For a "structure" (set, rule, query, ...) ς over atoms, by $atoms(\varsigma)$, $terms(\varsigma)$, and $vars(\varsigma)$ we respectively denote the set of atoms in ς, the set of terms in $atoms(\varsigma)$, and the set of variables in $atoms(\varsigma)$.

Given a database D and an ontology Σ, a *model* of $D \cup \Sigma$ is any instance $M \supseteq D$ such that, for each $\rho \in \Sigma$ and for each substitution μ, if $\mu(body(\rho)) \subseteq M$, then there exists a substitution μ' that agrees with μ on $\mathbf{X}$ for which $\mu'(head(\rho)) \subseteq M$. The set of all models of $D \cup \Sigma$ is denoted by $mods(D, \Sigma)$. Note that M might contain individuals (constants) that do not occur neither in D nor in Σ, to comply with the so-called open world assumption (OWA).

Example 4. Consider the Datalog$^\pm$ ontology Σ consisting of the following rule:

$$person(X) \; \to \; \exists Y \; hasFather(X, Y)$$

Given a database $D = \{person(john)\}$, a possible model of the knowledge base $D \cup \Sigma$ is the instance $M_1 = D \cup \{hasFather(john, luke)\}$. Moreover, the following expressions are conjunctive queries:

$$
\begin{aligned}
q_1(X, Y) &\equiv person(X), hasFather(X, Y) \\
q_2(X) &\equiv \exists Y \; hasFather(X, Y) \\
q_3() &\equiv \exists X \; hasFather(X, luke)
\end{aligned}
$$

In particular, q_1 has two free variables, namely X and Y, while q_2 has one free variable, namely X. Regarding q_3, it is usually called *Boolean* since it contains no free variable. Moreover, q_2 and q_3 are also called *atomic* since they consists of only one atom. □

We now introduce some Datalog$^\pm$ classes that can be handled by DLV and that we are going to mention in Sect. 4—namely, datalog [1], linear [15], j-acyclic [32], and shy [33]. Fix a Datalog$^\pm$ ontology Σ. We denote by $\mathcal{R}(\Sigma)$ the set of predicates occurring in Σ. A *position* $p[i]$ is defined as a predicate p of $\mathcal{R}(\Sigma)$ and its i-th attribute. Let $pos(p) = \{p[1], ..., p[|p|]\}$. We assume that different rules of Σ share no variable. A term t occurs in a set A of atoms at position $p[i]$ if there is $\alpha \in A$ s.t. $pred(\alpha) = p$ and $\alpha[i] = t$. Position $p[i]$ is *invaded* by an existential variable X if there is $\rho \in \Sigma$ s.t.: (1) X occurs in $head(\rho)$ at position $p[i]$; or (2) some $y \in \mathbf{UV}(\rho)$ *attacked* by X (i.e., y occurs in $body(\rho)$ only at positions invaded by X) occurs in $head(\rho)$ at position $p[i]$. A universal variable is *protected* if it is attacked by no variable. Then, Σ belongs to

- datalog if $\mathbf{EV}(\rho) = \emptyset$;
- linear if, for each $\rho \in \Sigma$, $body(\rho)$ contains at most one body atom;
- j-acyclic if $G_\exists(\Sigma)$ is is acyclic, with $G_\exists(\Sigma) = \langle N, A \rangle$ being the existential graph of Σ defined as follows: $N = \cup_{\rho \in \Sigma} \mathbf{EV}(\rho)$ and $(X, Y) \in A$ if the rule ρ where Y occurs contains a universal variable attacked by X and occurring in $head(\rho)$;
- shy if, for each $\rho \in \Sigma$: (1) X occurs in two different atoms of $body(\rho)$ implies X is protected; and (2) if X and Y occur both in $head(\rho)$ and in two different atoms of $body(\rho)$, then X and Y are not attacked by the same variable;

3.2   Description Logics and OWL

Description Logics (DLs) are a family of formal knowledge representation languages that model concepts, roles, individuals, and their relationships. Let N_C (*concepts*), N_R (*roles*), and N_I (*individuals*) be mutually disjoint discrete sets. A DL *knowledge base* (KB) in normal form is any pair $\mathcal{K} = (\mathcal{A}, \mathcal{T})$ where:

(i) $\mathcal{A}$, the ABox (assertional box), is a finite set of *assertions* of the form $A(a)$ or $R(a, b)$, with $a, b \in N_I$, $A \in N_C$, and $R \in N_R$. Roughly, an ABox can be transparently seen as a database.

(ii) $\mathcal{T}$, the TBox (terminological box), is a finite set of *concept inclusions* (CIs) together with a finite set of *role inclusions* (RIs). Table 1 and Table 2 report only those inclusions that are at the basis of the OWL 2 Web Ontology Language Profiles introduced below. Accordingly, we consider the following classes of Description Logics: $\mathcal{EL}$++ [5], Horn-$\mathcal{SHIQ}$ [29], $\mathcal{ELH}$ [11], DL-Lite$_R$ [40], and DLP [27]. The semantics of concept (resp., role) inclusions is given in Table 1 (resp., Table 2) in terms of Datalog$^\pm$.

Table 1. Concept inclusions, where $A, B, B_1, B_2 \in N_C$ and $R \in N_R$.

$\mathcal{EL}$++	Horn-$\mathcal{SHIQ}$	$\mathcal{ELH}$	DL-Lite$_R$	DLP	concept inclusions	Equivalent Datalog$^\pm$ rule
✓	✓	✓	✓	✓	$B \sqsubseteq A$	$B(X) \to A(X)$
✓	✓	✓		✓	$B_1 \sqcap B_2 \sqsubseteq A$	$B_1(X), B_2(X) \to A(X)$
	✓			✓	$B \sqsubseteq \forall R.A$ $\exists R^-.B \sqsubseteq A$	$B(X), R(X,Y) \to A(Y)$
✓	✓	✓		✓	$\exists R.B \sqsubseteq A$	$R(X,Y), B(Y) \to A(X)$
✓	✓	✓	✓	✓	$\exists R.\top \sqsubseteq A$ $\mathrm{dom}(R) \sqsubseteq A$	$R(X,Y) \to A(X)$
✓	✓		✓	✓	$\mathrm{ran}(R) \sqsubseteq A$	$R(X,Y) \to A(Y)$
✓	✓	✓	✓		$B \sqsubseteq \exists R.A$	$B(X) \to \exists Y R(X,Y), A(X)$
	✓		✓	✓	$B \sqsubseteq \neg A$	$B(X), A(X) \to \bot$
	✓			✓	$B \sqsubseteq {\leqslant} 1 R.A$	$B(X), R(X,Y_1), R(X,Y_2),$ $A(Y_1), A(Y_2), Y_1 \neq Y_2 \to \bot$

Table 2. Role inclusions, where $R, S, P \in N_R$.

$\mathcal{EL}$++	Horn-$\mathcal{SHIQ}$	$\mathcal{ELH}$	DL-Lite$_R$	DLP	Rule inclusions	Equivalent Datalog$^\pm$ rule
✓	✓	✓	✓	✓	$S \sqsubseteq R$	$R(X,Y) \to S(X,Y)$
	✓	✓	✓	✓	$S^- \sqsubseteq R$	$S(X,Y) \to R(Y,X)$
✓	✓			✓	$R^+ \sqsubseteq R$	$R(X,Y), R(Y,Z) \to R(X,Z)$
✓					$S \circ P \sqsubseteq R$	$S(X,Y), P(Y,Z) \to R(X,Z)$
	✓		✓	✓	$S \sqsubseteq \neg R$	$S(X,Y), R(X,Y) \to \bot$

The OWL 2 Web Ontology Language, informally OWL 2, is an ontology language for the Semantic Web with formally defined meaning. OWL 2 ontologies provide classes, properties, individuals, and data values and are stored as Semantic Web documents. The most expressive OWL 2 profile is called OWL 2 DL.

Reasoning over OWL 2 DL is a very expensive task, in general. To balance expressiveness and scalability, the World Wide Web Consortium (W3C, for short)[1] identified also the following profiles:[2] OWL 2 EL, OWL 2 QL, and OWL 2 RL, each exhibiting better computational properties. Moreover, we point out that that $\mathcal{EL}$++ is the logic underpinning OWL 2 EL, DL-Lite$_R$ is the logic underpinning OWL 2 QL, and DLP is the logic underpinning OWL 2 RL.

Among these three profiles, OWL 2 RL is the only one that does not admit the usage of existential quantification in superclass expressions in the right-hand side of concept inclusions (i.e., $B \sqsubseteq \exists R.A$ in DL notation). Therefore, the following question naturally arises: *Is OWL 2 RL powerful enough to express/specify real-world ontologies?* An answer to this question will be given in Sect. 5.

---

[1] See https://www.w3.org/.

[2] See http://www.w3.org/TR/owl2-profiles/.

4   Ontology-Based Query Answering

In this section we formally define *ontology-based query answering*, one of the most important ontological reasoning service needed in the development of the Semantic Web and requiring the OWA. After that, we give a comprehensive picture of all ontologies that ensure tractability of QEVAL (under data complexity) and that can be efficiently handled by DLV.

4.1   The Query Evaluation Problem

Consider a triple $\langle D, \Sigma, q \rangle$, where D is a database (resp., an ABox, with a little abuse of notation), and Σ is a Datalog$^\pm$ ontology (resp., a TBox). The *answer* to q over a model $M \in mods(D, \Sigma)$ is the set $ans(q, M)$ of $|\mathbf{X}|$-tuples $\mathbf{t}$ for which there is a substitution μ such that $\mu(\phi(\mathbf{t}, \mathbf{Y})) \subseteq M$. Accordingly, the *certain answer* to q under OWA is the set

$$ans(q, D, \Sigma) = \bigcap_{M \in mods(D, \Sigma)} ans(q, M).$$

Example 5. Let us consider again the knowledge base $D \cup \Sigma$ introduced in Example 4. Together with the model $M = D \cup \{hasFather(john, luke)\}$ one has also to consider (at least) all models of the form $M_c = D \cup \{hasFather(john, c)\}$, where c is an individual in the set $\mathbf{C}$. Hence, according to the above definitions: $ans(q_1, M) = \{(john, luke)\}$, $ans(q_1, D, \Sigma) = \emptyset$, $ans(q_2, M) = \{(john)\}$, $ans(q_2, D, \Sigma) = \{(john)\}$, $ans(q_3, M) = \{()\}$, and $ans(q_3, D, \Sigma) = \emptyset$.   □

As usual, we consider the following associated decision problem:

QEVAL: *Given a database D, an ontology Σ, a $\mathbb{C}$ query $q(\mathbf{X})$ with $|\mathbf{X}| = n$, and a tuple $\mathbf{t} \in \mathbf{C}^n$, decide whether $\mathbf{t} \in ans(q, D, \Sigma)$.*

4.2   Dealing with OWA in DLV

As said, on the one hand, reasoning over OWL 2 DL is a very expensive task, in general. More precisely, just fact entailment (i.e., checking whether an individual is an instance of a certain concept) is already 2NEXPTIME-hard. But, most importantly, no algorithm is known so far for the evaluation of conjunctive queries over OWL 2 DL ontologies. In other words, decidability of conjunctive query answering is still an open problem in OWL 2 DL. Therefore, this definitely suggests that it is nearly impossible to devise a general approach for answering, in an efficient way, conjunctive queries over arbitrary very-large OWL 2 DL ontologies. Moreover, to balance expressiveness and scalability, the W3C identified also the following tractable profiles: OWL 2 EL, OWL 2 QL, and OWL 2 RL, each exhibiting better computational properties. Indeed, the evaluation of conjunctive queries over ontologies falling in these OWL 2 fragments is

Table 3. DLV-tractable ontology classes.

Ontology class	Maximum arity	Data complexity	Combined complexity
j-acyclic	Arbitrary	PTIME-complete	2EXPTIME-complete
OWL 2 EL Horn-$\mathcal{SHIQ}$, $\mathcal{EL}$++	2	PTIME-complete	EXPTIME-complete
datalog, shy	Arbitrary	PTIME-complete	EXPTIME-complete
OWL 2 RL DLP, $\mathcal{ELH}$	2	PTIME-complete	NP-complete
linear	Arbitrary	in AC_0	PSPACE-complete
OWL 2 QL DL-Lite$_R$	2	in AC_0	NP-complete

in PTIME (resp., EXPTIME) in data complexity (resp., combined complexity).[3] Moreover, we point out that $\mathcal{EL}$++ is the logic underpinning OWL 2 EL, DL-Lite$_R$ is the logic underpinning OWL 2 QL, and DLP is the logic underpinning OWL 2 RL.

On the other hand, as mentioned in the introduction and formalized in Sect. 2.3, the DLV language is quite expressive. Indeed, it can express all problems in the complexity class Δ_3^P. Hence, from a theoretical point of view, it can be definitely used for OBQA under every OWL 2 profile, as conjunctive query answering can be solved in polynomial time (in data complexity), and it is well-known that problems in PTIME are much simpler than those in Δ_3^P. Moreover, by considering also its high declarative capabilities, DLV becomes a very suitable and powerful tool to reason over ontological knowledge bases since ontologies are natively expressed via logic rules, which in some cases are already equivalent to DLV rules. Under the OWA, however, when existential quantification (axioms of the form $B \sqsubseteq \exists R.A$ in DLs, or existential variables in the heads of Datalog$^\pm$ rules) is enabled, the high theoretical expressiveness of DLV might not always be enough to guarantee also good performances. Hence, whenever ontologies cannot be "easily" reduced to DLV programs (to be evaluated under the CWA), "ad hoc" techniques have been developed and implemented inside the system with the aim of natively supporting anonymous individuals (mainly exploited under the classes j-acyclic and shy defined later).

Currently, DLV is able to optimally perform (i.e., in polynomial time in data complexity) OBQA over Horn-$\mathcal{SHIQ}$ OWL 2 ontologies (and clearly over its subclasses $\mathcal{ELH}$, DLP and DL-Lite$_R$) as well as over a number of Datalog$^\pm$ classes, namely datalog [1], linear [15], shy [33] and j-acyclic [32] (see Sect. 2). Table 3 reports each ontology class that can currently be managed by DLV for OBQA in a tractable way (i.e., in polynomial time in data complexity), as well as the associated computational complexity of QEVAL.

---

[3] Following Vardi's taxonomy [41], the data complexity is calculated taking only the ABox as input, whereas the query and the TBox are considered fixed. The combined complexity is the complexity calculated considering as input, together with the ABox, also the query and the TBox.

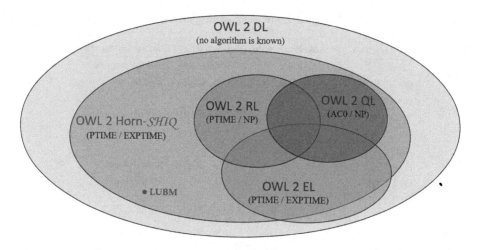

Fig. 1. Expressiveness and complexity of CQ answering on OWL 2 profiles.

In the following, we also provide two interesting Venn diagrams. The first one, in Fig. 1, shows how the three standard OWL 2 profiles are related with the OWL tractable ontologies that can be handled by DLV in polynomial time. Moreover, Fig. 2 shows how the above classes are related, and also which are their relationships with OWL 2 QL and OWL 2 RL.

5   Beyond OWL 2 RL: Expressiveness Issues

OWL 2 RL is a popular fragment of OWL, which shows some nice computational features. But, *is OWL 2 RL powerful enough to express/specify real-world ontologies?*

In this section we would like to shed some light on the impact of existential quantification in superclass expressions (i.e., $\exists R.A$) in the right-hand side of CIs. By having a closer look at Tables 1 and 2, one can observe that Horn-$\mathcal{SHIQ}$ (in practice, beyond OWL 2 EL) and DLP ($\approx$ OWL 2 RL) look rather similar, as they share all concept and role inclusion except for $B \sqsubseteq \exists R.A$. However, by looking at Table 3, one can also note the huge jump in computational complexity when moving from DLP to Horn-$\mathcal{SHIQ}$ (from NP to ExpTime). On the one hand, whenever this knowledge representation feature is not allowed, classical systems working under the CWA (e.g., RDFox [36] for OWL 2 RL, and DLV for both datalog and OWL 2 RL) can be profitably used. Conversely, whenever axioms of the form $B \sqsubseteq \exists R.A$ are needed—as in most of well-known ontologies in the Semantic Web (see below)—more sophisticated techniques have to be devised to deal with OWA, as mentioned in Sect. 4.2.

For example, consider LUBM [28], one of the most popular ontology for testing both capabilities and performances of OBQA systems. Due to the presence of some existential axioms, LUBM does not fall in any OWL 2 profiles, and it cannot be safely handled by OWL 2 RL reasoners (see Fig. 1). This implies that, contrarily to what happens with DLV, OWL 2 RL reasoners cannot be safely used for answering the LUBM

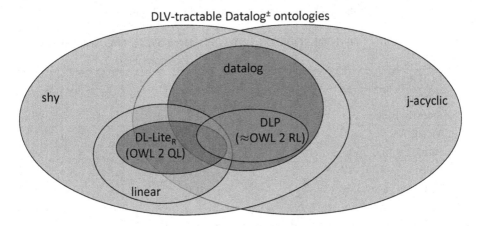

Fig. 2. DLV-tractable Datalog$^\pm$ classes and relationships with some OWL 2 profiles.

queries, since they ignore existential quantification in superclass expressions, and may return incomplete answers, even on very simple ABoxes. Consider for instance query #6 of the original LUBM suite asking for the set of all students:

PREFIX rdf: ⟨http://www.w3.org/1999/02/22-rdf-syntax-ns#⟩
PREFIX ub: ⟨http://swat.cse.lehigh.edu/onto/univ-bench.owl#⟩
SELECT ?X WHERE {?X rdf:type ub:Student }

Together with the following ABox (in Turtle format):

@prefix rdf: ⟨http://www.w3.org/1999/02/22-rdf-syntax-ns#⟩.
@prefix rdfs: ⟨http://www.w3.org/2000/01/rdf-schema#⟩.
@prefix owl: ⟨http://www.w3.org/2002/07/owl#⟩.
@prefix ub: ⟨http://swat.cse.lehigh.edu/onto/univ-bench.owl#⟩.

⟨http://www.University0.edu/GraduateStudent0⟩ a ub:GraduateStudent.

In other word, individual *GraduateStudent0* is a *GraduateStudent*. An OWL 2 RL reasoner would produce an empty answer, while

⟨http://www.University0.edu/GraduateStudent0⟩

should be returned because of the following axioms which are present in the LUBM TBox:

ta_1 : GraduateStudent $\sqsubseteq$ Person
ta_2 : GraduateStudent $\sqsubseteq$ $\exists$takesCourse.GraduateCourse
ta_3 : GraduateCourse $\sqsubseteq$ Course
ta_4 : Student $\equiv$ Person $\sqcap$ $\exists$takesCourse.Course[4]

---

[4] As usual in DLs, $A \equiv B$ is a shortcut form $A \sqsubseteq B$ together with $B \sqsubseteq A$.

Table 4. Classification of popular OWL ontologies.

	OWL2QL	OWL2RL	OWL2EL	Horn-$\mathcal{SHIQ}$ OWL ontologies (DLV-tractable)
LUBM				✓
Adolena	✓			✓
StockExchange	✓			✓
Vicodí	✓	✓	✓	✓
Path5	✓		✓	✓
Galen	✓			✓
NPD Fact Pages	✓			✓

In particular, individual *GraduateStudent0* should be a *Student* because (i) he is a *GraduateStudent*, (ii) every *GraduateStudent* is a *Person* who *takes* a *GraduateCourse*, (iii) every *GraduateCourse* is a *Course* and (iv) *Students* are all those *Persons* who *take* a *Course*. However, *GraduateStudent0* will never become a Student for these reasons because axiom ta_2 is completely ignored by any OWL 2 RL reasoner.

Analogously, it turns out that any OWL 2 RL reasoner is incomplete even on queries #7, #8, #9 and #10 over structurally simple ABoxes. For the remaining queries, instead, since they depend on a portion of knowledge base involving only axioms without existential quantification, they can be correctly answered by OWL 2 RL reasoners. More in general, one may define many additional queries where OWL 2 RL reasoners are incomplete over LUBM. However, this is rather difficult to appreciate while using the standard ABox generator provided with LUBM. Indeed, it seems that the aim of this generator is testing systems scalability rather than correctness.

It is worth pointing out, in addition, that most ontologies which are commonly used for testing OBQA systems are out of OWL 2 RL and, hence, they cannot be safely handled by OWL 2 RL reasoners. This is the case for instance of *Adolena*[5], *StockExchange*[6], *Path5*[7], *Galen*[8] and *NPD Fact Page*[9]. Among well-known ontologies, an exception is represented by *Vicodí*[10]. We close the section by highlighting, for each of the abovementioned ontologies, which are the OWL fragments including it (see Table 4). Note that all of them are DLV-tractable, while only one of them falls in OWL 2 RL.

---

[5] The Adolena (Abilities and Disabilities OntoLogy for ENhancing Accessibility) ontology [31] has been developed for the South African National Accessibility Portal. It describes abilities, disabilities and devices.

[6] StockExchange [38] is an ontology of the domain of financial institution in the EU.

[7] Path5 is a synthetic ontology [38] encoding graph structures, and used to generate an exponential blow-up of the size of the rewritten queries.

[8] Galen is an open source medical ontology that is widely used as stress test for OBQA systems since its TBox consists of about 50k/60k axioms. For more details, see https://bioportal. bioontology.org/ontologies/GALEN.

[9] NPD FactPages is an ontology describing the petroleum activities in the Norwegian continental shelf.

[10] Vicodí is an ontology of European history which falls in OWL 2 RL, developed within the Vicodì project. For more details, see https://cordis.europa.eu/result/rcn/34582_en.html.

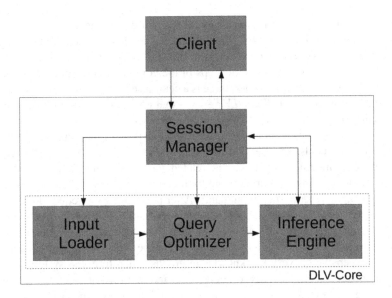

Fig. 3. Overall architecture of the DLV-Server infrastructure.

6   Implementation Details

In this section, we show the architecture of DLV by focusing on a branch of the system we recently developed on purpose for ontological reasoning. In this regard, it is worth pointing out that the architecture of the whole system is composed of further modules that will not be introduced here, as they are exploited by DLV to handle more complex problems going beyond OBQA and, as such, they are out of the scope of this paper. Anyway, we refer the reader to [2,3,17,34,35] for further information. Afterwards, we provide a description of the main query-oriented optimization techniques implemented by our reasoner.

6.1   System Architecture

The overall architecture of our system is depicted in Fig. 3. As one can observe, the core of DLV is composed of the following modules: *Input Loader*, *Query Optimizer* and *Inference Engine*. The Input Loader is in charge of loading the input data in main-memory. Then, the input query can be manipulated on the basis of the current ontology by the Query Optimizer with the aim of making the answering process faster. Eventually, the Inference Engine can evaluate either the original query over the whole knowl-edge base or the manipulated query over the initial set of data. In particular this latter module implements a bottom-up *inference* strategy based on the semi-naïve algorithm enhanced by advanced *indexing* and other optimization techniques aimed at improving the system performance. Around the core, we recently developed a sophisticated infras-tructure enabling a server-like behavior that allows to keep DLV alive and cache the main information produced at every steps of the computation (as, for instance, the input loading). The implemented framework is particularly useful in the context of reasoning over large-scale knowledge graphs. Handling huge knowledge bases in main-memory requires indeed a significant effort in terms of time and memory usage; hence, at times, it is worth caching the output of some steps of the computation to speed up the query answering process. In our framework, there is a central server (reachable at a specific IP address and port number) - called *DLV-Server* - that provides several functions to control the main computation of DLV. Within a private *working session* established with the *Session Manager*, any remote *Client* can invoke exposed functionalities by issuing proper XML commands. The Session Manager compiles the incoming XML requests and asks the core modules to perform the related actions. As an example, some of the functions that can be invoked on-demand by the user are "load and cache an ABox", "run a query" and "reset cached input data". After performing the required tasks, DLV is kept alive to avoid the loss of the materialized information. Potentially, the framework allows for a static *pre-materialisation* of the entire knowledge base, so that no further inference would be required at answering time. On the other hand, such an approach can be too expensive on very big knowledge graphs. Therefore, the system has been further empowered with dedicated optimizations and facilities oriented towards effective reasoning over extensive scenarios. In this regard, the most impactful optimization techniques implemented by the system are query-oriented and will be discussed in the next section.

6.2   Query-Oriented Optimization Techniques

Nowadays, many real-world semantic applications rely on very large knowledge graphs that cover several domains at the same time. As a consequence, an approach based on a static pre-materialisation of the full model of the knowledge base can be considerably expensive; even more resource-consuming if we consider a scenario where the underlying set of data may change frequently, requiring the model to be updated continuously. In addition, it is worth pointing out that queries are usually posed to retrieve specific information on particular (sub)domains. Hence, in this cases, a full materialisation of the model is not actually needed for answering the input query. To face such a challenging scenario, DLV provides an execution modality where no static pre-computation is performed, and the inference process is activated "on-demand" for every incoming query. In this case, a number of query-oriented optimization techniques are exploited by the system to single out only a portion of the considered knowledge graph that is actually relevant for answering the query at hand. In this context, *Magic Sets* [4, 19] are definitely the most impactful technique; it is indeed commonly exploited by commercial RDBMSs and logic-based systems for addressing the query answering task. The technique is translational and is implemented in DLV as a module (inside the Query Optimizer) independent from the other components of the system architecture. The main intuition here is to rewrite the initial ontology (a logic program) so that the subsequent bottom-up evaluation only materializes ground atoms that are relevant to answer the query in input. This is done by "pushing-down" possible bindings coming from the query to the underlying set of data. To this aim, new predicates are introduced in the rewritten ontology. In the following, we provide more details on the implemented algorithm by showing an example where a recursive definition of the concept of *ancestor* is given. Let us now consider the following ontology:

$$ancestor(X, Y) \leftarrow parent(X, Y)$$
$$ancestor(X, Y) \leftarrow parent(X, Z), ancestor(Z, Y)$$

and the following query asking for *mario*'s descendants:

$$q(X) \equiv ancestor(mario, X)$$

The Magic Sets rewriting start with the query seed *m#ancestor#bf*(*mario*), modifies the rules defining the intentional predicate *ancestor*, and introduces magic rules for every occurrence of intentional predicates in the modified rules. The final rewriting produced at the end of this process is the following:

$$m\#ancestor\#bf(mario).$$
$$ancestor(X, Y) \leftarrow m\#ancestor\#bf(X), parent(X, Y).$$
$$ancestor(X, Y) \leftarrow m\#ancestor\#bf(X), parent(X, Z), ancestor(Z, Y).$$
$$m\#ancestor\#bf(Z) \leftarrow m\#ancestor\#bf(X), parent(X, Z).$$

The rewritten program above is optimized for answering the specific query as its bottom-up evaluation only materializes *mario*'s descendants, rather than the full ancestor relation. It is straightforward to see that the above transformation of the initial ontology may have a strong impact on the system performance, as a possibly large portion of the search space is pruned in this case. To observe practical implications of the Magic Sets technique on a real ontology we refer the reader to Sect. 7 where the results of an experimental analysis are presented.

7 Experiments

In this section we report on some experiments we carried out in order to evaluate the efficiency and the effectiveness of DLV for OBQA. In particular, our analysis is aimed at showing that DLV can be effectively used for fast and powerful query answering over OWL 2 ontologies. According to our goal, we simulated a couple of typical real-world application scenarios where DLV is exploited as a powerful RAM-based reasoner in a client-server architecture. In the following, we first discuss the test scenarios along with the benchmark domain used for our experiments. We then show the attained results along with some final considerations about several system-extension proposals which would plenty pay off in the context of the Semantic Web.

7.1 Tested Scenarios Under OWL 2 Ontologies

As discussed in Sect. 6.1, the main tasks performed by DLV are: *loading, indexing, inference* and *answering*. Thus, to analyze the system performance in depth, we split overall timings in four different groups, one for each task listed above. However, it is worth noting that some of the aforementioned actions can be executed by DLV-Server just once, and their output can be kept in memory for answering the incoming queries. For example, in a static environment, keeping the output of the inference step already indexed in memory would surely speed up the evaluation of the queries. Conversely, in a dynamic environment it could be too expensive to frequently update the materialized model. In this case, only the initial data should be indexed and cached so that an efficient "query-driven" inference step can be performed on-demand for any incoming query.

According to the system configurations introduced above and in order to deeply investigate DLV performance, we simulated 2 different application scenarios:

1. The knowledge base is not subject to real-time updates;
2. The knowledge base is subject to real-time updates.

In scenario 1, loading, indexing and inference are performed at the system startup; after that, the materialized information are kept in memory in order to promptly answer the incoming queries. In this case, both the original and the inferred data are indexed once and for all. In scenario 2, we load and index only the initial set of data at the system startup. No preliminary inference is done here because the knowledge base may change frequently. For each incoming query, the system performs an efficient "query-driven" evaluation. Indeed, the query-oriented optimization techniques implemented by DLV (see Sect. 6.2) allow to single out a (hopefully small) portion of the knowledge base that is actually relevant for the query at hand.

In this regard, it is worth pointing out that the higher is the number of constants in the query and the more the research space can be pruned. This is the main reason why we retain that our optimization techniques may have a strong impact on real-world applications, where queries have typically several constants and their patterns are known in advance. As an example, consider a query asking Amazon for all the *XL-sized blue t-shirts made by "Versace"*. This is a realistic scenario where our Magic Sets technique would dramatically reduce the research space so that the computed model would be extremely smaller than the initial set of data. If the knowledge base is subject to frequent changes, making static pre-computation inapplicable, this latter approach could plenty pay off.

7.2   Benchmark Domain

Our experimental analysis relies on LUBM (Lehigh University Benchmark), one of the most popular OWL 2 ontologies widely used in academic contexts for testing OBQA system prototypes. LUBM has been specifically developed to facilitate the evaluation of Semantic Web reasoners in a standard and systematic way. In fact, the benchmark is intended to evaluate performances of those reasoners with respect to extensional queries over large data sets that commit to a single realistic ontology. The LUBM benchmark consists of a university domain OWL 2 ontology with customizable and repeatable synthetic data and a set of 14 input SPARQL queries. The main described concepts are (among others): universities, departments, students, professors and relationships among them. The LUBM ontology provides a wide range of axioms that are aimed at testing different capabilities of the reasoning systems. It is worth pointing out that the whole ontology falls in Horn-$\mathcal{SHIQ}$ and in none of the OWL 2 profiles (RL, QL and EL) since it makes use of several advanced properties as, for instance, existential quantification as superclass, inverse and transitive roles (see Sect. 5). Data generation has been carried out via the LUBM data generator tool whose main generation parameter is the number of universities to consider. In our experiments, we carried out a scalability analysis evaluating the trends in running times and memory consumption by increasing the

Table 5. DLV statistics about time (sec.) and memory (MBs) consumption over the LUBM queries at a growing number of universities (scenario 1, pre-materialization).

	lubm-50	lubm-100	lubm-500	lubm-1000
loading	25.37	51.48	262.73	543.09
inference	5.15	10.49	53.65	127.03
indexing	7.21	14.97	86.21	206.47
ans(Q1)	<0.01	<0.01	<0.01	<0.01
ans(Q2)	0.46	0.92	4.64	10.57
ans(Q3)	<0.01	<0.01	<0.01	<0.01
ans(Q4)	<0.01	<0.01	<0.01	<0.01
ans(Q5)	<0.01	<0.01	<0.01	<0.01
ans(Q6)	0.43	0.90	4.51	9.44
ans(Q7)	0.21	0.49	2.57	5.26
ans(Q8)	0.33	0.65	3.28	6.61
ans(Q9)	1.13	2.05	11.00	23.74
ans(Q10)	<0.01	<0.01	<0.01	<0.01
ans(Q11)	<0.01	<0.01	<0.01	<0.01
ans(Q12)	<0.01	0.02	0.09	0.22
ans(Q13)	<0.01	<0.01	0.01	0.02
ans(Q14)	0.33	0.69	3.55	7.82
ans(avg)	0.21	0.41	2.12	4.55
memory(max)	2,290.3	4,602.5	22,606.8	45,271.7

number of universities between 50 and 1000, specifically the generated data sets are: lubm-50, lubm-100, lubm-500 and lubm-1000, where "50", "100", "500" and "1000" in these acronyms indicate the number of universities used as parameter to generate the data. The number of statements (both individuals and assertions) stored in the initial data sets vary from about 6M for lubm-50 to about 120M for lubm-1000.

7.3   Results

Experiments were performed on a NUMA machine equipped with two 2.8 GHz AMD Opteron 6320 processors and 128 Gb RAM. Unlimited time and memory were granted to running processes.

Tables 5 and 6 show DLV performances over the 14 LUBM queries in scenarios 1 and scenario 2, respectively. We observe that the system scales linearly in both scenarios. Regarding scenario 1, it is worth highlighting that most of the benchmark queries (8 out of 14) are answered in up to 10^{-1} s when the biggest data set (lubm-1000) is considered. More precisely, 6 of them are answered in up to 10^{-4} s, one is answered in 10^{-2} s and the last one in 10^{-1} s. From our analysis it turns out that the most complex query of the benchmark is Q9 since it shows the highest timings in every data set.

Table 6. DLV statistics about time (sec.) and memory (MBs) consumption over the LUBM queries at a growing number of universities (scenario 2, on-the-fly inference).

	lubm-50	lubm-100	lubm-500	lubm-1000
loading	26.10	53.14	262.27	540.87
indexing(avg)	2.47	5.09	28.07	64.33
ans(Q1)	<0.01	<0.01	<0.01	<0.01
ans(Q2)	1.72	3.45	17.39	38.42
ans(Q3)	<0.01	<0.01	<0.01	<0.01
ans(Q4)	0.21	0.41	1.97	6.09
ans(Q5)	0.23	0.45	2.16	5.36
ans(Q6)	6.25	12.28	64.77	145.62
ans(Q7)	0.75	1.42	7.38	17.73
ans(Q8)	1.18	1.82	7.97	17.08
ans(Q9)	6.44	12.65	66.66	148.86
ans(Q10)	<0.01	0.02	0.10	0.19
ans(Q11)	0.02	0.03	0.14	0.28
ans(Q12)	0.41	0.50	2.64	6.30
ans(Q13)	0.42	0.77	4.14	8.96
ans(Q14)	0.52	1.07	5.39	10.75
ans(avg)	1.30	2.49	12.91	28.97
memory(avg)	1,318.8	2,647.4	13.183.53	26,392.66

This is mainly due to the fact that Q9 is the biggest query, with its 6 joined atoms, and does not feature any constant. Indeed, the presence of constant terms in the query usually allows to filter out a number of configurations which otherwise have to be considered. However, although input queries are evaluated against pre-materialized models composed of hundreds of millions of facts (about 100 millions of fact in case of lubm-500 and 200 millions of facts if lubm-1000 is considered), DLV managed to reply in milliseconds in most of the cases, even on complex queries (see, for instance, queries Q4 and Q5), and in a few seconds in average.

Regarding scenario 2, we specify that no rows for inference are reported in Table 6 because here we do not perform any pre-computation. The system stops after parsing the input data and waits for incoming queries. For each input query DLV produces a possibly different Magic Sets (query-oriented) rewriting of the input ontology, and then it evaluates the rewritten rules on-the-fly against the initial set of data (which has been already loaded in main-memory). Here, the actual inference is performed at query answering time. This implies that query answering timings are generally higher with respect to scenario 1. However, we point out that when the input knowledge base is subject to real-time updates no static pre-computation is applicable. In this setting, this latter approach is much more effective than the one adopted in scenario 1. Indeed, when no pre-computation is performed, the time taken for answering a single query in scenario 2 (i.e., the sum between query answering and indexing timings) is in general significantly lower than the time taken for answering the same query in scenario 1 (i.e., the sum of indexing, inferencing and answering timings). Improvements are mainly due to the query-oriented optimization techniques implemented by DLV (see Sect. 6.2). Such an approach may be performed rapidly even in case of huge input knowledge base. Of course, described advantages are more evident when highly selective queries are given (i.e., queries featuring several constant terms and depending on a small subset of ontology predicates). In our experiments, for example, most of the queries are highly selective. In fact, in several cases DLV manages to perform in milliseconds when lubm-1000 is considered (see, for instance, queries Q1, Q4, Q5, Q10 and Q11). Anyway, in many real-world applications it is common to have highly selective queries over huge knowledge bases that are subject to real-time updates.

In conclusion, the attained results confirm that DLV can be effectively exploited for answering complex queries over Horn-$\mathcal{SHIQ}$ ontologies in both static environments, where the knowledge base is not subject to real-time changes, and dynamic environments. From our experiments we realized that there are wide margins of improvement, both on the loading process and on the memory usage. Regarding the loading task, we can observe that our relational representation of ABoxes is much more verbose than OWL-Turtle, as IRIs are not encoded succinctly (no namespace management is provided). Hence, there are two options: either supporting namespaces in our data model or extending the DLV to handle OWL-Turtle files natively. Furhtermore, concerning the memory-related issue, there are a number of engineering aspects that can be improved, as for instance, succinctness of data representation and indexing.

8   Ongoing Work

Several software-engineering aspects of DLV are under investigation, and appear useful in this context. We next list some features which appear to be relevant for ontology-based query answering:

- enabling a server-like execution of DLV with a main-memory process which is kept alive, to separate off-line reasoning (loading, indexing, inference, etc.) from query answering;
- enhancing the query-oriented optimization techniques to improve efficiency of the evaluation process, and extending the supported language;
- reducing main-memory usage, so allowing DLV to deal with data sets of bigger dimension;
- implementing parallel evaluation, to speed up the reasoning tasks;
- evaluating DLV on different large domains;
- extending the system to deal with Big Data, by developing a hybrid approach which can work on data stored both in main-memory and secondary memory.

References

1. Abiteboul, S., Hull, R., Vianu, V.: Foundations of Databases. Addison-Wesley, Boston (1995). http://webdam.inria.fr/Alice/
2. Alviano, M., et al.: The ASP system DLV2. In: Balduccini, M., Janhunen, T. (eds.) LPNMR 2017. LNCS (LNAI), vol. 10377, pp. 215–221. Springer, Cham (2017). https://doi.org/10.1007/978-3-319-61660-5_19
3. Alviano, M., Dodaro, C., Leone, N., Ricca, F.: Advances in WASP. In: Calimeri, F., Ianni, G., Truszczynski, M. (eds.) LPNMR 2015. LNCS (LNAI), vol. 9345, pp. 40–54. Springer, Cham (2015). https://doi.org/10.1007/978-3-319-23264-5_5
4. Alviano, M., Leone, N., Manna, M., Terracina, G., Veltri, P.: Magic-sets for *datalog* with existential quantifiers. In: Barceló, P., Pichler, R. (eds.) Datalog 2.0 2012. LNCS, vol. 7494, pp. 31–43. Springer, Heidelberg (2012). https://doi.org/10.1007/978-3-642-32925-8_5
5. Baader, F., Brandt, S., Lutz, C.: Pushing the EL envelope. In: Kaelbling, L.P., Saffiotti, A. (eds.) Proceedings of the Nineteenth International Joint Conference on Artificial Intelligence (IJCAI), pp. 364–369. Professional Book Center (2005). http://ijcai.org/Proceedings/05/Papers/0372.pdf
6. Baader, F., Calvanese, D., McGuinness, D.L., Nardi, D., Patel-Schneider, P.F. (eds.): The Description Logic Handbook: Theory, Implementation, and Applications. Cambridge University Press, Cambridge (2003)
7. Baget, J., Leclère, M., Mugnier, M., Salvat, E.: On rules with existential variables: walking the decidability line. Artif. Intell. **175**(9–10), 1620–1654 (2011). https://doi.org/10.1016/j.artint.2011.03.002
8. Bárány, V., Gottlob, G., Otto, M.: Querying the guarded fragment. Log. Methods Comput. Sci. **10**(2) (2014). https://doi.org/10.2168/LMCS-10(2:3)2014
9. Bienvenu, M., ten Cate, B., Lutz, C., Wolter, F.: Ontology-based data access: a study through disjunctive datalog, CSP, and MMSNP. ACM Trans. Database Syst. **39**(4), 33:1–33:44 (2014). https://doi.org/10.1145/2661643
10. Bourhis, P., Manna, M., Morak, M., Pieris, A.: Guarded-based disjunctive tuple-generating dependencies. ACM Trans. Database Syst. **41**(4), 27:1–27:45 (2016). https://doi.org/10.1145/2976736
11. Brandt, S.: Polynomial time reasoning in a description logic with existential restrictions, GCI axioms, and - what else? In: de Mántaras, R.L., Saitta, L. (eds.) Proceedings of the 16th Eureopean Conference on Artificial Intelligence (ECAI), pp. 298–302. IOS Press, Amsterdam (2004)
12. Brewka, G., Eiter, T., Truszczynski, M.: Answer set programming at a glance. Commun. ACM **54**(12), 92–103 (2011). https://doi.org/10.1145/2043174.2043195
13. Calì, A., Gottlob, G., Kifer, M.: Taming the infinite chase: query answering under expressive relational constraints. J. Artif. Intell. Res. **48**, 115–174 (2013). https://doi.org/10.1613/jair.3873
14. Calì, A., Gottlob, G., Lukasiewicz, T.: Tractable query answering over ontologies with datalog$^\pm$. In: Grau, B.C., Horrocks, I., Motik, B., Sattler, U. (eds.) Proceedings of the 22nd International Workshop on Description Logics (DL). CEUR Workshop Proceedings, vol. 477. CEUR-WS.org (2009). http://ceur-ws.org/Vol-477/paper_46.pdf
15. Calì, A., Gottlob, G., Lukasiewicz, T.: A general datalog-based framework for tractable query answering over ontologies. J. Web Semant. **14**, 57–83 (2012). https://doi.org/10.1016/j.websem.2012.03.001
16. Calimeri, F., Cozza, S., Ianni, G., Leone, N.: Computable functions in ASP: theory and implementation. In: Garcia de la Banda, M., Pontelli, E. (eds.) ICLP 2008. LNCS, vol. 5366, pp. 407–424. Springer, Heidelberg (2008). https://doi.org/10.1007/978-3-540-89982-2_37

17. Calimeri, F., Fuscà, D., Perri, S., Zangari, J.: I-DLV: the new intelligent grounder of DLV. Intell. Artif. **11**(1), 5–20 (2017). https://doi.org/10.3233/IA-170104

18. Calvanese, D., De Giacomo, G., Lembo, D., Lenzerini, M., Rosati, R.: Data complexity of query answering in description logics. Artif. Intell. **195**, 335–360 (2013). https://doi.org/10.1016/j.artint.2012.10.003

19. Cumbo, C., Faber, W., Greco, G., Leone, N.: Enhancing the magic-set method for disjunctive datalog programs. In: Demoen, B., Lifschitz, V. (eds.) ICLP 2004. LNCS, vol. 3132, pp. 371–385. Springer, Heidelberg (2004). https://doi.org/10.1007/978-3-540-27775-0_26

20. Eiter, T., Gottlob, G., Mannila, H.: Disjunctive datalog. ACM Trans. Database Syst. **22**(3), 364–418 (1997). https://doi.org/10.1145/261124.261126

21. Faber, W., Leone, N., Ricca, F.: Answer set programming. In: Wah, B.W. (ed.) Wiley Encyclopedia of Computer Science and Engineering. Wiley, Hoboken (2008). https://doi.org/10.1002/9780470050118.ecse226

22. Faber, W., Pfeifer, G., Leone, N., Dell'Armi, T., Ielpa, G.: Design and implementation of aggregate functions in the DLV system. TPLP **8**(5–6), 545–580 (2008). https://doi.org/10.1017/S1471068408003323

23. Gelfond, M., Lifschitz, V.: Classical negation in logic programs and disjunctive databases. New Gener. Comput. **9**(3/4), 365–386 (1991). https://doi.org/10.1007/BF03037169

24. Gottlob, G., Kikot, S., Kontchakov, R., Podolskii, V.V., Schwentick, T., Zakharyaschev, M.: The price of query rewriting in ontology-based data access. Artif. Intell. **213**, 42–59 (2014). https://doi.org/10.1016/j.artint.2014.04.004

25. Gottlob, G., Orsi, G., Pieris, A.: Query rewriting and optimization for ontological databases. ACM Trans. Database Syst. **39**(3), 25:1–25:46 (2014). https://doi.org/10.1145/2638546

26. Gottlob, G., Pieris, A., Tendera, L.: Querying the guarded fragment with transitivity. In: Fomin, F.V., Freivalds, R., Kwiatkowska, M., Peleg, D. (eds.) ICALP 2013. LNCS, vol. 7966, pp. 287–298. Springer, Heidelberg (2013). https://doi.org/10.1007/978-3-642-39212-2_27

27. Grosof, B.N., Horrocks, I., Volz, R., Decker, S.: Description logic programs: combining logic programs with description logic. In: Hencsey, G., White, B., Chen, Y.R., Kovács, L., Lawrence, S. (eds.) Proceedings of the Twelfth International World Wide Web Conference (WWW), pp. 48–57. ACM (2003). https://doi.org/10.1145/775152.775160

28. Guo, Y., Pan, Z., Heflin, J.: LUBM: a benchmark for OWL knowledge base systems. J. Web Semant. **3**(2–3), 158–182 (2005). https://doi.org/10.1016/j.websem.2005.06.005

29. Hustadt, U., Motik, B., Sattler, U.: Data complexity of reasoning in very expressive description logics. In: Kaelbling, L.P., Saffiotti, A. (eds.) Proceedings of the Nineteenth International Joint Conference on Artificial Intelligence (IJCAI), pp. 466–471. Professional Book Center (2005). http://ijcai.org/Proceedings/05/Papers/0326.pdf

30. Johnson, D.S., Klug, A.C.: Testing containment of conjunctive queries under functional and inclusion dependencies. J. Comput. Syst. Sci. **28**(1), 167–189 (1984). https://doi.org/10.1016/0022-0000(84)90081-3

31. Keet, C.M., Alberts, R., Gerber, A., Chimamiwa, G.: Enhancing web portals with ontology-based data access: the case study of South Africa's accessibility portal for people with disabilities. In: Dolbear, C., Ruttenberg, A., Sattler, U. (eds.) Proceedings of the Fifth Workshop on OWL: Experiences and Directions (OWLED). CEUR Workshop Proceedings, vol. 432. CEUR-WS.org (2008). http://ceur-ws.org/Vol-432/owled2008eu_submission_7.pdf

32. Krötzsch, M., Rudolph, S.: Extending decidable existential rules by joining acyclicity and guardedness. In: Walsh, T. (ed.) Proceedings of the 22nd International Joint Conference on Artificial Intelligence (IJCAI), pp. 963–968. IJCAI/AAAI (2011). https://doi.org/10.5591/978-1-57735-516-8/IJCAI11-166

33. Leone, N., Manna, M., Terracina, G., Veltri, P.: Efficiently computable datalog$^\exists$ programs. In: Brewka, G., Eiter, T., McIlraith, S.A. (eds.) Proceedings of the Thirteenth International Conference on Principles of Knowledge Representation and Reasoning (KR). AAAI Press (2012). http://www.aaai.org/ocs/index.php/KR/KR12/paper/view/4521

34. Leone, N., et al.: The DLV system for knowledge representation and reasoning. ACM Trans. Comput. Log. **7**(3), 499–562 (2006). https://doi.org/10.1145/1149114.1149117

35. Maratea, M., Ricca, F., Veltri, P.: DLV^{MC}: enhanced model checking in DLV. In: Janhunen, T., Niemelä, I. (eds.) JELIA 2010. LNCS (LNAI), vol. 6341, pp. 365–368. Springer, Heidelberg (2010). https://doi.org/10.1007/978-3-642-15675-5_33

36. Nenov, Y., Piro, R., Motik, B., Horrocks, I., Wu, Z., Banerjee, J.: RDFox: a highly-scalable RDF store. In: Arenas, M., et al. (eds.) ISWC 2015. LNCS, vol. 9367, pp. 3–20. Springer, Cham (2015). https://doi.org/10.1007/978-3-319-25010-6_1

37. Ortiz, M.: Ontology based query answering: the story so far. In: Bravo, L., Lenzerini, M. (eds.) Proceedings of the 7th Alberto Mendelzon International Workshop on Foundations of Data Management (AMW). CEUR Workshop Proceedings, vol. 1087. CEUR-WS.org (2013). http://ceur-ws.org/Vol-1087/keynote3.pdf

38. Pérez-Urbina, H., Motik, B., Horrocks, I.: Tractable query answering and rewriting under description logic constraints. J. Appl. Logic **8**(2), 186–209 (2010). https://doi.org/10.1016/j.jal.2009.09.004

39. Rosati, R.: The limits of querying ontologies. In: Schwentick, T., Suciu, D. (eds.) ICDT 2007. LNCS, vol. 4353, pp. 164–178. Springer, Heidelberg (2006). https://doi.org/10.1007/11965893_12

40. Rosati, R., Almatelli, A.: Improving query answering over dl-lite ontologies. In: Lin, F., Sattler, U., Truszczynski, M. (eds.) Proceedings of the Twelfth International Conference on Principles of Knowledge Representation and Reasoning (KR). AAAI Press (2010). http://aaai.org/ocs/index.php/KR/KR2010/paper/view/1400

41. Vardi, M.Y.: The complexity of relational query languages (extended abstract). In: Lewis, H.R., Simons, B.B., Burkhard, W.A., Landweber, L.H. (eds.) Proceedings of the 14th Annual ACM Symposium on Theory of Computing (STOC), pp. 137–146. ACM (1982). https://doi.org/10.1145/800070.802186

Machine Learning-Assisted Cognition of Driving Context and Avoidance of Road Obstacles

Manolo Dulva Hina[1($\boxtimes$)], Andrea Ortalda[1], Assia Soukane[1],
and Amar Ramdane-Cherif[2]

[1] ECE Paris School of Engineering, 37 quai de Grenelle, 75015 Paris, France
manolo-dulva.hina@ece.fr
[2] Université de Versailles Paris-Saclay, 10-12 Avenue de l'Europe, 78140 Velizy, France

Abstract. In the vehicle of the future, an intelligent vehicle should be able to recognize the driving context so as it would be able to perform the necessary actions to continue the trip up to its intended destination. Moreover, such intelligent vehicle should also be able to detect and recognize road obstacles, as it is the failure to recognize an obstacle and avoid it that often lead to road accident, normally causing human fatalities. In this paper, knowledge engineering related to the cognitive processes of driving context detection, perception, decision and optimal action related to the driving context and avoiding road obstacles. Ontology and formal specifications are used to describe such mechanism. Different supervised learning algorithms are used for cognition of driving context and in recognizing and classifying obstacles. The avoidance of obstacles is implemented using reinforcement learning. The work is validated using driving simulator in the laboratory. This work is a contribution to the ongoing research in safe driving, and the application of machine learning leading to prevention of road accidents.

Keywords: Ontology · Formal specification · Machine learning · Safe driving · Smart vehicle · Cognitive informatics

1 Motivation

Several road accidents happen due to the loss of focus during driving [1]. This may be due to any of the following:

- Generally distracted or 'lost in thought' – About 62% of all accidents are due to this reason. A driver may be thinking of an incident, or is furious or angry over an issue, leading to being distracted while driving. A road accident due to this reason often leads to collision, leading to death of the driver or other actors involved in the event.
- Busy talking to the phone while driving – About 12% of all accidents are due to people driving and talking on the phone at the same time.
- Looking at someone or something outside the vehicle – This distraction accounts 7% of all accidents.

© Springer Nature Switzerland AG 2020
A. Fred et al. (Eds.): IC3K 2018, CCIS 1222, pp. 137–160, 2020.
https://doi.org/10.1007/978-3-030-49559-6_7

The global statistics of road accidents provided by the World Health Organization [2] dictates that the way we do driving should improve:

- Every year, about 1.24 million people die each year in road traffic accidents;
- Road traffic injury is the leading cause of death on young people, aged 15–29 years;
- If no remedy is employed, road traffic accidents are predicted to result in the deaths of around 1.9 million people annually by 2020.

The status quo in vehicular driving is inadequate and must be improved. For this reason, current solution such as ADAS [3–5] must be enhanced. Another solution is to put intelligence [6, 7] into our vehicles.

A non-smart or semi-autonomous vehicle is not capable of recognizing driving situations and therefore would not be able to assist the driver or the vehicle to prevent accidents. Driving assistance mechanisms are essential in the prevention of road accidents as they are integral parts of ADAS. ADAS may be used for both safe driving and green driving [8]. The embedded features of ADAS [9, 10] are however numerous and often expensive to implement. Often, ADAS is also closed to proprietary constraints, which makes it a specialized assistance system for a specific brand of vehicle but useless for another brand.

Considering the importance of injecting intelligence into our vehicles, this paper – the extended version of our previous paper [11] – intends to show how it would be possible for a vehicle to recognize a driving context and road obstacles. Given such situation, the intelligent vehicle should be able to perform action that is appropriate for the situation. The following processes are put in a firmer basis:

- The setting and structure of the environment that recognizes driving context is presented (Sect. 2). The functionalities of each component is also discussed.
- The knowledge representation related to the driving model is discussed (Sect. 3).
- Machine learning techniques for cognition of driving context and obstacles recognition and classification are discussed (Sects. 4 and 5).
- The concept of reinforcement learning as used in the avoidance of obstacle, as well as some experimental results are presented (Sect. 6)

Related works in learning algorithms used in intelligent transportation systems are presented in Sect. 7.

2 An Intelligent Human-Vehicle Interaction System

In order to understand driving context, it is necessary to collect various parameters that make up the driving context. To do so, we make used of a driving simulator capable of simulating a wide selection of driving scenarios: driving scenario in the city, in a rural area, along the expressway, etc. This simulator mimics a real vehicle as it has steering wheel, accelerator, brake, dashboard and other functionalities. The driving environment shows roads and lanes, traffic signs, obstacles, weather conditions, etc. Real-life obstacles, such as vehicles, pedestrians, and non-moving objects are also present in the driving scenario. Weather conditions, such as fog, rain, snow, and others are fully integrated. All traffic signs and signals are also present. The components of an intelligent interactive system for the cognition of driving context are shown in Fig. 1. The numbered steps involved are described below:

- Step 1: A user drives the driving simulator, yielding actual values for various parameters related to the driving event, such as the vehicle's speed, road's speed limit, etc.
- Step 2: Given the parameters obtained from the simulator, the driving event is identified. Machine-learning mechanism is used in the identification process.
- Step 3: Using optimization algorithms and reinforcement learning, we identify the optimal action apt for the given driving event. By optimal, we mean the action yields the highest score in safe driving.
- Step 4: The appropriate action for the driving event is implemented.
- Step 5 (A): The assistance mechanism for the driver is implemented. This may mean sending an audio, visual or vibration message to the driver. (B): The assistance mechanism for the vehicle is activated. This usually means sending a value to some vehicular signals (e.g. fog light = "on"). In the case of autonomous vehicle, Step 5(A) is not necessary anymore.
- Step 6: Repeat. The process continues until the destination is reached and the vehicle engine is turned off.

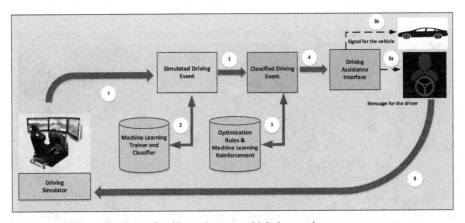

Fig. 1. An intelligent human-vehicle interaction system.

3   The Driving Model

The driving environment is a set of all the elements describing the driver, the vehicle and all entities, animate or inanimate, present during the conduct of a driving activity.

3.1 Environment Representation

Here, we identify the elements that are present during the conduct of a driving activity. We will describe these elements in a mathematical notion. The sets of elements present in the environment during a driving activity are: (i) the road object collection (**R**); (ii) the nearby object collection (**C**); and (iii) the obstacle object collection (**O**).

Let **R** be the set of all the road objects present in the environment **E**. Let **C** be the set of nearby road objects and **O** the set of the obstacles. Then **R** is an element of **E**, **C** is a subset of **R**, and **O** is a subset of **C**. Mathematically,

$$\mathbf{R} = \{r_1, r_2, \ldots, r_n\}, \ \mathbf{R} \subset \mathbf{E} \tag{1}$$

$$\mathbf{C} = \{c_1, c_2, \ldots, c_n\}, \ \mathbf{C} \subseteq \mathbf{R} \tag{2}$$

$$\mathbf{O} = \{o_1, o_2, \ldots, o_n\}, \ \mathbf{O} \subseteq \mathbf{C} \tag{3}$$

Let e be an environment object in the driving simulation platform, programmed using Unity 3D [12]. Every e related to the driving environment has a tag t, a notation used for identification purposes. For all e in **E**, if an element e has a tag of "RoadObject", then such e (denoted e_1) is a road object r_1. Mathematically, $\forall e \in \mathbf{E} \mid \exists ei \cdot t = $ "RoadObject" $\Rightarrow e_1 = r_1 \wedge \mathbf{R} \neq \emptyset$. Figure 2 shows the specimen environment **E** and all the elements $r \in \mathbf{R}$ (all elements that are found on the road) are highlighted.

Fig. 2. The specimen environment **E** and the entire road objects r's therein (**R** $\subset$ **E**) (diagram extracted from [11]).

Figure 3 shows the ontological representation of an element $r \in \mathbf{R}$. The subclasses describe the different types of r and every subclass of Thing can have one or more individuals. The arrows "*hasSubclass*" and "*hasIndividual*" show how this is done in Protégé [13].

3.2   The Nearby Road Object Collection

The nearby road objects are those elements that are within the vicinity of the referenced vehicle. See Fig. 4. They are parts of the road objects collection. By vicinity, we mean an element is located within the referenced radius (example: 50 m) of a referenced vehicle. Let m be the radius of the referenced sphere (as it is the case in Unity 3D), and d as the distance between our referenced vehicle and a road object. If the distance d of the road object is less than m then such road object is considered a nearby road object c. Mathematically, $\forall r \in R \mid \exists r_i \bullet d < m \Rightarrow r_i = c_i \wedge C \neq \emptyset$.

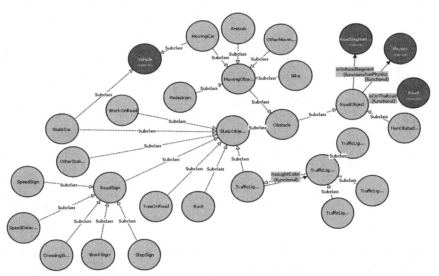

Fig. 3. The ontological representation of road object collection **R** (diagram extracted from [11]).

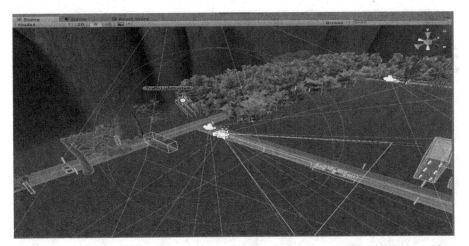

Fig. 4. The nearby road objects from the referenced vehicle's perspective (diagram extracted from [11]).

Figure 5 shows our specimen **E** with all elements c ∈ **C** highlighted. Take note that a radius from the referenced vehicle is shown. It is to be noted that this one is just one of the possible c to consider. Nearby road objects may be in front, at the back, on the left or on the right side of the referenced vehicles. Some of the nearby road objects may be obstacles while some may be not. Ontology creation is therefore important because it allows us to have a good vision of the closest road object that may be considered as road obstacles.

Figure 6 shows all elements c ∈ **C**. As shown, the ontology is much smaller than the previous one, given that we only consider objects that are present in the specified radius of a sphere with our vehicle as the point of reference, with radius = m.

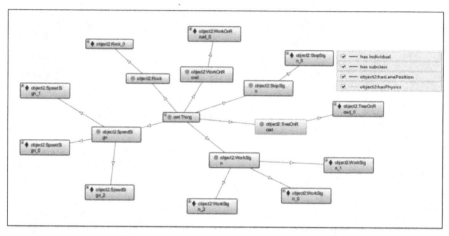

Fig. 5. The ontological representation of nearby road object collection **C** (diagram extracted from [11]).

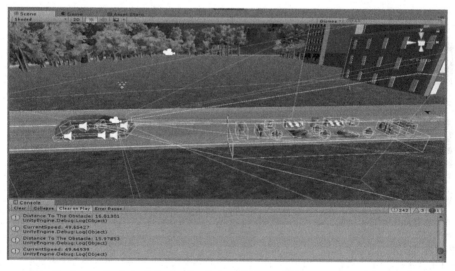

Fig. 6. A sample obstacle in the simulation platform (diagram extracted from [11]).

3.3 The Obstacle Object Collection

The nearby road objects are obstacles if they are in front of the vehicle (located in the same lane), the distance between it and the referenced vehicle is near, and the time to collision is near.

Let v = the current speed of our referenced vehicle, d = the distance between the vehicle and the road object r, t = the time to collision, m = radius of the sensor sphere, l = describes if the vehicle and the object r are on the same lane and p = the direction of the vehicle. For a nearby object $c_i \in C$ located within the vicinity of the referenced vehicle, and given that the speed of the vehicle divided by the distance between the vehicle and the nearby object is less than the time to collision, and that both the vehicle and the nearby object are on the same lane, then object c_i is an obstacle. Mathematically, $\forall c \in C \mid \exists c_i \bullet d < m \wedge v/d < t \wedge l = 1 \wedge d > 0 \Rightarrow c_i = o_i \wedge O \neq \emptyset$. Note that the parameter p is used in the computation of l.

Given that the simulation platform is in 3D coordinate system, the orientation is necessary in order to determine if vehicle s and nearby object c are on the same lane. Let dcr be the distance from the center of the road. Then:

- If p = North $\vee$ p = South $\Rightarrow$ dcr is taken on the x plane, else $\Rightarrow$ dcr is taken on the z plane.

Let dcr_s be the distance the vehicular system to the center of the road, and dcr_c be the distance of nearby object to the center of the road, then:

- $l = 1$, if (dcrs > 0 $\wedge$ dcrc > 0) $\vee$ (dcrs < 0 $\wedge$ dcrc < 0)
- $l = -1$, if (dcrs > 0 $\wedge$ dcrc < 0) $\vee$ (dcrs < 0 $\wedge$ dcrc > 0)

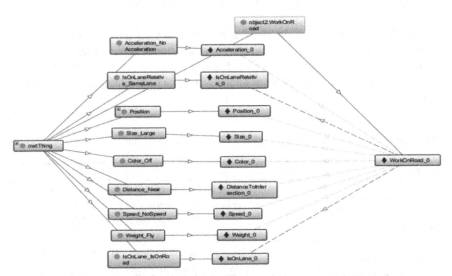

Fig. 7. Ontological representation of a sample obstacle (work on the road) (diagram extracted from [11]).

Figure 6 shows a sample road obstacle located in the same lane as the vehicle. Here, the ontology representation details are important. It is essential that all conditions for qualifying an object as an obstacle be verified. Figure 7 shows the properties of every obstacle $o \in \mathbf{O}$.

Here, the ontology is presented in details for obstacle roadwork $o_1 \in \mathbf{O}$. The legend shows the obstacle characteristics, such as speed or size. In this phase, the road obstacle is already detected. The next phase should be the identification of the obstacle. An obstacle may be another vehicle (static or moving), a pedestrian, a roadwork sign, a traffic light, etc. In general, when an obstacle is detected, the referenced vehicle should stop or slow down and try to avoid such obstacle. The manner to avoid is different, depending on the type of the obstacle. For example, we avoid pedestrian differently from a rock stuck on the road. Machine learning [14, 15] would be used to identify an obstacle.

4 Machine Learning Cognition of Driving Context

4.1 Basics of Machine Learning

Supervised learning and unsupervised learning are the two main learning types in which we can divide the machine-learning world [16], while reinforcement learning and deep learning can be seen as special application of supervised and unsupervised learnings.

Consider a normal x-y function, given a set of input x, we define y as the corresponding output value for a relation f between x and y. The differences between machine learning techniques may be explained using the basic notion of mathematics given below:

- In supervised learning, x and y are known and the goal is to learn a model that approximate f.
- In unsupervised learning, only x is given and the goal is to find f between the set of x.

Supervised learning is used for model approximation and prediction while unsupervised is used for clustering and classification [16]. Reinforcement learning is a particular case of supervised learning; it differs from the standard case not due to the absence of y but in the presence of delayed-reward r that allows it to determine f in order to get the right y. See Table 1.

Table 1. Basic mathematical representation for machine learning (table extracted from [11]).

ML Method	Relation	Comments
Supervised Learning	$y = f(x)$	x and y are known and the goal is to learn a model that approximates f
Unsupervised Learning	$f(x)$	x is given and the goal is to find f for a given set of x
Reinforcement Learning	$y = f(x); r$	r is a reward that allows determination of f in order to obtain the optimal y

Deep learning is a supervised or unsupervised work based on learning data representation. It uses an architecture based on multiple-layer structure for the data [17], using it for feature extraction and representation. Each successive layer uses as input the previous layer output [18].

4.2 Machine Learning Data Training

Machine learning algorithms need to learn from experience. Such data may already be available or not. If not, then these data need to be created (i.e. collected from the driving simulation). The realism and pertinence of the simulation data are important because it is from these data that the system will learn. Furthermore, the data should be large enough to accommodate variations in the values of parameters associated with certain event. After data collection, the event to which the data belong is specified (i.e. tagged). For our specimen events, we wish to classify some basic driving events: turn left, turn right, go straight, and stop. We then extract the features associated for each sample simulated driving event. These features – some of it – are shown in Table 2. One may opt to test other driving events, but the procedure remains the same.

Table 2. Some representative samples of simulation data.

Data name	Values	Comments
Image	PNG file	The screenshot of the situation, used to label the data
Look orientation	"front", "left", "right", "behind"	Current way the driver is looking
Steering angle	Float, between 1 and -1	Current steering wheel angle, -1 is maximum to the left, 1 is maximum to the right, 0 is neutral
Throttle	Float, between 0 and 1	Throttle force put on the acceleration pedal, 0 is none, 1 is maximum
Speed	Km/h	Speed of the vehicle
Orientation	"North", "South", "East", "West"	Current orientation of the vehicle
Speed limit	Km/h	Speed limit of the road
Next lane	-1 or positive	ID of the next road segment
Position on lane	-1, 0 or 1	Current lane. 1 = right lane, -1 = left lane, 0 = not on the road
hasStop	0 or 1	1 if there is a Stop the vehicle is aware of
Vehicle Speed	Km/h	Speed of the other vehicle
hasPedestrian	0 or 1	1 if there is a pedestrian that our vehicle is aware of

As a starting point, we sampled 8521 driving states (to be augmented in the future), the repartition is as follows: (i) Straight/Normal: 5707 samples (66.98% of all events);

(ii) Stop: 1288 samples (15.12% of all events); (iii) Turn Left: 812 samples (9.53% of all events); and (iv) Turn Right: 713 samples (8.35% of all events). See Table 3.

The next step is the processing of data. First, it is necessary to split the data into training and test sets. A good rule of thumb is to take 80% of data into training set and the remaining 20% into test set. If we need a validation set, the recommended split is 60% for training, 20% for validation and 20% for testing. Once the data are split, training the algorithm begins.

Table 3. Repartition of driving events.

Driving event	Number of events	Percentage of events
Normal	1138	66.98%
Stop	257	15.12%
Turn left	162	9.53%
Turn right	142	8.35%

Training data are split into data X and the target values y. For example, for simulation i with vehicle speed of 12.30 km/h, throttle of 0, and tag of Straight, then X_i would contain "*speed = 12.30; throttle = 0*" while y_i contains *Straight*. A representative sample of some features associated with the basic driving events is shown in Table 4.

Table 4. Distribution of sampled driving events.

Tag	Speed	Brake	Throttle	Steering angle
Straight (normal)	33.42	0.00	0.08	−0.66
Straight (normal)	32.08	1.00	0.00	0.00
Straight (normal)	32.27	0.00	0.08	0.02
Straight (normal)	19.12	0.00	0.11	−0.14
Straight (normal)	54.05	0.00	0.00	0.00
Turn right	2.76	0.00	0.00	1.00
Straight (normal)	17.35	0.00	0.00	0.00
Straight (normal)	20.86	0.00	0.00	0.00
Stop	5.043	0.00	0.00	0.00
Turn left	10.02	0.00	0.08	−0.44
Stop	5.61	0.23	0.00	0.00
Turn right	2.76	0.00	0.00	1.00

For the training of the algorithms, we use Python library scikit-learn and Decision tree as classifier. The fit function of the Decision Tree Classifier is the implementation of the CART (Classification and Regression Tree) algorithm. After training the algorithm, it is then validated. Avoiding over fitting is important. Next, we need to optimize the hyper parameters (the parameters used by the learning algorithm). For the decision tree, it is the criterion used for the split (i.e. "gini" measures the purity of the node or "entropy" which measures the information gain), and the splitter strategy (i.e. "best" chooses the best split or "random" for random split when algorithm takes time to train). The feature ranking of decision tree shows how purely a feature separates the classes. It indicates which proportion of each class is left in each node after the separation, where good purity signifies that everything has the same class. To validate the algorithm, the validation set is separated into X_valid and y_valid, use the prediction function of the model on the data set to get the y_predict, and finally compare y_predict vs. y_valid to determine the accuracy of the model.

4.3   Decision Tree Driving Event Classification

Decision tree uses a binary tree as a predictive model. See Fig. 8. A decision tree is a flowchart-like structure in which each internal node represent a "test" on an attribute, each branch represent the outcome of the test and each leaf represent a class label for classification tree. A tree can be created by splitting the training set into subset based on an attribute value test and repeating the process until each leaf of the tree contain a single class label (where entropy = 0) or we reach the desired maximum depth. One advantage of decision tree is that the results given by the model are explained by Boolean logic and are easy to use. We used the machine learning algorithms from the scikit-learn library. We choose decision tree and k-nearest-neighbor algorithms because of their speed and simplicity, the possibility of data analysis after learning and because they are the algorithms that gave the best results. We obtained results of 96.18% of precision for the decision tree algorithm on our test set and 92.65% with the k-nearest neighbor. Results indicate a good accuracy although the number of samples is low. For better results, we need more data with different variables.

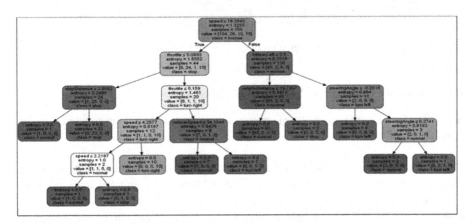

Fig. 8. Decision tree driving event classification.

4.4   Connecting Simulation and Applying the Machine Learning Result

To connect the simulation to the model, we use the TCP protocol. A python server is created; this server waits for a connection from the simulator. Once the simulation is connected, the server waits for an input from the simulation. The simulation sends data of the current driving event. The server then processes the data received, and then use them with the model it saved to predict which driving event corresponds to the sampled data. After predicting the result, the server displays messages and sends back current situation to the simulator to implement the necessary action that corresponds to the situation. Related message/s for driver is/are then displayed on the screen.

Figure 9 shows representative sample messages intended for the driver based on the given driving event. Figure 9 (top) shows an over speeding message (i.e. the driver's speed is 68.07 km/h while the road's speed limit is 50 km/h). Figure 9 (down) shows a message informing the driver to stay on the lane.

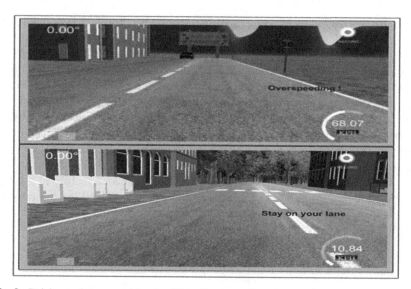

Fig. 9.   Driving assistance notification (Top: Over speeding, Down: Vehicle not on the lane).

4.5   Ensemble Learning and Validation of Classifiers

Here below is the summary of other learning algorithms and their appropriateness in our domain of application:

- Given that K Nearest Neighbor (KNN) is a "lazy" classifier in the sense that it takes more time to calculate the results, we believe that it is less suitable for a real-time system.
- We now use ensemble learning to classify driving events. We previously used decision tree (precision of 96.18%). As shown in examples, ensemble learning is effective and can improve learning results substantially by averaging the bias, reducing the variance

and their unlikeliness to overfit. Using random forest algorithm, we get a precision of 96.36%.

- Given that a decision tree is part of a random forest, we can still get an insight of the most useful features in our data by using a decision tree. The random forest, however, is better from a precision standpoint. We experimented with Adaboost algorithm to test boosting in our problem. We got a precision of 84.49%, which is worse than decision tree, even worse than simple Support Vector Machine. The weak classifier used was 50 decision trees.

- The Stratified random algorithm (we choose a random label with a distribution according to the frequency of each label) gives a precision of 64.63%. The Most frequent algorithm (we always choose the most frequent label) gives a precision of 77.44%. The Random algorithm (we choose randomly with uniform distribution) gives a precision of 22.68%. The support vector machine (SVM) learning algorithm gives a precision of 86.13%. The Naïve Bayes algorithm gives a precision of 30.08%.

- The best algorithm right now is still the random forest algorithm with a precision score of 96.36%.

5 Machine Learning for Obstacle Classification

In this section, the machine learning-assisted classification of obstacle is described in details. Various learning algorithms were tested for the authors to determine the optimal solution.

5.1 Obstacle Classification Using Decision Tree

As stated, decision tree learning uses a decision tree as a predictive model. A decision tree is a flowchart-like structure in which each internal node represent a "test" on an attribute, each branch representing the outcome of the test while each leaf representing a class label for classification tree. Many criteria can be used to divide a node into two branch, such as the information gain, which consist of finding the split that would give the biggest information gain, based on the entropy from the information theory [19].

Figure 10 shows the decision tree for the object classification. Gini impurity is a measure of how often a randomly chosen element from the set would be incorrectly labeled if it were randomly labeled according to the distribution of labels in the subset. The value signifies various obstacles considered, wherein value = [crossingSign, moving-Car, pedestrain, rock, speedSign, workOnroad, stopSign, traffickLightA, traffickLightB, treeOnRoad, staticCar, workSign].

Some features are important in classifying an obstacle using decision tree. From the simulation results, the features that are most important for the decision-tree classification algorithm are the obstacle's size and speed; all others features are insignificant. The data obtained are split as 80% for training, and 20% for testing. Accordingly, it obtains 97.8% accuracy in identifying obstacles in the training set and 97.1% in identifying the obstacles within the test set. The results are satisfactory.

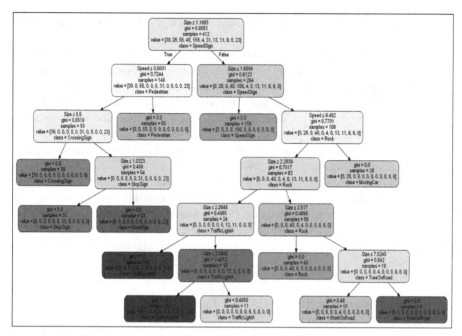

Fig. 10. Obstacle classification using decision tree (diagram extracted from [11]).

5.2 Obstacle Classification using K-Nearest Neighbors (KNN)

The k-nearest neighbor algorithm is a simple algorithm, which consists of selecting for an instance of data the k-nearest other instances and assigning to the first instance the most frequent label in the k instance selected. The value of k is user defined. The distance can be computed in different ways, such as the Euclidian distance for continuous variables like ours. The importance of each neighbor can be weighted; often the weight used is inversely proportional to the distance to give more importance to closer neighbor.

5.3 Obstacle Classification using Random Forest

Random Forest is a supervised learning algorithm. It creates a forest and makes it somehow random. The "forest" it builds is an ensemble of decision trees, most of the time trained with the "bagging" method. The general idea of the bagging method is that a combination of learning models increases the overall result [20]. From the simulation result, the features that are important for the random forest are: (i) object size, (ii) object acceleration, (iii) object color, and (iv) its distance from the vehicle.

As shown, the feature that is most important for the random-forest classification algorithm, as per simulation result, is the obstacle's size, acceleration, color and the obstacle's distance from the referenced vehicle.

The random forest algorithm uses 70% of the data for training, and 30% for testing. Accordingly, the simulation result yields 99.7% accuracy in identifying obstacles in the training set, and 99.4% in identifying the obstacles within the test set. The results are better than the ones obtained using decision-tree learning algorithm.

5.4 Obstacle Classification using Multilayer Perceptron

A multilayer perceptron (MLP) is a feedforward artificial neural network that generates a set of outputs from a set of inputs. An MLP is characterized by several layers of input nodes connected as a directed graph between the input and output layers. MLP uses back propagation for training the network. MLP is a deep learning method [21]. MLP uses 70% of the data for training, and 30% for testing. Accordingly, it obtains 99.7% accuracy in identifying obstacles in the training set and 99.4% in identifying the obstacles within the test set. The results are the same as the ones from random forest learning algorithm.

6 Obstacle Avoidance

After the obstacle detection, the system needs to avoid the obstacle. This will be done using a reinforcement learning application, building a Markov decision process (MDP) [22]. From a mathematical point of view, reinforcement-learning problems are always formalized as Markov decision process, which provides the mathematical rules for decision-making problems, both for describing them and their solutions. A MDP is composed by five elements, as shown in Table 5:

Table 5. Basic elements of Markov decision process (table extracted from [11]).

Variable	Definition
State	**S** is the finite set of the possible states in an environment T
Action	**A** is the possible set of action available for a state **S**
Environment	**T(S, A, S')**; **P(S'⎪A, S)** where **T** represents the environment model: It is a function that produces the probability P of being in state **S'** taking action **A** in the state **S**
Reward	**R(S, A, S')** is the reward given by the environment for passing from **S'** to **S** as a consequence of **A**
Policy	π(**S; A**) is the policy of the state (i.e. The solution of the problem) that takes as input a state **S** and gives the most appropriate action **A** to take

Given the MDP table above, the main idea here is the necessity to create a Markov Decision Process (MDP) based on the parameters state S, action A, and reward r in order to get a policy P capable of avoiding the obstacle in the environment **E**:

- Action set A = [Accelerate, Steer]
- The reward function r is based on the vehicle lane, and collision with obstacles
- Possible state set S (position of the vehicle in the environment).

The action set is composed of two actions of steering the vehicle, and accelerate (in a positive or negative way), while the reward function is based on the position of the vehicle with respect to the lane and collision with obstacles:

- The reward is positive if the vehicle stays on the road and no collision occurs.
- The reward is negative if the vehicle is no longer on the road and a collision is detected.

Finally, the vehicle at every time t in certain state s, would be represented by its position within the environment.

6.1   The Reinforcement Learning (RL) Scene

In order to test a working avoidance system, a new scene was created. The scene, for simplicity purposes, is composed of three main actors: a vehicle, an obstacle and an intended destination. The idea is simple: the vehicle must avoid (after detecting and classifying) the obstacle. It must be able to get back to its right lane afterwards. Figure 11 shows the intended RL scene. The vehicle would be able to detect the obstacle (Fig. 11(a)), avoid it (Fig. 11(b)) and get into its intended destination (Fig. 11(c)). With various tests and trials, we are able to achieve our goal at the end of the process.

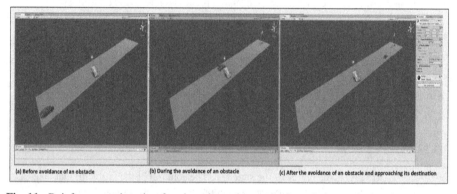

(a) Before avoidance of an obstacle   (b) During the avoidance of an obstacle   (c) After the avoidance of an obstacle and approaching its destination

Fig. 11. Reinforcement learning for obstacle avoidance: before, during and after the avoidance of obstacle (diagram extracted from [11]).

Reward Function. The notion of the reward function is to compensate a vehicle if it is able to avoid the obstacle and arrive at its intended destination. Equations 4 and 5 show the reward functions structure. Here, collision variable has a value of 1 if the vehicle reaches its target (intended destination) and 0 if collides with the obstacle; $isOnLane$ is a variable whose value is 1 as long as the vehicle is on the road, otherwise its value is 0 while $distanceToTarget$ and $previousDistance$ are variables that get updated every frame. They represent the current and the previous distance of the vehicle and its intended destination.

A key point in the reward function is the value for time penalty factor: -0.05 for function 1 and -0.01 for function 2. This small reward is added at every frame, expressed with the condition that time $t_i < t_{i+1}$. The time penalty factor is used in the RL reward function implementation, encouraging the agent to move and reach the target. The best performances were achieved using function 1, while function 2 showed high values for reward function but with worst performances.

$$r = \begin{cases} +1 \; if \; collision = 1 \\ +0.1 \; if \; distanceToTarget < previousDistance \\ -0.05 \; if \; distanceToTarget > previousDistance \\ -0.05 \; if \; ti < ti + 1 \\ -1 \; if \; collision = 0 || isOnLane = 0 \end{cases} \tag{4}$$

$$r = \begin{cases} +1 \; if \; collision = 1 \\ +0.05 \; if \; distanceToTarget < previousDistance \\ -0.05 \; if \; distanceToTarget > previousDistance \\ -0.05 \; if \; ti < ti + 1 \\ -1 \; if \; collision = 0 || isOnLane = 0 \end{cases} \tag{5}$$

Next, we present three different training results. For each result, a graph shows each of the two most important statistics for the training phase, given below:

- *Cumulative Reward*: This is the mean cumulative episode reward over all agents. It should increase on a successful training session.
- *Entropy*: It describes how random the decisions of the model are. It should slowly decrease during a successful training process.

All three trainings described below were made using same parameters with only two variations: the *reward function* used, and the *maximum step* that fixes the maximum number of steps for the training phase. The next discussion focuses on the problems and strong points in each training phase

Training 1: CarSimpleJ
Here, the first good performances were accomplished using the following parameters, using the 2-reward function:

```
default: trainer: ppo | batch_size: 4096 | beta: 1.0e-4 |
buffer_size: 40960 | epsilon: 0.1 | gamma: 0.99 | hidden_units:
256 | lambd: 0.95 | learning_rate: 1.0e-5 | max_steps: 2.5e6
| memory_size: 256 | normalize: false | num_epoch: 3 |
num_layers: 2 | time_horizon: 64 | sequence_length: 64 | sum-
mary_freq: 1000 | use_recurrent: false
```

Figure 12 shows the graphs for the Cumulative Reward and Entropy of CarSimpleJ. Here, the key point is that the reward is increasing overall, but has lot of peaks, both high and low. This is due to the Entropy that is not decreasing in the right way. This leads to a behaviour that sometimes gives us good results, and sometimes not, with the vehicle either reaching its destination or colliding with the obstacle.

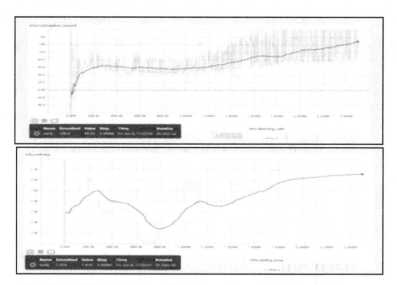

Fig. 12. CarSimpleJ training, (Top): Cumulative reward, (Down): Entropy.

Training 2: CarSimpleJ20
Here, some changes were made on the maximum step parameter, fixed at 20 million, in order to see if the reward and entropy would have followed the correct behaviour. Figure 13 shows the behaviour of the parameters, highlighting the correct trend, even with some low peaks for the reward.

From a numerical point of view, the results were very satisfying, but the problem was linked to the vehicle's behaviour. It was going too slow, taking positive reward thanks to the fact it was getting closer to the target destination. After the agent has avoided the obstacle, it was not, however, able to return on the correct lane. This overfitting behaviour was due to the reward given when the target is approaching the destination being too high relative to the value given to the final goal to achieve. Note the difference of the trend in the graph, Entropy for CarSimpleJ and CarSimpleJ20.

Training 3: CarSimpleJ25
The behaviour obtained in the previous simulations has suggested that a change in the reward function is necessary. Indeed, Eq. 1 was adopted, changing the value assigned for approaching the target and the time penalty. In Fig. 14, it is possible to notice the immediate stabilization of the reward function, while the entropy is decreasing in the correct way. The behaviour is almost perfect, with the agent able to avoid the obstacle and return in the correct lane, reaching the intended destination. In this simulation, the maximum step parameter was set to 25 million.

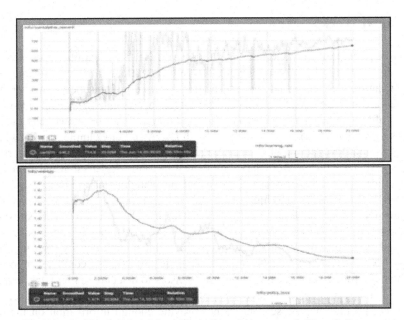

Fig. 13. CarSimpleJ20 training, (Top): Cumulative reward, (Down): Entropy.

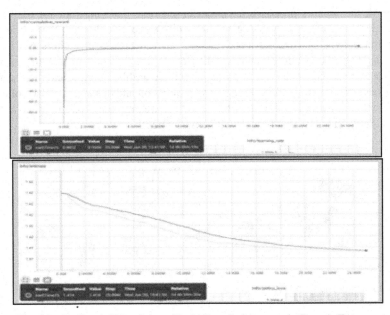

Fig. 14. CarSimpleJ25 training, (Top): Cumulative reward, (Down): Entropy.

7 Related Works

Supervised learning and unsupervised learning are the two main learning types in which we can divide the machine-learning world [16], while reinforcement learning and deep learning can be seen as special application of supervised and unsupervised learnings. Many researches have been made on obstacle detection, classification and avoidance as this type of system helps insuring road safety and therefore has become one of the key enablers in Advanced Driver Assistance System (ADAS). For example, the Euro New Car Assessment Program requires providing vehicles with a Front Collision Warning function [23]. Several carmakers started implementing obstacle detection and avoidance based systems such as Front Assist, Crash avoidance and Automatic Emergency Braking (AEB) in their middle and high range cars [24, 25]. Image processing techniques and computer vision models are extensively used in obstacle detection and classification researches [26–28]. This is justified by the use of different types of cameras such as stereo and monocular ones, which are less expensive than high-density laser scanners like LiDAR [29]. Other research works, such as [5, 30–33] use combined information obtained from several lasers and imaging sensors to detect road obstacles, namely vehicles and pedestrians. The main reason for the complementarity of different sensors is the fact that the imaging sensors do not provide enough information on the distance between the vehicle and the obstacles of the road, which is essential for obstacle avoidance systems.

In [34], the authors proposed a system based on a deep network for road scene visualization (Fig. 15). The system generates a bird's eye map showing the surrounding vehicles that are visible to the dashboard camera. To train the model, authors used a video game called GTAV to generate a massive dataset of more than one million images. Each image has two variants, one corresponding to vehicle dashboard view and the second to the bird's eye view. Other information like yaw, location and distance are also collected. The authors claims the usefulness of the system in helping the driver to make a better decision, being more aware of the driving environment.

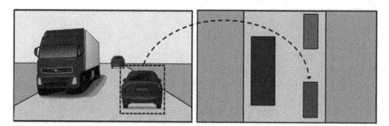

Fig. 15. Input and output of Bazilinskyy, P. et al. system (diagram extracted from [11]).

The authors in [35] worked on a real-time approach to detect and recognize road obstacles. A special focus has been made on three types of obstacles, namely abandoned objects, illegally parked vehicles and accident vehicles. The system follows three main consequent steps. It starts by removing the objects outside the road using a Flushed Region of Interest (FROI) algorithm. It then uses a Histogram Orientation Gradient

(HOG) descriptor to detect road obstacles based on the speed of tracked objects and finally applying a Support Vector Machine (SVM) algorithm to classify the ROI and to separate abandoned objects from vehicles (both accident and illegally parked vehicles). The two types of vehicles are then distinguished using a special algorithm for accident vehicles identification. Authors contend that the proposed system achieved a detection rate of 96%.

Most of collision avoidance systems start by detecting and classifying the obstacle that may cause the collision before calculating the time to collision (TTC) which indicates the remaining time that two consecutive vehicles are to collide. In the event of TTC, the system reacts either by alerting the driver or even by acting on the vehicle to cause brake [36]. In 2011, Volvo has commercialized its "Volvo S60" car with "Collision Warning with Auto Brake and Cyclist and Pedestrian Detection" feature to assist the driver in case of a risk of collision with a vehicle, cyclist or pedestrian [24]. Other auto manufacturers such as Ford, Honda, Toyota, and Nissan Mercedes-Benz have equipped their vehicles with Collision Avoidance Systems (CAS) [25].

The authors in [31] proposed an obstacle detection method that processes a data from a LIDAR sensor combined with single camera-generated images. The obstacles are then classified using the LIDAR point's height information after projecting the LIDAR point cloud onto the images. In [37], the authors proposed a system for real time Collision Warning based on a Multi-Layer Perceptron Neural Network (MLPNN). The input layer was composed of five input neurons: the distance between preceding and following vehicle, speed and acceleration of the following vehicle, speed and deceleration of the preceding vehicle. The final output used a threshold discriminator of 0.5 to come out with a value of zero or one indicating whether a rear-end collision warning should be displayed.

In [38], the authors worked on a Dynamic Bayesian Network (DBN) method to train a model using information gathered by IMU sensor and a camera. The system was designed to provide two types of support: warning on nearby vehicles and brake alert for potential collision with the calculation of the speed and acceleration of the vehicle. The test showed a convenient performance that can be improved by adding other sensors like radar and LIDAR. In addition, the vehicle detection capability may be extended via machine vision based algorithms such as Convolutional Neural Networks (CNN). Most features here have to be integrated in smart vehicle's intelligent component.

The ongoing project "Vehicle of the Future" [10] is an undertaking in which the proponents, including the authors, would like to contribute to safe driving, among others. This project makes use of various sources, including internet of things (IoT) [39, 40], to obtain driving parameters that will make up the driving context [41]. The paper in [42] shows that data mining algorithms can be used to make IoT more intelligent, thus providing smarter services. We make use of the various techniques in the cognition [43–45] of driving events to determine if such driving situation needs driving assistance. Multimodal fission [46–48] determines the details on how to implement such assistance. In this paper, supervised learning algorithms were used as tools for the cognition of driving events and recognition of obstacles. We also used reinforcement learning to determine the optimal action to avoid obstacles. The overall intent is to support both autonomous and semi-autonomous vehicles. In the area of intelligent transportation, connected and autonomous vehicles are a technological revolution. The core science and technology required to support cyber-physical vehicles [41] are essential for future economic competitiveness. This is where the work in this paper lies.

8 Conclusion

In this paper, we modeled the driving context using ontological approach. The values obtained from a simulation are taken and passed onto the ontological template in order to produce a real-time driving situation in which the actual values are those obtained from the simulator. Machine learning is invoked to identify the sampled driving event. Ours is a case of classification problem and we used supervised learning and to solve the issue at hand.

In our "Vehicle of the Future" project, the vehicle's intelligent component is able to detect, identify and avoid a road obstacle. The knowledge engineering part of this paper is the systematic detection and identification of obstacles. Knowledge representation is implemented using ontology and formal specification. Machine learning techniques are used to accomplish the goal. In particular, various supervised learning algorithms (i.e. decision tree, K-nearest neighbors, random forest and multilayer perceptron) are used for identification of obstacles, and experimental results of classification are satisfactory. Intelligent avoidance of obstacle is being implemented via reinforcement learning, using Markov decision process.

Future works involve the implementation of different driving events wherein reinforcement learning should be used to mimic the actions of the driver, including avoiding obstacles such as moving and static vehicles, pedestrians, and others.

References

1. SafeStart. Top 10 Causes of Distracted Driving—and What They All Have in Common, 10 January 2019. https://safestart.com/news/top-10-causes-distracted-driving-and-what-they-all-have-common/
2. WHO (World Health Organization). 10 Facts on Global Road Safety (2015). http://www.who.int/features/factfiles/roadsafety/en/
3. European_Commission. SMARTCARS: Low cost Advanced Driver Assistance Systems (ADAS): A cost affordable solution for improved road safety, 12 July 2018. https://trimis.ec.europa.eu/project/low-cost-advanced-driver-assistance-systems-adas-cost-affordable-solution-improved-road
4. Li, L., Wen, D., Zheng, N.-N., et al.: Cognitive cars: a new frontier for ADAS research. IEEE Trans. Intell. Transp. Syst. **13**, 395–407 (2012)
5. García, F., de la Escalera, A., Armingol, J.M.: Enhanced obstacle detection based on Data Fusion for ADAS applications. In: 16th IEEE International Conference on Intelligent Transportation Systems (ITSC) (2013)
6. Ithape, A.A.: Artificial intelligence and machine learning in ADAS. Presented at the Vector India Conference 2017, Pune, India (2017)
7. Saxena, A.: Machine Learning Algorithms in Autonomous Cars, 27 September 2017. http://visteon.bg/2017/03/02/machine-learning-algorithms-autonomous-cars/

8. Hina, M.D., Guan, H., Deng, N., Ramdane-Cherif, A.: CASA: safe and green driving assistance system for real-time driving events. In: Bi, Y., Kapoor, S., Bhatia, R. (eds.) IntelliSys 2016. LNNS, vol. 15, pp. 987–1002. Springer, Cham (2018). https://doi.org/10.1007/978-3-319-56994-9_67

9. Hina, M.D., Guan, H., Deng, N., et al.: Secured data processing, notification and transmission for a human-vehicle interaction system. In: ITSC 2016, IEEE Intelligent Transportation Systems Conference, Rio de Janiero, Brazil (2016)

10. Hina, M.D., Thierry, C., Soukane, A., et al.: Ontological and machine learning approaches for managing driving context in intelligent transportation. In: KEOD 2017, 9th International Conference on Knowledge Engineering and Ontology Development Madeira, Portugal (2017)

11. Ortalda, A., Moujahid, A., Hina, M.D., et al.: Safe driving mechanism: detection, recognition and avoidance of road obstacles. In: KEOD 2018, 10th International Conference on Knowledge Engineering and Ontology Development, Seville, Spain (2018)

12. Game_Engine. Unity 3D (2016). https://unity3d.com/

13. Protégé. Protégé: Open-source ontology editor (2016). http://protege.stanford.edu

14. Louridas, P., Ebert, C.: Machine learning. IEEE Softw. **33**, 110–115 (2016)

15. Mitchell, T.: Machine Learning. McGraw Hill, New York (1997)

16. Tchankue, P., Wesson, J., Vogts, D.: Using machine learning to predict driving context whilst driving. Presented at the SAICSIT 2013, South African Institute for Computer Scientists and Information Technologists, East London, South Africa (2013)

17. Lv, Y., Duan, Y., Kang, W., et al.: Traffic flow prediction with big data: a deep learning approach. IEEE Trans. Intell. Transp. Syst. **16**, 865–873 (2015)

18. Bengio, Y.: Learning Deep Architectures for AI. Université de Montréal, Montreal (2009)

19. Witten, I., Frank, E., Hall, M., Mining, D.: Practical Machine Learning Tools and Techniques. Morgan Kaufmann, Burlington (2011)

20. Niklas Donges: The Random Forest Algorithm (2018). https://towardsdatascience.com/the-random-forest-algorithm-d457d499ffcd

21. Technopedia. Multilayer Perceptron (MLP) (2018). https://www.techopedia.com/definition/20879/multilayer-perceptron-mlp

22. Sutton, R.S., Barto, A.G.: Reinforcement Learning: An Introduction, 2nd edn. MIT Press, Cambridge (2017)

23. Pyo, J., Bang, J., Jeong, Y.: Front collision warning based on vehicle detection using CNN. In: 2016 International SoC Design Conference (ISOCC), Jeju, South Korea, pp. 163–164 (2016)

24. Coelingh, E., Eidehall, A., Bengtsson, M.: Collision warning with full auto brake and pedestrian detection-a practical example of automatic emergency braking. Presented at the 13th IEEE International Conference on Intelligent Transportation Systems (ITSC) (2010)

25. ResearchNews. Key Technologies for Preventing Crashes, vol. 2. Thatcham, Berkshire (2013)

26. Bevilacqua, A., Vaccari, S.: Real time detection of stopped vehicles in traffic scenes. In: IEEE International Conference on Advanced Video Signal Based Surveillance, London, UK, pp. 266–270 (2007)

27. Zeng, D., Xu, J., Xu, G.: Data fusion for traffic incident detection using D-S evidence theory with probabilistic SVMs. J. Comput. **3**, 36–43 (2008)

28. Wolcott, R.W., Eustice, R.: Probabilistic obstacle partitioning of monocular video for autonomous vehicles. Presented at the British Machine Vision Conference 2016 (2016)

29. Levi, D., Garnett, N., Fetaya, E., et al.: StixelNet: a deep convolutional network for obstacle detection and road segmentation. In: British Machine Vision Conference (2015)

30. Bertozzi, M., Bombini, L., Cerri, P., et al.: Obstacle detection and classification fusing radar and visio. Presented at the 2008 IEEE Intelligent Vehicles Symposium (2008)

31. Shinzato, P.Y., Wolf, D.F., Stiller, C.: Road terrain detection: avoiding common obstacle detection assumptions using sensor fusion. In: IEEE Intelligent Vehicles Symposium Proceedings, pp. 687–692 (2014)

32. Linzmeier, D., Skutek, M., Mekhaiel, M., et al.: A pedestrian detection system based on thermopile and radar sensor data fusion. In: 8th International Conference on Information Fusion (2005)
33. Wang, X., Xu, L., Sun, H., et al.: Bionic vision inspired on-road obstacle detection and tracking using radar and visual information. In: 17th IEEE International Conference on Intelligent Transportation Systems (ITSC) (2014)
34. Bazilinskyy, P., Heisterkamp, N., Luik, P., et al.: Eye movements while cycling in GTA V. In: Tools and Methods of Competitive Engineering (TMCE 2018), Las Palmas de Gran Canaria, Spain (2018)
35. Lan, J., Jiang, Y., Fan, G., et al.: Real-time automatic obstacle detection method for traffic surveillance in urban traffic. J. Sig. Process. Syst. **82**, 357–371 (2016)
36. Rummelhard, L., Nègre, A., Perrollaz, M., Laugier, C.: Probabilistic grid-based collision risk prediction for driving application. In: Hsieh, M.A., Khatib, O., Kumar, V. (eds.) Experimental Robotics. STAR, vol. 109, pp. 821–834. Springer, Cham (2016). https://doi.org/10.1007/978-3-319-23778-7_54
37. Lee, D., Yeo, H.: Real-time rear-end collision-warning system using a multilayer perceptron neural network. IEEE Trans. Intell. Transp. Syst. **17**, 3087–3097 (2016)
38. Iqbal, A., Busso, C., Gans, N.R.: Adjacent vehicle collision warning system using image sensor and inertial measurement unit. In: 2015 ACM Proceedings on International Conference on Multimodal Interaction, pp. 291–298 (2015)
39. Miorandi, D., Sicari, S., De Pellegrini, F., et al.: Internet of things: vision, applications and research challenges. Ad Hoc Netw. **10**, 1497–1516 (2012)
40. Tsai, C.-W., Lai, C.-F., Chiang, M.-C., et al.: Data mining for internet of things: a survey. IEEE Commun. Surv. Tutor. **16**, 77–97 (2014)
41. Brioschi, G., Hina, M.D., Soukane, A., et al.: Techniques for cognition of driving context for safe driving application. In: ICCI*CC 2016, 15th IEEE International Conference on Cognitive Informatics and Cognitive Computing Stanford, CA, USA (2016)
42. Bin, S., Yuan, L., Xiaoyi, W.: Research on data mining models for the internet of things. Presented at the International Conference on Image Analysis and Signal Processing (2010)
43. Kelly III, J.E.: Computing, cognition and the future of knowing: how humans and machines are forging a new age of understanding (2015)
44. Haas, S., Weisner, K., Stone, T.C.: Car ride classification for drive context recognition. Presented at the Mobility 2014, 4th International Conference on Mobile Services, Resources and Users, Paris, France (2014)
45. Mitrovic, D.: Reliable method for driving events recognition. IEEE Trans. Intell. Transp. Syst. **6**, 198–205 (2005)
46. Costa, D., Duarte, C.: Adapting multimodal fission to user's abilities. In: Stephanidis, C. (ed.) UAHCI 2011. LNCS, vol. 6765, pp. 347–356. Springer, Heidelberg (2011). https://doi.org/10.1007/978-3-642-21672-5_38
47. Frédéric, L.: Physical, semantic and pragmatics levels for multimodal fusion and fission. In: 7th International Workshop on Computational Semantics, Tilburg, Netherlands (2007)
48. Adjali, O., Hina, M.D., Dourlens, S., et al.: Multimodal fusion, fission and virtual reality simulation for an ambient robotic intelligence. In: 6th International Conference on Ambient Systems, Networks and Technologies (ANT-2015), London, UK (2015)

The Evaluation of Ontologies for Quality, Suitability for Reuse, and the Significant Role of Social Factors

Marzieh Talebpour(✉), Martin Sykora, and Tom Jackson

School of Business and Economics, Loughborough University, Loughborough, UK
{m.talebpour,m.d.Sykora,t.w.Jackson}@lboro.ac.uk

Abstract. A frequent challenge faced by ontologists and knowledge engineers is the choice of the correct or most appropriate ontology for reuse. Despite the importance of ontology evaluation and selection and the widespread research on these topics, there are still many unanswered questions and challenges. Most of the evaluation metrics and frameworks in the literature are mainly based on a limited set of internal characteristics of ontologies, e.g., their content and structure, which ignore how the community uses and evaluates them. This paper used a survey questionnaire to investigate the notion of quality and reusability in ontology engineering, and to explore and identify the set of metrics that can affect the process of ontology evaluation and selection for reuse. Responses from 157 ontologists and knowledge engineers were collected, and their analysis suggests that the process of ontology evaluation and selection for reuse, not only depends on different internal characteristics of ontologies, but that it also depends on different metadata, and social and community related metrics. Findings of this research can contribute to facilitating and improving the process of selecting an ontology for reuse.

Keywords: Quality metrics · Ontology · Evaluation · Ontology selection · Ontology reuse

1 Introduction

Recent uptake in Semantic Web technology applications has urged researchers and ontology engineers to develop ontologies in different domains. Increase in the number of ontologies and the cost of developing them has urged researchers in this field to consider ontology reuse [1]. Ontology reuse can be defined as the process of using the available ontological knowledge as input to develop new ontologies. Building an ontology by reusing the available ones will not only facilitate the development process but will also make the outcome ontology reusable. Ontology reuse consists of different steps namely searching for adequate ontologies, evaluating the quality and fitness of those ontologies for the reuse purpose, selecting an ontology and integrating it in the project [2].

Regardless of all the advantages of reusing ontologies and the availability of different ontologies, ontology reuse has always been a challenging task. Guidelines for building ontologies are usually blamed for lack of reuse strategies and some argue that they are

© Springer Nature Switzerland AG 2020
A. Fred et al. (Eds.): IC3K 2018, CCIS 1222, pp. 161–177, 2020.
https://doi.org/10.1007/978-3-030-49559-6_8

not explicitly concerned with ontology reuse. Others consider the first steps of ontology reuse, that is the identification and evaluation of the knowledge sources which can be useful for an application domain, as the hardest step in the process of ontology reuse. Ontologists and knowledge engineers not only have to find the most appropriate ontologies for their search query but should also be able to evaluate those ontologies according to different implicit or explicit criteria. The lack of appropriate supportive tools and automatic measurement techniques for evaluating and assessing ontology features has been considered as a barrier for ontology reuse [3].

Ontology evaluation is at the heart of ontology selection and has received a considerable amount of attention in the literature. The term evaluation refers to the process of judging different technical aspects of an ontology namely its definitions, documentation and software environment [4]. Evaluation has also been described as the process of measuring the suitability and the quality of an ontology for a specific goal or in a specific application [3]. This definition refers to the approaches that aim to identify an ontology, an ontology module or a set of ontologies that satisfy a particular set of selection requirements [5].

This paper is an extended version of [6], and aims to determine some of the metrics that can be used to evaluate the suitability of an ontology for reuse. The fundamental research question of this study was whether or not social and community related metrics can be used in the evaluation process. Another question was how important those metrics were, compared to some of the well-known ontological metrics such as content and structure. Qualitative and quantitative research designs were adopted to provide a deeper understanding of how ontologists and knowledge engineers evaluate and select ontologies. This study offers some valuable insights into ontology quality, what it depends on and how it can be measured.

2 Background

Evaluation is one of the most popular and also defined terms in the field of ontology engineering. It is used to refer to several different activities including detecting faults in an ontology, assessing an ontology's quality, and measuring its fitness for a specific purpose. There are many different ways of defining ontology evaluation; one of the most popular and also the earliest definitions for ontology evaluation was provided by Gómez-Pérez where the term evaluation was used to refer to the technical judgment of an ontology considering its different aspects, namely its definitions, documentation, and software environment [4]. According to this definition, evaluation encompasses validation and verification; ontology validation is mainly concerned with the correctness of an ontology whereas ontology verification is more about determining how well an ontology corresponds to what it should represent [7]. In other words, ontology validation focuses on building the correct ontology whereas ontology verification is about building an ontology correctly [8].

Ontology evaluation has also been widely defined as the process of determining the adequacy and quality of an ontology for being used for a specific goal and in a specific context [3]. This definition is used to link the process of ontology evaluation to ontology selection. Ontology selection aims to identify an ontology, an ontology module or a set of ontologies that satisfy a particular set of criteria or selection requirements [5]. Some consider ontology evaluation as the core to ontology selection and argue that ontology evaluation is influenced by different components of the selection process, e.g., selection criteria, type of output, and the libraries that the selection is based on [5]. Ontology assessment is also used to refer to this particular definition of ontology evaluation and is commonly defined as the activity of checking and judging an ontology against different user requirements such as usability and usefulness [9]. Unlike the first definition of the ontology evaluation, in which the developer team is responsible for validating and verifying an ontology, ontology assessment and evaluation for selection is done by the end users [10].

Ontology evaluation can also refer to a function or an activity that aims to map an ontology or a component of an ontology to a score or a number, e.g., in the range of 0 to 1 [11]. The main aim of these types of processes is to measure and assess the quality of an ontology with regards to a set of predefined metrics and requirements [12]. This definition is somehow similar to what [9] defines as ontology quality assurance, which refers to the activity of examining every process carried out and every product built during the ontology development process and making sure that the level of their quality is satisfactory. Moreover and as it is seen in the literature, the expressions "Ontology Evaluation" and "Ontology Ranking" are sometimes used interchangeably. While they both tend to refer to a set of similar criteria, for us, ontology ranking is the process of sorting ontologies in descending order and according to the scores that are assigned to them in the evaluation process.

Ontology evaluation is important in the ontology development process, whether it is built from scratch, automatically or by reusing other ontologies [13]. While building an ontology from scratch, developers need to evaluate the outcome ontology, to measure its quality [14], to check if it meets their application requirements [13] and also to identify the potential refinement steps [15]. Evaluation is also helpful in checking the homogeneity and consistency of an ontology when it is automatically populated from different resources [13, 16]. Building an ontology from scratch is very costly and time-consuming [17, 18]; therefore, ontologists are urged to consider reusing existing ontologies before building a new one [19]. Ontology evaluation is and has always been a major concept when it comes to ontology reuse [20]. Some argue that ontology evaluation is one of the main issues that should be addressed if ontologies are to become widely adopted and reused by the community [15, 18, 20, 21].

Moreover, the number of ontologies on the web has been increasing rapidly [13], and users usually face multiple ontologies when they need to choose or use one in their everyday activities [12, 15, 22]. Before using an ontology in an application or selecting it for reuse, ontologists have to assess its quality and correctness and also compare it to the other available ones in the domain. This is when ontology evaluation comes into the picture; ontology evaluation is believed to be the core to the ontology selection process [5] and is used to select the best or the most appropriate ontology among many other candidates in a domain [15]. Evaluating an ontology is considered as a complicated process [12, 23]; it is believed that failure to evaluate ontologies or to choose the right ontology can lead to using the ontologies that are not right or have a lower quality [12].

Being one of the most popular and also important parts of the ontology engineering domain, ontology evaluation has long been at the centre of research attention in this field. Since 1995 to date, there has been a variety of research on different aspects of ontology evaluation including methodologies, tools, frameworks, methods, metrics, and measures [4]. However, much uncertainty and also disagreement still exists about the best way to evaluate an ontology generally or for a specific tool or application. As it is seen in the literature, there are many different ways of evaluating ontologies and also many ways of classifying those evaluation methods, algorithms and approaches. Some of the most popular ontology evaluation approaches are reviewed in the following part of this section. Ontology evaluation approaches can broadly be classified as follow:

User-Based Evaluation. Ontologists and knowledge experts can assess the quality of ontologies [8] in two different ways: one is the criteria-based evaluation approach in which the suitability of an ontology for a particular task or requirement is evaluated by being compared against a set of pre-defined criteria [18]. Peer review based evaluation, as the other type of user-based evaluation approach, allows ontologists and knowledge experts to link subjective information to ontologies by providing metadata and extra qualitative information about different aspects of them [24]. Despite their popularity, user-based ontology evaluation approaches are blamed for being solely based on different characteristics of ontologies and for ignoring the functionality of an ontology in an application [12].

Golden Standard. This approach refers to the type of evaluation that is performed by comparing an ontology to another ontology, also known as a "gold standard" ontology, and aims to find different types of similarities such as lexical as conceptual between them. This approach was first proposed by [25] and was then used in many other researches namely [11], where a fully automated evaluation approach was proposed by introducing a similarity measure called OntoRand index and comparing ontologies to a gold standard one using that measure. This kind of evaluation is typically applied to the ontologies that are generated semi-automatically and to measure the effectiveness of the ontology generation process [22]. A major problem with this approach is that comparing ontologies is not easy [5].

Data or Corpus Driven Evaluation. This approach is similar to the "gold standard" approach, but instead of comparing an ontology to another one, it compares it to a source of data or a collection of documents [15]. One of the most popular architectures for this type of evaluation is proposed by [19]; it is based on three main steps namely extracting keywords from a corpus, applying some query expansion algorithms on the ontology concept, and finally mapping the terms identified in the corpus to the concepts in an ontology. They will then analyse how well the ontology is covering the source of data [19].

Task-Based Evaluation. Also known as application-based [26] or black box evaluation [21]; this approach aims to evaluate an ontology's performance in the context of an application [19]. One of the main assumptions of this approach is that there is a direct link between the quality of an ontology and how well it serves its purpose as a part of a larger application [27]. The challenges of performing this type of evaluation includes the difficulty of assessing the quality of the performed task as well as making sure that the experimental environment is clean, and that the ontology is the only factor that is influencing the performance of the application [5].

Rule-Based (Logical). This type of evaluation is proposed by [16] and aims to validate ontologies and detect conflicts in them by using different rules that are either a part of the ontology development language or are identified by users. Rule-based evaluation is more relevant when evaluation aims to detect faults and inconsistencies in an ontology, rather than when the quality assessment or ontology selection is concerned.

Other Approaches. Besides the above-mentioned categories, that are very popular in the literature, there are some other ways of classifying ontology evaluation approaches. For example, ontology evaluation approaches can be classified into glass-box or black-box. Glass-box approaches tend to evaluate the internal content and structure of ontologies [20] and are blamed for not predicting how ontology might perform in an application. In contrast, black-box approaches do not explicitly use knowledge of the internal structure of ontologies and focus on the quality of an ontology performance and results [20]. Ontologies can also be evaluated as a whole or according to their different layers, e.g. data level, taxonomy level, and application level [15]. [17] has divided the concept of ontology quality into two broad types: "Total Quality" and "Partial Quality". Some argue that evaluating an ontology as a whole, especially automatically, is not possible or practical, especially considering the complex structure of ontologies [15].

From all the approaches mentioned above, much of the research in the ontology evaluation domain has concentrated on criteria-based approaches, and many have tried to identify and introduce a set of metrics that can be used for ontology evaluation. A more detailed account of criteria-based ontology evaluation is given in the next section.

3   Criteria-Based Evaluation

Criteria-based evaluation, also known as metric-based, multiple-criteria [15] or feature-based [16], is one of the most popular evaluation approaches in the literature. This type of evaluation is mostly based on identifying and selecting multiple attributes or features of ontologies and then evaluating them for ranking and selection purposes [15]. The outcome of this approach is usually an overall or an aggregated score that is computed by adding the scores that are assigned to each criterion [28]. Despite the wide use and popularity of criteria-based evaluation, identifying the right set of metrics for ontology evaluation and measuring them is still a challenge.

Criteria based approaches are different from each other in a number of respects. First, the type of the metrics they use to assess ontologies can be different. Some approaches are based on qualitative metrics and tend to rely on expert users' judgement and ratings about an ontology or a module in an ontology [29]. Qualitative approaches can also be used to evaluate an ontology based on the principles that are/were used in its construction [19]. Other are based on different quantitative criteria about different aspects of ontologies such as its structure and content. These approaches, that are also known as formal rational approaches, are usually concerned with technical and economical aspects of ontologies and use different goal-based strategies [18].

They can also be based on assessing internal and/or external attributes of ontologies. Internal attributes are concerned with the ontology itself and its internal organization whereas external measures mostly focus on how ontologies are taken-up or used within the user communities [30]. [31], for example, has followed software engineering measurement traditions and has proposed a method that aims to identify what they call key internal attributes of ontologies including consistency, richness and clarity. They have also mentioned maintainability and application performance as example for external quality attributes of ontologies [31].

Moreover, metrics used in the criteria-based evaluation can either be query dependent or query independent. Coverage, for example, aims to measure how well a candidate ontology match or cover a set of query term(s) and selection requirements [32, 33] and therefore, it depends on users' queries. Popularity, in contrast, is measured by checking the presence of an ontology in different well-known repositories as well as looking into the number of visits or page views of an ontology in ontology repositories in a recent specific period [28]; hence, it does not depend on the selection requirements.

For the purpose of this paper and according to the previous study conducted by [34], ontology evaluation quality criteria are broadly classified into three main sub groups including (1) Internal metrics that are based on different internal characteristic of ontologies such as their content and structure, (2) Metadata that are used to describe ontologies and to help in the selection process, and (3) Social metrics that focus on how ontologies are used by communities. The rest of this section moves on to explain different quality metrics for ontology evaluation in more details.

3.1 Internal Metrics

Internal aspects of ontologies have always been used as a mean of their evaluation. Different internal quality criteria such as clarity, correctness, consistency, and completeness have been used in the literature to measure how clear ontology definitions are, how different entities in an ontology represent the real world, how consistent an ontology is, and how complete an ontology is [12]. Coverage is yet another significant content related metric; the term coverage is mostly used in the literature to measure how well a candidate ontology match or cover the query term(s) and selection requirements [32]. Structure or graph structure [20] is the other important internal aspect of an ontology that can be used to measure how detailed the knowledge structure of an ontology is [35] and also to evaluate its richness of knowledge [5] density [22], depth and breadth [35].

3.2 Metadata

Besides the internal aspects of ontologies, some of the frameworks and tools have suggested evaluating ontologies using different types of metadata. Metadata or "data about data" is widely used on the web for different reasons namely to help in the process of resource discovery [36]. [37] believes that the primary connection between different elements of an ontology is in the mind of the people who interpret it; so, tagging an ontology with more data will help in making those mental connections explicit. Ontologies can be tagged and described according to their different characteristics, namely their type and version. The language that different ontologies are built and implemented with can also be used as a metric to evaluate, filter and categorize them [38].

There are different examples of using metadata in the literature to help with the process of evaluating, finding and reusing ontologies. Swoogle [39] was one of the very first selection systems in ontology engineering field to introduce the concept of metadata to this domain. There is a metadata generator component in this system that is responsible for creating and storing three different types of metadata about each discovered ontology including basic, relation, and analytical metadata [39]. [24] has also proposed two sets of metadata that can be used to evaluate ontologies: source metadata and third-party metadata.

Moreover, metadata is created and used to help interoperability between different applications and ontologies. Ontology Metadata Vocabulary (OMV) was proposed by [40] and is one of the most popular sets of metadata for ontologies. OMV is not directly concerned with ontology evaluation or ranking and its main aim is to facilitate ontology reuse. [41] have proposed a guideline for minimum information for the reporting of an ontology (MIRO) to help ontologists and knowledge engineers in the process of reporting ontology description and providing documentation. It is believed that MIRO can improve the quality and consistency of ontology descriptions and documentation.

3.3 Community Aspects of Ontologies

Besides how ontologies are built and what they are covering or even not covering, some believe that how they are used by different communities can be considered as a feature in their evaluation and selection. [8] define user-based ontology evaluation as the process of evaluating an ontology though users' experiences and by capturing different subjective information about ontologies. According to a study that was conducted by [42], relying on the experiences of other users for evaluating ontologies will lessen the efforts needed to assess an ontology and reduce the problems that users face while selecting an ontology. [23] have also highlighted the importance of relying on the wisdom of the crowd in ontology evaluation and believe that improving the overall quality of ontological content on the web is a shared responsibility within a community.

As it is seen in the literature, social or community features of ontologies have not been the main focus of the evaluation frameworks until recently. However, some of the very well-known frameworks for ontology evaluation consider social quality as one of the metrics, among others, that can be used in the evaluation process. [31], for example, applied a deductive method to identify a set of general, domain-independent and application-independent quality metrics for ontology evaluation. This approach proposed different social quality metrics namely authority and history to measure the role of community in ontology quality.

Another example of social based quality application was proposed by [43], in which the notion of the open rating system and democratic ranking were applied to ontology evaluation. According to this approach, users of this system can not only review the ontology, but they can also review the reviews provided by other users about an ontology. A similar approach was proposed by [42] where users' ratings are used to determine what they call user-perceived quality of ontologies.

[34] also attempted to investigate and explore how community and social aspects of ontologies can affect their quality. According to their findings, knowledge engineers consider different social aspects of ontologies when evaluating them. Those aspects include: (1) build related information, for example, who has built the ontology, why the ontology was built, do they know the developer team, (2) regularity of update and maintenance, and (3) responsiveness of the ontology developer and maintenance team and their flexibility and willingness toward making changes.

Overall, the above-mentioned studies highlight the importance of the criteria-based approaches in ontology evaluation. They also outline the most important or used quality metrics in the literature. The next sections discuss the methodology used to collect data and the findings of this research.

4 Methodology

From all the groups of quality related metrics mentioned in the previous section, the focus of this research is on different metadata and social characteristics of ontologies that can be used in the evaluation process. This study was built upon the findings of the previous interview study conducted by [34] and aims to clarify and confirm the metrics identified in that study. To do that a survey questionnaire was designed based on a mixed research strategy combining qualitative and quantitative questions.

The survey was sent to a broad community of ontologists and knowledge engineers in different domains. Different sampling strategies namely purposive sampling [44] were used in order to find the ontologists and knowledge engineers that were involved in the process of ontology development and reuse. The survey was also forwarded to different active mailing lists in the field of ontology engineering. The lists used are as follows:

- The UK Ontology Network
- GO-Discuss
- DBpedia-discussion
- The Protégé User
- FGED-discuss
- Linked Data for Language Technology Community Group
- Best Practices for Multilingual Linked Open Data Community Group
- Ontology-Lexica Community Group
- Linking Open Data project
- Ontology Lookup Service announce
- Technical discussion of the OWL Working Group
- This is the mailing list for the Semantic Web Health Care and Life Sciences Community Group

There was a total number of 31 questions broadly divided into four different sections. Each section consisted of different number of questions and aimed to explore and discover the opinion of ontologists and knowledge engineers regarding (1) the process of ontology development, (2) ontology reuse, (3) ontology evaluation and the quality metrics used in that process, and (4) the role of community in ontology development, evaluation and reuse. Different types of questions were used in the survey namely close-ended questions, Likert scale questions, open-ended questions, and multiple-choice questions. Screening questions were also used throughout the survey to make sure that respondents are presented with the set of questions that is relevant to their previous experiences.

The most important part of the survey aimed to explore the process of ontology evaluation and the set of criteria that can be used in this process. Respondents were first asked about the approaches and metrics they tend to consider while evaluating ontologies. They were then presented with four different sets of quality metrics including (1) internal, (2) metadata, (3) community and (4) popularity related criteria and were asked how important they thought those metrics were, by offering a 5-point Likert scale, ranging from "Not important" to "Very important". The criteria presented and assessed in this part of the survey were collected both from the literature and the previous phase of the data collection, that was an interview study with 15 ontologists and knowledge engineers in different domains [34].

5 Findings

As was mentioned in the previous sections, this research aimed to introduce different metrics that could be potentially used for ontology evaluation. Prior studies have identified many different quality metrics, mostly based on ontological and internal aspects of ontologies. This study was designed to determine the importance of those metrics and also to explore how communities can help in the selection process. The findings of this study are discussed in the following sections.

5.1 Demographics of Respondents

The aim of this section is to provide information on the profile of respondents to the survey. This study managed to access ontologists and knowledge engineers with many years of experience in building and reusing ontologies in different domains. Around 80% of the participants in the survey were actively involved in the ontology development process and all of them would consider reusing existing ontologies before building a new one. The 157 respondents of this study are categorized by the following demographics, all declared by responders:

Job Title. After conducting frequency analysis on the job titles provided by respondents, 78 unique job titles were identified, many of which were somehow related to different roles and positions in academia such as researcher, professor, lecturer, etc.

Type of Organization. According to the frequency analysis conducted on the organization types, 68.8% (108) of the respondents of the survey were working in academia. The other 31.2% of the respondents were working in other types of organizations including different companies and industries.

Years of Experience. Interestingly, most of the survey respondents were experts in their domain and only around 10% of them had less than two years of experience. Around 46% (73) of the respondents had more than ten years of experience. The second largest group of the respondents were the ontologists with five to ten years of experience (26.8%).

Main Domains They Had Built or Reused Ontologies In. Survey respondents had worked/were working in many different domains such as biomedical, industry, business, etc. Most of participants had mentioned more than one domain, some of which were not related to each other.

5.2 Evaluation Metrics According to Qualitative Data

Before presenting participants with four sets of quality metrics that can be used for ontology evaluation and asking them to rate those metrics, they were asked an open-ended question about how they evaluate the quality of an ontology before selecting it for reuse. This question aimed to provide further insight and to gather respondents' opinions on different evaluation metrics and approaches. The responses to this question were coded according to different categories of quality metrics namely (1) internal, (2) metadata, (3) community and popularity related metrics.

According to the analysis, quality metrics thought to be the most important were content and coverage (mentioned 51 times) and documentation (mentioned 41 times). The fact that an ontology has been reused previously and the popularity of the ontology on the web, or among community was the other frequently mentioned metric by the respondents (38 times). Community related metrics such as reviews about the quality of an ontology, existence, activeness and responsiveness of the developer team, and the reputation of the developer team or organisation responsible for ontology were also mentioned by many of the respondents (25 times).

The findings of the qualitative question in the survey confirmed the findings of the quantitative part and the interview study previously conducted by [34]. It should be noted that two of the metrics mentioned by the responders namely "fit" and "format" were not presented as a Likert item in the quantitative part of the survey. Format was only mentioned two times but how relevant an ontology is to an application requirement was mentioned 37 times. The reason fit was not used as a Likert item is that it cannot be used as a criterion to judge the quality of an ontology. However, it is a significant factor in the selection process.

One of the emerging themes in the analysis was "following or being a part of a standard". Interestingly, 19 respondents had mentioned following or complying with different design guidelines and principles or being a part of a standard like W3C, and OBO Foundry as a criterion in the evaluation process. Some had also mentioned that while evaluating an ontology, they check if it is built by using a method like NEON. A similar question was proposed as one of the Likert items and respondents were asked to rate how important "The use of a method/methodology (e.g. NEON, METHONTOLOGY, or any other standard and development practice)" is when evaluating an ontology. Surprisingly, it was ranked 30th (out of 31) with a mean of 2.80 and a median of 3.

5.3 Importance of Quality Metrics

Table 1 shows the descriptive statistics of all 31 quality metrics, sorted by standard deviation. The metrics are ranked from 1 to 31, with 1 being the most important and 31 being the least important metric considered when evaluating the quality of an ontology for reuse. Mean and median are used to show the center and midpoint of the data respectively. Standard deviation is used to express the level of agreement on the importance of each metric in the ontology evaluation process; the lower value of standard deviation represents the higher level of agreement among the survey respondents on a rating.

As it is seen in Table 1, ontology content including its classes, properties, relationships, individuals and axioms is the first metric ontologists and knowledge engineers tend to look at when evaluating the quality of an ontology for reuse. Other internal aspects of ontologies like their structure (class hierarchy or taxonomy), scope (domain coverage), syntactic correctness, and consistency (e.g. naming and spelling consistency all over the ontology) are also among the top ten quality metrics used for ontology evaluation.

Documentation is the second most important quality metric used in the evaluation process. Survey respondents have also given a very high rate, five and eight respectively, to other metadata related metrics such as accessibility and availability of metadata and provenance information about an ontology. In contrast to these metrics, other criteria in the metadata group like availability of funds for ontology update and maintenance, use of a method/methodology and ontology language are among the bottom ten least important metrics.

Community related metrics have some very interesting ratings. The results show ontologists and knowledge engineers would like to know about the purpose that an ontology is used/has been used for (e.g. annotation, sharing data, etc.) while evaluating and before selecting it for reuse. They have also rated "Availability of wikis, forums, mailing lists and support team for the ontology" as one of the very important quality metrics for ontology evaluation. Having an active, responsive developer community and knowing and trusting the ontology developers are among the other top-ranked community related aspects of ontologies that can be used for their evaluation.

Survey responders were also presented with a set of popularity related metrics. According to Table 1, the popularity of an ontology in the community and among colleagues has the highest median and mean compared to the other metrics that can be used for evaluating the popularity of an ontology. Respondents also tended to consider the reputation of the ontology developer team and/or institute in the domain while evaluating an ontology for reuse. Other popularity related metrics such as the popularity of the ontology in social media (e.g. in GitHub, Twitter, or LinkedIn), the popularity of the ontology on the web (number of times it has been viewed in different websites/applications across the web), and the reviews of the ontology (e.g. ratings), were among the metrics with the least mean and median.

Survey responders were also presented with a set of popularity related metrics. According to Table 1, the popularity of an ontology in the community and among colleagues has the highest median and mean compared to the other metrics that can be used for evaluating the popularity of an ontology. Respondents also tended to consider the reputation of the ontology developer team and/or institute in the domain while evaluating an ontology for reuse. Other popularity related metrics such as the popularity of the ontology in social media (e.g. in GitHub, Twitter, or LinkedIn), the popularity of the ontology on the web (number of times it has been viewed in different websites/applications across the web), and the reviews of the ontology (e.g. ratings), were among the metrics with the least mean and median.

Table 1. Descriptive statistics of all the quality metrics in the survey (extracted from [6]).

Rank	Metric	SD	Median	Mean
1	The Content (classes, properties, relationships, individuals, axioms)	0.57	5	4.59
2	The availability of documentation (both internal, e.g. adding comments and external)	0.79	5	4.38
3	The Structure (Class hierarchy or taxonomy)	0.82	4	4.29
4	The Scope (domain coverage)	0.84	5	4.42
5	The ontology is online, accessible, and open to reuse (e.g. License type)	0.85	5	4.52
6	The Syntactic Correctness	0.92	4	4.15
7	The Consistency (e.g. Naming and spelling consistency all over the ontology)	1.00	4	4.03
8	Availability of metadata and provenance information about the ontology	1.01	4	3.92
9	Availability of wikis, forums, mailing lists and support team for the ontology	1.03	4	3.45
10	Having information about the purpose that ontology is used/has been used for (e.g. annotation, sharing data, etc.)	1.03	4	3.77
11	The Semantic Richness and Correctness (e.g. level of details)	1.06	4	3.92
12	Having an active responsive (developer) community	1.09	4	3.62
13	Having information about the other individuals or organizations who are using/have used the ontology	1.1	3	3.12
14	Having information about the other projects that the ontology is used/has been used in	1.1	3	3.34
15	Knowing and trusting the ontology developers	1.11	4	3.42
16	Knowing and trusting the organization or institute that is responsible for ontology development	1.11	3	3.38
17	The reputation of the ontology developer team, and/or institute in the domain	1.12	3	3.31
18	The number of times the ontology has been reused or cited (e.g. owl:imports, rdfs:seeAlso, daml:sameClassAs)	1.13	3	3.40
19	The flexibility of the Ontology (being easy to change) and the ontology developer team	1.14	4	3.41
20	The frequency of updates, maintenance, and submissions to the ontology	1.16	3	3.22
21	The popularity of the ontology in social media (e.g. in GitHub, Twitter, or LinkedIn)	1.16	2	2.28

(continued)

Table 1. (*continued*)

Rank	Metric	SD	Median	Mean
22	The popularity of the ontology in the community and among colleagues	1.17	4	3.51
23	The number of updates, maintenance, and submissions to the ontology	1.19	3	3.13
24	Availability of published(scientific) work about the ontology	1.19	4	3.56
25	The size of the ontology	1.19	3	3.02
26	The number of times the ontology has been reused or cited (e.g. owl:imports, rdfs:seeAlso, daml:sameClassAs)	1.19	3	3.08
27	The availability of funds for ontology update and maintenance	1.23	3	2.77
28	The popularity of the ontology on the web (number of times it has been viewed in different websites/applications across the web)	1.24	3	3.05
29	The reviews of the ontology (e.g. ratings)	1.25	3	3.03
30	The use of a method/methodology (e.g. NEON, METHONTOLOGY, or any other standard and development practice)	1.26	3	2.80
31	The Language that ontology is built in (e.g. OWL)	1.30	4	3.70

6 Discussion

Finding a set of metrics that can be used for ontology evaluation and selection for reuse has always been a critical research topic in the field of ontology engineering. As mentioned in the introduction and background sections, many different ontology evaluation approaches and metrics for quality assessment have been proposed in the literature. However, these studies suffer from some limitations; for example, they have not dealt with ranking and the importance of the quality metrics, especially the community related ones. Therefore, the focus of this research was on constructing a criteria-based evaluation approach and determining a set of metrics that ontologists and knowledge engineers tend to look at before selecting an ontology for reuse. This study also set out with the aim of assessing the importance of the quality metrics identified in the literature and in a previous phase of this research [34].

Previous studies have mostly been concerned with identification and application of a new set of quality metrics [38]. However, the key aim of this study was not only to identify the quality metrics used in the process of evaluating ontologies but also to find how important each of the quality metrics are. The results of this survey study indicate that the internal characteristics of ontologies are the first to assess before selecting them for reuse. However, some other aspects of ontologies such as availability of documentation, availability and accessibility of an ontology (e.g. license type), availability of metadata and provenance information, and also having information about the purpose that ontology is used/has been used for previously (e.g. annotation, sharing data, etc.) are as important as the quality of the internal components of ontologies.

Popularity, as one of the most defined and used term in the literature, refers to the role of community in the quality assessment process. As a part of this study, respondents were asked to rate the importance of six different popularity related metrics, four of which were previously mentioned in the literature. The results suggest that ontologists and knowledge engineers tend to care more about the popularity metrics, as identified by [34, 45], such as popularity of an ontology in the community and among colleagues (ranked 14 out of 31, when sorted by median) and the reputation of the ontology developer team, and/or institute in the domain (ranked 21 out of 31, when sorted by median) than the popularity related metrics that have been widely used in the literature and by selection systems. Metrics used in the literature include the number of times an ontology has been reused or cited [46, 47], the popularity of an ontology on the web [28, 31], the reviews of an ontology [42] and the popularity of an ontology on social media [48]; while having a lower median and mean, some of these metrics were ranked higher when the quality metrics were sorted by standard deviation. Standard Deviation shows a higher level of agreement among the survey respondents about the lower rank of those metrics.

7   Conclusion

This paper set out to explore and clarify the notions of quality and reuse in the field of ontology engineering and to identify the set of metrics that ontologists and knowledge engineers tend to consider when assessing the suitability of an ontology for reuse. It also investigated the potential role of community and social interactions in the process of ontology evaluation and selection for reuse.

The results of this study suggest that the process of ontology evaluation and selection for reuse does not only depend on different internal characteristics of ontologies, such as their content and structure, but it also depends on many other metadata and community related metrics. Moreover, the results of this study indicate that ontologists and knowledge engineers find some of the metrics identified in this research more important and useful, compared to the ones proposed by the previous studies. The proposed ranking based on the metrics identified in this research were also found helpful and useful in the ontology evaluation and selection process.

Overall, the results suggest that the metadata and social related metrics should be used by different selection systems in this field in order to facilitate and improve the process of evaluating and selecting ontologies for reuse and also, to provide a more comprehensive and accurate recommendation for reuse. Moreover, definition of some of the quality metrics used in the literature, e.g., popularity and how they are currently measured, may benefit from updating.

References

1. Bontas, E.P., Mochol, M., Tolksdorf, R.: Case studies on ontology reuse. In: Proceedings of the IKNOW05 International Conference on Knowledge Management, vol. 74, p. 345, June 2005

2. d'Aquin, M., et al.: What can be done with the semantic web? An overview of watson-based applications. In: CEUR Workshop Proceedings, vol. 426 (2008)
3. Fernández, M., Cantador, I., Castells, P.: CORE: a tool for collaborative ontology reuse and evaluation. In: CEUR Workshop Proceedings, vol. 179 (2006)
4. Gómez-Pérez, A.: Some ideas and examples to evaluate ontologies. In: 11th Conference on Artificial Intelligence for Applications Proceedings, pp. 299–305. IEEE, February 1995
5. Sabou, M., et al.: Ontology selection: ontology evaluation on the real semantic web. In: Vrandecic, D., et al. (ed.) 4th International EON Workshop, Evaluation of Ontologies for the Web, EON 2006, (CEUR Workshop Proceedings), Edinburgh, Scotland, UK (2006)
6. Talebpour, M., Sykora, M.D., Jackson, T.: Ontology selection for reuse: will it ever get easier?. In: 10th International Conference on Knowledge Engineering and Ontology Development, 18–20 September, Seville, Spain (2018)
7. Gómez-Pérez, A., Facultad, D.I.: Evaluation of taxonomic knowledge in ontologies and knowledge bases (1999). http://sern.ucalgary.ca/KSI/KAW/KAW99
8. Hlomani, H., Stacey, D.: Approaches, methods, metrics, measures, and subjectivity in ontology evaluation: a survey. Semant. Web J. 1, 1–11 (2014). http://www.semantic-web-journal.net/system/files/swj657.pdf
9. Suárez-Figueroa, M.C., Gómez-Pérez, A.: First attempt towards a standard glossary of ontology engineering terminology. In: 8th International Conference on Terminology and Knowledge Engineering, TKE 2008 (2008). http://www.neon-project.org/. Accessed 17 Feb 2019
10. Gómez-Pérez, A.: From knowledge based systems to knowledge sharing technology: evaluation and assessment, differences, pp. 1–15 (1994). http://oa.upm.es/6498/
11. Brank, J., Mladenic, D., Grobelnik, M.: Gold standard based ontology evaluation using instance assignment. In: Workshop on Evaluation of Ontologies for the Web, EON, May 2006
12. Yu, J., Thom, J.A., Tam, A.: Requirements-oriented methodology for evaluating ontologies. Inf. Syst. 34(8), 766–791 (2009)
13. Tartir, S., Arpinar, I.B., Sheth, A.P.: Ontological evaluation and validation. In: Poli, R., Healy, M., Kameas, A. (eds.) Theory and Applications of Ontology: Computer Applications. Springer, Dordrecht (2010). https://doi.org/10.1007/978-90-481-8847-5_5
14. Ning, H., Shihan, D.: Structure-based ontology evaluation. In: 2006 IEEE International Conference on e-Business Engineering, ICEBE 2006, pp. 132–137. IEEE, October 2006
15. Brank, J., Grobelnik, M., Mladenic, D.: A survey of ontology evaluation techniques. In: Conference on Data Mining and Data Warehouses, SiKDD 2005, Ljubljana, Slovenia, p. 4 (2005)
16. Arpinar, I.B., Giriloganathan, K., Aleman-Meza, B.: Ontology quality by detection of conflicts in metadata. In: Proceedings of the 4th International EON Workshop, May 2006
17. Bandeira, J., et al.: FOCA: a methodology for ontology evaluation, vol. 3, pp. 1–3 (2016). http://arxiv.org/abs/1612.03353
18. Maiga, G., Ddembe, W.: A flexible approach for user evaluation of biomedical ontologies (2008)
19. Brewster, C., et al.: Data driven ontology evaluation. In: 4th International Conference on Language Resources and Evaluation, LREC 2004, Lisbon, Portugal, p. 4 (2004)
20. Gangemi, A., Catenacci, C., Ciaramita, M., Lehmann, J.: Modelling Ontology Evaluation and Validation. In: Sure, Y., Domingue, J. (eds.) ESWC 2006. LNCS, vol. 4011, pp. 140–154. Springer, Heidelberg (2006). https://doi.org/10.1007/11762256_13
21. Obrst, L., Ceusters, W., Mani, I., Ray, S., Smith, B.: The evaluation of ontologies. In: Baker, C.J.O., Cheung, K.H. (eds.) Semantic Web, pp. 139–158. Springer, Boston (2007). https://doi.org/10.1007/978-0-387-48438-9_8

22. Yu, J., Thom, J.A., Tam, A.: Ontology evaluation using wikipedia categories for browsing. In: Proceedings of the Sixteenth ACM Conference on Information and Knowledge Management, pp. 223–232. ACM, November 2007

23. McDaniel, M., Storey, V.C., Sugumaran, V.: The role of community acceptance in assessing ontology quality. In: Métais, E., Meziane, F., Saraee, M., Sugumaran, V., Vadera, S. (eds.) NLDB 2016. LNCS, vol. 9612, pp. 24–36. Springer, Cham (2016). https://doi.org/10.1007/978-3-319-41754-7_3

24. Supekar, K.: A peer-review approach for ontology evaluation. In: 8th International Protege Conference, pp. 77–79, July 2005

25. Maedche, A., Staab, S.: Measuring similarity between ontologies. In: Gómez-Pérez, A., Benjamins, V.R. (eds.) EKAW 2002. LNCS (LNAI), vol. 2473, pp. 251–263. Springer, Heidelberg (2002). https://doi.org/10.1007/3-540-45810-7_24

26. Fahad, M., Qadir, M.A.: A framework for ontology evaluation. ICCS Suppl. **354**, 149–158 (2008)

27. Netzer, Y., Gabay, D., Adler, M., Goldberg, Y., Elhadad, M.: Ontology evaluation through text classification. In: Chen, L., et al. (eds.) APWeb/WAIM -2009. LNCS, vol. 5731, pp. 210–221. Springer, Heidelberg (2009). https://doi.org/10.1007/978-3-642-03996-6_20

28. Martínez-Romero, M., Jonquet, C., O'connor, M.J., Graybeal, J., Pazos, A., Musen, M.A.: NCBO ontology recommender 2.0: an enhanced approach for biomedical ontology recommendation, J. Biomed. Semant., **8**(1), 21 (2017)

29. Porzel, R., Malaka, R.: A task-based approach for ontology evaluation. In: ECAI Workshop on Ontology Learning and Population, Valencia, Spain, pp. 1–6, August 2004

30. Kehagias, D.D., Papadimitriou, I., Hois, J., Tzovaras, D., Bateman, J.: A methodological approach for ontology evaluation and refinement. In: ASK-IT Final Conference. June (Cit. on p.), pp. 1–13, June 2008

31. Burton-Jones, A., Storey, V.C., Sugumaran, V., Ahluwalia, P.: A semiotic metrics suite for assessing the quality of ontologies. Data Knowl. Eng. **55**(1), 84–102 (2005)

32. Buitelaar, P., Eigner, T., Declerck, T.: OntoSelect: a dynamic ontology library with support for ontology selection. In: Proceedings of the Demo Session at the International Semantic Web Conference (2004)

33. Buitelaar, P., Eigner, T.: Ontology search with the ontoselect ontology library. In: LREC, May 2008

34. Talebpour, M., Sykora, M. Jackson, T.W.: The role of community and social metrics in ontology evaluation: an interview study of ontology reuse. In: 9th International Joint Conference on Knowledge Discovery, Knowledge Engineering and Knowledge Management, pp. 119–127 (2017) https://doi.org/10.5220/0006589201190127

35. Fernández, M., Overbeeke, C., Sabou, M., Motta, E.: What makes a good ontology? A case-study in fine-grained knowledge reuse. In: Gómez-Pérez, A., Yu, Y., Ding, Y. (eds.) ASWC 2009. LNCS, vol. 5926, pp. 61–75. Springer, Heidelberg (2009). https://doi.org/10.1007/978-3-642-10871-6_5

36. Gill, T.: Metadata and the Web: Introduction to metadata, vol. 3, pp. 20–38. Getty publications, Los Angeles (2008)

37. Sowa, J.F.: Ontology, metadata, and semiotics. In: Ganter, B., Mineau, G.W. (eds.) ICCS-ConceptStruct 2000. LNCS (LNAI), vol. 1867, pp. 55–81. Springer, Heidelberg (2000). https://doi.org/10.1007/10722280_5

38. Lozano-Tello, A., Gómez-Pérez, A.: Ontometric: a method to choose the appropriate ontology. J. Database Manage. (JDM) **15**(2), 1–18 (2004)

39. Ding, L.: Swoogle: a search and metadata engine for the semantic web. In: Proceedings of the Thirteenth ACM International Conference on Information and Knowledge Management, pp. 652–659. ACM, November 2004

40. Hartmann, J., Sure, Y., Haase, P., Palma, R., Suarez-Figueroa, M.: OMV–ontology metadata vocabulary. In: ISWC, vol. 3729, November 2005
41. Matentzoglu, N., Malone, J., Mungall, C., Stevens, R.: MIRO: guidelines for minimum information for the reporting of an ontology. J. Biomed. Semant. **9**(1), 6 (2018)
42. Lewen, H., d'Aquin, M.: Extending open rating systems for ontology ranking and reuse. In: Cimiano, P., Pinto, H.S. (eds.) EKAW 2010. LNCS (LNAI), vol. 6317, pp. 441–450. Springer, Heidelberg (2010). https://doi.org/10.1007/978-3-642-16438-5_34
43. Lewen, H., Supekar, K., Noy, N.F., Musen, M.A.: Topic-specific trust and open rating systems: an approach for ontology evaluation. In; Workshop on Evaluation of Ontologies for the Web, May 2006
44. Morse, J.M.: Mixed Method Design: Principles and Procedures. Routledge, London (2016)
45. Talebpour, M., Sykora, M., Jackson, T.: Social and community related themes in ontology evaluation: findings from an interview study. In: Fred, A., et al. (eds.) IC3K 2017. CCIS, vol. 976, pp. 320–336. Springer, Cham (2019). https://doi.org/10.1007/978-3-030-15640-4_16
46. Supekar, K., Patel, C., Lee, Y., Characterizing Quality of Knowledge on Semantic Web. In: FLAIRS Conference, pp. 472–478, May 2004
47. Wang, X., Guo, L., Fang, J.: Automated ontology selection based on description logic. In: Proceedings 2008 12th International Conference on Computer Supported Cooperative Work in Design, CSCWD, vol. 1, pp. 482–487 (2008)
48. Martínez-Romero, M., Vázquez-Naya, J.M., Pereira, J., Pazos, A.: BiOSS: a system for biomedical ontology selection. Comput. Methods Programs Biomed. **114**(1), 125–140 (2014)

Towards a Term Clustering Framework
for Modular Ontology Learning

Ziwei Xu[1(✉)], Mounira Harzallah[1(✉)], Fabrice Guillet[1(✉)], and Ryutaro Ichise[2(✉)]

[1] LS2N, Ecole Polytechnique de l'Université de Nantes, 44300 Nantes, France
{ziwei.xu,mounira.harzallah,Fabrice.Guillet}@univ-nantes.fr
[2] National Institute of Informatics, Tokyo 101-8430, Japan
ichise@nii.ac.jp

Abstract. This paper aims to analyze and adopt the term clustering method for building a modular ontology according to its core ontology. The acquisition of semantic knowledge focuses on noun phrase appearing with the same syntactic roles in relation to a verb or its preposition combination in a sentence. The construction of this co-occurrence matrix from context helps to build feature space of noun phrases, which is then transformed to several encoding representations including feature selection and dimensionality reduction. In addition, word embedding techniques are also presented as feature representation. These representations are clustered respectively with K-Means, K-Medoids, Affinity Propagation, DBscan and co-clustering algorithms. The feature representation and clustering methods constitute the major sections of term clustering frameworks. Due to the randomness of clustering approaches, iteration efforts are adopted to find the optimal parameter and provide convinced value for evaluation. The DBscan and affinity propagation show their outstanding effectiveness for term clustering and NMF encoding technique and word embedding representation are salient by its promising facilities in feature compression.

Keywords: Text mining · Feature extraction · Ontology learning · Term clustering

1 Introduction

Ontology building is a complex process composed of several tasks: term or concept acquisition, concept formation, taxonomy definition, ad-hoc relation definition, axiom definition [17]. The ever-increasing access to textual sources has motivated the development of ontology learning approaches based on techniques of different fields, like natural language processing, data mining and machine learning. Many works are focused on the taxonomy definition and more especially on the hypernym relation extraction. A term t1 is a hypernym of a term t2 if the former categorizes the later. This relation is also known as a terminological $is - a$ relation. For its extraction from texts, several approaches based on Harris' distributional hypothesis are proposed. This hypothesis states that words/terms in the same context can have similar meanings [27]. Then each term can be represented by a numeric vector in a vector space by taking into account the context, with different word embedding techniques (e.g. co-occurrence matrix, word2vec, NMF, etc.)

© Springer Nature Switzerland AG 2020
A. Fred et al. (Eds.): IC3K 2018, CCIS 1222, pp. 178–201, 2020.
https://doi.org/10.1007/978-3-030-49559-6_9

Based on the geometric similarity in a vector space, non-supervised methods are applied for term clustering. Due to the concerns about the semantic relation between terms upon the construction of vector space, each cluster is expected to include semantically similar terms (i.e. synonyms or related by the hypernym relation) or semantically connected terms.

In case that the semantic meaning of clusters could not match any existing concepts of ontology, these clusters are not suitable for ontology building. Moreover, these approaches may have poor performance due to the sparsity of the co-occurrence matrix [4]. Dimensionality reduction becomes a crucial issue. It can be performed by feature selection. In the statistical stage, feature selection could be achieved by the frequency of terms or the weighting of Tf-Idf (term frequency-inverse document frequency).

Clustering terms under the core concepts of ontology are demonstrated to be productive to build a modular ontology [33]. A core ontology of a domain is a basic and minimal ontology composed only of the minimal concepts (i.e core concepts) and the principal relations between them that allow defining the other concepts of the domain [5,40]. This step (i.e. term clustering under core concepts) is the first stage towards a taxonomy definition. Indeed, a term of each cluster is expected to be synonym or hyponym of the core concept that corresponds to its cluster. Later, inside of each cluster, other hypernym relations between terms have to be extracted.

In this paper, we will group terms under core concepts through clustering algorithms and to evaluate these clustered terms whether they are synonym, hypernym or semantically close to core concepts. Accordingly, we define and evaluate several frameworks for term clustering by varying feature representations (i.e. co-occurrence representation, weighted co-occurrence representation, NMF representation, and word embedding representation) and clustering techniques(i.e. k-means, k-medoids, affinity propagation, DBscan and co-clustering). We present the ontology building steps from core ontology in Sect. 2. The related works are discussed in terms of term clustering for ontology building in Sect. 3. We then describe the corpus and the pre-processing steps served for feature representation in Sect. 4. Sequentially, we discuss the parameters setting of these five clustering techniques, analysis their results. Finally, we conclude with the term clustering techniques recommendation for ontology building purpose.

The main differences between this paper and previous work [52] can be summarized regarding to the extension of content and the augmentation of experiments. We progressively describe the ontology building procedures from 'core ontology' to 'modular ontology', and to our proposed ontology in Sect. 2. Furthermore, we detail the interesting clustering methods about their advantages and disadvantages and show their utility over ontology building in previous work. In terms of experiments, we extend our operation with three additional clustering techniques: k-medoids, DBscan and co-clustering, and update the existing experiments with a much enlarged gold standard. Ultimately, five different clustering techniques are compared together with their fresh results in order to offer a broader comparison upon term clustering techniques.

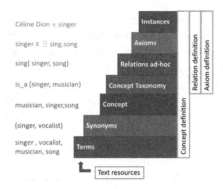

Fig. 1. The ontology learning cake from [3] with modification.

2 Ontology Building

Ontology building from text could be achieved by various approaches, it could be performed manually, automatically or semi-automatically. During the ontology construction procedures, respecting to the sequence of manipulation, ontology building is able to be divided into the bottom-up approach, top-down approach, and mixed approach. However, the step of human validation is irreplaceable at the end of ontology building, to ensure the accuracy of knowledge representation in the constructed ontology.

Ontology conceptualization is the core part of ontology building. It can be simplified into this "ontology learning layer cake" [3] in Fig. 1. As shown in this cake, starting with terms from text, several steps are followed to explore concepts and their corresponding relations. For example, in the music domain, the terms 'singer', 'vocalist', 'musician' and 'song' are extracted. Then, term synonyms are identified and grouped to form concepts (e.g. the synonyms terms 'singer' and 'vocalist' are grouped and constitute the concept). From these isolated terms, we can find their synonyms. At the same time, we can infer the relations between them. It could be the simple 'is-a relation' or more complex 'ad-hoc relation'. Once enough relations are dug out, it is interesting to find the axioms between these relations. In our approach, we concentrate on the bottom three steps, from term extraction to synonyms identification and to concept definition. From these stages, we are allowed to cluster the extracted terms to form concepts where each cluster includes synonyms or hypernyms of core concepts. Then within each cluster, further synonym or is-a relations between terms of the same cluster can be extracted.

2.1 Core Ontology

To steer the learning process of a domain ontology, we benefit from a domain core ontology. A core ontology of a domain is the basic and minimal concepts (i.e. core concepts) and the principle relations between them that allow defining the other concepts of the domain [5,21,38]. Scherp [46] considers that a core ontology should be characterized by a high degree of axiomatization and formal precision. Nevertheless, it could be presented by a concept taxonomy structure with is-a relation as Fig. 2 shows.

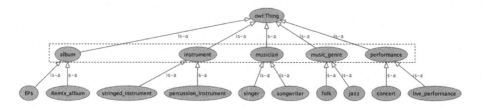

Fig. 2. The core ontology and its sub concepts.

Furthermore, in a core ontology, generally, each core concept (except 'Thing') represents (conceptualize) a sub-domain (a topic) of the ontology domain and it could be specialized on sub-concepts in order to define the sub-domains (see Fig. 3).

A core ontology could be considered as an upper ontology (i.e. top-level ontology or foundation ontology [5]) of domain ontology, which provides the high possibilities to be reused for extensive purpose. In most cases, the core ontology is predefined by a domain expert, in order to provide guidelines in terms of domain ontology construction.

On the basis of core ontology, Gruber [25] suggests using core ontology of a domain to build domain ontology. Additionally, several works define or reuse a core ontology to identify and further define the domain concepts by specialization. For instance, on the one hand, almost all OBOs (Open Biomedical Ontologies) have been originated by importing the BFO (Basic Formal Ontology) and the RO (Relation Ontology); Opdhal et al. [39] used BWW (Bunge Wand Weber) ontology to build the UEML ontology; Chulyadyo et al. [7] improved the ontology flatness by inferring hypernym relation between extracted terms and core concepts. On the other hand, some works map a core ontology to a given domain ontology, so as to better define the concepts of the domain and superimpose a structure of one domain ontology. For example, Deprès et al. [11] map the Core Legal Ontology (CLO) to legal Ontologies; Burita et al. [5] map NEC (Network Enabled Capabilities) core ontology to the NEC domain ontology.

2.2   Modular Ontology

Modular ontology is considered as a major topic to facilitate and simplify the ontology engineering process in the field of formal ontology developments [29]. If it is required to alter the structure of the ontology, we can just remove, add or enrich the target modules in modular ontology, without interference to other remaining parts of ontology. Moreover, the modular representations are easier to understand, reason with, extend and reuse [24]. Therefore, using these representations tends to reduce the complexity of designing and to facilitate ontology reasoning, development, and integration [13].

Gangemi [22] and Kutz [33] suggest to map core ontology to domain ontology for improving modularity. On this basis of core ontology, it is interesting to obtain a well-structured taxonomy where each sub-domain is defined by a separate module (Fig. 3). Then it becomes easier to define a modular regarding each core concept that represents its sub-domain. The constituted several main topics (i.e. core concepts) in a specific domain will lead the extension of sub-concepts (bottom layer in Fig. 3).

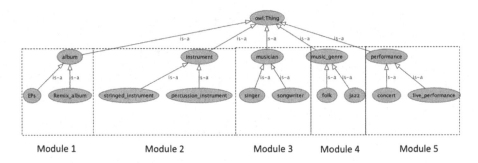

Fig. 3. The domain modular ontology.

2.3 Our Target Ontology

Concisely, we aim to build modular ontology from text using term clustering derived by core ontology. Following the top-down approaches from the core ontology to modular ontology in order to build an ontology, we would like to enrich each module by concepts/terms, through extracting terms and clustering them where each cluster should correspond to the terms/concepts of a module. We start by analysing term clustering frameworks and comparing their suitability to put terms semantically close to a core concept (i.e. synomym or hypernym terms of a core concept) in the same cluster. For that, it is required to evaluate whether the resulted clusters are close to a manual term classification.

In our work, a clustering framework concerning NPs as terms and it depends of three main components: 1) feature representation approaches, 2) dimension reduction techniques, 3) and clustering algorithms. These components allow to be substituted by the different related techniques, which brings the high flexibility for the entire term clustering framework.

3   Related Work

3.1   Feature Representations

In the field of knowledge acquisition from text, it is apparent that the functional entities of sentences and their clauses constitute the dominant linguistic elements for syntagmatic information collection. Cimiano [9] describe the local context by extracting triples of nouns, their syntactic roles, and co-occurred verbs. They consider only verb/object relations, so as to emphasize partial features of terms working as an object by a conditional probability measure, which calculate the conditional probability that a certain term appears as head of a certain argument position of a verb. Similarly, Jiang [31] and Riosalvarado [45] formed the triple term structure of noun phrases and verbs, in the shape as subject of the noun, verb, the object of the noun. Moreover, ASIUM [16] acquires semantic knowledge from the following canonical syntactic frames which include the verb, and their preposition or syntactic roles and the headword of noun phrases:

$$< to\,verb >\quad ((< preposition > | < syntactic\,role >)\quad < headword >)$$

For examples, the instantiated syntactic frame of the clause, "Bart travels by a huge boat", we get:

$$< to\ travel > \quad < subject > \quad < \mathbf{Bart} >$$

$$< by > \quad < \mathbf{boat} >$$

It is evident that their focus is based on the dependency between the verb (i.e. 'to travel') and features of the verb (i.e. 'Bart' with syntactic roles 'subject'; 'boat' with preposition 'by'). Except for the extraction of nouns and verbs, some work consider the involvement of adjectives as well, which would be considered as keywords of ontology learning [43,50].

Besides syntactic dependency, one recent work [19] extracts co-occurring couples of entities and present their semantic relations with pattern-based representation. To interpret these appearances, terms (entities) are presented by vectors with the frequent sequential pattern as components. Then pattern-based feature space is constructed for relation discovery. Moreover, according to Word2vec [36], a term is statistically encoded with analogies from its appearance in a different context, where the similarity of encoding vectors reflect the semantic relations between terms.

3.2 Dimensionality Reduction Techniques

After the choice of the feature representation and the building of term-feature matrix, often we have to deal with matrix sparsity problem using dimensionality reduction techniques. Church et al. [8] proposed to apply PMI weighting (pointwise mutual information) to reduce bias in rare contexts, in which values below 0 are replaced by 0. Tf-Idf (term frequency-inverse document frequency) also contribute to weight terms by their specificity to documents. The computational complexity grows exponentially with the size of the lattice, where NMF (non-Negative Matrix Factorization) [34] is dedicated to solving the dimensionality reduction problem by performing feature compression.

3.3 Clustering Techniques

K-Means. The most typical clustering technique is k-means, which starts with randomly selected centroids and performs iterative calculations to optimize the positions of the centroids for partition purpose [28]. It is easy to be implemented and widely used as a simple clustering solution. However, its drawbacks are also evident that 1) k-means is quite sensitive to the initial set of seeds; 2) its performance could be strongly impacted by the noisy elements. Despite that, k-means is always regarded as the baseline to compare with other clustering algorithms.

K-Medoids. Similar to k-means clustering algorithm, k-medoids also attempts to minimize the distance between centroids. In contrast to k-means, k-medoids choose the starting centroids as priori before calculation [32]. K-medoids provides many favorable properties: 1) it presents no limitations on attributes types, which means it is capable of numerical, categorical and binary attributes. 2) the choice of medoids is dictated by the location of a predominant fraction of points inside a cluster and, therefore, it is lesser sensitive to the presence of outliers. Briefly, it is more robust to noise and outliers as compared to k-means. However, this algorithm suffers from the negative effects of unsuitable initial seeds, because it does not allow reassigning seeds while changing mean values. Nevertheless, it could be a preferable clustering algorithm for us once we acknowledge the proper starting seed for each cluster.

Affinity Propagation. Like k-medoids, affinity propagation clustering algorithm finds centroids to represent their located clusters during iterations. Differ from the dissimilar distance in k-medoids, affinity propagation uses graph distance that performs in a 'message passing' way between data points [18]. With this approach, 1) it is not required to determine the number of clusters in advance and 2) the centroid of each cluster is specified after calculation, which turns out to be helpful for cluster interpretation. However, this algorithm is not friendly with big datasets because the time complexity of calculation increases dramatically along with the amount of clustered elements. Nevertheless, affinity propagation is still interesting as clustering algorithm for normal-size datasets.

DBscan. Despite those distance-based clustering methods, DBscan (Density-based spatial clustering of applications with noise) [15] is distinguished as a density-based clustering method. It groups together closely packed points and marks the low-density points as outlier points, in order to accentuate the high-density points into clusters and get rid of the negative impacts of outliers. DBscan clustering algorithm has some special benefits: 1) it is capable to find arbitrarily shaped clusters, because of the reduced single-link effect (different clusters being connected by a thin line of points) 2) no demand to specify the number of clusters as that of affinity propagation. In opposite, DBscan allows for points to be part of more than one cluster, which might induce overlapping between clusters. It requires the knowledge of domain expert during the selection of key parameters, such as the minimum number of points required to form a dense region (i.e. minPts) and the radius of a neighborhood with respect to some points (i.e. eps). It is desirable to apply DBscan clustering algorithm even with several pre-experiments for the selection of parameter.

Co-Clustering. In co-clustering algorithm (also called bi-clustering, block clustering), not only the targets but also the features of the targets can be clustered simultaneously, which preserves the existing relation between targets and their features. We are interested in the bi-clustering over contingency table [23]. Typically, the input matrix would be arranged as a two-way contingency table. This algorithm shows the encouraging performance on the contingency outcomes. The co-clustering has practical importance in gene research and also document classification. The resulted co-clusters are expected to overlap with each other, where these overlaps themselves are often of interest. It has two major shortcomings: 1) the problem of local optimization to each co-cluster individually; 2) the lack of a well-defined global objective during each iterations [40]. Despite these facts, the co-clustering algorithm is attractive because it takes into account the relation between clustered elements and the features of them.

In previous work, Clustering techniques have shown their favorable properties in terms of ontology learning. The K-means clustering algorithm was implemented to separate the domain knowledge for the purpose of domain ontology learning [47]. One adaptive k-medoids clustering method [14]could be applied to identify clusters by these medoids, which are representing the concepts of ontology from the knowledge database. Except for the typical clustering algorithm, there are many calculation approaches used for clustering purpose. The Weka data mining tool [51] helps to implement many algorithms for clustering purposes, such as viz., EM, Farthest First and k-Means. The previous research showed that the Farthest First clustering technique yielded rather better performance than the others in the attempt of concept clustering. The Farthest-First [37] is a variant of K-Means that differs in the initial centroid assignment, which places the cluster center at the point furthest from the existing centers. On the other hand, Hao [26] aimed to construct a hierarchy of ontology by using EM algorithm [10] to cluster the keywords from domain corpus. EM computes the distribution of parameters for each cluster by the maximum likelihood criteria. Hao [26] implemented EM several times to select the appropriate number of clusters and then summarized the subject of the cluster for the convenience of hierarchy construction and organization.

Briefly, many clustering algorithms have participated in the procedures of ontology learning. In previous work, the output of automatic term clustering for ontology building is hard to recognize the meaning of each cluster and label it relating to ontology domain. In the same time, the quality of clusters is not satisfying. In our work, our approach is based on a core ontology and aims at obtaining clusters, where each one includes terms that are synonyms, hypernyms of a core concept or strongly related to it. Meanwhile, little effort has been done in term clustering for ontology learning using core ontology.

4 Frameworks Comparison Approach

For the purpose of ontology building, we established a workflow for the comparison of approaches of term. The workflow is comprised of 5 stages to gradually transform corpus into the dedicated clusters of terms. The corpus (stage 1) provides resources for relation extraction of terms (stage 2). It brings two basic feature representations, co-occurrence representation and word embedding representation. With respect to feature transformation and dimension reduction techniques, the two initial features could be transformed into 4 extensive feature representations (stage 3). Based on those representations of terms, various clustering algorithms are employed to gather together the semantic similar terms (stage 4). Finally, the quality of clusters is assessed according to evaluation indices (stage 5).

4.1 Corpus Selection

With the aim of term clustering experiments, we choose two corpora in different domains: music domain and ontology learning domain. Each corpus possess the gold standard, which includes a set of extracted terms that are classified manually over the core concepts of the domain.

Music Corpus [6], is composed of 100M-word documents, includes Amazon reviews, music biographies and Wikipedia pages about theory and music genres.

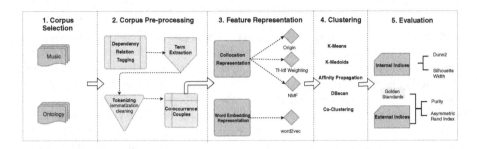

Fig. 4. The term clustering workflow. Adapted from Xu et al. [52].

Table 1. The corpus size and statistics.

Corpus	# Docs	Sampling	# Sentences	# Occurrence	# Unique tokens	$\frac{\#tokens}{docs}$	# Docs containing CC	$\frac{\#CCs}{docs}$
Music	105,000	2,000	28,286	703,519	51,327	351	1,879	4.9
Ontology	16	16	4,901	112,628	7,700	7,040	16	198.7

We deliberately selected 2000 documents from 105,000 documents, ensuring that the chosen content includes the great proportion of terms in the predefined gold standards. The Ontology Learning Corpus comprises of 16 scientific articles in the domain of ontology learning. As shown in Table 1, it presents the statistics of the number of documents, the number of documents after sampling, the number of sentences, the occurrence of tokens, the number of unique tokens, the number of tokens divided by the number of sampled documents, the number of documents containing a core concept(CC) and the number of core concepts(CCs) divided by the number of sampled documents. These two corpora are different in terms of domain and the amounts of docs, however, their evident contrast could help researchers to figure out whether it exists a relation between corpus and term clustering techniques.

The aforementioned core concepts are predefined for each domain in the gold standard. As shown in Table 2, the gold standard of Music Corpus is composed of 4,382 relevant terms (i.e nouns relevant for the music domain) labeled with one of the core concepts of music domain, while in the gold standard of Ontology Learning Corpus, 2953 terms (as nouns) are labeled with one of the core concepts of the ontology learning domain.

4.2   Corpus Pre-processing

Considering that only semantic similar terms are interesting to be clustered, it turns to be essential to extract the relations between terms from their context. Regarding to the utility of syntactic roles, the skeleton of a sentence is supposed to comprise the subject, the object and their related verb. In other words, terms with important syntactic roles are assumed to cover the most descriptive information in a sentence. Thus noun phrases (NP), acting as subject or object, are worth to be highlighted in concept extraction, while their contextual components, i.e. verbs, could present the concrete connection between NPs.

Table 2. The gold standard.

Corpus	# Core concepts	# Terms	Labels of core concepts
Music	5	4,382	Album, Musician, Music Genre, Instruments, Performance
Ontology Learning	8	2,953	Component, Technique, Ontology, Domain, Tool, User, Step, Resource

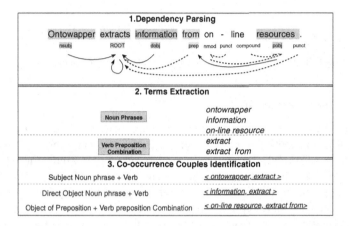

Fig. 5. The instantiated co-occurrence couples extraction. Adapted from Xu et al. [52].

In the procedure of relation tuples extraction based on dependency tagging, as shown in the stage 2 of Fig. 4, syntactic information is extracted to help identify NPs acting as a subject or object and their co-occurred verbs. In our experiment, we propose to use spaCy [48] as a parser tool. It could decompose an entire typical syntactic tree into structured information, which shows the overwhelming convenience in post-processing, comparing to other parser tools, such as cleanNLP [2] and coreNLP [35].

To explain how noun phrases (NPs) with subject and object role and verb-preposition combinations (VPCs) are extracted during the POS tagging, we provide an instance about co-occurrence couples extraction in Fig. 5. After the tokenization of a sentence, tokens will be cleaned and lemmatized. Following the pre-processing steps, we start with the recognition of skeleton terms. As shown in the top of Fig. 5, terms in a sentence are presented with dependency relation, where the shaded terms have been tagged as subject (nsubj), ROOT and object (dobj, pobj). The subject ('ontowrapper') and direct object ('information') point to the ROOT ('extract') with the solid lines, while the proposition object ('on-line resource') indirectly points to ROOT ('extract from') with the relay of dashed lines and solid lines. As for the non-skeleton dependency, they are connected in dashed lines. Furthermore, we need to pay attention to the distinction between the passive and active sentences. To simplify the composition of sentences, it is practical to record passive subject (nsubjpass) as direct object (dobj). With the help of head pointers, noun phrases (NPs) and verb-preposition combinations (VPCs) could be gathered and extracted in the compound format. Finally, the pairs of ROOT (verbs) and skeleton terms are tagged and recorded as the reconstruction resource taking the place of the raw corpus.

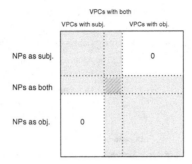

Fig. 6. The merged co-occurrenc matrix. Adapted from Xu et al. [52].

4.3   Feature Representation

After the pre-processing, the feature representation stage are following as shown in Fig. 4. We plant to experiment with 5 distinct strategies to build the word representation in a scalar vector space where each word is encoded as a numeric tuple/vector. We begins with two disparate approaches to build the basic feature representations. One of the fundamental vector spaces takes advantage of the frequency of NPs-VPCs pairs, while another feature representation uses the entire context to acquire the word embedding. They differ from each other in the range of terms co-location, for which the fundamental method facilitates syntactic roles for co-occurrence pairs within a sentence, while the word embedding method takes into account a certain length of context of all appearance places of a term. Additionally, to tackle the sparseness problem of numeric vectors, dimensionality reduction techniques are employed to condense feature representation.

Co-Occurrence Representation. To build up the co-occurrence representation, the aforementioned pairs are extracted and transformed into a co-occurrence frequency matrix, where VPCs are considered as the features of NPs. Since we notice that it exists a big gap in terms of the syntactic functionality between subject and object, their representation are supposed to be separated into different co-occurrence pairs, named subject co-occurrence and object co-occurrence.

As a ground truth, one kind of co-occurrence pairs, either subject or object, could only convey the partial linguistic knowledge from a sentence. It is profitable to deliberately combine subject and object co-occurrence pairs, with the intention of an entire coverage of context. Thus, we propose the merged co-occurrence matrix (in Fig. 6). In this model, we differentiate NPs and VPCs into 'pure subject', 'pure object' and common part. The common part means NPs and VPCs appear in both subject and object. On the whole, the merged matrix comprises 9 sub-parts, where the non-existing pairs present to be all zero (blank rectangles) and the 'pure pairs' (subject or object) present their frequency respectively in two blue rectangles. Common couples (shaded rectangles), the overlaps between subject rectangle and object rectangle, are filled with the accumulative frequency of subject pairs and object pairs. From any objective perspective, as long as subject and object co-occurrence pairs join together, the merged matrix

Table 3. The dimensionality reduction after the threshold. Adapted from Xu et al. [52].

	#NPs			#VPCs			Reduction with Frequency		Reduction with Tf-Idf	
							#NPs	#VPCs	#NPs	#VPCs
Corpus	subj.	obj.	both	subj.	obj.	both	Threshold δ_1:Summation of frequency		Threshold δ_2:Summation of value	
Music	3,138	7,272	1,560	254	3,054	532	$\delta_1 > 8$		$\delta_2 > 7$	
							573	660	582	456
Ontology	401	1,643	281	80	889	219	$\delta_1 > 3$		$\delta_2 > 4$	
							602	505	563	502

theoretically encompasses complete linguistic information. Hence, this merged model will work as a primary representation in the following part.

Dimensionality Reduction. The sparseness of a merged co-occurrence matrix becomes a significant issue, where the dimension reduction technique can be applied to solve it. For a sparse matrix, the reduction over row and column are both required to decrease the noise effect. In Table 3, we apply with the frequency-based thresholds to eliminate the most common and rare NPs and VPCs. On the right hand, Tf-Idf encoding representation also provides bi-directional selection respecting to NPs and their tf-df features.

– **Weighted Co-occurrence Representation.** Based on the co-occurrence representation, we would like to weight values to differentiate the importance of co-occurrence pairs. Tf-Idf, is designed with this discriminative purpose. Basically, this algorithm could extract the most descriptive terms from documents, which is able to be extended to weight the most significant NPs to specific VPCs, instead of documents. With certain thresholds in rows and columns, only prominent NPs and their co-occurred VPCs are kept at last. Owing to the derivation of Tf-Idf, the close connected NPs and VPCs are preserved through the thresholds in Table 3 so that the weighted co-occurrence matrix gets refined from the reduced dimensionality.
– **NMF Co-occurrence Representation.** Term co-occurrences could be separated into 3 levels according to the identity of words in context [20]. In the first-order co-occurrence, terms appear together in the identical context. As for two terms are associated by means of second-order co-occurrence, they share at least one-word context and have strong syntactic relations. Besides, terms do not co-occur in context with the same words but between words that can be related through indirect co-occurrences, namely third (higher) order co-occurrence. To capture those co-occurrences, NMF [34] is applied to condense the isolated VPCs into some encoded features. In this way, NPs with indirect co-occurrence are presented in the new dense feature space. We set the number of features to be 100 during experiments.

Word Embedding Representation. On the basis of contextual information, it allows to build feature vectors that are adapted for semantic similarity tasks. Word embedding representation was trained using word2vec [36] algorithm under the skip-gram model. In the local aspect, terms can be represented by vectors of its co-located words within

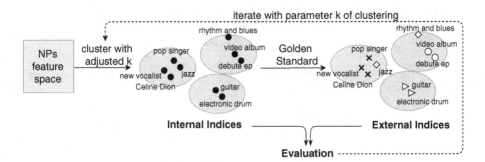

Fig. 7. The utility of gold standard. Adapted from Xu et al. [52]. Note: The symbol 'black dots' in green circle represent the unlabeled terms, on the right hand, the 'cross', 'diamond', 'circle' and 'triangle' symbols in green circles show that the terms are marked with different labels. (Color figure online)

certain window size, called co-locating vectors. The sum of co-locating vectors around the appearance place of a term constitutes the context vectors. In the global aspect, the sum of context vectors at all appearance places of a term gives the construction of word vectors. It integrates all the contextual features of a word and presents by the encoded similarity statistically. One of the advantages of word2vec is that it achieves dimension reduction purposes by indicating the required amount of features. To be comparable with NMF encoding technique, the number of features with word2vec is also given by 100.

4.4 The Clustering over Feature Representation

Heretofore, we have introduced all the alternative algorithms in the term clustering workflow, involving four different feature representations and five diverse clustering approaches. The composition of these alternatives is under interests for term clustering exploration, this effort assists to present a clear comprehension for the dominant possibilities of term clustering workflows.

In this stage, we analysis the combination of the different feature representation and clustering algorithms. The four feature representations have various concerns about relations between terms. As we discussed in previous section, the *co-occurrence representation* offers the co-occurrence relation between NPs and VPCs; the *weighted co-occurrence representation* discriminates the principle co-occurrence from the rare or extreme frequent pairs of NPs and VPCs; the *NMF co-occurrence representation* takes into account the indirect co-occurrence of pairs by encoded features; the *word embedding representation* emphasizes the co-occurrence within certain windows in sentences. These distinct features would generate different compactness with these five clustering algorithms, including *k-means*, *k-medoids*, *affinity propagation*, *DBscan* and *co-clustering*.

4.5 Evaluation Indices

A large number of indices provide possibilities to assess the clustering quality [1]. In order to simplify the discrimination process, we select two distinct indices respectively for internal evaluation and external evaluation.

Indices for Internal Evaluation. To evaluate the observations that are aggregated into clusters, one intuitive approach is to measure their compactness and separateness by their geometric similarity. Without any assistance of extra knowledge, the cluster could be evaluated with some distance-based indices, given the name as the internal evaluation. In Fig. 7, after applying the clustering algorithm over one of the NPs feature spaces, the terms could be directly evaluated by internal indices. However, in this situation, the clusters are difficult to be labeled with some human understandable concepts.

Silhouette width [44] and adjusted Dunn Index are chosen as indices of internal evaluation. Silhouette method specifies how well each observation lies within its cluster.

$$s(i) = \frac{b(i) - a(i)}{max(a(i), b(i))} \tag{1}$$

In Eq. 1, i represents one observation in clusters, $a(i)$ represents average dissimilarity between i and all other observations of the cluster to which i belongs. For each cluster C, $d(i, C)$ denotes average dissimilarity of i to all observations of C. In this basis, $b(i)$ is set by the smallest $d(i, C)$ and can be considered as the dissimilarity between an observation i and its "neighbor" cluster. A high average silhouette width indicates a good clustering according to features.

Adjusted Dunn Index proposed by Pal and Biswas [41] overcomes the presence of noise comparing to original Dunn Index [12]. In general, they are both dedicated to the identification of "compact and well-separated clusters". Higher values are preferred, which shows a good performance of compactness. Notably, the Dunn Index family does not exhibit any trend with respect to the number of clusters, of which this property is exceedingly welcomed since the number of clusters varies in different iterations.

Indices for External Evaluation. In the case of external evaluation, the indices are slightly different from the former because of the use of a gold standard. In the external indices section of Fig. 7, the terms are marked with different labels by the classes of gold standard, which becomes human interpretable. For instance, in the displaying of clusters, the left cluster includes terms as 'pop singer', 'new vocalist', 'Celine Dion' and 'jazz'. With the assistance of labels, it is straightforward to explain that this cluster is composed of 75% musician class and 25% music genre class. The top-right cluster is constituted by 33% music genre class and 66% album class. The bottom-right cluster is labeled with 100% instruments class. Further, in the approach of external evaluation, the clusters are capable to be label by classes from external evaluation, which provides the possibility for cluster labelling issues. According to the expected core concept classes, Purity and Asymmetric Rand Index are representative of clustering quality measurement.

Purity is one of the most simple and widely used indices. Each cluster firstly is assigned with a label that is most frequent, according to the gold standard, then this assignment is calculated by counting the number of correctly assigned elements dividing by all elements. High purity is easy to achieve when the number of clusters is large, because the number of terms in each cluster will significantly decease and the percentage of terms with the same label probably increases. A larger amount of clusters may refine the branches of structure in ontology building, however, it incurs complexity to label clusters with core concepts, performing as the first step of ontology learning. Thus we could not use only purity to trade off the quality of clustering against the number of clusters.

The Asymmetric Rand Index proposed by Hubert and Arabie [30] is also considered, for which it provides the comparison between the result of a classification and a correct classification. This index is developed from the idea of typical Rand Index (RI). Instead of counting single observation, the typical Rand Index (RI) counts the correctly classified pairs of observations. Then the rand index [42] is calculated by:

$$RI = \frac{a+b}{\binom{n}{2}}, \tag{2}$$

where $\binom{n}{2}$ is the number of un-ordered pairs in a sets of n observations. The a in the formula refers to the number of times that the pair of observation belongs to the same classification but exists in different clusters and the b indicates the opposite way, in which a pair belongs to different classification and exists in different clusters. Hence RI depends on both, the number of clusters and the number of observations [49].

However, we cannot get the lowest value (e.g. zero) for two random partitions by typical Rand Index. Thus Hubert and Arabie [30] made a modification with the null hypothesis, which means the value of Adjusted Rand Index (ARI) is expected to under the null hypothesis, with 0 for independent clustering and 1 for identical clustering. The Adjusted Rand Index (ARI) [30] is defined as follows:

$$ARI = \frac{\sum_{i=1}^{k} \sum_{j=1}^{l} \binom{m_{i,j}}{2} - t_3}{\frac{1}{2}(t_1 + t_2) - t_3}, \tag{3}$$

where $t_1 = \sum_{i=1}^{k} \binom{|C_i|}{2}$, $t_2 = \sum_{j=1}^{l} \binom{|C'_j|}{2}$, $t_3 = \frac{2t_1 t_2}{n(n-1)}$. In general, the i and j represents the cluster i and classification j. The m_{ij} indicates the number of observations in cluster i matching to classification j. The $|C_i|$ and $|C'_j|$ represent the total number of observations for each cluster i or for each classification j, respectively.

Additionally, ARI allows that the number of clustering can be different with the number of classification of gold standard. During experiments, the number of partitions are always larger than that of classification from gold standard, while the application of Asymmetric Rand Index allows for a more accurate analysis.

5   Experiment Settings and Evaluation

However, before the examination of the combination between clustering algorithms and feature representations, it is inevitable to preset the parameters regarding clustering methods. How to choose the optimal number of clusters? And is it valuable to choose the number of clusters according to core concepts? These puzzles would be tackled in the following subsections. On the grounds of these prepared settings, the related experiments are executed to provide the evaluation for each examination. The analysis of those outcomes will bring in the recommendation about the alternative algorithms for term clustering.

Table 4. The Parameters of 5 clustering algorithm.

Clustering	Similarity measure	R library	Function	k selection	Parameter selection	Other parameters
k-means	cosine	stats	kmeans()	2–50	–	–
k-medoids	cosine	cluster	pam()	2–50	–	medoids
Affinity propagation	cosine	apcluster	apclusterK()	2–50	–	maxits=2000;convits=200
DBscan	cosine	fpc	dbscan()	–	dbscan::kNNdistplot()	eps=0.2;minpts=3
Co-clustering	–	blockcluster	coclusterContingency()	9	–	–

5.1   Parameter Setting of Clustering

On the basis of various feature representation of terms, the inner relations between terms are able to be discovered by the clustering algorithms. The clustering algorithms differ from each other with regards to both their distance measurements and their preference on the optimal number of clusters.

Similarity Calculation of Clustering. Before applying these representations to clustering algorithms, it is essential to illustrate the choice of similarity/dissimilarity measure for each algorithm. For example, k-means, k-medoids and DBscan clustering algorithm make use of cosine distance for each representation. The cosine measurement has an outstanding favorable property as normalization, which fits well to the multi-nominal probability distributions in Bag-of-word assumption. On the contrary, the affinity propagation employs cosine similarity calculation as required by the executing algorithms. However, the similarity or dissimilarity calculation is skipped for the co-clustering approach, because its concentration is to explore the contingency of raw data with row and column effects.

Repetitions of Clustering. To weaken the impact of the randomness of clustering, the repetition of experiments is necessary as a proof for the subsequent analysis. Generally, to serve our purpose about selecting the optimal number of clusters, each experiment goes through all the parameters of k (the number of clusters) ranging from 2 to 50 for 10 repetitions. To get the convincing results, each index is statistically averaged to mean values for evaluation. As presented in Fig. 7, each iteration allows for analysis of clustering performance respecting to internal indices and external indices.

However, this method is not suitable for all of the clustering methods. On the one hand, as we mentioned that some clustering algorithms do not require the pre-setting of the number of clusters, instead, they are able to provide the choice of optimal number of cluster. As shown in Table 4, it depicts the experiment parameters for these five clustering algorithms. Theoretically, affinity propagation can be implemented without such prerequisite. However, from the experiments we obtained very poor performance based on the automatic assignment of k. In order to acquire the optimal setting for such clustering algorithm, we apply the k selection procedure to vary the number of clusters from 2 to 50. As for DBscan clustering algorithm, it could implement without such prerequisite of k, but it needs the parameter of the minimum number of points required to form a dense region (i.e. minPts) and the radius of a neighborhood with

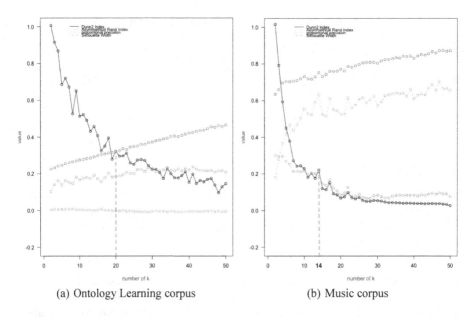

(a) Ontology Learning corpus   (b) Music corpus

Fig. 8. The examples of parameter selection with K-Means. Note: All values are statistically averaged from 10 times.

respect to some points (i.e. eps). Fortunately, it exist a function (parameter selection column of Table 4) to assist us to find a suitable value for DBscan by calculating the k-nearest neighbor distances in a matrix of points. In the aspect of co-clustering, the selection of these two parameters brings many complexity. To solve this problem, the expert knowledge of domain assists us to settle down these numbers. Hence, we can directly use the optimal number of clusters the same as the number of core concepts in the different corpus.

Eventually, k-means, k-medoids and affinity propagation clustering are capable to find their optimal number of clusters from a large range of candidates. To select the optimal amount of clusters, we attempt to solve the multi-criteria optimization problem. As Fig. 8 shows, it represents the evaluation results of k-means clustering with the co-occurrence feature representations, for Ontology Learning Corpus and Music Corpus separately. The two plots depict the fluctuation of all evaluation indices along with the increasing of the number of clusters. In order to address the multi-criteria optimization problem, we plan to find some evident peaks of one of the most fluctuating line and choose one from these candidate peaks to assure a rather higher summation over the entire indices. For instance, in the left sub-figure, we select the first 10 peaks of Dunn Index as candidates, and calculate the summation of all indices for those 10 candidates. Then we can choose the candidate with the highest summation as the optimal number of cluster. In Fig. 8, the dashed lines indicate the final parameter choice for this specific representation. In this figure, we select 20 as the optimal k of left experiment and select 14 for right experiment. Besides, the selection procedures of the rest feature representations follow the same rules.

Table 5. The evaluation of 5 clustering methods and 4 feature representations (Ontology Learning Corpus). Note: All values are statistically averaged.

	Clustering	Feature representation	# Selected k	Purity	Asymm Rand Index	Dunn2 Index	Silhouette Width
Corpus	K-Means	NP-VPC	20	32.3%	−0.1%	32.3%	18.6%
		NP-VPC-tfidf	44	60.3%	−2.6%	22.2%	−2.0%
		NP-VPC-NMF	37	43.3%	−1.0%	24.7%	<u>47.0%</u>
		NP-w2v	37	<u>62.1%</u>	**51.2%**	<u>64.7%</u>	13.9%
	K-Medoids	NP-VPC	25	36.2%	−0.5%	70.2%	24.3%
		NP-VPC-tfidf	18	36.2%	−0.5%	70.2%	24.3%
		NP-VPC-NMF	21	38.7%	1.0%	**99.4%**	<u>25.7%</u>
		NP-w2v	17	<u>51.8%</u>	<u>9.7%</u>	85.5%	7.8%
Ontology	Affinity Propagation	NP-VPC	47	48.2%	−0.3%	76.8%	34.7%
		NP-VPC-tfidf	–	–	–	–	–
		NP-VPC-NMF	26	41.0%	3.1%	10.5%	**50.0%**
		NP-w2v	43	**62.2%**	<u>7.2%</u>	<u>87.1%</u>	13.0%
	DBscan	NP-VPC	7	27.2%	−0.6%	–	1.6%
		NP-VPC-tfidf	1	25.6%	−1%	–	17.6%
		NP-VPC-NMF	76	<u>56.6%</u>	<u>3.5%</u>	79.4%	45.5%
		NP-w2v	16	35.8%	0.7%	73.3%	−12.2%
	Co-clustering	NP-VPC	9	26.6%	<u>0.8%</u>	49.0%	−10.7%
		NP-VPC-tfidf	–	–	–	–	–
		NP-VPC-NMF	9	<u>26.6%</u>	−0.4%	**99.4%**	4.2%
		NP-w2v	–	–	–	–	–

In other words, it seems better to choose a locally optimal k around the number of core concepts, so as to restrict the number of clusters within a suitable range for ontology learning purpose. This assumption takes into consideration of number of core concepts. However, it rejects the possibilities of high-quality clustering along with smaller clusters. Therefore, in replace of the local optimization approach, global optimization of all indices is preferred to choose parameters of k-means and affinity propagation clustering for each feature representation.

5.2   Evaluation of Clustering

Obviously, to complete the experiments, we need to apply the 5 different clustering methods upon the 4 diverse feature representations. Thus around 20 experiment outcomes are presented for each corpus. On the basis of these statistics, we have made multiple comparisons to discover the valuable matching from corpus to clustering algorithms and to feature representations for term clustering. The Table 5 and Table 6 indicate the evaluation of 5 clustering methods and 4 feature representations. The *co-occurrence representations* are denoted as 'NP-VPC', while their extended embedding techniques *weighted co-occurrence representation* and *NMF representation* are denoted by 'NP-VPC-tfidf' and 'NP-VPC-NMF'. To be short, these 3 representations are called by a joint name 'NP-VPC representation family'. Besides, the *word embedding representations* is said to 'NP-w2v'.

Table 6. The evaluation of 5 clustering methods and 4 feature representations (Music Corpus). Note: All values are statistically averaged.

	Clustering	Feature representation	# Selected k	Purity	Asymm Rand Index	Dunn2 Index	Silhouette Width
Corpus	K-Means	NP-VPC	14	75.1%	<u>63.3%</u>	22.1%	<u>20.8%</u>
		NP-VPC-tfidf	10	48.2%	0.1%	28.0%	13.3%
		NP-VPC-NMF	14	70.4%	24.4%	64.6%	19.0%
		NP-w2v	13	<u>81.1%</u>	59.9%	<u>79.7%</u>	16.1%
	K-Medoids	NP-VPC	23	78.9%	67.9%	72.3%	16.0%
		NP-VPC-tfidf	17	53.1%	5.2%	-	<u>22.2%</u>
		NP-VPC-NMF	25	75.1%	**74.5%**	**98.7%**	16.7%
		NP-w2v	27	<u>80.9%</u>	59.5%	87.1%	5.8%
Music	Affinity Propagation	NP-VPC	33	85.3%	<u>74.3%</u>	86.0%	**39.3%**
		NP-VPC-tfidf	37	69.9%	8.9%	11.1%	30.9%
		NP-VPC-NMF	19	75.2%	59.1%	<u>98.2%</u>	26.9%
		NP-w2v	37	**89.6%**	73.8%	91.4%	23.3%
	DBscan	NP-VPC	14	65.3%	19.1%	<u>83.8%</u>	2.6%
		NP-VPC-tfidf	12	48.2%	2.2%	–	<u>20.7%</u>
		NP-VPC-NMF	60	<u>78.2%</u>	<u>22.1%</u>	78.2%	14.2%
		NP-w2v	26	56.6%	7.0%	75.1%	−12.0%
	Co-clustering	NP-VPC	9	<u>49.5%</u>	−3.4%	59.9%	−8.7%
		NP-VPC-tfidf	–	–	–	–	–
		NP-VPC-NMF	9	48.5%	<u>−0.5%</u>	<u>96.7%</u>	<u>1.7%</u>
		NP-w2v	–	–	–	–	–

Table 7. The resulted combination of clustering and feature representation.

clustering	Feature representations	
	Ontology Learning Corpus	Music Corpus
K-Means	NP-w2v	NP-w2v
K-Medoids	NP-w2v	NP-VPC-NMF
Affinity Propagation	NP-w2v	NP-VPC
DBscan	NP-VPC-NMF	NP-VPC-NMF
Co-clustering	NP-VPC-NMF	NP-VPC-NMF

Generally, in the aspect of the corpus, it is evident that Music Corpus (see Table 6) reaches a much higher purity and higher Asymmetric Rand Index than that of Ontology Learning Corpus (see Table 5). It can be due to that bigger corpus (Music Corpus) provides significant contextual features to cluster terms.

For the difference between 5 clustering methods, first of all, there is no overwhelming clustering approach according to those evaluation indices. The performance of k-medoids is comparable or better than that of k-means, which conforms to our intuition somehow. The k-medoids clustering methods need the knowledge of centroids before calculation, whose results are expected to be more accurate than that of k-means. Moreover, co-clustering has a rather poor performance than others. During experiments, some feature representations are even failed with this algorithm, due to the contingency requirement of input data. While the affinity propagation algorithm achieves the relatively best performance of clustering, and the DBscan clustering methods are slight deficient than that of k-means, k-medoids and affinity propagation.

As for the evaluation indices, we notice that it occurs negative values in asymmetric Rand Index and silhouette width. In this situation, the former index reflects a worse elements labeling of clusters comparing to Gold Standard, while the latter index shows that there are overlapping parts between different partitions, which means feature similar terms probably share different labels. That is inevitable in linguistic because the similar context of terms could not straightly infer to the same meaning of them.

In terms of the encoding representations, Tf-Idf representations provide unevenly lower accuracy in clusters. While the NMF representations and the word embedding representations have a good clustering quality overall. On the other hand, the performance of co-occurrence representations varies along with different corpus. From the results of evaluation, we observe a rather better performance in Music corpus than that in Ontology Learning corpus. Due to that the bigger corpus(the Music corpus) contains more frequent NP-VPC pairs, the co-occurrence matrix can present more distinguishing values to accentuate their features for term clustering purpose.

In the aspect of the combination of clustering and feature representations, it is preferable to list the most outstanding feature embedding technique for each clustering method. In Table 5 and Table 6, we select the required feature representations for each clustering approach only if the amount of the underlined indices for that feature is as many as possible (the underlines are used to mark the highest value for each clustering method). According to the bold values in Table 5 and Table 6, we are able to choose the best combination for each corpus. The selected results are presented in Table 7. From these voted combinations, we aware that the majority of feature representation lies in NMF embedding technique. Except for k-means and affinity propagation, the other clustering methods are prone to fit well with NMF in at least one corpus. From Table 7, we notice several outperforming combinations of clustering and feature representation, including k-means with word embedding representation and DBscan or co-clustering with NMF embedding technique. However, for the counterpart of k-medoids and affinity propagation clustering algorithm, it does not exist a dominant feature representation for the different corpus, however the word embedding representation can achieve a rather good performance in small size corpus.

In general, NMF embedding technique and word embedding representations are prominent in most clustering situations. The word embedding representations show an enhanced quality of clustering with K-Means. The DBscan clustering algorithm accompanying with NMF encoding technique achieves a rather good performance in both corpus. On the other hand, the co-occurrence representations reach comparatively good performance with affinity propagation clustering, which shows the affinity propagation's feasibility over co-occurrence pairs.

6   Conclusions

Many works suggest making use of core ontology to build modular ontology. However, most of these efforts are manually constructed and seldom in the automatic approach. Term clustering according to a core ontology supports modular ontology construction without artificial demands. Taxonomic relations are constructed by gathering of NPs appearing with prominent syntactic roles after VPCs respecting to core concepts. Successfully we constructed feature space with these characteristics from two specialized corpora. To tackle the problem of sparsity, we benefit from feature selection and feature extraction techniques, such as adjusted Tf-Idf algorithm and NMF technique. Apart from that, word2vec is also compared as a benchmark. Along with all the extended representations, terms are clustered by 5 different clustering algorithms, which contains k-means, k-medoids, affinity propagation, DBscan and co-clustering algorithm. We found that the original co-occurrence feature space appearing with syntactic roles is not the most outstanding feature representation, while the usage of Affinity propagation clustering based on this original representation could prominently improve clustering performance. It is proved that the word embedding representations show an enhanced quality with K-Means and NMF encoding technique achieves a rather good performance with DBscan clustering algorithm. While the k-medoids and affinity propagation clustering algorithm have their preference to feature representations depending on the size of corpus.

From the comparison of term clustering frameworks, we recommend to start with a bigger domain-specific corpora. The syntactic relations between noun phrases and verbs are sufficient as features representation, with the assistance of encoding techniques, it gives rather convincing results in term clustering, which provides us a guideline for modular ontology building.

In the future work, we would like to explore the relations between terms in each module of ontology, so as to construct the concept hierarchy in modules. On the other hand, the relation between modules is still under our interests, in order to form a complete domain modular ontology.

References

1. Aggarwal, C.C., Zhai, C.: A survey of text clustering algorithms. In: Aggarwal, C., Zhai, C. (eds.) Mining Text Data. Springer, Boston (2012). https://doi.org/10.1007/978-1-4614-3223-4_4
2. Arnold, T.: A tidy data model for natural language processing using cleanNLP. R J. 9(2), 1–20 (2017). https://journal.r-project.org/archive/2017/RJ-2017-035/index.html
3. Buitelaar, P., Cimiano, P., Magnini, B.: Ontology learning from text: an overview. In: Buitelaar, P., Cimiano, P., Magnini, B. (eds.) Ontology Learning from Text: Methods, Evaluation and Applications, vol. 123, pp. 3–12. IOS press, Amsterdam (2005)
4. Buitelaar, P., Olejnik, D., Sintek, M.: A protégé plug-in for ontology extraction from text based on linguistic analysis. In: Bussler, C.J., Davies, J., Fensel, D., Studer, R. (eds.) ESWS 2004. LNCS, vol. 3053, pp. 31–44. Springer, Heidelberg (2004). https://doi.org/10.1007/978-3-540-25956-5_3
5. Burita, L., Gardavsky, P., Vejlupek, T.: K-gate ontology driven knowledge based system for decision support. J. Syst. Integr. 3(1), 19–31 (2012)
6. Camacho-Collados, J., et al.: SemEval-2018 Task 9: hypernym discovery. In: Proceedings of the 12th International Workshop on Semantic Evaluation, SemEval-2018, New Orleans, LA, United States. Association for Computational Linguistics (2018)
7. Chulyadyo, R., Harzallah, M., Berio, G.: Core ontology based approach for treating the flatness of automatically built ontology. In: KEOD, Portugal, pp. 316–323, September 2013

8. Church, K.W., Hanks, P.: Word association norms, mutual information, and lexicography. Comput. Linguist. **16**(1), 22–29 (1990)
9. Cimiano P., de Mantaras, R.L., Saitia, L.: Comparing conceptual, divisive and agglomerative clustering for learning taxonomies from text. In: 16th European Conference on Artificial Intelligence Conference Proceedings, vol. 110, p. 435 (2004)
10. Dempster, A.P., Laird, N.M., Rubin, D.B.: Maximum likelihood from incomplete data via the EM algorithm. J. Roy. Stat. Soc.: Ser. B (Methodol.) **39**(1), 1–22 (1977)
11. Despress, S., Szulman, S.: Merging of legal micro-ontologies from Europen directives. Artif. Intell. Law **15**(2), 187–200 (2007). https://doi.org/10.1007/s10506-007-9028-2
12. Dunn, J.C.: Well-separated clusters and optimal fuzzy partitions. J. Cybern. **4**(1), 95–104 (1974)
13. El Ghosh, M., Naja, H., Abdulrab, H., Khalil, M.: Application of ontology modularization for building a criminal domain ontology. In: Pagallo, U., Palmirani, M., Casanovas, P., Sartor, G., Villata, S. (eds.) AICOL 2015-2017. LNCS (LNAI), vol. 10791, pp. 394–409. Springer, Cham (2018). https://doi.org/10.1007/978-3-030-00178-0_27
14. Esposito, F., Fanizzi, N., d'Amato, C.: Partitional conceptual clustering of web resources annotated with ontology languages. In: Berendt, B., et al. (eds.) Knowledge Discovery Enhanced with Semantic and Social Information. Studies in Computational Intelligence, vol. 220. Springer, Heidelberg (2009). https://doi.org/10.1007/978-3-642-01891-6_4
15. Ester, M., Kriegel, H.P., Sander, J., Xu, X., et al.: A density-based algorithm for discovering clusters in large spatial databases with noise. KDD **96**, 226–231 (1996)
16. Faure, D., Nédellec, C., Rouveirol, C.: Acquisition of semantic knowledge using machine learning methods: The system "asium". Universite Paris Sud, Technical report (1998)
17. Fernández-López, M., Gómez-Pérez, A., Juristo, N.: Methontology: From ontological art towards ontological engineering. In: AAAI (1997)
18. Frey, B.J., Dueck, D.: Clustering by passing messages between data points. Science **315**(5814), 972–976 (2007)
19. Gábor, K., Zargayouna, H., Tellier, I., Buscaldi, D., Charnois, T.: Unsupervised relation extraction in specialized corpora using sequence mining. In: Boström, H., Knobbe, A., Soares, C., Papapetrou, P. (eds.) IDA 2016. LNCS, vol. 9897, pp. 237–248. Springer, Cham (2016). https://doi.org/10.1007/978-3-319-46349-0_21
20. Gamallo, P., Bordag, S.: Is singular value decomposition useful for word similarity extraction? Lang. Resour. Eval. **45**(2), 95–119 (2011). https://doi.org/10.1007/s10579-010-9129-5
21. Gangemi, A., Catenacci, C., Battaglia, M.: Inflammation ontology design pattern: an exercise in building a core biomedical ontology with descriptions and situations. Stud. Health Technol. Inform. **102**, 64–80 (2004)
22. Gangemi, A., Catenacci, C., Ciaramita, M., Lehmann, J.: Modelling ontology evaluation and validation. In: Sure, Y., Domingue, J. (eds.) ESWC 2006. LNCS, vol. 4011, pp. 140–154. Springer, Heidelberg (2006). https://doi.org/10.1007/11762256_13
23. Govaert, G., Nadif, M.: Latent block model for contingency table. Commun. Stat. Theory Methods **39**(3), 416–425 (2010)
24. Grau, B.C., Horrocks, I., Kazakov, Y., Sattler, U.: A logical framework for modularity of ontologies. IJCAI **114**, 298–303 (2007)
25. Gruber, T.R.: A translation approach to portable ontology specifications. Knowl. Acquis. **5**(2), 199–220 (1993)
26. Hao, J., Zhang, C., Wang, H.: Using keywords clustering to construct ontological hierarchies. In: Proceedings of the 2009 IEEE/WIC/ACM International Joint Conference on Web Intelligence and Intelligent Agent Technology-Volume 03, pp. 247–250. IEEE Computer Society (2009)
27. Harris, Z.: Distributional structure. Word **10**(23), 146–162 (1954)
28. Hartigan, J.A., Wong, M.A.: Algorithm as 136: a k-means clustering algorithm. J. Roy. Stat. Soc.: Ser. C (Appl. Stat.) **28**(1), 100–108 (1979)

29. Hois, J., Bhatt, M., Kutz, O.: Modular ontologies for architectural design. In: FOMI, pp. 66–77 (2009)
30. Hubert, L., Arabie, P.: Comparing partitions. J. Classif. **2**(1), 193–218 (1985). https://doi.org/10.1007/BF01908075
31. Jiang, X., Tan, A.H.: Mining ontological knowledge from domain-specific text documents. In: Fifth IEEE International Conference on Data Mining, pp. 665–668. IEEE (2005)
32. Kaufman, L., Rousseeuw, P.J.: Finding Groups in Data: An Introduction to Cluster Analysis, vol. 344. Wiley, Hoboken (2009)
33. Kutz, O., Hois, J.: Modularity in ontologies. Appl. Ontol. **7**, 109–112 (2012). https://doi.org/10.3233/AO-2012-0109
34. Lee, D.D., Seung, H.S.: Learning the parts of objects by non-negative matrix factorization. Nature **401**(6755), 788 (1999)
35. Manning, C.D., Surdeanu, M., Bauer, J., Finkel, J., Bethard, S.J., McClosky, D.: The Stanford CoreNLP natural language processing toolkit. In: Association for Computational Linguistics (ACL) System Demonstrations, pp. 55–60 (2014)
36. Mikolov, T., Chen, K., Corrado, G., Dean, J.: Efficient estimation of word representations in vector space. arXiv preprint arXiv:1301.3781 (2013)
37. Nancy, P., Ramani, R.G.: Discovery of patterns and evaluation of clustering algorithms in socialnetwork data (face book 100 universities) through data mining techniques and methods. Int. J. Data Min. Knowl. Manage. Process **2**(5), 71 (2012)
38. Oberle, D., Lamparter, S., Grimm, S., Vrandečić, D., Staab, S., Gangemi, A.: Towards ontologies for formalizing modularization and communication in large software systems. Appl. Ontol. **1**(2), 163–202 (2006)
39. Opdahl, A., Berio, G., Harzallah, M., Matulevičius, R.: Ontology for enterprise and information systems modelling. Appl. Ontol. **7**, 49–92 (2011)
40. O'Connor, L., Feizi, S.: Biclustering using message passing. In: Ghahramani, Z., Welling, M., Cortes, C., Lawrence, N.D., Weinberger, K.Q. (eds.) Advances in Neural Information Processing Systems 27, pp. 3617–3625. Curran Associates, Inc. (2014). http://papers.nips.cc/paper/5603-biclustering-using-message-passing.pdf
41. Pal, N.R., Biswas, J.: Cluster validation using graph theoretic concepts. Pattern Recogn. **30**(6), 847–857 (1997)
42. Rand, W.M.: Objective criteria for the evaluation of clustering methods. J. Am. Stat. Assoc. **66**(336), 846–850 (1971)
43. Rani, M., Dhar, A.K., Vyas, O.: Semi-automatic terminology ontology learning based on topic modeling. Eng. Appl. Artif. Intell. **63**, 108–125 (2017)
44. Rdrr.io: Silhouette: Compute or extract silhouette information from clustering (2019). https://rdrr.io/cran/cluster/man/silhouette.html. Accessed 10 May 2019
45. Rios-Alvarado, A.B., Lopez-Arevalo, I., Sosa-Sosa, V.J.: Learning concept hierarchies from textual resources for ontologies construction. Expert Syst. Appl. **40**(15), 5907–5915 (2013)
46. Scherpa, A., Saathoffa, C., Franza, T., Staaba, S.: Designing core ontologies. Appl. Ontol. **3**, 1–3 (2009)
47. Song, Q., Liu, J., Wang, X., Wang, J.: A novel automatic ontology construction method based on web data. In: 2014 Tenth International Conference on Intelligent Information Hiding and Multimedia Signal Processing, pp. 762–765. IEEE (2014)
48. spaCy: Spacy:industrial-strength natural language processing (NLP) with python and cython, explosion AI (2019). https://github.com/explosion/spaCy. Accessed 10 May 2019
49. Wagner, S., Wagner, D.: Comparing clusterings: an overview. Universität Karlsruhe, Fakultät für Informatik Karlsruhe (2007)

50. Wang, W., Barnaghi, P.M., Bargiela, A.: Learning SKOS relations for terminological ontologies from text. In: Wong, W., Liu, W., Bennamoun, M. (eds.) Ontology Learning and Knowledge Discovery Using the Web: Challenges and Recent Advances, pp. 129–152. IGI Global, Hershey (2011)
51. Witten, I.H., Frank, E., Hall, M.A., Pal, C.J.: Data Mining: Practical Machine Learning Tools and Techniques. Morgan Kaufmann, Burlington (2016)
52. XU, Z., Harzallah, M., Guillet, F.: Comparing of term clustering frameworks for modular ontology learning. In: Proceedings of the 10th International Joint Conference on Knowledge Discovery, Knowledge Engineering and Knowledge Management - Volume 2: KEOD, Seville, Spain, pp. 128–135. SCITEPRESS - Science and Technology Publications, September 2018

A Semantic Approach
to Constraint-Based Reasoning
in Geographical Domains

Gianluca Torta[1]([✉]) [iD], Liliana Ardissono[1] [iD], Daniele Fea[1], Luigi La Riccia[2] [iD],
and Angioletta Voghera[2] [iD]

[1] Dipartimento di Informatica, Università di Torino, Turin, Italy
{gianluca.torta,liliana.ardissono}@unito.it, daniele.fea@edu.unito.it
[2] Dipartimento Interateneo di Scienze, Progetto e Politiche del Territorio, Turin, Italy
{luigi.lariccia,angioletta.voghera}@polito.it
http://www.unito.it
http://www.polito.it

Abstract. Various models have been developed to manage geographic data but most of them integrate heterogeneous techniques to support knowledge representation and reasoning. This is far from optimal because it requires mapping data between different representation formats; moreover, as it fragments knowledge, it limits the possibility to use complete information about the problem to be solved for the execution of inferences.

In order to address this issue, we adopt a unified approach, in which we use Semantic Web techniques to manage both knowledge representation and reasoning rules with particular attention to constraint verification that is central to several geographic reasoning tasks. Our model exploits an ontological description of spatial constraints which supports the specification of their properties, facilitating the automated selection of the relevant ones to be applied to a given problem. The model supports different types of inferences, such as checking the compliance of a given geographical area to a set of constraints, or suggesting a suitable aggregation of land patches that satisfy them.

We test our model by applying it to the management of Ecological Networks, which describe the structure of existing real ecosystems and help planning their expansion, conservation and improvement by introducing constraints on land use.

Keywords: Geographic knowledge · Geographical constraints · GeoSPARQL ecological networks · Urban planning

1 Introduction

With the convergence of GIS and Semantic Web, various models have been developed to manage geographic information; however, most of them integrate differ-

This work is funded by the University of Torino, projects "Ricerca Locale" and "Ricerca Autofinanziata".

© Springer Nature Switzerland AG 2020
A. Fred et al. (Eds.): IC3K 2018, CCIS 1222, pp. 202–227, 2020.
https://doi.org/10.1007/978-3-030-49559-6_10

ent techniques to support knowledge representation and reasoning. For instance, they describe the application domain by means of ontologies but they use specialized reasoners, such as constraint solvers or rule-based systems, to make inferences. This approach is far from optimal because it fragments knowledge in multiple data sources characterized by heterogeneous representation formats. Therefore, it limits the possibility to use complete information about the problem to be solved for the execution of inferences.

In order to address this issue, we propose a geographic reasoning model that adopts a unified knowledge management approach to represent both geographic information and reasoning rules with particular attention to constraint verification, which is central to several geographic reasoning tasks. We adhere to the GeoSpatial Semantic Web paradigm [29] that promotes standard knowledge representation languages to maximize the interoperability of data and applications. Specifically, our model uniformly represents the application domain and its constraints as OWL ontologies [57] in order to benefit from the expressiveness and reasoning tools provided by standard Semantic Web languages. Moreover, it offers a set of specialized reasoners that take as input these ontologies in order to solve different types of constraint verification problems on a selected geographical area. As a proof-of-concept, the current implementation offers two reasoners optimized to solve specific types of tasks: i.e., finding paths that connect geographical areas by traversing land patches that satisfy a given set of constraints, and clustering land patches that satisfy the same constraints to summarize the distribution of homogeneous areas in a territory.

A novel aspect of our model is the representation of constraint types as classes of an OWL ontology. In this way, we employ a single, well-known knowledge representation standard and we avoid the introduction of a new language that would require ad-hoc tools to manage constraint information. Our Constraint ontology supports a detailed description of the different kinds of constraints (e.g., soft and hard, part-of and relational, aggregation and individual) by qualifying their scope, purpose and relationships. This meta-information enables the development of automated reasoners that can autonomously retrieve and apply the relevant constraints for the task to be completed.

We test our model on the management of Ecological Networks (ENs) [6], which describe the structure of existing real ecosystems and help planning their expansion, conservation and improvement by imposing restrictions on land use. ENs have been traditionally specified as large sets of Natural Language guidelines requiring a manual design of public policies for the proposal of land use transformations. We aim at providing an interactive tool that helps the human decision-maker by automatically designing the structure of the EN of a geographic region and by suggesting suitable aggregations of land patches that satisfy a given set of constraints; e.g., having medium or low levels of irreversibility and extroversion. These functions help the design of the structure of the EN and of urban and regional transformation plans and projects to improve the compliance of a geographical area with the EN specifications. Those activities are needed to construct the social awareness on bindings and opportunities related to Ecological Networks for quality of life. The present paper brings the following main contributions:

- It provides an ontological representation of Ecological Networks (EN ontology) and of the related constraints on land use (Constraint ontology) which supports knowledge sharing and semantic reasoning.
- It presents an extensible framework for reasoning about geographical constraints, based on a semantic knowledge representation.

The present paper extends the work described in [49] in the following ways: first, it refines the EN ontology defined in that article by describing different types of linear infrastructures; e.g., roads ranging from natural paths to highways that can represent serious obstacles to connecting land patches. Moreover, the present paper significantly extends the Constraint ontology proposed in [49] by defining more complex types of conditions to be used in constraints. Finally, by exploiting a number of examples that make use of the extensions to the ontology, this paper provides more detail about the reasoners we developed.

In the following, Sect. 2 provides background information and positions our work in the related one. Section 3 presents our knowledge representation and reasoning model. Section 4 describes the reasoners we developed. Section 5 describes the framework implementation. Section 6 concludes the paper and presents our future work.

2   Background and Related Work

2.1   Semantic Knowledge Representation

According to Gruber, an ontology is an explicit specification of a conceptualization [24]. Moreover, in [25], Guarino et al., explain that ontologies "may be classified into different types, depending on the way they are used. For instance, the primary purpose of *top-level ontologies* lies in providing a broad view of the world suitable for many different target domains. *Reference ontologies* target the structuring of ontologies that are derived from them. The primary purpose of *core ontologies* derives from the definition of a super domain. *Application ontologies* are suitable for direct use in reasoning engines or software package." In this paper, we define two application ontologies: the former, henceforth denoted as the EN ontology, specifies the types of elements that constitute an Ecological Network; the latter, denoted as Constraints ontology, defines geographical constraints.

The GeoSpatial Semantic Web vision advocates for representing geographical information by means of ontologies suitable for explicitly describing concepts and relations among concepts [29]. This supports a conceptual notion of data interoperability, which goes beyond the adoption of a common representation format and is aimed at enabling correct data interpretation and inferences in geographical reasoning. The interoperability issue has been studied in other works, related to information sharing and retrieval: for instance, Fonseca et al. propose an ontology to classify geographic elements with respect to geometric characteristics and attribute values [17]. They also analyze the impact of semantic granularity, i.e., the level of detail at which geographic objects are described, on interoperability [18]. On a similar perspective, Mauro et al. analyze the impact of semantic granularity on geographic information search support [36] and Palacio et al. investigate spatial granularity to describe toponyms at different levels of detail [40]. Some ontologies support the sharing of toponyms and generic geographic concepts; e.g., the GeoNames Mappings ontology [19] based on the GeoNames database [20]. Furthermore, specific ontologies describe fine-grained aspects of geographical objects; for instance, GeoSPARQL [38] defines geographical objects supporting the specification of their geometry, as well as topologic relations among different objects. Finally, other ontologies provide a semantics of Volunteer Geographical Information; for instance, LinkedGeoData links crowsourced OpenStreetMap (OSM) information to GeoNames and others ontologies [30].

Moving from knowledge representation to reasoning, in [48] and [50] Torta et al. propose the GeCoLan language for constraint-based reasoning on semantic geographical data, applied to the validation of Ecological Networks. Similarly, some Semantic Web languages allow the definition of constraints as generic rules (e.g., SWRL - Semantic Web Rule Language - [27] and RuleML [8]) or as logic formulas (e.g., see logical/functional languages such as the CIF Constraint Interchange Format [22]). All these works are affected by two main limitations: first, they require ad-hoc reasoners to perform inferences. Second, they fail to characterize the properties of constraints as needed to automatically retrieve and apply them to specific reasoning tasks. Our current work addresses both limitations because it represents ENs and constraints in the same language and it supports a detailed specification of the latter by qualifying their scope, purpose, relationships, so that an automated reasoner can retrieve and apply the appropriate ones, given the task to be completed. These characteristics associate our work to some recent research about spatial reasoning that investigates the homogeneous representation of different types of knowledge supporting complex tasks. For instance, Lazoglou and Angelides propose an ontology to model actors and tasks for spatial planning systems [32]; moreover, Abrahao and Hirakawa propose a task ontology for agriculture operations [1]; furthermore, the Spatial Decision Support Consortium promotes an ontology specifying spatial decision making [44]. Indeed, we have a similar perspective but a different purpose because we aim at reasoning about constraints.

Our work also differs from the path finding approaches adopted in location-based services and recommender systems. Given a graph representing the travel map of a geographical area, those models suggest paths suiting individual preferences by composing road segments which, globally, maximize one or more measures associated to the selected properties; e.g., the shortest path between two endpoints, or a path maximizing pleasure, calm, or other properties of an area [43]. Those models solve a specific task by taking a pre-defined set of constraints into account. Differently, we aim at supporting multiple reasoning tasks and at retrieving relevant constraints from a semantic knowledge base by using their description as classes of an OWL ontology.

2.2 Ecological Networks

Urban land use has dramatically extended towards natural spaces: external urban areas, such as uncultivated or abandoned cultivated land, burnt areas and degraded forests, have often been confined from urban and regional planning to a secondary position and sometimes simply considered as "waiting areas for a new urbanization" [53].

Ecological Networks (ENs) have been proposed to preserve biodiversity and enhance ecosystem services [28] by reducing the process of nature and landscape fragmentation and vulnerability caused by the development of new urbanizations, infrastructural networks and intensive agriculture [31]. As reported in [6], ecological networks share two generic goals: firstly, they are aimed at "maintaining the functioning of ecosystems as a means of facilitating the conservation of species and habitats". Secondly, they are aimed at "promoting the sustainable use of natural resources in order to reduce the impacts of new urbanizations on biodiversity and/or to increase the biodiversity value of managed landscapes".

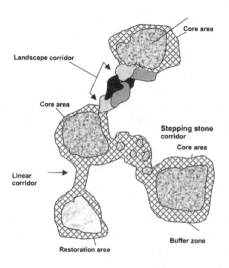

Fig. 1. Ecological Network representation, from [6].

Even though the Protected Areas and *Natura 2000* sites are now considered the backbone of European policy for biodiversity, the increasing expansion of urbanization and infrastructural networks is challenging the conservation of natural habitats for the preservation of animal species and plant varieties. It is thus necessary to develop policies for the improvement of Ecological Networks in order to overcome the fragmentation of habitats and natural areas, which is the main cause of biodiversity loss in Europe. The consequences of these processes can be summarized as follows [5]:

- Degradation of wetlands, which compromise the following ecological functions: control of water flows, ability to block sediments, support to plant and animal species (stepping stone function), ability to provide nutrients for the ecosystems.
- Loss of natural areas due to urban development and fragmentation of natural areas into smaller, disconnected patches that become isolated.
- Inability of ecosystems to respond to changes and find a new ecological balance; the effect is a significant reduction of resilience.
- Loss of ecosystem services: natural systems are considered essential "services", such as the control of water, the filter functions for pollutants, the preservation of climate change and environmental risks.
- The increased economic costs for public services, caused by the response to natural disasters deriving from human footprint.

An Ecological Network can be defined as an interconnected system consisting of territorial areas that include natural and semi-natural habitats. As shown in Fig. 1, the typical representation of an EN is a network of core areas interconnected by corridors. According to Bennet and Mulongoy [6]:

- *Core Areas* are the areas "where the conservation of biodiversity takes primary importance, even if the area is not legally protected".
- *Adjoining Areas*, also known as *Buffer Zones* are the areas that "protect the network from potentially damaging external influences and which are essentially transitional areas characterized by compatible land uses". They are important to safeguard and increase the stability of the core areas; see also [53].
- *Corridors* "serve to maintain vital ecological or environmental connections by maintaining physical (though not necessarily linear) linkages between the core areas".
- *Sustainable-use areas* are zones "where opportunities are exploited within the landscape mosaic for the sustainable use of natural resources together with maintenance of most ecosystem services".

Until now, the research on Ecological Network management has focused on the following main topics:

- Providing evaluation frameworks to simulate the evolution of an EN starting from its initial state. This is aimed either at predicting the future state of a given geographical area or at simulating the effects of some planned actions on the area. For instance, some researchers propose mathematical simulations to model the interaction between organisms within an ecosystem, the dynamics of the relations among species, the existence of dynamical bottlenecks in the functioning of the ecosystems, etc.; e.g., see [15,15,21,34,41,51]. These works are complementary to our own: in fact, EN simulation helps foresee the consequences of actions on a geographical area; however, it does not support the assessment of the status of the area, given its properties. Therefore, these works could support the identification of land use constraints to be imposed in order to safeguard an ecologic area, but they cannot support the identification of obstacles to the satisfaction of such constraints, or the suggestion of how to resolve the obstacles.

- Implementing ENs at different scales, from European ones down to small-scale ones such as those developed by the municipalities. The results of these implementations, built on the basis of a thorough analysis of the involved geographical areas, are guidelines on land use and planning documents; for instance, see [6,7,13] and the example used in this work [11]. Unfortunately all these documents are written in Natural Language, posing different challenges to the human planner: first, the lack of a formal specification makes it difficult to check the consistency among guidelines in the cases where they have to be jointly applied. Second, the EN elements of a geographical area have to be manually identified, posing a heavy burden on the decision-maker and exposing her/him to the risk of making mistakes. A formal representation of the concepts underlying Ecological Networks and of the properties of geographical areas is the missing building block for the development of any automated tool aimed at supporting this type of task.

Our work is concerned with the second topic above and aims at helping human planners through ICT. In our previous work [48,50], we proposed a semantic representation of ENs for their automated validation. However, as previously discussed, we introduced an ad-hoc constraint satisfaction language for the verification of ENs; e.g., to check whether a certain area, identified as a Buffer zone in a pre-defined EN, complies with the definition given in the specifications, or not. In the present work, we go one step forward by introducing a uniform representation of domain knowledge and inference rules, based on Semantic Web technologies, in order to provide a unified approach to the management of ENs.

Before concluding this section it is worth noting that, as far as the representation of Ecological Networks is concerned, some ontologies model the types of *land use/cover*; e.g., LBCS-OWL2 [37] and HarmonISA [26]. While those ontologies are interesting models, in our work we use a taxonomy based on the Land Cover Piemonte (LCP) cartography [42] because the experimental data available to us is tagged according to it; see project [11]. However, our approach is general and could be adapted to work on the basis of other specifications.

3 Knowledge Representation: Ontology and Graph Models

3.1 OWL Representation of Ecological Networks

The EN ontology describes the main concepts and relations of Ecological Networks starting from two main sources of information:

- The former is the set of Natural Language specifications produced in project "Experimental activity of participatory elaboration of ecological network" [11]. This project was carried out by the Metropolitan City of Turin (Italy) [12] in collaboration with Polytechnic of Turin and ENEA [14]; it aimed at defining a proposal for the Ecological Network implementation at the local level in two pilot municipalities near Turin. The goals were guiding local Public Administrations with measures to limit anthropogenic land use and, where possible, orienting and qualifying the conservation of ecosystem services.
- The latter is the GeoSPARQL ontology [38], which defines the *Feature* class to represent geographical information. A *Feature* has a *Geometry* on the 2D plane and can thus be used to represent points, lines and areas on a map, known in the literature as Simple Features [39]. GeoSPARQL also defines a set of topological geometric relations between *Features* that correspond to basic relations such as *intersects* (to represent geometric intersection), *equals* (to represent equality of geometries) and *contains* (to represent the fact that a geometry includes another one).

The EN ontology is defined using the OWL language [57] and it is composed of two main portions:

- The EN Domain ontology defines the concepts related to types of land use, land patches, and similar.
- The EN Task ontology describes the types of intervention that can be planned on a geographical region.

Figure 2 shows the main classes of the EN Domain ontology and of the portion of the GeoSPARQL ontology we used.[1] Following the graphic notation described in [52], the arrows with open heads symbolize subclass relationships between classes, while regular arrows connect domains and ranges of properties.

The top class is *Feature*, imported from the GeoSPARQL ontology. In order to define ENs, we introduce four subclasses of *Feature* that are the roots of the hierarchies of classes describing the core of the domain. In the figure, *Feature* is depicted in dark grey and the roots of the hierarchies of EN elements are depicted in light grey for easy identification. Specifically:

- *ENElement* represents a generic element of the EN and can be either a Core Area (*CoreArea*), a Sustainable-use area (*SustArea*), or a Priority Expansion Element (*PriorExpEl*). In turn, Priority Expansion Element has Corridor (*Corridor*) and Buffer Zone (*Buffer*) as more specific classes.
- *Patch* represents a small geographical area characterized by a specific land use. It is worth noting that each instance of *Patch belongsTo* an instance of *EcologicalNetworkElement*; conversely, each instance of *EcologicalNetworkElement* is *madeOf* one or more instances of *Patch*.
- *LinearObstacle* represents the linear obstacles that can separate land patches. There are various types of linear obstacles, represented as more specific

---

[1] All the graphs describing portions of the EN and Constraint Ontologies have been produced using the Dia Editor [35].

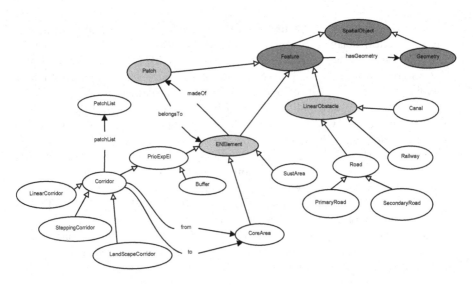

Fig. 2. A portion of the EN Domain Ontology.

classes. In the EN ontology we represent canals (*Canal*), railways (*Railway*), and roads (*Road*). In turn, roads can be primary ones, to denote highways and other major ones (*PrimaryRoad*) and secondary ones (*SecondaryRoad*).

The *LandUseElement* hierarchy of the EN Domain ontology describes the types of land use: each instance of *Patch* is *describedBy* a *LandUseElement*, i.e., it is associated with a specific land use. See Fig. 3, where the *describedBy* relation

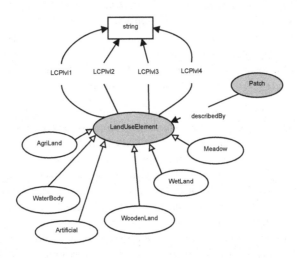

Fig. 3. A portion of the LandUseElement Hierarchy (EN Domain Ontology), from [49].

links the *Patch* class to the *LandUseElement* one. Each class of this hierarchy is a singleton and includes exactly one representative object characterized by:

- A specific type of land use; e.g., wetland (*WetLand*), wooden land (*Wooden-Land*), and similar, as defined in the Land Cover Piemonte (LCP) cartography [42]. The LCP defines a hierarchy of land use types organized in 4 levels that describe land use at different specificity levels: the first one (*LCPlvl1*) is the less detailed one and includes 5 general classes of land use; the second one (*LCPlvl2*) is more specific and includes 15 classes; the third one (*LCPlvl3*) includes 45 classes; the last one (*LCPlvl4*) is the most specific one and it includes 97 classes of land use.
- The score obtained with respect to five evaluation criteria taken from [53]. We represent these criteria as OWL properties of *LandUseElement* in the ontology but we do not show them in Fig. 3 for brevity:
  - *naturalness* (how close the element is to a natural environment);
  - *relevance* (how relevant it is for the conservation of the habitat);
  - *fragility* (how fragile the element is with respect to anthropogenic pressure);
  - *extroversion* (how much pressure it can exert on the neighboring patches);
  - *irreversibility* (how difficult it would be to change the use of the element).
  The value for each criterion ranges from 1 to 5 and 1 is the maximum value.

The EN Task ontology includes the *Intervention* and *Operation* subclasses of *Feature* (see Fig. 4), which describe the types of activity related to the planning of improvements and expansions of Ecological Networks. More specifically:

- *Intervention* represents an intervention for building, improving or conserving the Ecological Network.

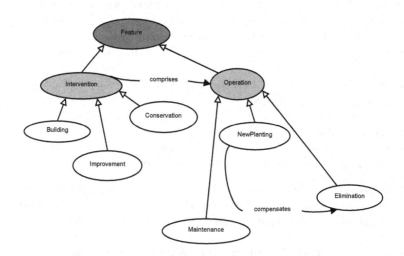

Fig. 4. A portion of the EN Task Ontology.

– *Operation* represents a specific operation of elimination (*Elimination*), construction (*NewPlanting*), or maintenance (*Maintenance*) that is part of an intervention; see the *comprises* relation between *Intervention* and *Operation*.

The current version of the EN ontology models interventions and operations at a coarse granularity level. However, we plan to refine them on the basis of recent work about spatial planning [32] and Spatial Decision Support Systems [44] which supports the automated management of activities by modeling actors and tasks in a detailed way.

3.2   OWL Representation of Geographical Constraints

As discussed by Louwsma et al. in [33], constraints in a geographical domain must be able to express restrictions on the instances of the classes of the domain ontology by specifying logic, geometric, and numeric requirements. For example, constraints can define the allowed values of categorical attributes of areas, they can be used to compute the sum of the sizes of a set of areas, or they can restrict the topological relations between pairs of areas.

In order to support the specification of constraints related to Ecological Networks, we define a Constraint ontology whose classes refer to the classes and properties of the EN ontology[2]. Moreover, we provide a flexible representation to compose constraints that allows to define both simple constraints and complex ones. The representation takes inspiration from the typical types of constraints that may appear in a generic configuration knowledge base; e.g., see [16,45,46].

Figure 5 shows a portion of the Constraints ontology, which is structured as a hierarchy rooted by class Constraint (in dark gray):

– *PartOfConstraint* (shortened to *PartOfCons* in the figure) describes the constraints that apply to one or more parts of a given object. It should be noticed that a part may be shared by different objects; thus, the semantics of this type of constraint is similar to the *aggregation* of UML [23].
  - *SingleAttributeConstraint* (*SingleAttrCons*) involves a single (part-of) attribute of the object.
  - *MultiAttributeConstraint* (*MultiAttrCons*) involves more than one (part-of) attribute of the object.
– *RelationConstraint* (*RelationCons*) describes the constraints that apply to a relationship between more than one object.
– *PreferenceConstraint* (*PreferenceCons*) represents soft constraints, which augment regular constraints with functions to be optimized.

Let us focus on the *SingleAttributeConstraint*s, henceforth denoted as SACs. They refer to a single class (*appliesToClass*) and attribute of that class (*appliesToAttribute*). Note that an *attribute* of class C is an OWL property with

---

[2] In OWL, referring to classes and properties as values of other properties is problematic; see [54]. We avoid these difficulties by only using such references in SPARQL [56] queries.

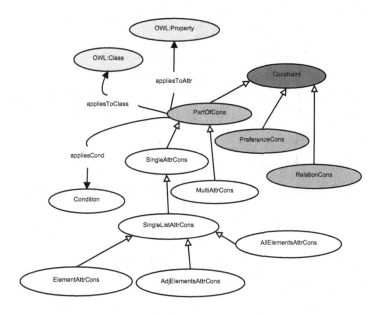

Fig. 5. A portion of the Constraints Ontology.

class C as a possible domain. A special kind of SAC, *SingleListAttributeConstraint*, applies to attributes that are ordered lists of objects or values. In that case, it is important to distinguish among the cases when the constraint applies to the individual elements of the list (*ElementAttributeConstraint*), to pairs of adjacent elements (*AdjElementsAttributeConstraint*), or globally to all the elements of the list (*AllElementsAttributeConstraint*).

A SAC specifies a condition by means of the *appliesCondition* property; see Fig. 6. We distinguisch between two types of conditions:

- *AggregateConditions* (*AggregateCond*, in gray) specify restrictions on some aggregate quantity computed from the elements of a list attribute or from a subset of them.
- *IndividualConditions* (*IndividualCond*) apply to each element (or pair of elements) of a list attribute, or to the unique value of a scalar attribute.

Individual conditions can be created by composing *AtomicConditions* into *CompositeConditions* with the usual logic connectives: *and, or* and *not*. Moreover, *QuantifierConditions* specify a quantified *variable* (*QVar*) to be used within an inner *subcondition*. A *QVar* has several properties that make it a powerful concept:

- a quantifier *quant* (*forall, exists*);
- a *class* from which the variable takes values (this is the domain of the variable);
- a *type* (*part, other*), which for *PartOfConstraint*s specifies whether the variable ranges over the parts involved by the constraint or not;

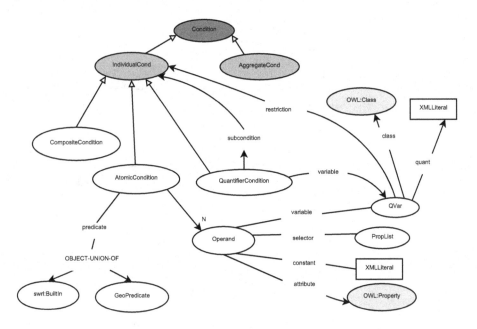

Fig. 6. A portion of the Condition Hierarchy (Constraints Ontology).

- an optional *restriction* that puts a further condition on the values over which the variable should range.

An *AtomicCondition* has a *predicate*, that can be either an SWRL built-in predicate (e.g., *equal, lessThen, add, subtract, ...*) or a *GeoPredicate*, i.e., a predicate that relates the geometric properties of two or more *Features*. The *GeoPredicate* class contains both GeoSPARQL and additional properties defined and implemented in the present work[3]. The condition has one or more *Operands*, which can specify:

- a quantified *variable* (*QVar*);
- a *selector* modeled as a list of properties;
- a *constant* value; i.e., *XMLLiteral*;
- an *attribute*.

As a SAC applies to an attribute A of a class C, by default an operand refers to the value of A in the objects O of class C. However, things can be customized by specifying a *constant* value, the *attribute* of O to consider, or the *selector* (list of properties) that should be followed from A to get to the value of the operand. Moreover, it is possible to specify a quantified *variable* (*QVar*) of an enclosing *QuantifierCondition*; in that case, the operand refers to the value taken by the variable.

---

[3] So far, we added one custom property (named *separates*) that will be used in the examples below.

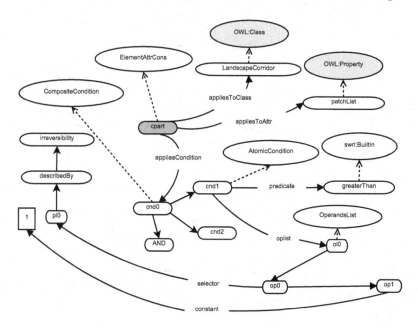

Fig. 7. The *cpart* (Corridor Part) constraint.

It should be noticed that the main goal of this representation is the specification of various metadata about constraints; for instance, see the distinction between part-of, relation and preference constraints. The ontology can be extended and refined as needed to express additional metadata. This is a key element for the development of reasoners that automatically retrieve suitable constraints to perform constraint solving, given the characteristics of the input problem.

Example 1. Let us consider the *LandScapeCorridor* class of the EN Domain ontology (see Fig. 2). The guidelines for the Local EN implementation devised in project [11] state that:

> *Corridors avoid areas with maximum irreversibility and areas with maximum extroversion.*

A landscape corridor is therefore made of patches that must exhibit the specified characteristics. Figure 7 depicts the specification of the constraint that enforces these prescriptions: we associate the constraint *cpart* with class *LandScapeCorridor*[4]. Constraint *cpart* is an *ElementAttributeConstraint* because it applies to each element of the *patchList* property of *Corridor*. It specifies a *CompositeCondition cnd0* that consists of the conjunction of two *AtomicConditions*:

---

[4] Following the graphic notation described in [52], the rounded rectangles represent individuals, while dashed arrows symbolize instance-of relationships.

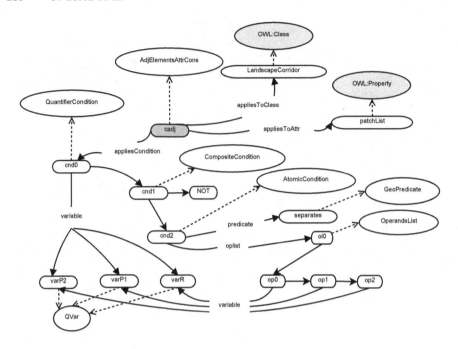

Fig. 8. The *cadj* (Corridor Adjacency) constraint.

- The former *AtomicCondition*, *cnd1*, requires a non-maximum irreversibility and it specifies:
  - the *predicate* as *swrlb:greaterThan*;
  - the operation list (*ol0*) that specifies the two operands of *cnd1* as a linked list. Specifically:
    * the first *Operand* is element *op0* in *oplist ol0*; *op0* is a *selector* and points to a *PropertyList pl0* that contains as its elements properties *describedBy* (from *Patch* to *LandUseElement*) and *irreversibility* (from *LandUseElement* to the value of the irreversibility criterion);
    * the second *Operand op1* is the *constant* value 1.
- The second *AtomicCondition cnd2* is similar to the first one but it requires non-maximum extroversion and is not detailed in Fig. 7 for shortness.

Example 2. Let us consider again the *LandScapeCorridor* class in the EN Domain ontology. A specification taken from [42] states that:

> *The design of Corridors should avoid major linear obstacles (highways, high-speed railways, large artificial canals).*

We can associate a suitable constraint with class *LandScapeCorridor*. The *cadj* constraint, depicted in Fig. 8, has the following traits:

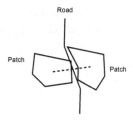

Fig. 9. The *Separates* predicate.

- it is an *AdjElementsAttributeConstraint*, because it constrains adjacent elements of the *patchList* property;
- it specifies a *QuantifierCondition cnd0* that quantifies the following *QVars*:
  - *varR*, ranging *forall* the *Road*s with *hasTraffic* property greater than 2;
  - *varP1*, ranging *forall* the *Patch*es that can constitute *single_parts* of the *patchList*;
  - *varP2*, ranging *forall* the *Patch*es that can constitute *single_parts* of the *patchList*;
- the subcondition of *cnd0* is a *CompositeCondition cnd1* that negates (*NOT*) its own subcondition *cnd2*;
- *AtomicCondition cnd2* specifies:
  - the predicate *separates*, which takes value *true* iff its first operand (a *Road*) separates the second and the third operands (two *Patch*es); this corresponds to checking whether the segment conjoining the centers of the two patches intersects the road, as shown in Fig. 9;
  - the *oplist ol0* containing operands that refer to *variables varR, varP1*, and *varP2*.

3.3 Representation of Constraints and of Individual Information Items

The instances of the constraints classes representing the actual constraints that apply in the domain, such as the sample ones described at the end of the previous section, are stored in RDF format [55] in a triple store that represents the knowledge base used by the system. The triple store also contains the instances of the classes defined in the EN Domain ontology, such as the *Patch*es of land that form the map of a specific geographic area of interest. As far as geographic items are concerned, the translation from input data-sets (typically available as ESRI shapefiles) to RDF triples is carried out by our data import functions described in Sect. 5.

3.4 Supporting Efficient Geographic Reasoning: The Adjacency Graph Model

While, starting from the RDF representation of domain knowledge, an automated reasoner can obviously perform the appropriate inferences to solve an input problem, several basic inferences could be pre-compiled to speed up exe-cution. In particular, the adjaciency relations between the land patches of a geographical area are expected to change very rarely; therefore, they can be pre-processed and made available to the automated reasoners as aggregated data.

In this perspective, beside the OWL representation of knowledge described in the previous sections, we consider a graph model that can be derived from the RDF instances of the knowledge base and is particularly useful for the rea-soning features of our system; see Sect. 4. The graph $\mathcal{G} = (N, E)$, denoted as the Adjacency Graph, is structured as follows:

– the nodes N correspond to areas of a map;
– the arcs E connect nodes whose associated areas are adjacent in the map.

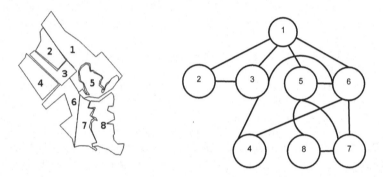

Fig. 10. A map and its corresponding Adjacency Graph, from [49].

Figure 10 shows a map and its Adjacency Graph. Each node of the graph is associated with an area of the map; moreover, areas and nodes are numbered consistently to show their correspondences. For example, node 1 corresponds to an area that is adjacent to the areas associated to nodes 2, 3, 5 and 6. It can be noticed that, in the generation of the Adjacency Graph, some noise in the map data has been removed. For instance, nodes 5 and 8 are connected in the Adjacency Graph even though the borders of their areas are not exactly adjacent in the map. This type of abstraction is needed to deal with real-world, imperfect GIS data, and is a basic pre-processing task that can be performed by our system. Specifically, when a new area A is inserted into the knowledge base of the system, standard geometric algorithms are used to compute an expansion A' of A which extends A with a border of a given thickness, and to determine the adjacent areas as the ones that intersect with A'.

It might be questioned why, instead of exploiting standard geographic reason-ing functions such as those offered by GeoSPARQL, we developed our own ones. Indeed, while GeoSPARQL provides a set of functions to compute the *Simple Features* topological relations it defines, those functions require that the involved geometries exactly satisfy the corresponding relations. For instance, according to

GeoSPARQL, an area *touches* another area *iff* they share some common points on their borders, but they do not share any internal points. This function is clearly too restrictive to determine the adjacency of two geographical areas in a meaningful way for our purposes because the specification of both areas could be noisy.

Overall, we use the Adjacency Graph of a geographical area to store more information than the association between nodes and areas. Specifically:

- Each node $n \in N$ can have attributes representing meta-information about the area $\mathcal{A}_n$ associated with it. In the EN domain, this may include:
  - the values of the evaluation criteria and the LCP levels of the *LandUseElement* describing $\mathcal{A}_n$;
  - information such as the area size and perimeter of $\mathcal{A}_n$;
  - the identity of the EN element to which $\mathcal{A}_n$ belongs; e.g., a *CoreArea*.
- Each arc $e = (n_i, n_j) \in E$ can have attributes that represent meta-information about the relationship between $\mathcal{A}_{n_i}$ and $\mathcal{A}_{n_j}$. For example, the arc can have:
  - the length of the perimeter shared by the two areas;
  - a numeric "cost" that describes how difficult is to move from $\mathcal{A}_{n_i}$ to $\mathcal{A}_{n_j}$. This cost is determined by the presence of an obstacle (instance of class *LinearObstacle* of the EN Domain ontology) between the two areas.

4   A Portfolio of Reasoners

4.1   Reasoning Tasks

Our model supports reasoning tasks based on the following kinds of inputs:

- the EN and Constraints ontologies, which describe the domain concepts, the constraints hierarchy and their relationships;
- the RDF data representing the instances of domain classes of the EN ontology; e.g., individual land patches included in the geographic area of interest;
- the RDF data representing the instances of the constraints (classes of the Constraints ontology) that apply to the specific domain;
- further requirements provided by the user to specify the desired reasoning task and its parameters.

Ideally, we would like that the system automatically extracts all the data needed to perform a requested task from the above listed sources of information, and use it to drive a generic reasoning engine that computes the answer by exploiting the RDF domain instances. However, this type of generality would be extremely hard if not impossible to achieve in practice. Therefore, we equip the system with a pre-defined (but extensible) set of reasoning capabilities that can be reused in different tasks and fill the details of specific reasoning task requests.

Definition 1. *A Reasoner* $\mathcal{R}(\Omega, \Delta, \rho)$ *is a function that takes as inputs an OWL ontology* Ω, *a RDF graph* Δ, *and a request* ρ, *where* Ω *is partitioned in two sets* Ω_{DOM} *(EN Domain ontology classes) and* Ω_{CONS} *(EN Constraint ontology classes), and, similarly,* Δ *is partitioned in two sets* Δ_{DOM} *and* Δ_{CONS}. *The reasoner performs the following steps:*

1. *it extracts from* Δ_{CONS} *(driven by ontology* Ω_{CONS} *and request* ρ*), a relevant set of constraints:*

$$\mathcal{C} = \mathcal{C}_G \cup \mathcal{C}_R$$

   denoting, respectively, graph constraints and reasoning constraints;
2. *using* $\mathcal{C}_G$, *it extracts from* Δ_{DOM} *the data* $\mathcal{D}_G$ *useful for building the Adjacency Graph model;*
3. *using* $\mathcal{D}_G$, *it builds the Adjacency Graph model* $\mathcal{G}$;
4. *using* $\mathcal{C}_R$, *it extracts from* Δ_{DOM} *the additional data* $\mathcal{D}_R$ *useful to support the reasoning task;*
5. *using* $\mathcal{D}_R$, *it performs a reasoning task on* $\mathcal{G}$ *by enforcing the constraints in* $\mathcal{C}_R$;
6. *it returns a result* α *that answers the request* ρ, *given* Ω *and* Δ.

The extraction of constraints (step 1 above) is done by issuing SPARQL queries [56] on the RDF data Δ_{CONS} using the vocabulary of ontology Ω. The retrieved constraints are represented as internal data structures that the reasoner can use to perform steps 2, 4 and 5 above. Specifically:

- $\mathcal{R}$ uses the constraints $\mathcal{C}_G$ to automatically generate SPARQL queries that extract from Δ_{DOM} the data $\mathcal{D}_G$ needed to build the nodes of graph $\mathcal{G}$;
- $\mathcal{R}$ uses the constraints $\mathcal{C}_R$ to automatically generate SPARQL queries that extract from Δ_{DOM} other, additional data $\mathcal{D}_R$ needed by the reasoner;
- finally, $\mathcal{R}$ directly evaluates in-memory the constraints $\mathcal{C}_R$ by using data $\mathcal{D}_R$ while it searches for a solution by visiting graph $\mathcal{G}$.

Specific tasks are requested by executing *Commands* that are translated to one or several invocations of the reasoner with specific values of request ρ.

Currently, we have implemented the following two reasoners:

- $\mathcal{R}_{CLUST}$: starting from a given *Patch*, it computes a clustering of the surrounding patches that satisfy the constraints associated with a given property. The reasoner can be used to implement the command *BUILD(CoreArea, id)*, which creates an instance of the *CoreArea* class by clustering the patches that have high or medium *ecological functionality*. The ecological functionality depends on their *naturality* and *relevance*.
- $\mathcal{R}_{PATH}$: given two *CoraAreas*, this reasoner computes a path that is composed of patches satisfying the constraints associated with a given property. The next section describes $\mathcal{R}_{PATH}$ in detail.

4.2   The $\mathcal{R}_{PATH}$ Reasoner

The $\mathcal{R}_{PATH}$ reasoner receives (through the request ρ) two identifiers id_s and id_e of *CoreAreas* that aggregate *Patches*, and the name of a property *prop* that is a list of *Patches*. It then computes a path of adjacent elements from element id_s to id_e taking into account the constraints associated with property *prop*.

This reasoner can be used to implement the command *BUILD(Landscape-Corridor, id_s, id_e)* which assigns id_s, id_e to the *from* and *to* attributes of *LandscapeCorridor*, and computes the value of the *patchList* attribute by invoking reasoner $\mathcal{R}_{PATH}$ with $\rho = (id_s, id_e, patchList)$.

1. First of all, the reasoner issues a number of SPARQL queries to retrieve the constraints associated with *LandscapeCorridor* and retrieves the following constraints:
   - a *ElementAttributeConstraint cpart* associated with *patchList* described in Example 1;
   - an *AdjElementsAttributeConstraint cadj* associated with *patchList* described in Example 2.

   Constraint *cpart* is a $\mathcal{C}_G$ constraint, i.e., it is used to identify the nodes of the adjacency graph $\mathcal{G}$. Constraint *cadj* is a $\mathcal{C}_R$ constraint, i.e., it is used directly by the reasoner during the search for a solution.
2. Then, the reasoner builds an Adjacency Graph $\mathcal{G}$ in such a way that the nodes of $\mathcal{G}$ are associated to patches that satisfy *cpart*; i.e., they have non-maximum irreversibility and extroversion.
3. After that, $\mathcal{R}_{PATH}$ considers constraint *cadj* and realizes that, for its enforcement, it needs to retrieve the additional data $\mathcal{D}_R$ consisting of all the *Roads* with *hasTraffic* ≥ 2.
4. Finally, the reasoner applies a simple path-finding algorithm based on the well-known *Dijkstra* algorithm [2] to identify a corridor between the id_s and

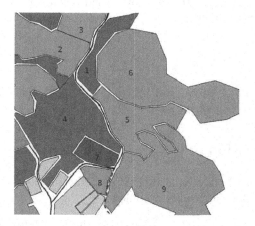

Fig. 11. Sample map with patches and roads.

id_e elements, if any. As the *cadj* constraint is of type *AdjElementsAttribute-Constraint*, $\mathcal{R}_{PATH}$ applies it whenever it explores any further nodes that are adjacent to the currently considered node. In particular, a node N' is considered adjacent to a node N iff there is no road selected by $\mathcal{D}_R$ that *separates* N and N'. Note that, in order to evaluate this condition, the reasoner needs to invoke an in-memory function that implements the *separates GeoPredicate*, with nodes N and N', as well as data $\mathcal{D}_R$, as arguments.

Example 3. As an example of the use of reasoner $\mathcal{R}_{PATH}$, let us consider the map depicted in Fig. 11, where:

- patches 2,3,5,6,8, and 9 (lighter gray) are *describedBy LandUseElements* of type *WoodenLand*
- patches 1,4, and 7 (darker gray) are *describedBy LandUseElements* of type *Meadow*
- the dashed-line road is a local road (with *hasTraffic* equal to 1)
- the solid-line road is a secondary road (whose *hasTraffic* equal to 3)

Let us further assume that patches 1 and 8 correspond to two *CoreAreas*. Reasoner $\mathcal{R}_{PATH}$ can then be invoked with $id_s = 1$ and $id_e = 8$ in order to try to find a path of suitable adjacent patches that connects them. First of all, we note that all the numbered patches in Fig. 11 satisfy constraint *cpart*, i.e., they have admissible levels of *irreversibility* and *extrovarsion*. Therefore, they are returned as elements of the data set $\mathcal{D}_G$ used to build the Adjacency Graph $\mathcal{G}$. As for the roads in the map, only the solid-line roads are returned as elements of the data set $\mathcal{D}_R$ because the *hasTraffic* property of the dashed-line roads has a value that is too low for such roads to be relevant for constraint *cadj*. When the reasoner starts searching for a path from patch 1 to patch 8, it first considers the patches that are adjacent to patch 1, namely: 2,3,4,5, and 6. However, by applying constraint *cadj*, the reasoner immediately discards patches 2,3, and 4, since they are *separated* from patch 1 by a road belonging to data set $\mathcal{D}_R$. The search for the path to patch 8 has therefore to continue from patches 5 and 6. A possible solution is the following path:

$$(5, 9)$$

that leads from patch 1 to patch 8 by crossing a local road that can be safely ignored according to constraint *cadj*.

5 Implementation

We have implemented the model described in the previous sections as a Java library consisting of the following modules:

- *data-import* contains functions supporting the import/export of shape files to/from a triple store (e.g., Parliament [4]), the pre-processing, optimization, and conversion of the reference system of the geometries associated with geo-SPARQL *Features*, and the transfer of RDF triples between disk and the in-memory model of the Jena library [3] used to query the triple store. The metadata associated with the geometries in the shape file is exploited to associate such geometries with the appropriate concepts in the EN ontology (in particular, *Roads* and *Patches* described by *LandUseElements*);

- *reasoning* contains the functions for the creation of the Adjacency Graph data model. Moreover, it collects all the specific reasoners provided by the system (currently, the $\mathcal{R}_{PATH}$ and $\mathcal{R}_{CLUST}$ reasoners described above);
- *commands* implements the parsing of commands (currently, the two forms of the *BUILD* command described above) and interfaces with the *reasoning* and *data-import* functions to execute them;
- *shared* provides the definitions and implementations of elements relevant across the other system modules; e.g., the geometric feature and triple store manager, as well as utility functions used by the other modules.

By exploiting the *data-import* module, we have populated the Parliament triple store with 395 patches and 307 roads defined in the shape files of a portion of map situated at the north of the Italian city of Turin. We have then used the implementation of the $\mathcal{R}_{CLUST}$ reasoner contained in the *reasoning* module to generate the Core Areas as clusters of patches with given characteristics. The reasoner has generated 74 clusters. Finally, we have used the implementation of the $\mathcal{R}_{PATH}$ reasoner to generate a number of landscape Corridors between pairs of Core Areas specified by us.

6   Conclusions and Future Work

This paper has presented a semantic framework for the specification and management of constraints on a geographical domain. Our framework supports the validation of conditions on a geographic area, the composition of land patches into broader areas having homogeneous properties and the identification of paths satisfying given sets of constraints for connecting land patches. We represent both the domain knowledge and the constraints as OWL ontologies based on standard languages for knowledge representation and reasoning. This approach has several advantages: first of all, it does not introduce any special language for the management of constraints. Second, it fully exploits the knowledge representation and reasoning interoperability provided by Semantic Web languages. Third, it opens the avenue to the classification of constraints for their automated management within reasoners that can adapt to solve a possibly large range of reasoning problems.

As a test-bed we use the Ecological Networks domain. In this context, we aim at supporting both the compliance verification with respect to a pre-defined Ecological Network and the generation of a new one by suggesting suitable aggregations of land patches into EN elements. Moreover, our approach is designed to support full-fledged implementations of creation and modification tasks in order to enable the automated suggestion of *modifications* to existing EN elements through suitable interventions. Whereas we implemented reasoning about ENs as a stand-alone model, the main motivation and application of our work lies in its possible integration within Participatory Geographical Information Systems (PGIS [47]), in order to support online interaction with stakeholders in inclusive urban planning and design processes aimed at collecting feedback and EN project proposals from stakeholders.

Our work can be extended in several directions to provide a suitable decision support system. For instance, we plan to:

- Extend the EN ontology to model finer-grained concepts. For instance, we currently describe a land patch by exclusively considering its use; e.g., wetland and wooden land. In our future work we may consider the association of more specific information with patches by exploiting existing ontologies to model further environment and ecology concepts, e.g., ENVO [10] and EcoCore [9].
- Extend the Constraint ontology to specify more types of constraints, such as *soft* constraints for guiding the automated reasoners offered by the framework to compute solutions that maximize some preference criteria, and *geometric* constraints about the shape, size, and other properties of given areas.
- Extend our reasoning framework with the ability to handle soft constraints, and with additional reasoners; e.g., for proposing maintenance and modification interventions on an EN.

Acknowledgements. We thank Adriano Savoca and Marco Corona for their contributions to this work.

References

1. Abrahao, E., Hirakawa, A.: Complex task ontology conceptual modelling: towards the development of the agriculture operations task ontology. In: Proceedings of 10th International Joint Conference on Knowledge Discovery, Knowledge Engineering and Knowledge Management (KEOD 2018). SCITEPRESS, Seville (2018)
2. Ahuja, R.K., Mehlhorn, K., Orlin, J., Tarjan, R.E.: Faster algorithms for the shortest path problem. J. ACM (JACM) **37**(2), 213–223 (1990)
3. Apache: Apache jena (2019). https://jena.apache.org/
4. Battle, R., Kolas, D.: Enabling the geospatial Semantic Web with Parliament and GeoSPARQL. Semant. Web **3**(4), 355–370 (2012)
5. Benedict, M., McMahon, E.: Green Infrastructure: Smart Conservation for the 21st Century. Watch Clearinghouse Monograph Series, Sprawl (2002)
6. Bennett, G., Mulongoy, K.: Review of Experience with Ecological Networks, Corridors and Buffer Zones. Technical Series, vol. 23 (2006)
7. Bennett, G., Wit, P.: The Development and Application of Ecological Networks: A Review of Proposals, Plans and Programmes. AIDEnvironment (2001)
8. Boley, H., Tabet, S., Wagner, G.: Design rationale of RuleML: a markup language for semantic web rules. In: Proceedings of the First International Conference on Semantic Web Working, pp. 381–401. CEUR-WS. org (2001)
9. Buttigieg, P.L.: Ecology Core Ontology (2018). https://github.com/EcologicalSemantics/ecocore. Accessed 28 July 2018

10. Buttigieg, P.L., Pafilis, E., Lewis, S.E., Schildhauer, M.P., Walls, R.L., Mungall, C.J.: The environment ontology in 2016: bridging domains with increased scope, semantic density, and interoperation. J. Biomed. Semant. **7**(1), 57 (2016). https://doi.org/10.1186/s13326-016-0097-6

11. Città Metropolitana di Torino: Misura 323 del PSR 2007–2013 (2014). http://www.cittametropolitana.torino.it/cms/territorio-urbanistica/misura-323/misura-323-sperimentale

12. Città Metropolitana di Torino: Torino Metropoli - Città Metropolitana di Torino (2019). http://www.cittametropolitana.torino.it

13. Council of Europe: General guidelines for the development of the Pan-European Ecological Network. Nature and environment, no. 107 (2000)

14. ENEA: Agenzia nazionale per le nuove tecnologie, l'energia e lo sviluppo economico sostenibile (2019). http://www.enea.it/it

15. Fath, B., Sharler, U., Ulanowicz, R., Hannon, B.: Ecological network analysis: network construction. Trends Ecol. Evol. **208**, 49–55 (2007)

16. Felfernig, A., Friedrich, G., Jannach, D., Zanker, M.: Configuration knowledge representation using UML/OCL. In: Jézéquel, J.-M., Hussmann, H., Cook, S. (eds.) UML 2002. LNCS, vol. 2460, pp. 49–62. Springer, Heidelberg (2002). https://doi.org/10.1007/3-540-45800-X_5

17. Fonseca, F., Egenhofer, M., Agouris, P., Câmara, G.: Using ontologies for geographic information systems. Trans. GIS **3**, 231–257 (2002)

18. Fonseca, F., Egenhofer, M., Davis, C.A., Câmara, G.: Semantic granularity in ontology-driven geographic information systems. Ann. Math. Artif. Intell. **36**(1–2), 121–151 (2002). https://doi.org/10.1023/A:1015808104769

19. GeoNames.org: Geonames mappings ontology (2018). http://www.geonames.org/ontology/mappings_v3.01.rdf

20. GeoNames.org: Geonames (2019). http://www.geonames.org/

21. Gobluski, A., Westlund, E., Vandermeer, J., Pascual, M.: Ecological networks over the edge: hypergraph trait-mediated indirect interaction (TMII) structure. Trends Ecol. Evol. **31**(5), 344–354 (2016)

22. Gray, P., Hui, K., Preece, A.: An expressive constraint language for semantic web applications. In: E-Business and the Intelligent Web: Papers from the IJCAI-01 Workshop, pp. 46–53 (2001)

23. Object Management Group: Unified Modeling Language (UML) (2008). http://www.uml.org

24. Gruber, T.: Towards principles for the design of ontologies used for knowledge sharing. Int. J. Hum.-Comput. Stud. **43**(5–6), 907–928 (1995)

25. Guarino, N., Oberle, D., Staab, S.: What Is an ontology? In: Staab, S., Studer, R. (eds.) Handbook on Ontologies. IHIS, pp. 1–17. Springer, Heidelberg (2009). https://doi.org/10.1007/978-3-540-92673-3_0

26. Hall, M., Mandl, P.: Spatially extended ontologies for a semantic model of harmonised landuse and landcover information, April 2006

27. Horrocks, I., Patel-Schneider, P., Boley, H., Tabet, S., Grosof, B., Dean, M.: SWRL: A semantic web rule language combining OWL and RuleML. W3C Member Submiss. **21**, 1–31 (2004)

28. Ingaramo, R., Salizzoni, E., Voghera, A.: La valutazione dei servizi ecosistemici forestali per la pianificazione e il progetto del territorio e del paesaggio. Valori e valutazioni **19**, 65–78 (2018)

29. Janowicz, K., Scheider, S., Pehle, T., Ha, G.: Geospatial semantics and linked spatiotemporal data - past, present, and future. Semant. Web **3**(4), 321–332 (2012). On linked spatiotemporal data and geo-ontologies

30. Janowicz, K., Scheider, S., Pehle, T., Ha, G.: LinkedGeoData: a core for a web of spatial open data. Semant. Web **3**(4), 333–354 (2012). Interoperability, Usability, Applicability
31. Jongman, R.: Nature conservation planning in Europe: developing ecological networks. Landsc. Urban Plann. **32**(3), 169–183 (1995)
32. Lazoglou, M., Angelides, D.C.: Development of an ontology for modeling spatial planning systems. Curr. Urban Stud. **4**(02), 241 (2016)
33. Louwsma, J., Zlatanova, S., van Lammeren, R., van Oosterom, P.: Specifying and implementing constraints in GIS - with examples from a geo-virtual reality system. GeoInformatica **10**(4), 531–550 (2006). https://doi.org/10.1007/s10707-006-0345-5
34. Lurgi, M., Robertson, D.: Automated experimentation in ecological networks. Autom. Exp. **3**(1), 1 (2011)
35. Macke, S.: Dia diagram editor (2019). http://dia-installer.de/
36. Mauro, N., Di Rocco, L., Ardissono, L., Bertolotto, M., Guerrini, G.: Impact of semantic granularity on geographic information search support. In: Proceedings of 2018 IEEE/WIC/ACM International Conference on Web Intelligence (WI), pp. 323–328. IEEE, Santiago (2019)
37. Montenegro, N., Gomes, J., Urbano, P., Duarte, J.: An OWL2 land use ontology: LBCS. In: Murgante, B., Gervasi, O., Iglesias, A., Taniar, D., Apduhan, B.O. (eds.) ICCSA 2011. LNCS, vol. 6783, pp. 185–198. Springer, Heidelberg (2011). https://doi.org/10.1007/978-3-642-21887-3_15
38. OGC: Geosparql vocabulary (2012). http://schemas.opengis.net/geosparql/1.0/geosparql_vocab_all.rdf
39. Open Geospatial Consortium, et al.: OpenGIS Implementation Standard for Geographic information-Simple feature access-Part 1: Common architecture (2011)
40. Palacio, D., Derungs, C., Purves, R.: Development and evaluation of a geographic information retrieval system using fine grained toponyms. J. Spatial Inf. Sci. JoSIS **11**, 1–29 (2015)
41. Pilosof, S., Porter, M., Pascual, M., Kefi, S.: The mulutilayer nature of ecological networks. Nat. Ecol. Evol. **1**(4), 1–9 (2017). article 101
42. Provincia di Torino: Linee guida per le reti ecologiche (2014) (in Italian). http://www.provincia.torino.gov.it/territorio/file-storage/download/pdf/pian_territoriale/rete_ecologica/lgsv_lgre.pdf
43. Quercia, D., Schifanella, R., Aiello, L.: The shortest path to happiness: recommending beautiful, quiet, and happy routes in the city. In: Proceedings of the 25th ACM Conference on Hypertext and Social Media (HT 2014), pp. 116–125. ACM, New York (2014)
44. SDS Consortium: Spatial decision support ontology (2017). http://sdsportal.sdsconsortium.org/ontology/
45. Soininen, T., Tiihonen, J., Männistö, T., Sulonen, R.: Towards a general ontology of configuration. AI EDAM **12**(4), 357–372 (1998)
46. Stumptner, M., Friedrich, G.E., Haselböck, A.: Generative constraint-based configuration of large technical systems. AI EDAM **12**(4), 307–320 (1998)
47. Sun, Y., Li, S.: Real-time collaborative GIS: a technological review. ISPRS J. Photogramm. Remote Sens. **115**, 143–152 (2016)
48. Torta, G., Ardissono, L., Savoca, A., Voghera, A., La Riccia, L.: Representing ecological network specifications with semantic web techniques. In: Proceedings of 9th International Joint Conference on Knowledge Discovery, Knowledge Engineering and Knowledge Management (KEOD 2017), pp. 86–97. SCITEPRESS, Funchal (2017)

49. Torta, G., Ardissono, L., Corona, M., La Riccia, L., Angioletta, V.: Ontological representation of constraints for geographic reasoning. In: Proceedings of 10th International Joint Conference on Knowledge Discovery, Knowledge Engineering and Knowledge Management (KEOD 2018), pp. 136–147. SCITEPRESS, Seville (2018)
50. Torta, G., Ardissono, L., Corona, M., La Riccia, L., Savoca, A., Voghera, A.: GeCoLan: a constraint language for reasoning about ecological networks in the semantic web. In: Fred, A., et al. (eds.) IC3K 2017. CCIS, vol. 976, pp. 268–293. Springer, Cham (2019). https://doi.org/10.1007/978-3-030-15640-4_14
51. Ulanowicz, R.: Quantitative methods for ecological network analysis. Comput. Biol. Chem. **28**, 321–339 (2004)
52. Van Hage, W.R., Malaisé, V., Segers, R., Hollink, L., Schreiber, G.: Design and use of the simple event model (SEM). Web Semant. **9**(2), 128–136 (2011). Science, Services and Agents on the World Wide Web
53. Voghera, A., La Riccia, L.: Ecological networks in urban planning: between theoretical approaches and operational measures. In: Calabrò, F., Della Spina, L., Bevilacqua, C. (eds.) ISHT 2018. SIST, vol. 101, pp. 672–680. Springer, Cham (2019). https://doi.org/10.1007/978-3-319-92102-0_73
54. W3C: Representing classes as property values on the semantic web (2017). https://www.w3.org/TR/2005/NOTE-swbp-classes-as-values-20050405/
55. W3C: Resource description framework (RDF) (2017). https://www.w3.org/RDF/
56. W3C: SPARQL query language for RDF (2017). https://www.w3.org/TR/rdf-sparql-query/
57. W3C: Web ontology language (OWL) (2017). https://www.w3.org/OWL/

DHPs: Dependency Hearst's Patterns for Hypernym Relation Extraction

Ahmad Issa Alaa Aldine[1,3(✉)], Mounira Harzallah[2], Giuseppe Berio[1],
Nicolas Béchet[1], and Ahmad Faour[3]

[1] University Bretagne Sud, IRISA Lab, Vannes, France
ahmad_alaa_eddein@hotmail.com
[2] Nantes University, LS2N Lab, Nantes, France
[3] Lebanese University, Beirut, Lebanon

Abstract. Hearst's patterns are lexico-syntactic patterns that have been extensively used to extract hypernym relations from texts. They are defined as regular expressions based on lexical and syntactical information of each word. Here,
we propose a new formulation of Hearst's patterns using dependency parser,
called Dependency Hearst's Patterns (DHPs). They are defined as dependency
patterns based on dependency relations between words. This formulation allows
us to define more generic Hearst's patterns that match better complex or ambiguous sentences. To evaluate our proposal, we have compared the performance of
Dependency Hearst's patterns to lexico-syntactic patterns: Hearst's patterns and
an extended set of Hearst's patterns applied on two corpora: Music and English.
Dependency Hearst's patterns yield to a considerable improve in term of recall
and a slight decrease in term of precision.

Keywords: Dependency Hearst's Patterns · Hypernym relation extraction ·
Dependency relations

1 Introduction

The Web has become a very huge store of resources, especially textual resources. Therefore, automated knowledge extraction becomes very necessary to address the challenge
of knowledge acquisition. Ontology learning techniques have been proposed to address
this automation. These techniques concern the automatic extraction of knowledge from
texts such as concepts, relations (hypernym and ad-hoc), and axioms. In this paper, we
focus our interest on the automatic extraction of hypernym (*is-a*) relations. Broadly
speaking, hypernym relation is a semantic relationship between two concepts: C_1 is
a hypernym of C_2 means that C_1 categorizes C_2 (e.g. "instrument" is a hypernym
of "Piano"). In the last decades, extracting hypernym relations gains a large interest
because of their importance for understanding content as required in several applications such as question answering, machine translation, information retrieval, and so on.
Besides that, hypernym relations are useful for building taxonomies that are considered
the backbone of ontologies.

In the last decades, two distinct kinds of approaches have been proposed for automatic extraction of hypernym relations from the text: pattern-based and distributional.

© Springer Nature Switzerland AG 2020
A. Fred et al. (Eds.): IC3K 2018, CCIS 1222, pp. 228–244, 2020.
https://doi.org/10.1007/978-3-030-49559-6_11

These two kinds of approaches can be considered as complementary: pattern-based methods extract hypernym relations based on what the text states while distributional ones discover implicit hypernym relations i.e. not necessarily stated in the text. Earlier distributional approaches are unsupervised approaches based on Distributional Inclusion Hypothesis (DIH) [10,26]. Recent approaches are supervised models relying on term embedding [12,15] to represent the feature vectors between term (word) couples. Various vector representations have been used such as concatenation [1] and difference [18,25]. Pattern-based approaches are heuristic methods that extract hypernym relations based on patterns matching. The most popular patterns have been introduced by Hearst [5], and currently known as Hearst's patterns. Original Hearst's patterns are lexico-syntactic patterns that rely on shallow linguistic techniques such as tokenization and POS tagging to include lexical and syntactic information about words. For instance, the pattern: "NP such as (NP, * or | and NP)" means that a noun phrase (NP) must be followed by term "such", term "as", and then by a NP or a list of NPs. In general, Hearst's patterns suffer from low recall due to their few numbers (6 patterns). Moreover, they are prone to make errors due to their limitation in dealing with sentence ambiguity or complexity.

In this paper, our interest is focused on improving the performance of Hearst's patterns. More specifically, we are going to study the impact of reformulating Hearst's patterns as dependency patterns instead of lexico-syntactic patterns on precision and recall. For that purpose, we manually reformulate Hearst's patterns as dependency patterns. A dependency pattern is an ordered set of *dependency relations* where each dependency relation is a binary grammatical relation between two words of a sentence. Dependency patterns are expected to be more general, potentially leading to recall improvement (see Sect. 2.2). In addition, they are expected to be more precise because dependency relations provide closer meaning to the semantics of the sentence. An evaluation is performed using Music and English corpora provided for the task of hypernym discovery in SemEval2018 [3]. The obtained results confirm that considerable improvement is achieved by dependency Hearst's patterns in term of recall but with a slight decrease in precision.

The rest of the paper is organized as follows. Section 2 presents prominent existing methods for hypernym relation extraction based on patterns. Then, we introduce and describe dependency Hearst's patterns in Sect. 3. In Sect. 4, we present the performed experiments. In Sect. 5, we introduce and discuss the results. Finally, conclusions and perspectives of this work are presented in Sect. 6.

2   Related Works

2.1   Pattern-Based Approaches

The first work to extract hypernym relations from a corpus based on patterns was introduced by Hearst at 1992 [5]. Her approach was to handcraft several lexico-syntactic patterns that suggest hypernym relations between noun phrases (NPs). These patterns are currently known as Hearst's patterns. In general, Hearst's patterns have a reasonable precision, but their recall is very low [2] because they are few in number, while there are several syntactical ways to express the same relationship between terms in a sentence.

In the last decades, several works have been proposed to improve recall and precision of Hearst's patterns. Most of the works to increase recall are based on extending Hearst's patterns [7–9, 14, 16, 22]. In [7], the authors introduce new variant patterns for each lexico-syntactic Hearst's pattern by substituting some terms of the patterns by other terms with close meaning or by adding new more terms to the pattern. For example, they replace the terms "such as" in the Hearst's pattern "NP_x such as NP_y" by the term "like" to produce a new pattern "NP_x like NP_y". Another example, they add the term "any" to the pattern "NP and other NP" to produce a new pattern "NP_y and any other NP_x". In [14], Hearst's patterns are extended by manual extraction of new patterns that occur frequently between known hypernym relations in a corpus (e.g. "NP_y is an example of NP_x"). In [22], an extended set of Hearst's patterns (59 patterns) collected from the past literature are used to build a large database of hypernym relation extracted from the web. Moreover, an approach was proposed to improve the recall by applying inference rules to extract additional hypernym relations [17]. The rule is that if y is hypernym of x, and z is similar to x, then it is probable that y is hypernym of z. In [16], an approach was proposed to improve precision first by identifying meronym (not hypernym) patterns, then by removing hypernym pairs if they match meronym patterns more than hypernym patterns. More recently, Roller et al. [19] use an extended set of Hearst's patterns and propose statistical measures based on the frequency of the extracted hypernym relations to improve both precision and recall.

The approaches mentioned above are based on lexico-syntactic patterns. Snow et al. [24] originally proposed an approach to automatically predict hypernym relation between terms using dependency parser. They extract all *dependency paths* that occur between labeled noun pairs. Then, they learn a logistic regression classifier model using the occurrence frequencies of the dependency paths. Dependency paths with higher weights in the classifier model are considered as relevant dependency patterns to indicate hypernym relations. Using their method, they were able to rediscover Hearst's patterns and discover new patterns. More recently, similar approaches to the one of Snow et al. [24] were proposed [20, 23]. In [20], authors compared between dependency patterns and lexico-syntactic patterns, and they have concluded that there is no much difference in performance and with a high cost of computation time using dependency patterns. While in [23], the approach was proposed to discover meronym patterns in addition to hypernym patterns. In [13], another approach was proposed to automatically extract hypernym relations based on dependency patterns. The authors extract all shortest dependency paths between named entities, and then they generalize these paths by replacing words with syntactic, lexical, and semantic information.

Despite the interest of previous approaches that use dependency parsing for automatic learning of dependency patterns [20, 23, 24], it was not possible to analyze and compare each dependency pattern to its corresponding lexico-syntactic pattern, because these approaches are supervised methods that use a large number of automatically extracted dependency patterns as features to learn a classifier model. Our work here focuses on understanding to what extent dependencies can improve the performance of lexico-syntactic patterns. In other words, we will study the strong and weak point dependency patterns over lexico-syntactic patterns by comparing each dependency pattern to its corresponding lexico-syntactic pattern. Therefore, we manually reformulate lexico-syntactic Hearst's patterns as dependency Hearst's patterns and compare their performance pattern by pattern. In addition, we compare each dependency pattern to a set of lexico-syntactic patterns that are extensions of the corresponding Hearst's pattern.

2.2 Extended Set of Hearst's Patterns

As mentioned in Sect. 2.1, Seitner et al. [22] have collected a large set of lexico-syntactic patterns (59 patterns) from literature to build a large database of hypernym relations extracted from the web. The extended set consists of Hearst's patterns, extended Hearst's patterns, and additional lexico-syntactic patterns. Table 1 shows some examples of patterns from the collected patterns. NP_{ho} refers to the hyponym noun phrase and NP_{hr} refers to the hypernym noun phrase.

Table 1. Some examples of patterns collected from the past literature.

Pattern
NP_{hr} such as NP_{ho}
NP_{ho} and other NP_{hr}
NP_{ho} is a NP_{hr}
NP_{ho} is example of NP_{hr}
examples of NP_{ho} is NP_{hr}
NP_{ho} and any other NP_{hr}
NP_{ho} and some other NP_{hr}
NP_{hr} which is called NP_{ho}
NP_{hr} like NP_{ho}
NP_{hr} like other NP_{ho}

From the set of collected patterns, we notice that some of these patterns are extensions of other patterns by adding one or more words and these additional words do not change the dependency path between "NP_{ho}" and "NP_{hr}". For instance, "NP_{ho} and any other NP_{hr}" is an extension of the Hearst's pattern "NP_{ho} and other NP_{hr}" by adding the word "any" before the word "other" and it has no effect on the dependency path between "NP_{ho}" and "NP_{hr}". Consequently, we expect that a dependency pattern replaces several lexico-syntactic patterns, leading to recall improvement. Table 2 shows two of Hearst's patterns and their extended patterns that are expected to be replaced by only two dependency patterns. The examples of extended patterns shown in the Table 2 are mentioned in the past literature, while our expectation is that dependency patterns are more generic patterns that may include lexico-syntactic patterns that are not extended before. For instance, "NP_{ho}, appositive phrase, is a NP_{hr}" is included in the dependency pattern corresponding to the Hearst's pattern "NP_{ho} is a NP_{hr}", because the appositive phrase does not affect the dependency path between NP_{ho} and NP_{hr} (e.g. "Lion, the king of the forest, is a dangerous animal").

3   Dependency Hearst's Patterns

3.1   Dependency Parsing and Relations

Dependency parsing is a Natural Language Processing (NLP) technique that provides the syntactic structure of a sentence. The syntactic structure of a sentence is described in

Table 2. Two of Hearst's patterns and their extended patterns that are expected to be replaced by two dependency patterns.

Hearst's pattern	Extended pattern
NP$_{ho}$ and|or other NP$_{hr}$	NP$_{ho}$ and|or any other NP$_{hr}$
	NP$_{ho}$ and|or some other NP$_{hr}$
	NP$_{ho}$ and|or like other NP$_{hr}$
NP$_{ho}$ is|are|was|were a NP$_{hr}$	NP$_{ho}$ is|are|was|were example of NP$_{hr}$
	example of NP$_{hr}$ is|are|was|were NP$_{ho}$

terms of directed binary grammatical relations that hold between the words. These grammatical relations are also known as dependency relations each one comprising one head word and one dependent word. $Rel(Head, Dependent)$. A major advantage of dependencies is the ability to deal with languages that have a relatively free word order. Another advantage of dependencies is that the dependency relations associate distant words in a sentence; in this sense, they are closer to the semantic meaning of a sentence [11].

Recently, additional and enhanced dependency relations have been presented in [21]. Examples of enhanced relations are the augmented modifiers, where all nominal modifiers in enhanced representation comprise the preposition e.g. nmod:such_as. Such relations facilitate the extraction of relationships between words. Figures 1 and 2 show the enhanced typed dependency tree for sentences "I like musical instruments invented in Spain, such as guitar" and "A march, as a musical genre, is a piece of music with a strong regular rhythm" respectively. Below, some dependency relations used in the remainder of the paper are explained:

– **nmod:such_as:** nmod refers to nominal modifier, associating a non-head noun that serves as a modifier of a head noun. "such_as" is the preposition name of "nmod". For instance, the dependency relation "nmod:such_as(instrument, guitar)" (see Fig. 1) is useful to indicate the hypernym relation "guitar *is-an* instrument".
– **cop:** cop refers to copula, i.e. a relation between a copula verb and its complement (all verbs "to be" are copula verbs). For instance, for a sentence reported above, the dependency parser provides the relation cop(is, piece).
– **nsubj:** nsubj refers to nominal subject, i.e. it represents the subject of a clause. The head in the relation is not always a verb, it can be an adjective or a noun when the verb is copula verb. For instance, for a sentence reported above, the dependency parser provides the relation nsubj(march, piece).

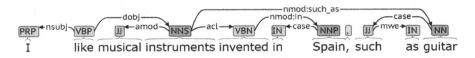

Fig. 1. Enhanced typed dependency tree [6].

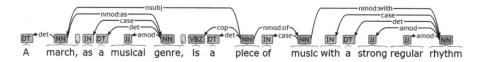

Fig. 2. Enhanced typed dependency tree [6].

3.2 Patterns Formulation

To reformulate Hearst's patterns in term of dependency relations (resulting in what we name Dependency Hearst's Patterns), we performed the following steps for each Hearst's pattern:

i. selecting from a corpus a random set of matching sentences with the lexico-syntactic pattern[1].
ii. applying the dependency parser on each sentence to extract enhanced dependency relations.
iii. analyzing manually the set of parsed sentences of one pattern.
iv. defining a general dependency pattern corresponding to the Hearst's pattern.

Table 3 shows the 6 Hearst's patterns, and their corresponding dependency patterns (DHPs). Each dependency pattern is an ordered set of dependency relations. However, dependency relations represent syntactic relations between words, while a sentence expresses semantic relations between noun phrases rather than between words. For instance, the hypernym relation between "instrument" and "guitar" or that between "piece" and "march" are less semantically rich (even not correct) than those respectively between "musical instrument" and "guitar" and "piece of music" and "march". DHPs enable to extract hypernym relations between noun phrases instead of words using the notion of $NPHead$ (headword of a noun phrase). DHPs first suggest hypernym relations between words, then they check if the words are headwords of noun phrases to suggest hypernym relations between the noun phrases. $NP_{ho}Head$ and $NP_{hr}Head$ refer to the headwords of hyponym and hypernym noun phrases respectively.

4 Hypernymy Extraction by DHPs

In this section, we describe the process of extracting hypernym relations between noun phrases using DHPs.

4.1 Corpus Pre-processing

Each DHP is a set of dependency relations that should match a sentence based on its syntactical structure (its dependency relations) to suggest hypernym relations between noun phrases. Thus, a pre-processing step is necessary to obtain the syntactical structure for each sentence in a corpus. For that purpose, we have implemented a Java process

---

[1] we select 10 sentences.

Table 3. Hearst's patterns and their corresponding dependency patterns.

Hearst's patterns	Dependency Hearst's patterns
NP_{hr} such as NP_{ho}	case($NP_{ho}Head$, such) nmod:such_as($NP_{hr}Head$, $NP_{ho}Head$)
Such NP_{hr} as NP_{ho}	amod($NP_{hr}Head$, such) case($NP_{ho}Head$, as) nmod: as($NP_{hr}Head$, $NP_{ho}Head$)
NP_{hr} including NP_{ho}	case($NP_{ho}Head$, including) nmod:including($NP_{hr}Head$, $NP_{ho}Head$)
NP_{ho} and|or other NP_{hr}	cc($NP_{ho}Head$, and|or) amod($NP_{hr}Head$, other) conj($NP_{ho}Head$, $NP_{hr}Head$)
NP_{hr} especially NP_{ho}	advmod($NP_{hr}Head$, especially) dep($NP_{hr}Head$, $NP_{ho}Head$)
NP_{ho} was|were|is|are a NP_{hr}	nsubj($NP_{hr}Head$, $NP_{ho}Head$) cop($NP_{hr}Head$, was|were|is|are)

using CoreNLP Library[2]. The process applies on a given corpus the following NLP techniques: Sentence Splitter, Tokenizer, Lemmatizer, POS tagger, and Dependency Parser. Besides that, the process extracts all noun phrases in each sentence and identify the headword of each noun phrase to be used by DHPs to suggest hypernym relations between noun phrases using their headwords.

Extraction of Noun Phrases. For a sentence, in order to extract its noun phrases that can be involved in a hypernym relation, we use the phrase structure tree of the sentence. Figure 3 shows the phrase structure tree of the sentence "I like musical instruments invented in Spain, such as guitar". The noun phrases of the sentence are tagged by "NP". In a nested noun phrase where a noun phrase comprises the smallest noun phrases, we select the smallest ones. For instance, "musical instrument invented in Spain" is a noun phrase that comprises the two smallest noun phrases: "musical instrument" and "Spain". On the contrary, in case of nested noun phrases linked by preposition "of", we consider those noun phrases as a unique noun phrase (e.g. "piece of march") based on our assumption that "NP of NP" is more semantically rich than each noun phrase alone.

Noun Phrase Headword Identification. A noun phrase headword is one of the noun phrase words that complies the following rules[3]:

- it is a noun.
- it is not a modifier of another noun within the parsed sentence (nmod).
- it is not a compound of another noun within the parsed sentence (compound).

For instance, consider the noun phrase "keyboard instrument", "keyboard" and "instrument" are both nouns, but "keyboard", according to dependency relations, is the "compound" of "instrument", then we consider "instrument" as NPhead.

---

[2] https://stanfordnlp.github.io/CoreNLP/.

[3] These rules are language dependent, they are defined for English. Thus, they should be adapted to be used for other languages (e.g French).

```
(ROOT
  (S
    (NP (PRP I))
    (VP (VBP like)
      (NP
        (NP (JJ musical) (NNS instruments))
        (VP (VBN invented)
          (PP (IN in)
            (NP (NNP Spain))))
        (, ,)
        (PP (JJ such) (IN as)
          (NP (NN guitar))))))
    (. .)))
```

Fig. 3. Phrase structure tree [6].

4.2 Hypernymy Extraction Between Noun Phrases by DHP Matching

One DHP could match a sentence and suggests hypernym relations between its noun phrases. It matches a sentence if each dependency relation in the pattern also occurs as dependency relation in the syntactical structure of the sentence, and the order of the dependency relations in the pattern is the same to that of the syntactical structure of the sentence. For example, if a DHP dependency relation of index i exists in the sentence set of dependency relations at index j, then the pattern dependency relation of index $i + 1$ should exist in the sentence set of dependency relations at index $j + k$, with i, j, & $k > 0$. After matching, DHP suggests one hypernym relations between pair of noun phrases by associating $NP_{ho}Head$ and $NP_{hr}Head$ of the pattern to the relevant noun phrases of the sentence.

However, lexico-syntactic Hearst's patterns are defined to match a sentence and extract one or more hypernym relations (one or more hyponyms for one hypernym). In order to identify one or more hyponyms for one hypernym when matching one DHP on a sentence, we use the conjunction dependency relation "conj($NP_{ho}Head$, $NP_{ho'}Head$)". Indeed, whenever a hypernym relation (ho, hr) is extracted by a pattern, we look for occurring relations as conj(ho, ho') and state that (ho', hr) is also a hypernym relation extracted by the pattern. Let us consider the following sentence: "I like musical instruments such as piano and guitar". Table 4 shows the extracted enhanced dependency relations [6]. A subset of these dependencies matches with the dependency pattern corresponding to "NP such as NP" where "piano" and "instrument" are the headwords of the hyponym and hypernym noun phrases respectively ($NP_{ho}Head$ & $NP_{hr}Head$). Then, a hypernym relation between the hyponym noun phrase "piano" and the hypernym noun phrase "musical instrument" is extracted. And by using the conjunction relation "conj:and(piano, guitar)", hypernym relation between "guitar" and "musical instrument" is also extracted.

Table 4. The enhanced dependency relations [6].

nsubj(like, I), root(ROOT, like)
amod(instruments, musical), dobj(like, instruments)
case(piano, such), mwe(such, as)
nmod:such_as(instruments, piano), cc(piano, and)
conj:and(piano, guitar)

4.3   Hypernymy Extraction Tool Using DHPs

In this section, we will provide our implemented tool for using DHPs to extract hypernym relations from a corpus. It is a simple user interface (UI) tool implemented using Python[4]. The tool consists of two dependent models: the first model takes as input a corpus and apply on it the pre-processing step (see Corpus Pre-processing in Sect. 4.1), the second model takes as input the result of the first model (pre-processed corpus file) and then match the formulated dependency patterns to extract hypernym relations between noun phrases. The final result of the second model is a list of unique hypernym relations extracted from the corpus and a frequency measure for each relation refers to the number of times the relation is extracted by the patterns. Figure 4 shows the interface of the tool. Figure 5 shows some hypernym relations with the highest frequency extracted by the tool from Music corpus where each line represent a hypernym relation in the form "hyponym, hypernym, frequency".

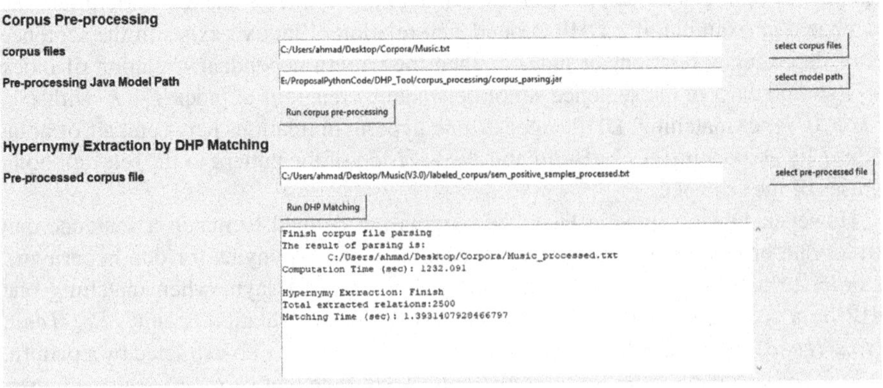

Fig. 4. UI tool for hypernym relation extraction using DHPs.

5   Experimental Setup

5.1   Corpus and Dataset

For the purpose of evaluating the performances of DHPs listed in Table 3, we perform some experiments using two corpora and two datasets made available from the

---

[4] https://github.com/AhmadIssaAlaa/Dependency-Hearsts-Patterns.

```
jazz, genres, 38
voice, instrument, 35
rock, genres, 32
australia, countries, 23
pop, genres, 21
music, rock, 20
blues, genres, 18
united states, countries, 16
france, countries, 16
germany, countries, 16
jazz, styles, 15
rock, styles, 13
spain, countries, 13
hip-hop, genres, 13
folk, genres, 13
metal, genres, 13
guitar, instrument, 13
canada, countries, 13
switzerland, countries, 11
album, work, 11
blues, styles, 10
belgium, countries, 10
punk, genres, 10
japan, countries, 10
korn, band, 10
rock, music, 9
funk, genres, 9
```

Fig. 5. Extracted hypernym relations by the tool.

organizers of hypernymy discovery task at SemEval2018 [3]. The first corpus (Music) contains English sentences representing music domain knowledge and the second corpus (English) contains English sentences representing general knowledge (non-specific domain corpus).

Each corpus is provided with a dataset (DS) that comprises hyponym-hypernym couples (more precisely, for each hyponym a list of hypernyms are provided) that were extracted from the corpus. The Music corpus contains 4.5 million sentences and the Music dataset comprises 5,675 couples. The English corpus contains 270 million sentences and the English dataset comprises 11,689 couples.

Before launching experiments and establishing an evaluation protocol, we analyze carefully both each corpus and its dataset. Indeed, to correctly evaluate precision and recall, each corpus and its dataset need to be compatible in the sense we explain hereinafter. Our analysis reveals that:

1. There are ho-hr couples in the dataset that do not indicate correct hypernym relation, they are errors i.e:

$$\exists \, (ho, hr) \in DS, (ho, hr) \in Errors$$

2. There are ho-hr couples in the dataset that do not occur in any sentence (patterns suggests couples that occur only in the same sentence) i.e:

$$\exists\,(ho, hr) \in DS, \forall\, S \in Corpus, (ho, hr) \text{ does not occur in } S$$

3. There are true ho-hr couples in the dataset occurring in sentences of the corpus, but the sentences do not convey the expected meaning i.e:

$$\exists\, true\,(ho, hr) \in DS\ \&\ \exists\, S \in Corpus, (ho, hr) \text{ occurs in } S$$
$$\implies S \text{ does not express hypernym relation between } ho\ \&\ hr$$

4. There are sentences containing true ho-hr couples (true couples according to some dictionaries or human judgment) but the couples are not comprised in the dataset i.e:

$$\exists\, S \in Corpus\ \&\ \exists\, true\,(ho, hr) \in S,\ where\ (ho, hr) \notin DS$$

The consequence is that it is impossible to evaluate precision and recall correctly by using the provided couples in the dataset. We have therefore defined an adapted protocol to estimate as better as possible precision/recall related to patterns. The protocol employs the given dataset for labeling the sentences in the corpus, then precision and recall are evaluated in terms of the number of sentences matching/non-matching with patterns (and not in terms of the number of couples, both found and expected, in the dataset because of the problems listed above).

5.2 Corpus Labeling

The underlying idea is to label as positive, sentences in which true ho-hr couples occur and conveying the expected meaning (i.e. the sentence semantically states that a couple of noun phrase occurring in it is related by hypernym relation). More formally, for a sentence S:

$$Positive(S)\ iff\ \exists\,(ho, hr) \text{ occurs in } S \text{ where } (ho, hr) \in DS$$
$$\&\ S \text{ expresses the hypernym relation between } ho \text{ and } hr$$

Positive sentences are required to estimate recall as better as possible: in other words, positive sentences enable to estimate the number of expected sentences matching patterns as we explain in Sect. 5.3. Additionally, it is evident that a pattern, if correct, should not match with a sentence not conveying the expected meaning even if the sentence contains a ho-hr couple found elsewhere. For instance, let us consider this sentence "By the 7th century, the koto (a zither) and the biwa (a lute) had been introduced into Japan from China"; the sentence contains the couple (zither, lute) but the sentence does not convey the meaning of hypernym relation between the couple terms. Indeed, as said in the Introduction, patterns extract what is semantically stated in single sentences.

However, there is the need to automate as much as possible the labeling of corpus sentences. Indeed, we cannot manually check each sentence for verifying the conditions above because this is a time-consuming activity; the availability of a dataset also introduces additional complexity for manual labeling because the dataset may represent a kind of ground truth, specific to a knowledge domain. We have therefore introduced the following heuristics, listed below, leading to automatically check the main condition of labeling sentences as positive:

S expresses the hypernym relation between ho and hr

Hereafter are the list of Heuristics to check the condition:

1. hyponym and hypernym are noun phrases.
2. hyponym and hypernym are distant less than 10 words.
3. hyponym and hypernym are not related by conjunction (conj dependency relation).
4. hyponym and hypernym do not occur in distinct brackets within the sentence.

Therefore, a sentence is labeled positive if at least one dataset ho-hr couple occurs in the sentence being this couple constrained by the heuristic provided above. On the contrary, if none of the dataset ho-hr couples occurs in the sentence, the sentence is labeled negative.

The corpus labeling is achieved using the provided dataset for it. But as mentioned in Sect. 5.1, the dataset contains some wrong ho-hr couples. Thus, a preliminary step (Dataset refining) was necessary to refine the dataset from the wrong couples before corpus labeling. Additionally, there are many sentences containing true ho-hr couples but the couples are not included in the provided dataset. Thus, we propose another step (Dataset enriching) to enrich the dataset with new couples. The refining step should prevent the wrong labeling of positive sentences. The enriching step should mitigate the wrong labeling of negative sentences.

- **Dataset Refining:** manual remove of wrong ho-hr couples from the dataset.

$$\forall (ho, hr) \in DS \ \& \ \neg \ True \ (ho, hr) \implies DS - (ho, hr)$$

- **Dataset Enriching:** addition of new ho-hr couples automatically extracted by lexico-syntactic Hearst's patterns (HP). When one pattern matches one sentence, and at least one of the extracted ho-hr couples exists in the dataset, we add the other extracted ho-hr couples by the same pattern on the same sentence to the dataset.

$$\forall S \in corpus \ \& \ \exists \ HP \in Hearst's \ patterns \ where$$
$$HP \ match \ S \ and \ extracts \ [(ho_1, hr_1), ..., (ho_n, hr_n)]$$
$$if \ \exists \ i \ (ho_i, hr_i) \in DS \implies \forall j \ (ho_j, hr_j), DS + (ho_j, hr_j)$$

5.3 Evaluation Protocol

In this section, we target the evaluation of precision, recall, and f-measure for patterns applied to corpus sentences. For that purpose, sentences are classified into True Matched (TM), False Matched (FM) and False Not Matched (FNM).

- **TM:** a matched sentence (positive or negative) with a pattern; and at least one of the extracted hypernym relations by the pattern is validated True.

- **FM:** a matched sentence (positive or negative) with a pattern; and none of the extracted hypernym relations by the pattern is validated True.
- **FNM:** a non-matched positive sentence by any of the patterns.

$$Precision = \frac{TM}{TM + FM}$$
$$Recall = \frac{TM}{TM + FNM}$$
$$F - measure = 2 * \frac{Precision * Recall}{Precision + Recall}$$

It should be noted that positive sentences are used to estimate recall (FNM). However, for precision, positive sentences are taken into account by considering if the extracted couple is validated true (TM) or not (FM). Indeed, a pattern matching a positive sentence may extract any couple which is not found in the dataset but also is not a valid elsewhere (WordNet) or not judged valid (by humans). An extracted hypernym relation is validated true if it exists in the given dataset or it exists in the WordNet [4]. The remaining ones that neither exists in the dataset nor the WordNet are validated manually.

6   Results and Analysis

In this section, we provide the results of applying Dependency Hearst's Patterns (DHPs), lexico-syntactic Hearst's Patterns (HPs), and the extension of lexico-syntactic Hearst's Patterns (extHPs)[5] on the two corpora (Music and English) after corpus labeling. After labeling, the Music corpus consists of 12416 sentences (6208 positive and 6208 negative) and the English corpus consists of 8370 sentences (4185 positive and 4185 negative). After that, an analysis of the results is provided also in this section.

6.1   Results

Table 5 and 6 show the performance for each lexico-syntactic Hearst's pattern (HP) and its corresponding dependency Hearst's pattern (DHP) when applied on Music and English corpora respectively. We can notice the increase of sentences that are true matched (TM) for the most of dependency Hearst's patterns that will lead to increase their recall. The results also show that there is no big difference in term of precision between HPs and DHPs.

Tables 7 and 8 show the precision, recall, and f-measure of HPs, extHPs, and DHPs when applied on Music and English corpora respectively. In both corpora, DHPs outperform other types of patterns in term of recall with a slight decrease in term of recall.

DHPs match sentences based on dependency relations. Thus, to use such type of patterns, a considerable cost will be paid in term of computation time. Table 9 shows the computation time (in seconds) it takes each type of patterns when applied on Music and English corpus. We can notice from the table results the high cost in computation time we have paid when using DHPs.

---

[5] The extHP contains all 59 patterns mentioned in the work of Seitner et al. [22].

Table 5. Pattern by pattern comparison on music corpus.

Pattern	HP			DHP		
	TM	FM	Pre (%)	TM	FM	Pre (%)
NP such as NP	426	**78**	**84.5**	**508**	134	79.1
NP including NP	**170**	**96**	**63.9**	157	107	59.5
NP and/or other NP	119	**42**	**73.9**	**145**	52	73.6
NP is a NP	214	**483**	30.7	**466**	1004	**31.7**
NP especially NP	**5**	**2**	**71.4**	2	4	33
Such NP as NP	28	**4**	**87.5**	**41**	9	82

Table 6. Pattern by pattern comparison on English corpus.

Pattern	HP			DHP		
	TM	FM	Pre (%)	TM	FM	Pre (%)
NP such as NP	24	**17**	**58.5**	**31**	30	50.8
NP including NP	9	33	21.4	**20**	46	**30.3**
NP and/or other NP	54	42	56.3	**65**	40	**62.9**
NP is a NP	75	**216**	**25.7**	**181**	563	24.3
NP especially NP	**3**	**0**	**100**	3	2	60
Such NP as NP	2	**6**	25	**3**	8	**27.3**

Table 7. All patterns comparison on Music corpus.

Patterns type	Precision	Recall	F-measure
HPs	57.8	15.4	24.3
extHPs	**58.9**	18.8	28.5
DHPs	50.2	**20.9**	**29.5**

Table 8. All patterns comparison on English corpus.

Patterns type	Precision	Recall	F-measure
HPs	33.9	3.9	7.0
extHPs	**35.5**	4.7	8.3
DHPs	30.5	**7.2**	**11.6**

Table 9. All patterns computation time on both Music and English corpora.

Patterns type		HPs	extHPs	DHPs
Computation time (sec)	Music	200	201	2454
	English	126	125	665

6.2 Qualitative Analysis

In order to understand the obtained results especially the considerable increase in recall when applying DHPs, we select and analyze some positive sentences that are true matched (TM) with DHPs, while not matching (FNM) or false matched (FM) with HPs. In contrast to HPs, DHPs are capable of matching and identifying correct hypernym relations where non-pattern words occur between hyponym and hypernym noun phrases because DHPs are based on dependency relations and they match sentences without words order restriction. For instance, in these two sentences "A march, as a musical genre, is a piece of music with a strong regular rhythm" and "Piano (pianoforte) is a musical instrument"; the existence of "as a musical genre" and "(pianoforte)" in the two sentences respectively prevents HPs and extHPs to match the sentences, while DHPs correctly match them. Such sentences are frequent and especially to the dependency pattern corresponding to "NP is a NP" which explain its high recall. The number of sentences true matched (TM) with DHP corresponding to "NP is a NP" is 466, while it is 214 for HP (see Table 5). Furthermore, DHPs perform better than HPs dealing with some ambiguous sentences. For instance, in this sentence "I like musical instruments invented in Spain, such as guitar"; HPs match the sentence and identify wrong hypernym relation between "Spain" and "guitar", while DHPs identify the correct hypernym relation between "instruments" and "guitar" thankful to the dependency relation "nmod:such_as(instruments, guitar)" obtained from the dependency parsing.

6.3 Error Analysis

Although, dependency parsing gives a better understanding of the meaning of sentences, it also prone to make errors when applied on complex sentences. These parsing errors may lead DHPs to either match positive sentences and identify wrong hypernym relations or never match the sentence. Additionally, dependency patterns as defined in this work are more generic patterns and they are prone to match sentences and suggest wrong hypernym relations. For example, the defined dependency pattern corresponding to "NP is a NP" is a generic pattern that includes patterns such "NP is in NP" and "NP is with NP", since the occurrence of "in" and "with" do not affect the dependency path between the two noun phrases (e.g. "the lounge revival was in full swing"). This explains the high number of FM by the dependency pattern corresponding to "NP is a NP".

Moreover, while manually validating the extracted hypernym relations for both DHPs and HPs, we notice many matching errors that are common between both types of patterns. The followings are some of these errors:

- errors in identifying named-entities using noun phrase chunker; e.g. "Alice In Chains were the band that made me discover music". We may mitigate such errors by using Named-Entity recognition tool.
- errors in distinguishing between hyponym and hypernym noun phrases, so many inverted hypernym relations are extracted; e.g. "This instrument was a guitar". Such errors are frequently noticed in the pattern "NP is a NP" and they are difficult to be managed by patterns.

– errors in matching ambiguous sentences, where there are some ambiguous sentences that are also very difficult to be managed by both types of patterns; e.g "I like musicians playing keyboard instruments such as Beethoven".

7   Conclusion and Perspectives

We have introduced a new formulation of Hearst's patterns based on dependency relations resulting what we named Dependency Hearst's patterns (DHPs). DHPs are formulated manually by extracting from a corpus some good sentences that were matched by lexico-syntactic Hearst's patterns and then analyzing their syntactical structure. And based on previous works to extend Hearst's patterns, DHPs are defined to be more generic patterns to cover some extended patterns of Hearst's. By reusing two corpora provided at SemEval2018, we propose an evaluation protocol to compare between Hearst's patterns, the extension of Hearst's patterns, and our formulated dependency Hearst's patterns. After analyzing the results, we can state that it is difficult to conclude which type of patterns is better than the others. However, in general, we can state that DHPs achieve a considerable improvement in term of recall with a slight decrease in term of precision. Besides that, a high cost in computation time must be paid for pre-processing sentences with dependency parser to be matched by DHPs.

We are convinced that to achieve a robust approach for hypernym relation extraction, pattern-based and distributional approaches should be integrated together. Therefore, our future work will be focused on integrating them together beside improving pattern-based approaches based on the error analysis interpreted in this paper. For improving pattern-based approaches, our work will be focused to find some additional information lexical or syntactical to be concatenated with DHPs to avoid the decrease in precision.

References

1. Baroni, M., Bernardi, R., Do, N.Q., Shan, C.C.: Entailment above the word level in distributional semantics. In: EACL, pp. 23–32 (2012)
2. Buitelaar, P., Cimiano, P., Magnini, B.: Ontology learning from text: an overview. In: Ontology Learning from Text: Methods, Applications and Evaluation, pp. 3–12 (2005)
3. Camacho-Collados, J., et al.: SemEval-2018 Task 9: hypernym discovery. In: Proceedings of the 12th International Workshop on Semantic Evaluation (SemEval 2018). Association for Computational Linguistics, New Orleans (2018)
4. Fellbaum, C.: WordNet: An Electronic Lexical Database. MIT Press, Cambridge (1998)
5. Hearst, M.A.: Automatic acquisition of hyponyms from large text corpora. In: Proceedings of the 14th International Conference on Computational Linguistics, pp. 539–545 (1992)
6. Aldine, A.I.A., Harzallah, M., Berio, G., Bechet, N., Faour, A.: Redefining Hearst patterns by using dependency relations. In: Proceedings of the 10th International Joint Conference on Knowledge Discovery, Knowledge Engineering and Knowledge Management - Volume 2: KEOD, pp. 148–155. INSTICC, SciTePress (2018). https://doi.org/10.5220/0006962201480155
7. Jacques, M.P., Aussenac-Gilles, N.: Variabilité des performances des outils de tal et genre textuel. Cas des patrons lexico-syntaxiques **47**, 11–32 (2006)

8. Kamel, M., dos Santos, C.T., Ghamnia, A., Aussenac-Gilles, N., Fabre, C.: Extracting hypernym relations from Wikipedia disambiguation pages: comparing symbolic and machine learning approaches. In: IWCS (2017)

9. Klaussner, C., Zhekova, D.: Pattern-based ontology construction from selected Wikipedia pages, pp. 103–108 (2011)

10. Kotlerman, L., Dagan, I., Szpektor, I., Zhitomirsky-Geffet, M.: Directional distributional similarity for lexical inference. NLE **16**, 359–389 (2010)

11. Marneffe, M.C.D., MacCartney, B., Manning, C.D.: Generating typed dependency parses from phrase structure parses. In: Proceedings of the 5th International Conference on Language Resources and Evaluation (LREC 2006), pp. 449–454 (2006)

12. Mikolov, T., Sutskever, I., Chen, K., Corrado, G.S., Dean, J.: Distributed representations of words and phrases and their compositionality. In: NIPS, pp. 3111–3119 (2013)

13. Nakashole, N., Weikum, G., Suchanek, F.: PATTY: a taxonomy of relational patterns with semantic types. In: Proceedings of the 2012 Joint Conference on Empirical Methods in Natural Language Processing and Computational Natural Language Learning (EMNLP-CoNLL 2012), pp. 1135–1145. Association for Computational Linguistics, Stroudsburg (2012). http://dl.acm.org/citation.cfm?id=2390948.2391076

14. Orna-Montesinos, C.: Words and patterns: Lexico-grammatical patterns and semantic relations in domain-specific discourses, vol. 24, Jan 2011

15. Pennington, J., Socher, R., Manning, C.D.: Glove: global vectors for word representation. In: EMNLP, pp. 1532–1543 (2014)

16. Ponzetto, S.P., Strube, M.: Taxonomy induction based on a collaboratively built knowledge repository. Artif. Intell. **175**(9), 1737–1756 (2011). https://doi.org/10.1016/j.artint.2011.01.003. http://www.sciencedirect.com/science/article/pii/S000437021100004X

17. Ritter, A., Soderland, S., Etzioni, O.: What is this, anyway: automatic hypernym discovery. In: AAAI Spring Symposium - Technical Report, pp. 88–93, Jan 2009

18. Roller, S., Erk, K., Boleda, G.: Inclusive yet selective: supervised distributional hypernymy detection. In: COLING, pp. 1025–1036 (2014)

19. Roller, S., Kiela, D., Nickel, M.: Hearst patterns revisited: Automatic hypernym detection from large text corpora. In: Proceedings of the 56th Annual Meeting of the Association for Computational Linguistics (Volume 2: Short Papers), pp. 358–363. Association for Computational Linguistics (2018). http://aclweb.org/anthology/P18-2057

20. Sang, E.T.K., Hofmann, K.: Lexical patterns or dependency patterns: which is better for hypernym extraction? In: Proceedings of the Thirteenth Conference on Computational Natural Language Learning (CoNLL 2009), pp. 174–182. Association for Computational Linguistics, Stroudsburg (2009)

21. Schuster, S., Manning, C.D.: Enhanced English universal dependencies: an improved representation for natural language understanding tasks. In: LREC (2016)

22. Seitner, J., et al.: A large database of hypernymy relations extracted from the web. In: LREC (2016)

23. Sheena, N., Jasmine, S.M., Joseph, S.: Automatic extraction of hypernym and meronym relations in English sentences using dependency parser. Procedia Comput. Sci. **93**, 539–546 (2016)

24. Snow, R., Jurafsky, D., Ng, A.: Learning Syntactic Patterns for Automatic Hypernym Discovery, pp. 1297–1304. MIT Press, Cambridge (2005)

25. Weeds, J., Clarke, D., Reffin, J., Weir, D., Keller, B.: Learning to distinguish hypernyms and co-hyponyms. In: COLING, pp. 2249–2259 (2014)

26. Weeds, J., Weir, D.: A general framework for distributional similarity. In: EMLP, pp. 81–88 (2003)

Knowledge Management and
Information Sharing

Investigating Knowledge Management Within Small and Medium-Sized Companies: The Proof of Concept Results of a Survey Addressed to Software Development Industry

Nelson Tenório[1,2,3(✉)], Danieli Pinto[1], Mariana Oliveira[1], Flávio Bortolozzi[1,2], and Nada Matta[3]

[1] UniCesumar, Maringá, Paraná 87050900, Brazil
{nelson.tenorio,flavio.bortolozzi}@unicesumar.edu.br,
danicne@gmail.com, mariana_santosoliveira@hotmail.com
[2] Institute Cesumar of Science, Technology, and Innovation, Maringá, Paraná 87050900, Brazil
[3] University of Troyes, Troyes Aube, France
nada.matta@utt.fr

Abstract. Due to the dynamism and complexity of software development, software vendors need to use their knowledge as an essential competitive advantage to keep themselves innovative in a demanding market. In this sense, when the knowledge is well managed and applied, it brings to the organization business sustainability. Knowledge Management (KM) processes can avoid the loose of knowledge once they provide improve the flow of knowledge for the whole organization. Those processes are supported by practices and tools which stimulate the creation, retention, and dissemination of the knowledge within the organizational environment. Therefore, this article shows the findings of a survey assessment through a proof of concept (POC) aimed to investigate the processes, practices, and tools of KM in small and medium-sized software development companies (SME-Soft). The survey was evaluated by fifty-one professionals from the software industry and KM experts. Our findings point out that the survey is widely suitable for software industry organizations to diagnose their knowledge management processes.

Keywords: Diagnose · Process · Software industry · Questionnaire

1 Introduction

Over the last years, companies recognized the knowledge as a relevant asset which adds value to products and services. In this sense, knowledge has been considered the most important asset for businesses growth [1]. Thus, the individuals are responsible for encouraging content creation and for updating of the existing knowledge [2]. Thus, KM offers a set of practices and tools to ensure the usage of the organization's expertise [3] which is crucial to enhance its performance [4, 5].

© Springer Nature Switzerland AG 2020
A. Fred et al. (Eds.): IC3K 2018, CCIS 1222, pp. 247–263, 2020.
https://doi.org/10.1007/978-3-030-49559-6_12

The software industry companies are characterized as highly competitive and dynamic [6]. The knowledge circulating within a software development teams is dynamic and evolves according to technology, organizational culture, and changes in software development processes [7]. Thus, KM prevents of knowledge loss for software development companies [8]. Therefore, considering the company size, the successful accomplishments concern to create and maintain their product depends on the KM once the individuals' expertise is directly related to the software development, management, and technology [7].

Facing this scenario, SME-Soft depends on the knowledge, experience, and skills of their employees and owners [9]. So, SME-Soft is not able to practice KM in the same way of large organizations due their organizational culture and structure. In this sense, investigate the practices, processes, and tools within SME-Soft is relevant since it can offer means to keep their knowledge flowing actively.

Previous research such as [10–13], has established means to investigate KM processes within organizations suggesting sort of diagnosis for KM processes and practices. However, those works were not mainly designed to investigate KM within the SME-Soft. Those researches follow specifics methodologies to be carried on offering a set of extend questionnaires to be answered which requires a KM expert help. In addition, the outcomes of those proposals also require much time to be understood and interpreted.

Considering this scenario, our work validated and refined a survey based on a questionnaire addressed to SME-Soft to investigate processes, practices, and tools of KM. by mean of a proof of concept (POC). The POC is the best way to practice and improve surveys based on questionnaires or tools in both experimental studies and commercialization of new products, helping to identify issues which compromises the study results [14]. Moreover, the POC works as a 'short launch' of the questionnaire, showing deficiencies, such as ambiguous, poorly designed, or double questions [15]. Therefore, the POC provides the sense concerned in its structure, content, applicability, and the time which each participant takes to answer it.

The remainder of this paper is structured as it follows. In the next section, we present a contextualization regarding software industry and KM. Following, we present previous related works which proposed surveys to investigate KM within organizations. Next, we present our methods to design a survey and to carry on the POC within SME-Soft. Finally, we present our results and our conclusions followed by the bibliography references.

2 The Software Industry as a Knowledge Organization

The software industry plays a significant role in the information technology (IT) sector since the intensive use of knowledge in the software development have contributed to advance technologies, desirable for the growth and development of any economy in the global market [16]. The software industry has a set of activities related to the products and services addressed to satisfy costumer's requirements.

There are different categories of software products such as systems (e.g., operating systems and database management systems), support (e.g., middleware, network management, and software development tools), and applications (software for office, smartphones, and tablets). Software services include the integration of a system's information, operating, maintenance, and software assessment [17]. In this sense, the software development companies sell products formed mainly from ideas embedded in code lines [21]. Therefore, the main 'material' of those organizations is the knowledge of their employees, who use creativity and their intellectual capacity to develop suitable solutions for specific purposes [22].

So, software development companies are peculiar when compared to other companies' segment once they carry on knowledge-intensive activities and generating high added-value products [8]. They are characterized by low entry and exit barriers, minimal costs of production and rapid disruptive innovations [18]. Characterized by the constant technological changes and by increasingly requirements of the clients, who are looking for fast and efficient solutions to meet their needs, the software development industry has a complex environment embedded [6, 8]. Thus, the software industry companies try to adapt promptly what already exists to a new environment and/or computational technology [19]. Therefore, software development activities are so peculiar that sometimes they cannot fit in all projects due the characteristics of the product. Thus, each project is different from the other and requires the use of existing knowledge or the creation of new knowledge since they use different techniques and programming languages [6]. Moreover, new knowledge is needed to support the continuous adoption of new technologies and practices by software development companies [20].

Since the software industry develops knowledge-intensive activities, they understand that the knowledge is their central resource and that it is strictly related to individuals [8]. Therefore, the activities performed by the software industry involve the accumulation of knowledge of the employees, individual technical qualification, accomplishment of methodological efforts, and interaction with sophisticated clients. In this way, knowledge is essential to understand deeply the problems of the client to build the best solution [23].

The knowledge which circulates within a software development organization is dynamic and evolves according to technology, organizational culture, and changes in software development processes [7]. Therefore, software companies need a KM system to prevent knowledge from being lost [8].

The main challenge for the software industry, in particular SME-Soft, is the correct use of the knowledge to address management issues and other organizational needs. To overcome this challenge, the software development companies can adopt KM processes, practices, and tools to increase their ability to learn from their own environment and incorporate new knowledge into their business process [7].

Considering this scenario, we find SME-Soft that manage their knowledge differently relating to large organizations, due the culture and organizational structure differences. Thus, SME-Soft differs from large organizations in aspects such as less complicated decision-making, the closeness of staff, lack of funding and lack of adequate leadership. Therefore, the success of SME-Soft is directly related to the knowledge, experience, and skills of owners and their employees [9].

For the knowledge to generate value for an organization, it must be embedded in services, processes, and products. Thus, organizations must be able to quickly find the right kind of knowledge to propose the best solutions to their problems, providing conditions for innovation [24]. Innovation is understood as the 'implementation of new ideas that create value' for a given organization [25]. The ability of an organization to innovate depends on the knowledge of the individuals working in it, on the experience embedded in its products and services, and on the relationship established with the clients [22]. Therefore, innovation is strongly dependent on knowledge and this knowledge must be managed efficiently. The organizations which manage their knowledge efficiently are more innovative and, consequently, more productive, achieving better performance [26].

According to the OECD (Organization for Economic Co-operation and Development), 'the generation, exploitation, and diffusion of knowledge are fundamental to economic growth, development and the well-being of nations' [27]. The growing discussion about innovation is presented in the Frascati Handbook [28], so according to that handbook, innovation is due 'among other reasons to the process of globalization and the rapid increase in the number of countries and companies that started investing in research and development activities. This manual also shows that the innovation process can take place anywhere on the planet and that research and development activities are carried out to ensure long-term sustainable leadership.

As knowledge-intensive organizations, the software industry needs to invest in research and development, facilitating innovation [29]. Thus, in software development companies, for a project to be considered innovative it requires the 'scientific or technological progress, and it must aim to dissipate scientific or technological uncertainty in a systematic way' [28]. Researches and development in the software industry are advancing quickly technology of operating systems, programming languages, data management, communication software, and software development tools. Furthermore, the software industry is constantly looking for methods of software design, development, installation, and maintenance [28].

Considering that the knowledge of the software industry is based on technology, the shortening of product life cycles directly affected its productivity dynamics. Innovation has become a crucial factor in the success of an organization, ensuring the production of new products [30]. Thus, to remain competitive in the market, companies in the software industry must be able to innovate, satisfying the expectations of their customers and providing new products with competitive prices [31]. In this scenario, companies must develop innovative capacity to manage the changing process, from the creation of ideas to the commercialization of the product created [32].

Concerning the innovation process in the SME-Soft, the challenges are constantly once involving limitations concern financial, cultural, and process [9]. Thus, SME-Soft are not able to invest in ideas, products, or services promptly. One of the challenges to innovation includes the effectiveness of KM processes, which are most often owner-driven. However, the owner has not always deployed KM processes for change in his company. Thus, the flow of the knowledge in the software industry is fundamental for the creation of new products, services, and generate innovation. Therefore, the KM becomes primordial to maintenance of knowledge practices, processes, and tools within SME-Soft.

3 Related Works

One way to find knowledge and how individuals use it within the organization is identifying the KM process. As important as understanding the revealing of knowledge is to know where knowledge is established [33]. So, evaluate KM practices within an organization means measure what has been done by them [34].

KM means understanding and deepening knowledge about organizational processes and what are their contributions to knowledge generation [35]. The author emphasizes that knowledge is an asset of constant evolution and as organizations share new experiences, they learn and advance, so later new understandings can be gained. Furthermore, the need to map the relationship between theory and KM practices, carried out by the organization, to show how it works, how it performs its operations and also the path covered by the information and knowledge [36]. Thus, many organizations are practicing KM, but they do not recognize their practices as a relevant organizational context, while other organizations even speak about practices but use minimal efforts to achieve success [34]. In this sense, KM is not just a management of intellectual assets, but also the processes that act on them including the development, storage, use and, especially, sharing knowledge which, in this case, involves the identification and analysis of availability and desirable assets, with the sole purpose of achieving the organizational objectives [37].

Different KM models were proposed by [10–13, 38] to investigate KM processes and practices aimed to diagnosis how the organization manages and controls its knowledge through an organizational knowledge overview. For instance, the KM diagnosis model offers a set of individual questions to the organization which are ranked, tabulated, interpreted, and discussed. KM diagnosis model is proposed by [10]. The model is divided in two dimensions, namely tactical and strategic. The tactical dimension is consisting of knowledge obtaining, using, learning, and contributing. The strategic dimension consisting of the evaluate, build and maintain the knowledge within the organization.

Through a detailed roadmap, [11] presents strategies to help organizations design, implement, and sustain their knowledge addressed either by organizations that are implementing or have already implemented KM. First, the model provides the step-by-step for the development and implementation of the strategy. Second, the model acts as an adjustment tool, providing a diagnosis of the knowledge status in the organization. Finally, the model presents four phases namely 'call to action', 'development of the KM strategy', 'design and implementation', and 'expansion and support'.

The model known as OKA (Organizational Knowledge Assessment Methodology) offers means to assess and measure the performance of an organization concerning KM through a questionnaire [12]. The model has three dimensions based on people, processes, and systems, and the results, presented in a radar chart, show the strengths and weaknesses of the KM in the organization. The Knowledge Management Facilitators' Guide, suggested by [13], brings a methodology for the implementation of KM addressed to small and medium-sized companies. That model consists of three levels namely accelerators, KM processes, and results.

While supporting KM investigation and diagnosis through the survey questionnaires, most of the models are splitted in different dimensions. Those dimensions are concerned to identify some improvement points categorizing the results of the KM models used for facilitating its interpretation and understanding. In this sense, [39] suggest six dimensions to investigate KM within SME-Soft as follows.

KM Perception Dimension. KM has to support companies' strategic plans explicitly. Moreover, KM establishes the understanding regarding individuals' knowledge to be used and aid the decision-making processes within the companies [21, 23]. Thus, this dimension is focused to investigate the participant's perception regarding KM within their organization.

Organizational Knowledge Identification Dimension. This dimension is essential to investigate whether the individuals know where they can find the knowledge which they need in the company's environment. So, the companies' experience is unique; i.e., there are not two or more companies with the same knowledge [40], and it is crucial to identify the organizational knowledge and map it in the corporate environment. Therefore, this dimension is addressed to investigate the flow of organizational knowledge and show the origin of that knowledge.

Organizational Knowledge Storage Dimension. This dimension is addressed to store personal knowledge getting it explicit through different means such as documents, manuals, databases in which the companies' knowledge should be stored in knowledge databases or repositories to become explicit and accessible [41]. Thus, knowledge associated with abstract concepts is coded and indexed by the experts to make it more tangible into the knowledge database and available for the whole organizational members. Thus, this dimension investigates 'where' and 'how' the knowledge is stored, and what kind of tools the companies could use to store their knowledge.

Organizational Knowledge Recovery Dimension. This dimension consists of retrieving the stored knowledge to supply individual's needs regarding information [42]. Moreover, the data retrieved give to individuals the means to build new knowledge [43]. Thus, this dimension investigates the knowledge recovery checking whether individuals usually recover the knowledge stored in the organization.

Organizational Knowledge Sharing Dimension. It considers that organizational knowledge is dynamic and dependent on social relationships for knowledge creation, sharing, and use [44]. Furthermore, organizations have different individuals with different expertise, experience, and necessities. So, the knowledge cannot be lost, and it is necessary for the organization to stimulate sharing practices offering favorable conditions for creation and use of the knowledge [45]. Therefore, this dimension enhances the organizational knowledge among individuals.

Finally, *KM Practices and Tools Dimension.* KM practices are a set of activities conducted by the organization to improve the effectiveness and efficiency of the organizational knowledge resource [46]. On the other hand, those tools aim to support those practices in which "tools must support communication appropriately, collaboration, sharing and searching activities related to relevant information and knowledge" [47]. Therefore, this dimension is addressed to identify how often companies are using the KM practices and what sort of tools they are using to subsidize those practices.

While offering useful means to investigate and diagnosis KM within the organizations, the questionnaires suggested by the previous works are too extensible and not focused on SME-Soft once those questionnaires do not contain specific questions concerned to software development companies. In this sense, we present our survey addressed to SME-Soft which was validated and refined by a POC.

4 Method

The survey was grounded based on previous works by [10–13, 39], and the questions were addressed investigate KM processes, practices, and tools within SME-Soft. We present the complete survey in the Appendix.

4.1 The Survey Design

We designed our survey according to the steps suggested by [15]. Afterward, we organized the questions in the Google Forms which was divided in two sections in order to simplify our data collection and analysis. The first section brings questions concern participants' profile through sixteen questions regarding education, age, gender, how long the participant works in the organization, and position. The second section is divided in six dimensions as proposed by [39]. The dimensions were structured considering the knowledge belonging to organizations is found in their employees and needs to be identified, whenever organized, and stored so that it can be recovered and shared when necessary.

Table 1 presents an overview of the survey, before the POC, showing the sections and dimensions followed by goals and a question's description. Finally, the Appendix shows the complete survey.

Table 1. Overview of the survey before the POC.

Section	Dimension	Goal	Description
Background questions	Sample characteristics	Identify the profile of the participants	Sixteen questions concern to age, gender, education, the position held in the company, time of experience in the position, and working time
KM within SME-Soft	KM Perception (KMP)	This dimension aims to show the participant's perception of the knowledge and the KM within the organizational environment	Thirteen yes or no assertions and one open question to investigate the perception of the KM's concept, relevance of the knowledge for the organization, knowledge usage within the organization, practice of KM, department/sectors where KM is practiced, KM practices and monitoring by the organization, and if KM is part of the organization strategy

(continued)

Table 1. (*continued*)

Section	Dimension	Goal	Description
	Organizational Knowledge Identification (OKI)	This dimension aims to verify if knowledge identification is a practice within the organization	Eight questions which six adapted Likert Scale [49], two yes or no, and two open questions. All of them addressed to investigate the frequency in which the organizational problems are solved, how often problem solvers use the sources of knowledge, whether team members know where to get a knowledge required, whether all team members express their ideas, and whether ideas are used in the software development process
	Organizational Knowledge Storage (OKST)	This dimension aims to investigate if the organization stores a knowledge acquired	One open question, one adapted Likert Scale question [49], and two yes or no questions. All of them related to the storage and maintenance of knowledge within the organization
	Organizational Knowledge Recovery (OKR)	This dimension shows if stored knowledge is recovered within the organization	There was one adapted Likert Scale question [49], and one open question to investigate knowledge recovery by the individuals
	Organizational Knowledge Sharing (OKSH)	This dimension investigates if the knowledge is shared and comprehensive among the team members within the organization	Five yes or no questions and one adapted Likert Scale question [49] regarding organizational motivation to store knowledge, exchange information between team members and other individuals in the organization or the external environment
	KM Practices and Tools (KMPT)	This dimension presents which practices and tools, currently used by people, are aligned with KM within the organization	Twenty Likert Scale assertion [49] related to the KM practices carried out in the organization (e.g., knowledge coffee, capturing ideas, coaching, bank of individual skills, evaluation of competencies management system and reporting questions). There were nineteen Likert Scale [49] assertion concern tools to support KM practices (e.g., database, blogs, skype, handbooks, notice board, chat, Facebook messenger, reports, bulletin board, video, virtual forums, Kanban, virtual collaboration, text, intranet, Canvas, e-mail, WhatsApp, official documents)

Source: Adapted from [50].

4.2 Data Collection

The participants were invited to cooperate with this research during a software local productive arrangement meeting attended by companies' members located in the Northwest Region of Paraná, Brazil. The local productive arrangement has more than four hundred small and medium-sized companies associated. At the meeting, fifty-three company's members were present, in which ten of them got interested in collaborating with our research. All participating companies were software vendors which have been ten to twenty-five years in business with local clients and also clients across Brazil.

After the meeting, we e-mailed the participants a brief of the research containing goals, methods, needing data to collect, and the time estimation for each participant to answer and assess the survey. The companies could decide the individuals participating in the POC according to their availability. The survey was assessed following a scheduled. We designed seven questions which were used as a driver of the survey assessment as it follows.

- How long did you take to answer the questionnaire? Do you think this time to respond was reasonable?
- Do the questions fit for the software industry?
- Does the questionnaire fit the software industry?
- Would you rule out an issue? Why?
- Would you add any questions? Why?
- Is the questionnaire relevant to your organization?

We carried on data collection between July and August of 2016. We visited each company, we accessed the survey in the Google Forms, and then we 'gave' the poll to each participant answer it by themselves in a private room. All participants data were kept in secret, and we could not identify them through the solutions. Each participant also received a hard copy of the survey, which made it possible to follow up the questions and some notes during the POC. We also invited a KM expert to assess the survey, which we just emailed it to this person.

4.3 Data Analysis

We organized all collected data into spreadsheets. Firstly, we analyzed the profile of the participants - first section of the survey - e.g., education, age, gender. Secondly, we analyzed the answers of the six dimensions to identify the processes, practices, and tools used by the participants within the organization. Finally, we analyzed the survey assessment by the participants carefully through the content analysis technique as suggested by [48], and our empirical findings are described following.

5 Results

The POC was answered by fifty-one workers from different software companies and one KM expert with over 20 years of experience in academic research. The profile of the POC participants is presented in Fig. 1.

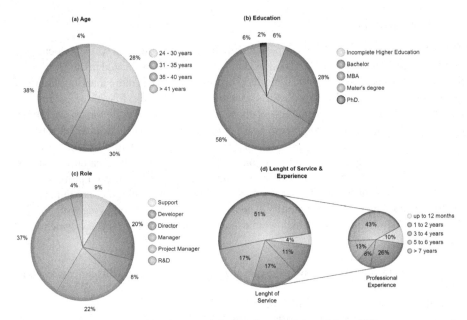

Fig. 1. Profile of the participants. Source: Adapted from [50].

Figure 1(a) shows the age of participants ranged between 24 and 50 years old. The largest age group was between 36 and 40 years, i.e., 38% of the participants. The Fig. 1(b) presents the degree of education of the participants in which 28% are bachelors, 57% have MBA in the area in which they work, and 8% have master's or Ph.D.

Moreover, the Fig. 1(c) shows that 37% of the participants are project managers, 16% are software development, and 28% is responsible for any area, e.g., leadership team, director, and CEO. Finally, the Fig. 1(d) shows that 85% of them have worked for the current company for more than three years, and 43% of them have experience in their current position for more than seven years. Therefore, all research participants have a precise knowledge of their position within the organization.

5.1 POC Findings

The POC of the survey resulted in exciting findings in which we divided into five categories such as *answer time, remove questions, add questions, the relevance of the issue, importance SME-Soft, and further considerations.*

Answer Time. One of our survey strengths reported by the participants was concerned by the answer time. We measured the answer time of the participants, and they took around 18 min to answer all questions on average. The shortest measured time was 14 min (P13, project manager) and the highest of was 42 min (P14, user support manager). Considering the answer time of our survey, the KM expert pointed out that it was quite reasonable.

Similar Questions Removal. The participants suggested removing items in the dimension namely OKI (Organizational Knowledge Identification). One development leader observed two questions that was investigating similar topics, i.e., questions 2.4 and 2.8 (see Appendix). Others two participants, one human resource manager and one project manager, also observed those similar questions, and the project manager highlighted that "similar questions could discourage the participants from continuing answering the questionnaire." Moreover, three of the participants suggested to keep one of the questions and throw out the other one, since both were similar, but none of them indicate which question should be excluded. Inversely, the KM expert observed that, although some topics are similar, there were no reasons to take out one of those questions since they appear in different dimensions with different goals. However, the KM expert suggested changing the order of the questions in the first dimension, observing that the sequence could be more systematic and logical.

Relevant Questions to Add. When we asked the participants regarding the necessities to add questions, one project manager suggested adding an item exploring which companies adapt to address the problems that arise when performing their daily activities. One operation manager said he would not add anything, however, stressed that the terms used to investigate actions and practices sometimes could be confused. Still, for that manager, this is a disadvantage for those who do not know what KM is. An administrative leader said that some open question should be added in the KMPT (KM Practices and Tools) dimension to investigate the use of other practices that are not listed in the survey. Also, another project manager missed some questions about the results obtained with the KM tools usage and the performing of KM practices. Inversely, the KM expert did not miss any question in KMPT dimension.

Importance of the Survey for SME-Soft. All participants observed that the study is entirely relevant for SME-Soft. For instance, one of the project managers considered conducting the survey to his team to 'perceived what needs to be improved.' In this context, the participant whose role was a human resource manager stressed that the survey provides a step forward. Another project manager and the administrative manager pointed out that the survey is provocative once they need to think about the whole organizational processes.

Further Considerations. The participants made additional considerations regarding our survey. One software developer observed that the questions in dimension OKST (Organizational Knowledge Storage) and OKSH (Organizational Knowledge Sharing) looked like similar, and those dimensions could be unified. Besides, one support manager suggested changing the word 'organization' for all questions by 'your department' or 'your team' in order to be more specific and to get the questions clearer. Curiously, all the participants observed that they got some insights while answering our survey. For them, the questions increased the visibility of the respondents regarding KM processes, practices, and tools leading them to reflect about the organization processes, recognizing KM tools usage, and getting ideas how the KM could open new grounds if applied within their team. This thought reinforces the relevance of our survey addressed specifically for SME-Soft.

5.2 Refining the Survey

After the POC, we analyzed all the participants' considerations and carried out the following adjustments to refine the questions of the survey.

Firstly, we updated the question's order. We changed the order of the items in the dimension KMP following the KM expert's suggestion facilitating the understanding of the issues once it begins from the specific to the general theme. Also, question 2.5 in the OKI dimension was moved to dimension OKSH once that question was related to knowledge dissemination (see Appendix).

Secondly, we removed some questions. Based on our analysis, we decided to withdraw of the three questions as follows. The question 2.4 from dimension OKI once it was similar to question 2.8 of the same dimension. Also, we removed the question 2.2 from dimension OKI since it was similar to question 4.2, the dimension OKR (see Appendix).

Thirdly, we added two new questions into the dimension KMPT. The questions enable the participants to inform other practices and tools adopted by the organization and also not listed in that dimension. Thus, the question added is 'Could you inform other practices/tools which your team use daily and are not listed above?', aiming to investigate different practices and tools used by the participant that is not listed in the survey (see Appendix).

Finally, we decided not unify the dimensions OKST and OKSH once they have different objectives, as observed by the KM expert. Moreover, while KM requires a holistic view, we also decided not to change the term 'organization' by different terms as suggested one of the participants.

Therefore, the results achieved here show that our survey is relevant and adequate for the SME-Soft. The participants highlighted that the survey helps them to understand KM processes, practices, and tools within SME-Soft, getting some insights to carry on KM with their team within the organization.

6 Conclusions

This paper carried out a POC to refine and validate a survey addressed to investigate KM in SME-Soft. Our result showed some relevant points to improve our survey such as the time of answer, irrelevant questions, pertinent questions to add, the importance of the survey for SME-Soft, and further considerations. Curiously, we disclosed that while the participants were assessing the study, they had some insights regarding KM processes and practices performed by their organization. Thus, all the participants considered the survey relevant to investigate KM within SME-Soft. However, the limitation of this work is the lack of conducting interviews with participants. In future work, we intend to conduct our survey broadly in different SME-Soft companies and carry out statistical analysis regarding KM processes, practices, and tools.

Acknowledgments. Our special thanks to Cesumar Institute of Science, Technology, and Innovation (ICETI - Instituto Cesumar de Ciência, Tecnologia e Inovação), Maringá, Paraná, Brazil. We also thanks to Programa de Suporte a Pós-Graduação de Instituições de Ensino Particulares (PROSUP) of Coordination for the Improvement of Higher Education Personnel (CAPES - Coordenação de Aperfeiçoamento de Pessoal de Nível Superior), Brazil.

Appendix

* Questions removed (strikethrough).
Δ Questions added.
• Questions moved to another dimension.
† Questions coming from another dimension.
‡ Likert Scale: (1) Strongly disagree; (2) Disagree; (3) Neither agree nor disagree; (4) Agree; (5) Strongly agree

KM Survey to SME-Soft

KM Perception Dimension (KMP)
1.1 Have you heard about knowledge management in any lecture, course, meeting, or conference? Y/N
1.2 Do you know what knowledge management is? Y/N
1.3 Is knowledge management currently a topic of interest to the organization? Y/N
1.4 Does the organization understand that knowledge is a resource of the organization? Y/N
1.5 Is it fact that knowledge is stored in people? Y/N
1.6 Does conduct knowledge management practices by the organization? Y/N
If the answer is YES
   1.6.1 How long are knowledge management practices in the organization?
   1.6.2 Are all areas aware of the organization's knowledge management practices? Y/N
   1.6.3 Are knowledge management practices carried out in all areas of the organization? Y/N
   1.6.4 Does the organization have a defined vision or justification for the practice of knowledge management? Y/N
   1.6.5 Knowledge management is aligned with and is part of the organization's management model?Y/N
   1.6.6 Does the organization continually and systematically assess knowledge management practices, identify weaknesses, and define and use methods to eliminate them? Y/N
If the answer is NO:
   1.6.7 Do you know if there are plans to implement projects on knowledge management in the organization? Y/N
   1.6.8 How soon will the project be implemented?

Organizational Knowledge Identification Dimension (OKI)
2.1 How often do employees often turn to colleagues within the organization to solve problems? Always/Frequently/Sometimes/Rarely/Never
* 2.2 How often do employees use other sources of knowledge (intranet, internet, database, manuals) to solve their problems? Always/Frequently/Sometimes/Rarely/Never
2.3 Employees know "who knows what" within the organization, making it clear where to look for specific information? Y/N
* 2.4 What resources do employees use to obtain information?
• 2.5 Do all employees express their ideas? Always/Frequently/Sometimes/Rarely/Never
2.6 Are employees' ideas taken into account for the organization's decision-making? Always/Frequently/Sometimes/Rarely/Never
2.7 Is the involvement of customers in the process of creating and developing new products and services a well-established practice in the organization? Always/Fre-

quently/Sometimes/Rarely/Never
2.8 How does the organization disseminate information or knowledge to its employees?

Organizational Knowledge Storage Dimension (OKST)
3.1 What resources does the organization use to store knowledge?

3.2 Knowledge storage media is updated: Always/Frequently/Sometimes/Rarely/Never
3.3 Does the knowledge storage space in the organization have a structure that enables everyone to contribute? Y/N
3.4 Is the knowledge stored in the organization intended for all sectors of the organization? Y/N

Organizational Knowledge Recovery Dimension (OKR)
4.1 When people are given the task of researching information in the organization, are they able to do it? Always/Frequently/Sometimes/Rarely/Never
4.2 Where do people usually look for information on the company?

Organizational Knowledge Sharing Dimension (OKSH)
5.1 Does the organization motivate its employees to share information with each other? Y/N
5.2 Do all employees in the organization share information with each other? Y/N
5.3 Is the workspace designed to promote the flow of ideas between workgroups? Y/N
5.4 Are people afraid to share their knowledge with other colleagues in the organization? Y/N
5.5 Does the organization support group activities? Y/N
† 5.6 (*previously 2.5*) Do all employees express their ideas? Always/Frequently/Sometimes/Rarely/Never

KM Practices and Tools Dimension (KMPT)
‡ *KM Practices*

Knowledge coffee (1/2/3/4/5)
Communities of practice (1/2/3/4/5)
Knowledge map (1/2/3/4/5)
Mentoring (1/2/3/4/5)
Brainstorming (1/2/3/4/5)
Capturing ideas (1/2/3/4/5)
Adoption of best practice (1/2/3/4/5)
Peer Assist (1/2/3/4/5)
Peer Review (1/2/3/4/5)
Storytelling (1/2/3/4/5)
Coaching (1/2/3/4/5)
Internal Benchmarking (1/2/3/4/5)
External Benchmarking (1/2/3/4/5)
Meetings (1/2/3/4/5)
Competency management system (1/2/3/4/5)
Bank of individual skills (1/2/3/4/5)
Technical improvement courses (1/2/3/4/5)
Lectures, training and workshops (1/2/3/4/5)
Balanced Scorecard (1/2/3/4/5)
Reporting (1/2/3/4/5)
Δ Could you inform other practices which your team use daily and are not listed above?

References

1. Del Giudice, M., Maggioni, V.: Managerial practices and operative directions of knowledge management within inter-firm networks: a global view. J. Knowl. Manag. **18**(5), 841–846 (2016)
2. Chang, C.L., Lin, T.C.: The role of organizational culture in the knowledge management process. J. Knowl. Manag. **19**(3), 433–455 (2015)
3. Dalkir, K.: Knowledge Management in Theory and Practice, 2nd edn. The MIT Press, Cambridge (2011)
4. Muthuveloo, R., Shanmugam, N., Teoh, A.P.: The impact of tacit knowledge management on organizational performance: evidence from Malaysia. Asia Pac. Manag. Rev. **22**(4), 192–201 (2017)
5. Colomo-Palacios, R., Fernandes, E., Soto-Acosta, P., Larrucea, X.: A case analysis of enabling continuous software deployment through knowledge management. Int. J. Inf. Manag. **40**, 186–189 (2018)
6. Nawinna, D.P.: A model of knowledge management: delivering a competitive advantage to small & medium scale software industry in Sri Lanka. In: 6th International Conference on Industrial and Information Systems, pp. 414–419 (2011)
7. Aurum, A., Daneshgar, F., Ward, J.: Investigating knowledge management practices in software development organizations - an Australian experience. Inf. Softw. Technol. **50**(6), 511–533 (2008)
8. Bjornson, F.O., Dingsoyr, T.: Knowledge management in software engineering: a systematic review of studied concepts, findings and research methods used. Inf. Softw. Technol. **50**(11), 1055–1068 (2008)
9. Wee, J.C.N., Chua, A.Y.K.: The peculiarities of knowledge management processes in SMEs: the case of Singapore. J. Knowl. Manag. **17**(6), 958–972 (2013)
10. Bukowitz, W.R., Willians, R.L.: The Knowledge Management Fieldbook. Pearson Education Limited, London (1999)
11. Vestal, W.: Measuring Knowledge Management. American Productivity & Quality Center, Houston (2002)
12. Fonseca, A.F.: Organizational Knowledge Assessment Methodology. Word Bank Institute, Washington (2006)
13. Nair, P., Prakash, K.: Knowledge Management: Facilitator's Guide. APO, Tokyo (2009)
14. Kendig, C.E.: What is proof of concept research and how does it generate epistemic and ethical categories for future scientific practice? Sci. Eng. Ethics **22**(3), 735–753 (2016). https://doi.org/10.1007/s11948-015-9654-0
15. Aaker, D.A., Kumar, V., Day, G.: Marketing Research. Wiley, New York (2008)
16. Binuyo, G.O., Oyebisi, T.O., Olayinka, A., Afolabi, B.S.: Evaluation of the factors influencing the indigenous software products development in Nigeria. Int. J. Adv. ICT for Emerg. Reg. **7**(3), 1–8 (2015)
17. Kewen, L., Changyuan, G.: A model for coopetition evolution of software industrial virtual cluster. Int. J. Grid Distrib. Comput. **9**(3), 145–155 (2016)
18. de Souza Bermejo, P.H., Tonelli, A.O., Galliers, R.D., Oliveira, T., Zambalde, A.L.: Conceptualizing organizational innovation: the case of the Brazilian software industry. Inf. Manag. **53**(4), 493–503 (2016)
19. Pressman, R., Maxim, B.: Engenharia de Software: uma abordagem profissional, 8nd edn. McGraw Hill, São Paulo (1999)
20. Mehta, N.: Successful knowledge management implementation in global software companies. J. Knowl. Manag. **12**(2), 42–56 (2008)

21. Davenport, T.H., Prusak, L.: Working Knowledge: How Organizations Manage What They Know. Harvard Business School Press, Boston (1998)
22. Kalkan, A., Bozkurt, Ö.Ç., Arman, M.: The impacts of intellectual capital, innovation and organizational strategy on firm performance. Procedia – Soc. Behav. Sci. **150**(150), 700–707 (2014)
23. Serna, E., Bachiller, O., Serna, A.: Knowledge meaning and management in requirements engineering. Int. J. Inf. Manag. **37**, 155–161 (2017)
24. Bhatt, G.D.: Knowledge management in organizations: examining the interaction between technologies, techniques, and people. J. Knowl. Manag. **5**(1), 68–75 (2001)
25. Linder, J.C., Jarvenpaa, S., Davenport, T.H.: Towards an innovative sourcing strategy. MIT Sloan Manag. Rev. **44**(4), 43–49 (2003)
26. Bari, M.W., Fanchen, M., Baloch, M.A.: The relationship between knowledge management practices, innovativeness and organizational performance (a case from software industry). Sci. Int. (Lahore) **28**(1), 463–475 (2016)
27. OCDE: Oslo Manual-Guidelines for collecting and interpreting innovation data. Organisation for Economic Cooporation and Development, Paris (2005)
28. OECD.: The Measurement of Scientific and Technological Activities Frascati: Proposed Standard Practice for Surveys on Research and Experimental Development. Cambridge University Press, Cambridge (2002)
29. Tian, D.: Evaluation model and empirical study for innovation efficiency of software industry. In: Fourth International Conference on Digital Manufacturing & Automation, pp. 29–30. IEEE, Qingdao (2013)
30. Edison, H., Bin Ali, N., Torkar, R.: Towards innovation measurement in the software industry. J. Syst. Softw. **86**(5), 1390–1407 (2013)
31. Rejeb, H.B., Morel-Guimarães, L., Boly, V., Assiélou, N.G.: Measuring innovation best practices: Improvement of an innovation index integrating threshold and synergy effects. Technovation **28**(12), 838–854 (2008)
32. Aryanto, R., Fontana, A., Afiff, A.Z.: Strategic human resource management, innovation capability, and performance: an empirical study in indonesia software industry. Procedia – Soc. Behav. Sci. **211**, 874–879 (2015)
33. Oliva, F.L.: Knowledge management barriers, practices and maturity model. J. Knowl. Manag. **18**(6), 1053–1074 (2014)
34. Khatibian, N., Hasan, T., Jafari, H.A.: Measurement of knowledge management maturity level within organizations. Bus. Strategy Ser. Bus. Process Manag. J. ISS J. Knowl. Manag. **11**(6), 793–808 (2010)
35. Demchig, B.: Knowledge management capability level assessment of the higher education institutions: case study from Mongolia. Procedia – Soc. Behav. Sci. **174**, 3633–3640 (2015)
36. Siadat, S.H., Kalantari, H., Shafahi, S.: Assessing knowledge management maturity level based on APO approach (a case study in Iran). Int. J. Soc. Sci. Hum. Res. **4**(3), 629–638 (2016)
37. Freeze, R., Kulkarni, U.: Knowledge management capability assessment: validating a knowledge assets measurement instrument. In: Proceedings of the 38th Annual Hawaii International Conference on System Sciences, pp. 1–10 (2005)
38. APO: Knowledge management: facilitator's guide. http://www.apo-tokyo.org/00e-books/IS-39_APO-KM-FG.htm. Accessed 21 Jan 2019
39. Pinto, D., Bortolozzi, F., Menegassi, C.H.M., Pegino, P.M.F, Tenório, N.: Design das etapas a serem seguidas em um instrumento para a coleta de dados para organizações do setor de TI. In: VI Congresso Internacional de Conhecimento e Inovação– CIKI (2016)
40. Capaldo, A., Petruzzelli, A.M.: Origins of knowledge and innovation in R&D alliances: a contingency approach. Technol. Anal. Strateg. Manag. **27**(4), 461–483 (2015)

41. Wiig, K.: Knowledge Management Foundations. Schema Press, Arlington (1993)
42. Yagüe, A., Garbajosa, J., Díaz, J., González, E.: An exploratory study in communication in Agile Global Software Development. Comput. Stand. Interf. **48**, 184–197 (2016)
43. Choo, C.W.: The Knowing Organization as Learning Organization, 2nd edn. Oxford University Press, New York (2006)
44. Ipe, M.: Knowledge sharing in organizations: a conceptual framework. Hum. Resour. Dev. Rev. **2**(4), 337–359 (2003)
45. Zhang, X., Jiang, J.Y.: With whom shall I share my knowledge? A recipient perspective of knowledge sharing. J. Knowl. Manag. **19**(2), 277–295 (2015)
46. Andreeva, T., Kianto, A.: Knowledge processes, knowledge intensity, and innovation: a moderated mediation analysis. J. Knowl. Manag. **15**(6), 1016–1034 (2011)
47. Perez-Aros, A., Barber, K.D., Munive-Hernandez, J.E., Eldrige, S.: Designing a knowledge management tool to support knowledge sharing networks. J. Manuf. Technol. Manag. **18**(2), 153–168 (2007)
48. Neuendorf, K.A.: The Content Analysis Guidebook. Sage, Newbury Park (2016)
49. Likert, R.: A technique for the measurement of attitudes. Arch. Psychol. **22**(140), 5–55 (1932)
50. Pinto, D., Oliveira, M., Bortolozzi, F., Matta, N., Tenório, N.: Investigating knowledge management in the software industry: a proof of concept findings from a data collection instrument for field research within small and medium-sized companies. In: 10th International Conference Knowledge Management Information Sharing - KMIS. Insticc, Seville, pp. 1–10 (2018)

Author Index

Printed in the
United States
by Baker & Taylor

Printed in the United States
By Bookmasters